THE ENCYCLOPEDIA OF
FRENCH
COOKING

THE ENCYCLOPEDIA OF
FRENCH COOKING

General Editor
JENI WRIGHT
Author
ELISABETH SCOTTO

CRESCENT BOOKS
New York

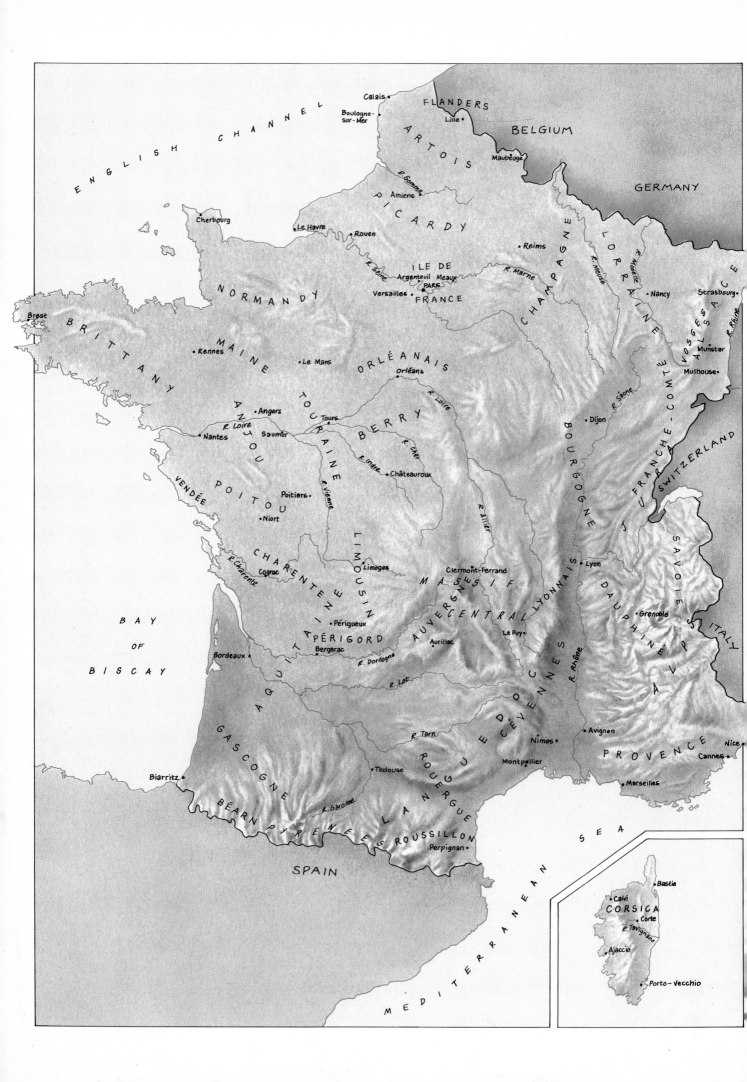

CONTENTS

INTRODUCTION

RECIPES

Introduction by Jeni Wright
Original recipes and wine information written by Elisabeth Scotto
Recipes translated by Jeni Wright
Special photography by Robert Golden

© MCMLXXXII Octopus Books Limited,
First published 1982 by
Octopus Books Limited,
59 Grosvenor Street, London W1

Library of Congress Catalog Card No: 82-70577
Scotto, Elisabeth
The encyclopedia of French cooking
NY: Crescent Books 192p. 8106 801120
ISBN 0-517-36958-3

Produced by Mandarin Publishers Limited
Printed in Hong Kong

HISTORY

The cooking of France enjoys the reputation of being the finest cuisine in the world. France is frequently described as 'the gastronomic centre of the world', but it is important to realize there are two very distinct and different types of French cooking – *la haute cuisine* and *la cuisine regionale*. 'French cooking' should therefore only be used as a generalization.

La haute cuisine owes its heritage to such great names as Taillevent, La Varenne, Carême and Escoffier, and the traditions of these great cooks are still carried on by the famous French chefs of today, in some of the finest and most celebrated restaurants and hotels all over the world. To cook *à la haute cuisine* takes years of dedication and professional training, plus a considerable amount of artistic skill; it is therefore a style of cooking best left to the experts.

In contrast, *la cuisine regionale* is a natural cuisine, developed over the centuries from a basic need to utilize the produce of the land to its best advantage (France has always been a predominantly agricultural country). It is the simple cooking of the provinces or regions of France, cooked by French housewives with a minimum amount of fuss, and a maximum amount of care and attention – often in modest kitchens with very little in the way of sophisticated cooking equipment. It is a style based on the use of the simplest, albeit the finest, of natural ingredients.

To trace the history of cooking in France, we must go back as far as the Roman Apicius, the first known 'cookery writer' and author of *De Re Coquinaria*, written some time between the first and third centuries. Thanks to Apicius's book, we know something about the eating habits in western Europe during those times. Herbs and spices were used in abundance, and the mixing of sweet and sour flavours together in one dish was immensely popular. Meat was eaten, but fish was more abundant – numerous different varieties were caught and prepared for the table. Apicius himself was fond of fish; he invented a method of force-feeding trout with honeyed wine and dried figs. Apicius was also the first 'chef' to succumb to madness in his passion for food – the story goes that after spending a fortune on one single meal, he committed suicide for fear of starving to death!

Throughout the whole Gallo-Roman era, fish remained a popular staple food. Meat and game were still eaten and *charcuterie* was as much-loved by the Gauls as it is today by the modern Frenchman. There were few revolutionary changes in eating habits for centuries after Apicius. There then followed a period of general decline and regression in all areas – and naturally this was reflected in changes in eating habits. Misery, want and famine lasted well into the Middle Ages, and cereals took the place of fish and meat as the main part of a meal; at least 90 per cent of Frenchmen lived only on their 'daily bread'. These were hard times for everyone, with few new developments in the culinary arts.

By the 13th century, however, life in France was at least a little improved, and the towns, if not the remote villages, had regular supplies of food, particularly fresh water fish. A century later Taillevent, the most famous

cook of the Middle Ages – some say 'the father of French cookery' – began his career. He started as kitchen boy at the court of the French Queen, Jeanne, ending it as master chef to King Charles VI. His book *Le Viandier* is one of the oldest and most celebrated of French cookbooks, and from it we learn that food was again highly spiced and seasoned, and that elaborate concoctions were popular once more. No expense was spared in cooking for the royal household, but what the average French peasant had to eat was a very different matter. Not for him the delicacies of roast peacock and suckling pig; his diet was based almost entirely upon vegetables – frowned upon and hardly ever eaten by the rich.

Despite Taillevent's influence, some historians claim it was not before the middle of the 16th century that French cooking really began to develop. This they attribute to the arrival in Paris of Catherine de Medici, for her marriage to the Dauphin in 1533. Catherine brought Italian cooks with her from the Florentine court, and there is little doubt that the French are

ABOVE: **French confectionery shop's painted ceramic front depicting an old farming scene.**
RIGHT: **Nineteenth Century painting 'The Market Place' by L'Hermitte.**

indebted to Italian culinary expertise; until this time there was no other cuisine in Europe with such a high degree of sophistication as that of Florence. From the Renaissance onwards, spurred on by the Italians, a spirit of innovation gradually developed in French cuisine – and recipes began to emerge. In 1651, La Varenne wrote *Le Cuisinier François*, the first real cookbook since *Le Viandier* nearly 300 years before. He was one of France's great chefs, and a founder member of French classical cooking.

At the beginning of the 19th century another great chef emerged. This was Antonin Carême, prolific writer of cookery books, chef to foreign minister and gourmet Talleyrand, and one-time chef to the English Prince Regent and the Russian Czar Alexander. Carême followed La Varenne in the classic *haute cuisine* style; 'King of cooks and cook of Kings', he is considered by many purists to have been the greatest and most talented cook of all. From Carême's time, *la haute cuisine* and *la cuisine regionale* are seen to emerge as separate styles of cooking.

The early 19th century witnessed a massive new interest in food in France, with restaurants springing up all over the capital, and gastronomes and food critics (most notably Brillat-Savarin) becoming very much a part of the culinary scene. Chefs and cooks were no longer the exclusive property of royal households – they turned to cooking in their own hotels and restaurants for a sparkling clientele of royals and celebrities. Eating out at smart restaurants became the fashionable thing to do – amongst the nobility.

In the late 1800s, Auguste Escoffier became the next 'chef of kings' after Carême – he was a favourite of the Prince of Wales (the future King Edward VII). At the height of his career, Escoffier went into partnership with César Ritz of the Grand Hotel Monte Carlo. Together they made the perfect team – Ritz with his ability to attract the fashionable set of the day and Escoffier with his gift for creating new and exciting dishes. Yet despite his flamboyance and flair, Escoffier was responsible for simplifying many of the dishes of *la haute cuisine*. Escoffier believed that food should look and taste like food, that it should be simple and fresh-tasting not pretentious. There is little doubt that he set a fine example for today's *nouvelle cuisine* and professional chefs all over the world still regard his *Guide Culinaire* (published as long ago as 1902) as the culinary 'bible' for classic dishes, sauces and garnishes.

Michel Guérard and Paul Bocuse, two of today's great chefs, cannot claim to have transformed French cooking, but they play a positive role in its modern-day development. Simplification of preparation and an emphasis once more on natural taste are now the order of the day. In today's top restaurants, *la grande cuisine* of the master chefs moves closer to the produce of the land and *la cuisine regionale* then ever before.

REGIONAL COOKING

THE NORTH
Flanders, Artois, Picardy

The north is too often made out to be grey, flat and depressing, for it is the traditional home of coal-mining and the textile and metallurgical industries. The skyline is also crowded with silos, sugar refineries, flour mills and tips. But do not be misled by such a landscape, because here they also grow corn and wheat, rye, potatoes and sugar beet (producing one fifth of French sugar), and the fields of corn and beet add much colour to the region.

On the Channel coast, in the *département* of Pas-de-Calais, is France's largest fishing port, Boulogne-sur-Mer. The main catch is herring, which is sold smoked, salted, marinated and canned, as well as fresh. The fish is sent from the port in refrigerated lorries to all parts of the country.

The cooking of this region is made up of simple, hearty fare, with a preponderance of strong flavours. Wholesome dishes predominate, with vegetables providing the filling ingredients. Amongst the most commonly used vegetables are leeks, chicory (known in the north and Belgium as *chicons*), red and white cabbage, potatoes, and the dried haricot beans known as *haricots de soissons*, which are much sought after for their size and flavour. Frogs and eels abound in the lakes and rivers of the region, and are used to make such famous dishes as *potage de grenouilles* (soup from the marshlands of Picardy), and *anguilles au vert* (eel cooked with herbs – page 85) which is eaten hot or cold and is equally as popular in Belgium as it is in northern France.

The favourite drink of this region is not wine, but beer, and both brown and pale ales are brewed. Lille and Maubeuge are the largest brewery towns, producing one third of all French beers. Half are light beers, the others the so-called 'de luxe' beers. Light beers are served with meals, de luxe beers are drunk on their own. Beer is also used in cooking, particularly in casseroles and stews of the *carbonnades flamandes* type (page 128).

Another popular drink is the local *genièvre* or gin. A spirit distilled from grain and flavoured with juniper berries, it is drunk neat as a liqueur and used as an ingredient in many cooked dishes. Made since the 13th century, it is sold in square bottles called *sarcopages*, and is at least 40° proof. A *bistouille* or coffee made with *genièvre*, is a very popular after-dinner drink in the north of the region.

Desserts are much loved in the north, and local specialities include *gaufres* or waffles, which are served dusted with icing (confectioner's) sugar, or topped with whipped cream flavoured with alcohol. *Gaufres* are traditional at New Year and Mardi Gras (Shrove Tuesday), but they are enjoyed on other occasions throughout the year. *Cramique*, another local dessert, is a kind of brioche with raisins and, like many other dishes of northern France, it seems to be just as popular in Belgium.

THE NORTH-EAST
Alsace

Rich plains of cereals and vegetables, green fields for grazing, vine-clad hillsides, orchards of fruit trees, deep forests rich in game and innumerable rivers (including the Rhine) teeming with fish – all these make Alsace a region where eating well comes as naturally as breathing.

Alsatian cooking is rich and varied, though sometimes heavy, with many of the traditional dishes having a Germanic character. This is partly due to the proximity of the German border and past German domination of the region, but it also stems from the influence of Jewish colonies within Alsace. These people have added German, Austrian and, to a lesser extent, Eastern European flavours to Alsatian cookery. The local *choucroute* is a case in point. Like its German counterpart, *sauerkraut*, it is a dish of shredded pickled cabbage, served with *charcuterie*. In Alsace this will be bacon, Strasbourg sausages, smoked ham and smoked pork chops. Other celebrated Alsatian dishes which include pickled cabbage are *chou rouge aux pommes* (braised red cabbage with apples – page 158) and *chou au lard* (white cabbage with bacon – page 155).

Another equally famous Alsatian speciality is *pâté de foie gras*, made from the specially fattened livers of geese. Like Périgord, Alsace breeds vast quantities of geese for *foie gras*. Often the livers are served simply on their own (*foie gras naturel*), more elaborately they are encased in pastry (sometimes with truffles added) to become *pâté de foie gras en croûte*, a dish that Curnonsky once described as 'one of the greatest wonders of gastronomy'.

Next to goose, pork is the most commonly eaten meat, and apart from being eaten fresh, it is widely used to make the many kinds of local *charcuterie*, of which the Strasbourg hams and sausages are the most famous. (Strasbourg is almost equally as famous for its Munster cheese – see page 36.) The fresh beef is good, and there is also a large amount of game – wild boar, venison and wild duck, in particular. Fish – salmon, trout and pike – are abundant in the rivers, lakes and streams of the region, adding freshness and variety to the Alsatian diet. Desserts are also varied, but the most famous by far is *Kugelhopf* (page 186), a kind of brioche with almonds, which has come to be as much a symbol of the region as the Alsatian stork. *Kugelhopf* is traditionally cooked in a decorative glazed earthenware mould, with a grooved funnel in the centre. In the past, it was the custom to bake it in different shapes

also distilled, but the spirit is not as highly prized as *Mirabelle*. As for kirsch, distilled in Lorraine as well as Alsace, its name and popularity have spread far beyond their borders, both as an after-dinner liqueur and for its uses in cooking, particularly in desserts. As in Alsace, there is an abundance of freshwater fish – eel, pike, carp, crayfish and trout, and plenty of game – wild boar, hare and wild duck. Beetroots, cabbages and potatoes are the main vegetables grown in Lorraine.

The cooks of Lorraine use lots of fresh cream, known locally as *meurotte* or *murotte*, vital in the preparation of that most famous of Lorraine dishes, the quiche. There are numerous different fillings for quiche, but *quiche lorraine* (page 65), with its pastry case filled with diced bacon, cream and eggs, must be the best known. Some recipes for *quiche lorraine* use cheese in the filling, but this is not authentic. Sometimes, *quiche lorraine* is served with a cup of hot bouillon, a practice said to have been introduced by Stanislas Leczinski, Duke of Lorraine. The two great desserts of Lorraine are also attributed to him: the *baba* and the *madeleine* (page 187). The *baba*, so the story goes, was originally a *kugelhopf* that the Duke soaked in sweet Malaga wine. *Madeleines* are said to have been invented by a serving girl called Madeleine, who made them during one of the Duke's dinners.

– a heart for weddings, a baby for christenings, a fleur-de-lys for Twelfth Night and a star for Christmas.

The prolific orchards of the region provide fruit for tarts and pies – strawberries, raspberries, bilberries, quetsch plums and mirabelles being the most commonly used. These fruits are also made into the celebrated *eaux-de-vie*, without which no Alsatian meal is complete. Best likened to liqueurs, *eaux-de-vie* are in fact pure fruit spirits, and their powerful bouquet is quite unique. They are also used widely in cooking. Kirsch is undoubtedly the best known, but *framboise*, with its almost overpowering scent of raspberries, deserves to be more so. *Tutti-frutti*, a distillation of several fruits, is a great Alsatian speciality.

Lorraine

With its gentle landscape, Lorraine is characterized by its cattle-rearing pastures and its vast orchards, where the region's most famous fruit, the mirabelle plum, is grown. The mirabelle is eaten fresh or dried. It goes into the making of enormous tarts, *quatre-quarts* (a type of rich Madeira cake), cold soufflés and, above all, the spirit that bears the name of the fruit, *Mirabelle*. The quetsch plum, another important regional product, is

Champagne

The cooking of the Champagne region has always been overshadowed by the fact that its wine is so famous. But there are many good dishes from this region and those that are cooked *au champagne* (that have champagne as an ingredient) have an incomparable creamy richness and aroma. Game is abundant in the form of wild boar, deer, pheasant, hare and woodcock, and the rivers are rich with fish – notably eel, pike, carp, perch, trout and crayfish. Champagne is the home of the famous *truites aux amandes* (trout with almonds – page 91), and of different varieties of *matelotes* (page 91), soups made with freshwater fish in champagne wine.

The meats most commonly eaten are pork and mutton. Pork is used in the local charcuterie, to make the famous *andouilles* and *andouillettes de Troyes* (chitterling sausages). Offal (variety meat) too, is popular – and the favourite way to cook oxtail and pigs', calves' and sheeps' trotters, is *à la Saint Menehould*. This involves boiling the meat in stock, coating it with butter or a mixture of herbs and breadcrumbs, then cooking it until crisp and golden under the grill (broiler). Another regional speciality worth mentioning is *potée champenoise*, a mixture of meats and vegetables which is enhanced by the famous mustard from the town of Meaux, *moutarde de Meaux*, sold in the distinctive stone jars. Desserts are varied and, of course, fruit and champagne go into their making. In Reims, capital of Champagne, they sell *bouchons de champagne*, delicacies of chocolate or praline made in the shape of champagne corks.

Franche-Comté

Franche-Comté is a small region with a beautiful landscape of contrasting features – plateaux, plains and mountains. The Jura mountains are covered with dense forests, and wood provides an important source of revenue. Mountain streams and rivers score the region, which is subsequently rich in freshwater fish, most notably crayfish.

Long cold winters give the cooking a hearty, solid and warming character. However, there are delicate dishes in the region, especially those made with wild mushrooms like morels (page 152), which grow in abundance. And as in all mountain areas, *charcuterie* is popular, especially the raw Mortean sausage. Local game is eaten – venison, boar and wild hare, but the pride of Franche-Comté is its cattle, which give rich milk, thick cream and, above all, the exquisite *Comté* cheese (page 35). These cows are of the Montbéliard breed which are amongst the very best of dairy cattle; they graze in rich pastures above an altitude of 1200 metres. Another source of pride to the region is the *poulet de Bresse*, a small, delicate chicken with a flavour all of its own – exported to other regions in France as a great delicacy. Local desserts are often based on the fruit of the region – blackberries, bilberries, blackcurrants and plums.

Ile de France

A region with a long history, the Ile de France includes the centre of the Parisian basin, as well as encompassing the *départements* that surround the capital.

In the past, when links between the various regions were fraught with difficulty, the people of Paris, as elsewhere, relied almost exclusively on local produce – butter from Clamart, asparagus from Argenteuil, cherries from Montmorency and wines from Montmartre or Saint-Cloud. Inspired cooks created dishes that have now become all but household words: recipes for *sauce Béchamel* (page 44), *sauté de veau marengo* (page 136), *entrecôte Bercy* (page 125), *Gâteau Saint-Honoré* (page 185), *crème Chantilly* (page 50) and many, many more. Paris was the birthplace of *la haute cuisine*, the home of countless grand chefs, and one of the great, if not the greatest culinary centres in the world. But nowadays, Paris is a vast city, and its cooking has become international. Despite the fertility of the region, the richness of the soil in the fields, meadows and woods and the abundance of fish in the rivers and streams, the demands of the city now far outweigh the region's resources, and produce has to be brought in from all over France and abroad to supply its needs.

THE NORTH-WEST
Normandy

A largely coastal region, Normandy is drained by the Seine, which flows into the Channel at Le Havre. It is a rich province, with a wealth of raw materials. Milk, cream, butter and cheese are produced and exported in large quantities. Farm poultry, especially duckling; lamb, tenderest mutton and pork; saltwater fish and shellfish with an incomparable flavour . . . the list of local produce is seemingly endless.

The two most famous products associated with Normandy come from the apples, which grow in abundance. These are cider and *calvados* or apple brandy. Cider, as popular in Normandy as it is in Brittany, goes into the making of many dishes. There is a cider made from pears known as *poiré*, but the cider for which Normandy is so well-known is made from the juice of several varieties of apple, mixed together. Normandy cider is divided into four main categories: sweet cider (approximately 3° proof), which is excellent with desserts; *brut* (4.5° proof), which goes very well with meat and is often combined with the rich Normandy cream to make dishes *à la Normande*; dry and semi-dry (without sugar), good with all savoury dishes; and bottled cider, a quality cider, which is also excellent with desserts.

Calvados is an apple or cider brandy which, according to the archives, has been produced in Normandy since 1553. It is made from two to three year-old cider – *vieux calvados* is two years old; *vieille reservé* three years old. After six years, it is classed as *hors d'age* or over-age. It can be served at the end of a meal, like all brandies, but there is also the traditional *trou normand*, the drinking of calvados in the middle of a meal to whet the appetite.

Brittany

Divided into *pays* or countries, Brittany is an immensely diverse region, with some areas orientated towards the sea, others exclusively towards the soil.

Fish and shellfish are prolific along the entire length of the coast. Anchovy, bream, cod, mackerel, skate, sole, turbot and tuna are eaten cooked in a *court-bouillon*, fried, grilled (broiled), baked *au gratin* or made into soups (*matelotes*) and the famous *cotriade* (page 94). The seafood and shellfish is amongst the best anywhere in France; a dish of Breton *fruits de mer* is a real feast – fresh oysters, mussels, lobsters, sea urchins, winkles, scampi, shrimp(s), clams, crabs, spider-crabs and scallops are all caught locally. The rivers of Brittany are also rich in fish – particularly pike, eels and elvers, trout, salmon trout and salmon. The salmon from the Aven is much sought after.

Inland, Brittany is predominantly stock-farming country. Lamb and mutton are highly prized, especially the famous *pré-salé* or salt-meadow variety which comes from animals that graze in salty pastures, fields flooded by the sea at spring tide. These fields are rare, so the meat is correspondingly in short supply – and expensive. Pork is a close rival to lamb and

mutton, and plays a decisive role in the cooking of the region, both fresh as joints and chops, and in the making of *andouilles, andouillettes*, hams, black puddings, sausages and pâtés. Beef takes pride of place in the traditional dish of Brittany *kig ha farz* – boiled beef, cabbage and *farz* (a paste of buckwheat flour mixed with prunes or raisins). This dish has many different versions throughout the region. Another great Breton speciality is the salted butter, which gives the famous *beurre blanc* (page 48) of the Nantes area.

No description of the food of Brittany would be complete without a mention of the ubiquitous *crêpes* or pancakes (page 171), known also as *galettes* in the northern part of the region. Made from wheat or buckwheat flour, they are paper-thin and served simply sprinkled with salt or sugar, spread with jam or honey, or stuffed with savoury or sweet mixtures.

Like Normandy, Brittany produces cider, but also *hydromel*, a honey-based mead, drunk both as an *aperitif* and as a *digestif*. Once made with buckwheat, it is now more often made from heather.

THE LOIRE COUNTRY
Orléanais, Touraine, Anjou, Maine

These four large regions, drained by the Loire and its many tributaries, form the fertile 'garden of France'. Market gardens, fruit farms and vineyards are numerous and bountiful, the climate is mild, and the sun often shines. The landscape is varied: the vast plain of la Beauce, north of Orléans, is the centre of the corn and maize growing industry; sugar beet is produced here too. The Touraine plateau is covered with woods and heathland, scattered here and there with cultivated clearings and fertile valleys – the Val de Loire, the valleys of the Cher, the Indre and the Vienne. The regions of Maine and Anjou resemble Brittany in their geography and cooking.

Fruit and vegetables grow in abundance in this delightful château country along the banks of the river Loire, which itself provides the region with a plentiful supply of fish. Shallots (scallions) are used in almost all savoury dishes, and cream and butter are everyday ingredients. The Touraine is the home of the classic *beurre blanc* (page 48), a whisked combination of wine vinegar and butter, often claimed by the Bretons to be their own. Plums and apples are served in pies; cherries, apricots and pears are baked in shortcrust pastry at Angers, and in flaky pastry at Saumur. Nuts, especially walnuts, are used widely in cake making. It goes without saying, therefore, that this is a rich region in its gastronomic traditions.

Poultry and pig breeding are widespread throughout the whole of the Touraine, and potted and preserved meats and pâtés are great local specialities. *Rillettes de porc* (page 66) and *rillons d'oie* (potted goose) are exported all over the world from the Touraine, with Tours and Le Mans being the undisputed *rillettes* 'capitals'. In Tours, the *rillettes* are made from pure pork. The *rillettes* of Le Mans combine pork and boned goose meat.

Wine growing in the Anjou region is substantial. It is also the home of a wide variety of spirits and liqueurs: peach leaf, sloe and hazelnut being the most unusual. Angers, capital of Anjou, is also the home of the famous orange-flavoured liqueur – *cointreau*.

Vendée, Poitou, Charente

The grouping of these three regions together is traditional: Vendée, which borders on Brittany; Poitou, south of the Loire country; and Charente, close to Bordeaux and the south-west. The cooking is as varied as the landscape. Vendée and Charente, lying on the Atlantic coast, are fishing regions. Seafood is the predominant feature of the local cuisine, and the oyster beds of Marenne-Oléron are famous throughout France. Mussels, too, are everywhere along this coastline and are served in countless different ways. The most famous of all the mussel dishes is undoubtedly *mouclade* (page 98), usually a combination of mussels, white wine and cream, although recipes vary considerably, depending on whether it is a Charente or a Vendée *mouclade*.

This is also the land of *mojhettes* (dried white beans), of *cagouilles* or *lumats* (snails), charentais melon and locally churned butter. The town of Niort is the home of angelica, used for its tonic and curative properties, but also turned into sweets by confectioners, and used as the base of an aromatic liqueur. Angelica is probably best known in its crystallized form, cut into little green sticks, to become *angelique confite*. Crystallized angelica is sculpted into ingenious shapes – frogs, snails, rabbits and ducks . . . on sale in all the confectioner's shops in the town of Niort.

The local wines are not known for their distinction but the area is noted for two very special drinks. *Cognac* is distilled from the white wines of Charente and Charente Maritime and aged in oak casks. It is sold in different qualities, from V.O. (very old) right through to V.V.E.S.O.P (very, very extra superior old pale). *Pineau* is the second most famous drink of the area, quite unique and something of an acquired taste. It is a blend of cognac and charentais grape juice (20° to 22° proof), and is served chilled, as an aperitif.

THE CENTRE
Berry, Auvergne, Limousin

These three regions at the heart of France are relatively poor compared with the rest of the country. Berry, with the town of Châteauroux, is a stock-breeding region of plains and small valleys. Auvergne consists of volcanic plateaux and mountains – the Puy chain with the Puy de Dôme rising to 1465 metres, the Dore mountains with the Puy de Sancy at 1886 metres, and the plomb du Cantal with its peak at 1858 metres. The main Auvergne towns are Clermont-Ferrand, Le Puy and Aurillac. Limousin is a plateau covered with dense forests, and stock farming, especially sheep, is widespread; its best known towns are Limoges and Guéret.

The cooking here is rustic and solid, as is to be expected from a region with a rocky, mountainous and volcanic landscape, often combined with harsh weather conditions. In their cooking, self-reliance is the keynote, for the people seem to exist almost exclusively on local produce, with little contribution from outside. Potatoes, mushrooms, cabbages and turnips are the most commonly used vegetables. Walnuts and chestnuts form the basis of many dishes and desserts, especially in Auvergne and Limousin. Many of France's rivers find their source here, therefore freshwater fish, crayfish, carp, perch, pike, salmon and trout in particular, are plentiful.

There is good grazing land and pastures high on the plateaux, and sheep are reared, both for their meat and for their milk, which is turned into many excellent cheeses. Pigs are a common sight on small-holdings and, as in all mountainous areas, are cured and smoked for *charcuterie* – hams and sausages are therefore always in plentiful supply.

Cattle farming is expanding in the region. Charolais cattle are bred for meat, as well as dairy cows for milk and cheese. Cantal (page 35) is the best known cheese outside the region. Breast of veal is used to make the famous *falette*, with its stuffing of chopped veal and herbs. *Tripoux*, made with tripe, is another local speciality and considered a great delicacy in the region, although arguments are rife as to which is the most authentic way to make it, and there are numerous different recipes.

Poultry farming is widespread, and chickens and geese can be seen pecking away on virtually every small-holding in the region. *Sanguette*, seasoned and cooked chicken blood, is a great local delicacy. *Confit d'oie* (preserved goose) and *foie gras* (goose liver) are much liked, although not quite to the same extent as they are in Périgord. The local soups are thick and filling – *metonnée berrichone* from Berry, for example, with its thickening of bread, is typical of the region.

Clafoutis (page 172), a kind of baked cherry pudding and one of France's best known desserts, comes from Auvergne. Traditionally made during the cherry season, with ripe black cherries baked in batter, recipes vary from one part of the region to another. It is known locally as *millard*. The town of Clermont-Ferrand produces an unusual cherry sweet; called *guignolette*, it is made of cherries soaked in kirsch, wrapped in a cherry pastry.

Rouergue and Cévennes
Although hinging geographically with the south of the country, the cooking of Rouergue and Cévennes is more like that of the centre.

Rouergue comprises the *département* of Aveyron and part of Lot-et-Garonne; its main towns are Rodez, Millau (the glove capital) and Villefranche-de-Rouergue. The landscape is varied: mountains and plateaux are separated by the wide valleys of the Lot and Tarn rivers, and a volcanic massif, the Aubrac, that stretches up into Auvergne. Cévennes is a land of rivers and vast chestnut forests.

Both regions have game, freshwater fish and cattle farming. In the Aveyron is the town of Roquefort, which gives its name to the unique and succulent cheese ripened in limestone grottoes, which is famous all over the world (see page 37). At Rodez, as in Auvergne, *tripoux* is a staple dish and the town of Privas, in the Ardèche is famous for delicious *marrons glacés* (candied chestnuts).

THE RHÔNE-ALPS
Bourgogne and Lyonnais
Bourgogne, or the region of Burgundy as it is best known, is most famous for its wines. Formed by four *départements* – Côte-d'Or, Saône-et-Loire, Nièvre and Yonne, the countryside is one of vine-clad hillsides, valleys and plateaux covered with meadows. The Charolais plateau feeds the cattle of the same name that give some of the tenderest of French beef, and the hills of Bresse, in Saône-et-Loire, supply the famous Bresse poultry, so highly prized throughout the whole of France. There are many orchards and market gardens in this region, and in the Côte-d'Or, they grow hops. Dijon, famous for its mustard and gingerbread, is the main town of the Côte-d'Or, where the names of so many of the little towns evoke the great wines of the region: Nuits-Saint-Georges, Meursault, Volnay, Puligny-Montrachet.

The Lyonnais, the region around Lyon to the south of Bourgogne, is rightly classed alongside Paris as one of France's greatest gastronomic centres, and the vineyards of Burgundy and Beaujolais, close to Lyon have given many great wine-based recipes to the cooking of the region. The most famous by far are *coq au vin* (page 102), *boeuf bourguignon* (page 128) and *entrecôte beaujolaise* (steak cooked in Beaujolais wine) although *tanches au beaujolais* (tench in Beaujolais), i not so well known, is equally as good.

Truffles are one of the wonders of this region's cuisine: sautéed or cooked in a cream sauce, they are prolific enough to be served as a vegetable! Frogs, snails and freshwater fish are widely used and pork provide *charcuterie* of a quality second to none.

Lyon itself produces a variety of desserts and sweetmeats of which the most famous is the *beignet* or fritter, known locally as *bugne*; one variety of which is made with acacia flowers. Blackcurrants are used in many desserts, but the majority of them go into the making of that famous blackcurrant liqueur – *cassis*. Other delicacies include *tendresses*, pieces of rum-flavoured nougat wrapped in meringue, and *cocons* liqueur-flavoured marzipan sweets, shaped like a silk-worm's cocoon. Lyon was once the capital of silk-weavers or *canuts*, and there is actually a type of cheese made with *fines herbes* called *la cervelle de canut* or 'the silkweaver's brain'!

Dauphiné and Savoie
On the borders of Switzerland and Italy are Dauphiné and Savoie, both mountainous regions and important tourist centres. People come here from all over France, and further afield, to ski. The olympic town of Grenoble is in the Dauphiné, and there are several popular winter and spring ski-resorts in Savoie.

Both regions boast many lakes and mountain streams, with such well known fish as carp, crayfish and trout, as well as others that are unknown elsewhere – féra, lavaret and char. These fish are rare – and correspondingly expensive. The milk from the cows grazing in the rich pastures gives an excellent butter and delicious cheeses. Mushroom-picking is a great attraction, and the potato goes to make the famous *gratin dauphinois* (page 166).

As for desserts, dried fruit and nuts are used extensively, but the region is perhaps best known for its *gâteau de Savoie* (page 187), a whisked sponge cake served plain, or with fruit, and/or whipped cream.

AQUITAINE
Bordeaux, Périgord, Gascogne, Béarn

Aquitaine occupies the Atlantic face of the *bassin aquitain*; the coast forms a straight line bordered with sand dunes and salt pools. To the north is the estuary of the Gironde, guarded by the town of Bordeaux, and the Arcachon basin where mussels and oysters are bred; to the east is the plateau of Périgord, intersected by wide valleys; south-west is Gascogne (Gascony), and a vast triangle of the Landes forest sloping gently down to the Atlantic Ocean. To the far south lies the French Basque country at the edge of the Pyrenees with its main town – Bayonne.

The cooking of the whole Aquitaine region is rich and varied, both in ingredients and flavour. Bordeaux produces some of the very best of French wines, and food and drink are of more than prime importance to the Bordelais. The area is unique for its different types of wild mushrooms, cèpes from Périgord being the most highly prized. Truffles are also found in this region, and are used in numerous different dishes, but especially in stuffings and wonderful pâtés and terrines.

The whole of Périgord is known for its gastronomic richness. Its geese are bred for their oversized livers (*foie gras*). Pigs go to make an enormous range of *charcuterie*, and game are hunted in the forests. Fish too are prolific, from exotic oysters and crayfish, to the more usual types of freshwater fish found in the many streams and rivers. Cultivated snails, which fatten themselves on the vine leaves, are also highly regarded.

In the *département* of Gers, one of France's most famous brandies is distilled – *armagnac*. Local white wine, heated in distilling, produces a white brandy that acquires its characteristic golden colour during a ten-year ageing period in oak casks.

THE SOUTH
Toulouse

Part of the Midi-Pyrenees, the town and area of Toulouse border onto the Pyrenees, the inland *bassin aquitain*, and Languedoc. A town all its own, called the '*ville rose*', because of its pink-tiled rooves, Toulouse is the capital of Occitanie (the Languedoc area in south-west France) and has a past rich in history. A speciality of the town is *violettes en sucre*, violets coated in sugar. They have been made in Toulouse since 1879, when water of violet was used for its various medicinal properties – for curing fevers and digestive problems.

The region has plenty of fruit and vegetables and, as in Aquitaine and Périgord, there are truffles, *foie gras* and *confit d'oie*. Its position, between the Mediterranean and the Atlantic, ensures an ample supply of fish.

The most important traditional dish of this region, however, is *cassoulet* (page 144), the preparation of which varies from town to town. For example, in Castelnaudry, where it is said to have originated, it is made with pork; in Toulouse mutton and *confit* are added, in Carcassone, mutton and partridge (when in season). But no matter what the meat, haricot beans (*fèves blanches*) are always the main ingredient in a *cassoulet*. Their introduction is attributed to the Arabs, who brought them to Occitanie in the 7th century, and taught the local people to make a ragoût of mutton '*aux fèves blanches*', the precursor of today's *cassoulet*. The name *cassoulet* most probably derives from *cassoule*, a sort of glazed earthenware casserole, reddish in colour, which is manufactured near Castelnaudry.

Languedoc–Roussillon

This region is made up of the *départements* of Aude, Gard, Hérault, Lozère and Pyrenées Orientales, and is noted for its clear luminous atmosphere, hot dry summers, and cold, often violent winter winds. The Mediterranean coast is lined with tourist resorts, amongst which is Sète, the second largest French Mediterranean port to Marseille. Here there is a large-scale fishing industry, and the *Etang de Thau* is a mussel and oyster breeding centre. Olive trees grow in profusion, producing the strong-flavoured olive oil that is an indispensable part of French cooking in the south-east.

The cooking of this region is rich in fish and shellfish, in mutton and suckling kid, in fruit and vegetables – sweet peppers, courgettes (zucchini), aubergines (eggplant), artichokes and tomatoes chief amongst them. In Nîmes, the great speciality is *brandade de morue* (page 94), made by adding garlic, milk and olive oil to a purée of cod. This dish was traditionally served on Christmas Eve, occasionally enhanced with a few slices of fresh truffle. Cod was brought to the area by the fishermen of Brittany who came south to buy salt, Mediterranean salt being more plentiful and thus less expensive than the salt of the Atlantic coast. In order not to sail south with empty holds, they filled their boats with cheap cod, and the people of Languedoc preserved this cod in salt. *Brandade* and many other dishes using salt cod were thus invented to make good use of plentiful supplies.

In Montpellier, *oreillettes* are a popular local speciality. These are delicious fritters flavoured with orange blossom, although recipes vary enormously from one district to another.

Provence – Côte d'Azur

This region is formed by six *départements* – Alpes-de-Haute-Provence, Hautes-Alpes, Alpes-Maritimes, Bouches-du-Rhône, Var and Vaucluse. The two largest cities are Marseille and Nice, but other major towns with familiar names to the foreigner and tourist are Toulon, Avignon, Valence, Montelimar, Saint-Tropez, Cassis, Antibes, Juan-les-Pins. To the west is the Rhône valley, which opens out in the south into the Camargue and borders the Alps to the east. To the south-east, in sharp contrast with the Golfe du Lion coast, is the mountainous and jagged *côte d'azur*. The light, as in Languedoc, is intensely bright and the infamous Mistral wind blows from time to time with fierce intensity through the whole of the Rhône corridor. The climate is extremely dry and irrigation is always a problem.

Provence is a unique region; its people essentially Mediterranean rather than French, with a language of their own. The local agriculture is intensive, both for local consumption and for export, the main markets being at Cavaillon and Château-Renard. Fruit and vegetables grow in abundance, and flower-growing is fast becoming a highly developed industry, as is the making of perfume, especially in Grasse. Rice grows in the fields of the Camargue, and the Crau plain supplies milk and meat for the whole region. This is also France's major sheep-breeding area.

As in the Languedoc, local dishes are heady with the flavour of olive oil, garlic and herbs. Fruit, vegetables, fish and shellfish, lamb, mutton and kid are among the staple ingredients. In the Nice area in particular,

famous for its *ratatouille* (page 157), there are many unusual varieties of courgettes (zucchini) – round and light-skinned, and aubergines (eggplant) – long and round, white and very pale violet in colour. Peppers come in all shades of green, red and yellow, and tomatoes are huge, juicy and full of sweet flavour. But garlic, most often used with oil, is one of the prides of Provence. Sold in plaits at the late spring markets, it lasts the year through, but is at its very best when 'new' in early spring, eaten raw or cooked. It flavours countless Provençal dishes, but is most predominant in *aïoli* (page 48).

Fresh basil is also an essential ingredient in the cooking of Provence, exquisite in both flavour and aroma in tomato salads, and meat and vegetable stuffings. But basil is not the only 'Provençal' herb, all aromatic herbs play an important role in the cuisine of this region – thyme, rosemary, savory, oregano and fennel are all used widely. In and around Nice, a popular salad is *mesclum*, from the Latin verb *mesclare* meaning 'to mix'. This salad, which originated in Italy, is a mixture of thirteen kinds of salad ingredients.

Along the coast, fish and shellfish are prolific, and used in numerous different dishes, from simple grilled (broiled) fresh sardines and giant prawns simply tossed in olive oil, garlic and cognac, to the more complicated fish soups and stews, recipes for which differ from one

tiny fishing village to another. *Bouillabaisse* (page 92) from Marseille is undoubtedly the most famous of these, with *bourride* (page 95) running a close second. Made with an incredible variety of locally caught Mediterranean fish (sold straight from the fishing boats in the early morning at the port of Marseille), these soups are difficult to imitate outside the area.

Pine trees grow all over the region, yielding pine seeds that go into the making of many local desserts, of which *croissants aux pignons* (also known as *pignoulats*) are probably the best known. The variety of regional desserts also includes *tarte aux blettes de Nice*, a sweet tart made with beets, garnished with raisins, pine seeds and flavoured with rum, and *navettes*, traditional Candlemas cakes sold in Marseille in front of the abbey of Saint-Victor. At Christmas, the traditional sweet is *treize desserts* (thirteen desserts), representing Christ and the twelve Apostles. It consists of dried fruits, nougats, biscuits and a bread-based cake called *pompe a l'huile* (oil pump). This is sometimes replaced by a yeast cake known as *fougasse* or *fougassons* (page 187).

CORSICA

Occupied for a long time by the Italians and sold to France two years before the birth of Napoleon by the Republic of Genoa (Napoleon was actually born on the island), Corsica is a Mediterranean island that is best described as a mountain in the sea. Just 170 kilometres south of Nice, and despite its chequered history of occupation, it still remains unmistakably French in atmosphere. It is an island of breathtaking natural beauty, with mountains descending to the sandy beaches and clear blue shores of the Mediterranean.

Outside the main towns and tourist resorts – Ajaccio, Bastia, Calvi, Porto-Vecchio, Propriano – most of the population lives in the mountains or deep valleys in between, where a traditional pastoral existence seems to thrive happily in almost tranquil oblivion, in contrast to the bustle of the town centres. Sheep and goats are raised to make cheese, herbs grow wild on the hillsides amongst the *maquis*, a unique heather-like plant that seems to cover the whole of the island like a perfumed carpet.

Olive, almond, plum, citron and mandarin trees grow anywhere and everywhere; so too do the vines, which are cultivated both for their grapes and for making wine. Corsican fruit is mainly peaches, apricots and pears, and other less well known fruit such as medlars, pomegranates and jujubes. But there is one tree that is absolutely vital to the cooking of Corsica, and that is the chestnut. Used in both savoury dishes and desserts, the chestnut is found to be a most useful and versatile ingredient in Corsican cookery – and is even ground into flour and used in baking.

WINES

Today, all wine lovers and connoisseurs are well aware that most of the world's great wines come from France. For centuries it has been the centre of the world's wine trade and from north to south, east to west, the different regions produce all manner of splendid wines – red, white, rosé and sparkling. Many of the more famous names are known to us all – the light fruity red Beaujolais, the popular dry white Muscadet and, of course, the sparkling wine of Champagne.

There is no doubt that France is the only country in the world that produces so many different varieties of quality wine – about two-thirds of the land surface is given over to viticulture. Wine is a delicate product that requires very specific and complex development conditions. Its quality depends as much on the professional art of the vine-growers as on the climate, type of soil and variety of grape used.

As the popularity of wine-drinking has increased, so many methods of winemaking and production have been modernised. Laws have also been introduced in France to guarantee the quality of the wine.

THE CLASSIFICATION OF WINES

How can you tell a good wine from an average one? How do you know if it is 'elegant', 'nervy', 'supple', or conversely, if it is 'dumb' or 'flat'? A few basic guidelines are indispensable when choosing a French wine.

Vins Délimités de Qualité Supérieure (V.D.Q.S)

This secondary rating is for good, but basically local, wines. Obtained after analysis and tasting, this classification is subject to a decree from the *Institut National des Appellations d'Origine*. These wines are often delicate and do not travel well.

Appellation Contrôlée (A.C. or A.O.C.)

There are 251 *Appellation Contrôlées* in France. And if not all A.C. wines are necessarily great wines, all great wines are A.C. *Appellation Contrôlée* is a guarantee not only of origin but also of a certain standard and it can only be granted by the *Institut National des Appellations d'Origine*. For wines to receive this recognition, they must reach a precise condition, so an *Appellation Contrôlée* is a good indication for the wine buyer.

Châteaux and Domaine Wines

These are the 'wine of wines', the finest, the most famous . . . and the most expensive wines. They too carry the *Appellation Contrôlée* label because they do not have their own administrative status. As far as these great wines are concerned, it is their property of origin (*Château or Domaine*) which makes their reputation. The wines are further ranked by *crus*. *Grand cru* is the highest grade, then *premier, deuxième, troisième cru* etc.

Blended wines (vins de coupage) and vins de pays

These are either blended wines of mixed origin, or local wines which do not qualify for any of the *Appellations* above. They are table wines which must have a minimum alcohol content of 9°5, and must by law state this content on the bottle.

The Vintage

The vintage is the year the grapes were picked. The word 'vintage' is often erroneously used to mean 'a very good year'. In fact, it only means very good wine when applied to champagne. Other wines (V.D.Q.S. or A.C.) always carry the vintage on the bottle, whether it was a good year or not. There are good vintages and bad ones. To tell them apart, is a matter of long experience of the appearance, smell and taste of a wine.

The Label

Labels can tell you a great deal if you know how to read them. To find out what is in the bottle, you have to open it and costly mistakes can result from relying on luck alone. A label can provide certain guarantees, provided a few simple rules are followed. For example, be wary of excessively ornate labels, or ones with over-wordy descriptions and prolific information. Look for simple labels which give only the essential details: place of origin and grower's name. It is also worth noting that only '*vins ordinaires*' actually have the word '*vin*' on the label (unlike most of the *Appellation* wines) together with a figure: 9°5, 12°, etc.

THE WINE REGIONS OF FRANCE
Alsace and Lorraine

Alsace, which incorporates the two *départements* of Haut-Rhin and Bas-Rhin, is one of the oldest wine-growing areas in France. Alsace wines are white, dry and fruity, and can be drunk very young. Unlike other *Appellation* wines, they are not known by their area or estate of origin but by the name of their variety of grape, or '*cépage*', which falls into one of three main categories.

The *cépages courants* or common grapes category includes the light semi-sparkling wine, Chasselas.

Cépages fins or fine grapes includes Sylvaner and Pinot blanc. Sylvaner is a very dry wine with a delicate bouquet and is ideal with fish and shellfish. Pinot blanc is dry and fruity and is perfect with *foie gras* and meats.

The *cépages nobles* or noble grapes provide some of the best known wines of the region, including Riesling, Pinot gris or Tokay d'Alsace, Muscat and Gewürztraminer. Riesling is undoutedly the most popular wine of the region. It is fruity, dry and full-bodied and makes the perfect accompaniment to hors d'oeuvre and fish. Pinot gris, a dry spicy wine, is excellent with *foie gras* and game. The light musky taste of Muscat is the ideal complement to desserts and cheeses. The dry and mellow Gewürztraminer is one of the very few wines that can be served with highly-flavoured dishes and strong cheeses.

From Lorraine, there are two V.D.Q.S. wines worthy of note: Côtes de Toul, a very pleasant light and fruity wine, and Côteaux de Moselle, subtle and fragrant in its good vintages.

Champagne

Champagne is not only the most famous wine in the world, it is also a unique wine in that it owes much to the talent of the grower, for champagne is as much a recipe as it is a product of the soil and climate. Between the pressing of the different types of grape (black and white) and the sale of bottles on the market, there are many intermediate stages, some of them very delicate procedures. And champagne needs time: it spends

about three years in the cellar before going on sale.

Unlike other French wines, the wines of Champagne do not have *crus*. It is the careful selection of grapes which determines the 'value' of champagne. They also differ from other wines in that their labels do not give either the type of grape or the origin, but merely the brand name. So you have to go by the reputation of the particular brand.

Champagne does not improve with age, so there is no point in laying it down in the cellar. It can be drunk at any time of day and, although the custom has been to drink champagne at the end of a meal with the dessert, more and more wine-lovers are drinking it before and even during a meal.

Champagne can be *brut* (bone-dry), *extra-sec* (dry), *sec* (slightly sweet), *demi-sec* (sweet) or *doux* (very sweet), according to the amount of *liqueur d'expédition* that is added at the last moment. This liqueur is a mixture of old champagne, sugar and sometimes cognac.

The Loire Valley

For almost 500 kilometres, from Nevers to Nantes, the banks of the Loire and of some of its tributaries produce all kinds of wines, with a lightness and grapiness which is both appetizing and refreshing. Most of the wines are white and they are, quite literally, 'charming' wines.

Noteworthy among the nine wine-growing sub-divisions of the region are Muscadet, Pouilly-sur-Loire, Sancerre, Anjou and Touraine. Muscadet has an excellent reputation as a fresh dry white wine and it is particularly pleasant with fish and shellfish. Pouilly-sur-Loire is best known for Pouilly-Fumé, an excellent dry white wine. Sancerre is a justly famous dry white, perfect with poultry in sauce. Much of the wine of Anjou is pink, with an excellent bouquet.

The wines of Touraine, white, rosé and red, are sweeter. The one-time Bishop of Tours, Saint-Martin, owned many vineyards in Touraine, and the story goes that the art of dressing the vines was discovered by his donkey. One year the donkey grazed on some of the young vinestocks, and the following year it was noticed that those particular vines were giving better grapes – and more of them. Since then, on the feast of Saint-Martin, November 11th, the wine-growers taste the new wine and call it 'martining'.

One Touraine wine stands out above all others: the world-famous Vouvray, a sparkling accompaniment to almost any dish – or on its own! Apart from Vouvray there is Montlouis, its younger brother which is almost as good. As for red wines, there are two outstanding *Appellations Contrôlées*. Bourgueil, a light wine with a delicate raspberry bouquet is good with meats in sauce, game and cheeses. Chinon, soft and violet-scented, was once described as 'a wine for intellectuals' and goes well with the same dishes as Bourgueil. Both of these wines are normally drunk young, although Bourgueil ages well.

Bordeaux

Wine-lovers have always waxed lyrical about Bordeaux, describing it as a 'feminine' wine because of its delicate complexity, as opposed to the 'virile' wine of burgundy. Louis XIV even described it as 'nectar of the gods'. In praising the finesse, subtlety and mellowness of these wines, adjectives and epithets have almost run dry.

There is great variety among the wines of Bordeaux, all of which come from the *département* of Gironde, the best of them from along the banks of the rivers. Bordeaux improves with age – its great longevity (up to 100 years or more) is one of its main characteristics, together with its distinctive bouquet: the freshness of undergrowth or violets.

It is difficult to tell one Bordeaux from another, with three dozen *Appellations Contrôlées*, five *crus*, and the *appellations générales*. The labels on the bottles must carry the name of the *Appellation Contrôlée* and the name and address of the proprietor, but the name of the *château*, the *cru* and vintage are optional.

For the red wines there are four *appellations générales*: Bordeaux, Bordeaux Supérieur, Bordeaux Rosé or Claret, and Bordeaux Mousseux; 42 *appellations régionales*, including Saint-Emilion, Pomerol, Médoc and Haut-Médoc; and *communales* (Saint-Estèphe, Margaux, Pauillac, etc). White Bordeaux includes Entre-Deux-Mers, Côtes de Blaye, Cadillac, Sauternes, Barsac, Graves Supérieures.

The great variety of Bordeaux wines means that they can accompany many different dishes. Saint-Emilion, dark in colour, full-bodied and with a distinctive bouquet, is good with aspics and terrines, and makes a good accompaniment to *cèpes à la bordelaise* (page 152). Pomerol is brightly coloured, full and supple and goes well with omelettes and other egg dishes – *oeufs frits aux aubergines* (page 71) in particular. The delicate and discreet Médoc is ideal to serve with *agneau rôti de pauillac* (roast leg of lamb with potatoes – page 140) and perfect with Munster cheese. Bordeaux claret is the wine to drink with *charcuterie*; Graves Supérieures and Sauternes with *foie gras*, fish and shellfish. Barsac, with its pretty yellow colour, enhances the delicate flavour of shellfish and the classic lobster dish *homard à l'américaine* (lobster a l'américaine – page 96).

If the name of Bordeaux is in the main synonymous with great wine, it should also not be forgotten that some of the so-called 'little' table wines, like the *appellations générales* Bordeaux Rouges and Supérieurs Rouges, are good light wines that in a good year can

rival certain *crus*, and at a much lower price. The same is true of the white Bordeaux Supérieurs (11° minimum) which are dry, light and fruity.

Bergerac

The wines of the Bergerac region are often wrongly assumed to be Bordeaux. But the grapes which go to produce these wines are grown in the Dordogne, and only the wines of the Gironde have the right to the Bordeaux *appellation*. There are ten *Appellation Contrôlée* wines in this region, the best known of which is Bergerac (red and rosé). Others include Pécharmant, full-bodied and generous, and Montravel, dry or sweet and very fruity. Monbazillac, the best of the Bergerac wines, is a wonderful white wine to serve with desserts – and keeps for thirty years.

Bourgogne

The name of Bourgogne, or Burgundy, is synonymous throughout the world with great wine. Superlatives abound where the wines of Burgundy are concerned. And rightly so. The people of Burgundy who

have been cultivating vineyards on the same soil for 2000 years, are unrivalled (except perhaps at Bordeaux) for the loving care with which they nurture their wines.

Burgundy wine is the wine of kings: the kings of France prized it above all others, especially the Beaune. It is claimed that when Philippe VI was crowned at Reims, he arranged for Burgundy wine to pour from the nostrils of a bronze horse in front of the cathedral! Unfortunately though, the world-wide reputation of these famous wines, richly deserved as it is, lends itself all too easily to abuse. All over the world unscrupulous dealers think nothing of sticking a Burgundy label onto any old wine. So beware of imitations, the only wines that deserve this prestigious name are those from the Côte d'Or region and from the Chalonnais.

The greatest wines (*crus*) of Burgundy come from the sunny slopes of the Côte d'Or and are produced in the two main sectors: Côte de Nuits and Côte de Beaune. Among the Côte de Nuits wines, Chambolle-Musigny (red) compared in fragrance with Fixin, or Vosne-Romanée, full-bodied yet mellow. All meat and poultry, potato and flageolet (bean) dishes are ideal fare to serve with these wines. The more delicate Clos de Vougeot, with its scent of truffles, and Gevrey-Chambertin, with its full bouquet, are wonderful accompaniments to truffle and mushroom omelettes. If your purse and palate permit, serve *dinde aux marrons* (turkey with chestnuts), roast lamb or hare with the full-bodied Nuits-Saint-Georges, or, better still, with Romanée-Conti, the prince of all the Burgundy red wines.

As to the Côte de Beaune wines, Beaune is a peerless accompaniment to roast beef, guinea fowl and goose; Pommard is ruby-coloured, firm and elegant; Volnay, subtle and delicate, is the perfect wine to drink with *chou au lard* (white cabbage with bacon – page 155). Of the wines of Chalonnais, Givry and Mercurey are very close to the Côte de Beaune wines.

Great Burgundian wines age well, some for 50 years and more, by which time, unfortunately, they are extremely rare and extremely expensive. Less pricey are the so-called 'appellations génériques' Burgundies, which although not so great as those from the Côte d'Or and the Chalonnais are very respectable table wines. The Bourgogne Clairet, Bourgogne Passe-tout-grain, Bourgogne Ordinaire and Grand Ordinaire (9° minimum) are pleasant accompaniments to hearty soups, such as the famous *soupe à l'oignon gratinée* (page 55).

Burgundy produces excellent white wines as well as red ones. Montrachet and Meursault – with its nutty taste, are two of the best-known Burgundian wines. However, the most famous white wine from this region must be Chablis which, according to the connoisseurs, is the only wine to drink with fish and shellfish. The less well-known Bourgogne-Aligoté is another good white to serve with shellfish.

Finally, it is worth noting that the great Burgundies, as well as the less exalted ones, are incomparable with soft cheeses like Munster, Pont-l'Evêque, Livarot, Camembert and Brie.

Beaujolais and Mâconnais
The Beaujolais region, south of Burgundy, produces probably the most popular wines in the world. Beaujolais is no longer considered a Burgundy wine,

for the simple reason that it is produced with a different grape (*gamay*). Beaujolais wines are characterized by their lightness and fruitiness and all, except for Morgon, should be drunk young. There are twelve Beaujolais, three *appellations* and nine *crus*. Beaujolais, Beaujolais Supérieur and Beaujolais-Villages, the *appellation* wines, are basically refreshing and satisfying. The nine *crus*, equally refreshing if a little fruitier, go well with fairly simple dishes. Chénas and le Fleurie, both fine young and light red wines, complement dishes like *potage au cresson* (cream of watercress soup – page 59), *saucisson en brioche* (hot sausage in pastry – page 68) and *entrecôte bercy* (page 125). Chiroubles, Juliénas, Morgon and Brouilly, with their fuller body and richer colour, go well with thick soups, *charcuterie* and dishes like *coq en pâte* (stuffed chicken in pastry – page 105) and *foie de veau à la lyonnaise* (calf's liver with onions – page 148).

Moulin-à-vent, considered by some connoisseurs to be the king of the Beaujolais, is a strong wine but one which loses some of its fruitiness quite early. It is recommended to drink with fish pâtés, beef in aspic and *civet de lièvre* (jugged hare – page 112).

The geographical border between Mâconnais and Beaujolais is hard to determine. The two noteworthy reds to come from the Mâconnais are Mâcon and Pinot-Chardonnay-Mâcon, but the area is better known for its white wines. Pouilly-Fuissé is the outstanding white wine of the area. Dry and light, with a lovely pale golden colour, it is best drunk young, with fish and shellfish. It is particularly good with *filets de sole à la normande* (page 84).

The Rhône Valley
The wines of the Rhône valley are produced along the banks of the river, between Lyon and Avignon. In the main, less subtle than the Burgundy or even the Beaujolais wines, they are full and heady. For their quality in relation to price, they are amongst the best value French wines.

The *appellation Côtes du Rhône* applies to most of the wines produced in the 138 communes of the five *départements* that make up the region. The best wines go by the name of their commune of origin. The outstanding red wine is Châteauneuf-du-Pape, full-bodied and strong, with a high alcohol content. It is excellent with pâtés, terrines and galantines, and with *homard à l'américaine* (lobster a l'américaine – page 96). A Gigondas will also go well with this dish. Other good red wines, like Côte-Rôtie, with a hint of violets, or Ermitage with its raspberry-like scent, are heady complements to turkey, guinea-fowl and game.

The white wines of the Rhône valley are equally as good as the reds. Château-Grillet is dry and heady when mature, and does great justice to shellfish and dishes such as *loup au fenouil* (charcoal-grilled bass with fennel – page 89). A white Crozes-Ermitage goes perfectly with all fried and cold fish dishes.

The most famous French rosé is a Côte du Rhône called Tavel. With its bouquet of wild strawberries, it is perfect with *brandade de morue* (creamed salt cod – page 94). Another quality rosé to look for is Lirac. A review of Rhône wines would be incomplete without a mention of the Côtes de Ventoux. These red, white and rosé wines lack the reputation of Côtes du Rhône, but are none the less interesting. Clairette de Die, a dry white sparkling wine, is noted for its freshness.

The Jura and Savoie

Although some good-quality red wines are produced in this region, the speciality of the Jura is undoubtedly its 'yellow' wine. Produced from white grapes, it owes its name to its characteristic colour. Château-Chalon, the best of the yellow wines, is quite exceptional in that it can be enjoyed throughout a meal, no matter what types of dishes are served. It is, however, particularly to be recommended as an accompaniment to veal escalopes, crayfish, *morilles à la crème* and *tarte aux amandes*.

In Savoie, Seyssel (sparkling or still) and Crépy are *Appellation Contrôlée* white wines; Bugey (red, white and rosé) is a V.D.Q.S. wine, pleasantly light and fruity.

Languedoc and Roussillon

This area, known as the Midi, has more vineyards than any other area of France. The twenty-one V.D.Q.S. wines produced in the Languedoc represent almost half of France's production of this category of wines. Although there are few *Appellation Contrôlée* wines, the *vins du pays* are legion.

The Clairette de Languedoc (A.O.C.) is a pleasant dry white to go with fish and shellfish. Clairette de Bellegarde (A.O.C.), a firm dry white, is ideal with *brandade de morue* (creamed salt cod – page 94). The dry and full-bodied Fitou (A.O.C.) – some say the best red wine of Languedoc – suits game dishes. The Corbières, in terms of quantity, is the main V.D.Q.S. wine in France and it goes well with strong flavoured soups. With desserts, especially *pâtisserie* and melon, the

Muscat de Frontignan is tempting, so too is the Blanquette de Limoux. A peculiarity of the Languedoc is the *vin de sable* or sand wine, so called because it grows on the sandy shore of the Mediterranean. It is a simple little local wine (the best-known is sold under the name Listel), that goes very well with roast chicken. From the Haut-Languedoc, Cahors (A.O.C.), a full-bodied, fruity wine, is excellent with *cassoulet toulousain* (page 144).

In the Roussillon, the best wines are the fortified dessert wines which have an alcohol content of at least 15°. Banyuls, Banyuls Grand Cru and Muscat de Rivesaltes are all best served as aperitifs or with dessert. Some reds, like Collioure or the Catalan wines, are equally pleasant to taste.

Provence and Corsica

Provence, land of sunshine, is best known for the rosé wines which are its main produce. Lively and refreshing, they are definitely wines to be drunk rather than sipped, and are perfect with such regional dishes as *mouton gardianne* (lamb chops with potatoes and garlic – page 140), *sardines farcies au vert* (sardines stuffed with spinach – page 86) and *bouillabaisse* (page 92). Provence has five *Appellation Contrôlée* wines: Bandol (white, rosé and red), Bellet (white and red), Cassis (white and one of the best rosés), Palette (white, rosé, and red) and Côtes de Provence (especially the rosés).

Corsica produces its own wines, but few of these are exported. The red Côteaux d'Ajaccio and the rosé Patriomonio are naturally ideal with *rougets à la bonifacienne* (Corsican red mullet – page 86).

COOKING EQUIPMENT

Bain Marie: There are two types of *bain marie*. One is a large pan similar to a roasting pan which usually has two handles for easy lifting and is mainly used for baking custards, pâtés and terrines in the oven. The dish in which the food is cooked is placed in the *bain marie*, which is then filled with water to come halfway·up the sides of the dish. The water may be hot or cold, depending on the food that is to be cooked (see *au bain marie* – page 38). It is not essential to buy a special *bain marie* pan, a large roasting pan will do just as well.

The other type of *bain marie* is for use on top of the stove, to keep sauces warm. It is like a large saucepan with a close fitting lid. The sauce is placed in a heatproof bowl or small pan, which is then placed inside the *bain marie*. Water is poured into the pan to come halfway up the sides of the bowl and a lid is placed on top; the water can then be left to simmer gently without the sauce forming a skin. Any large heavy-based saucepan or double boiler (see opposite) can be used for this purpose. A metal stand is often used in conjunction with this type of *bain marie*. It is placed on the bottom of the *bain marie* so that the bowl or pan containing the sauce does not come·in direct contact with the heat – ideal for sauces containing cream or egg yolks which curdle or separate easily.

Balloon Whisk: The favourite whisk of French chefs for incorporating air into mixtures. The balloon shape, where the loops of wire are wider at the bottom than the top, is the most efficient way to whisk because it allows plenty of air to be forced in quickly – balloon whisking can increase the volume of egg whites by as much as seven times. The combination of a balloon whisk and a round-bottomed copper bowl (see opposite) is best for whisking eggs. One small and one large balloon whisk is adequate for most kitchens.

Birch Whisk: Simply a bunch of birch twigs tied together tightly at one end. Used mainly for whisking eggs and in sauce-making. A birch whisk gives a rustic look to the kitchen if nothing else, although some cooks prefer the action of the birch to the balloon whisk. Hold between the palms of both hands and rub together to produce a twirling action.

Cannelle Knife: A knife for making channels, or *cannelles*, in the rind of citrus fruit, mostly oranges and lemons. Useful for removing thin strips of rind for flavouring sauces, etc., and making attractive garnishes.

Casserole: Used extensively in French kitchens, for long, slow cooking of meat dishes. Many French casserole dishes are cooked on top of the stove, therefore the flameproof cast iron variety in which the vegetables and meat can be fried before adding liquid, is the most sensible kind to buy. Casseroles with domed lids are traditional for cooking game, whereas the casserole with a concave lid called a *doufeu*, is used for pot roasting cuts of meat which tend to dry out during cooking. The lid is filled with water and the resulting evaporation helps keep the meat moist. French earthenware casseroles, usually glazed on the inside, look attractive but are not all flameproof – check before buying. See also *Cocotte*, Copper pans and *Marmite*.

Charlotte Mould: This is like a deep metal cake tin (pan), but with sloping sides and usually with small handles on each side. It is indispensable for making charlottes: the mould is lined with sponge fingers (lady fingers), filled with a mousse mixture and allowed to set. Charlottes are turned out before serving. Decorative charlotte moulds are also available which give a pattern to the top layer of jelly when turned out. Charlotte moulds are also useful for setting plain mousses and soufflé mixtures, and for baking *crème caramel* (page 172). Available in two sizes – 15 cm/6 inch and 18 cm/7 inch.

Cheesecloth (Muslin): Used for draining and straining sauces to give them a fine consistency – a sieve (strainer) is lined with cheesecloth, then the sauce passed through slowly. Also sometimes used for lining cheese drainers.

Cheese Drainer: Small mould used to drain off whey from curd cheese and for making *crémets* (page 173). Sometimes lined and/or covered with cheesecloth (muslin), cheese drainers are made of china, earthenware and metal. Heart-shaped moulds are also available for making the classic *coeur à la crème* – cream cheese, cream, egg white and sugar.

Chinois: A conical strainer with a fine stainless steel or wire mesh. Used mostly for straining sauces, to make them smooth. Swedish stainless steel conical sieves (strainers) are the most practical to clean, and have a hook opposite the handle which grips onto the lip of bowls and pans.

Cocotte: A general term used to describe any round or oval cooking utensil, from a large casserole to individual dishes, in which food is both cooked and served. Large *cocottes*

...re usually made of cast iron or earthenware, ...ith a handle on each side for easy lifting and ...close-fitting lid. They are used for the same ...urpose as a casserole. Small *cocottes*, also ...lled ramekins, are generally made of fire-...roof china, porcelain or earthenware. A set ...f these is useful for individual servings.

...opper Bowls: An unlined copper bowl ...ith a rounded bottom is traditionally used ...y French chefs for beating egg whites – the ...ombination of copper and a wire balloon ...hisk gives the greatest volume. An expen-...ve but worthwhile investment, especially ...r soufflé making.

...opper Pans: These not only look attrac-...ve, they are the best conductors of heat and ...set of copper saucepans is therefore a good ...iy. They must be tin-lined, or the copper ...ill give off toxic compounds and taint food. ...are must be taken with cleaning (never use ...scouring pad), and they will need to be ...tinned professionally whenever the lining ...ears thin.

...rêpe Pan: For best results a special pan ...iould be reserved for cooking *crêpes*. French ...*pe* pans are usually made of steel or cast ...on. They are very shallow and have a ...irved lip to make it easy to slide the *crêpe* ...it after cooking. Different sizes are ...ailable, but the traditional size is about ...5 cm/6 inches. Never wash out a *crêpe* pan ...ter use – simply wipe clean with kitchen ...iper towels and salt.

...ouble Boiler: An important piece of ...quipment when making sauces and cus-...rds, since direct contact with the heat ...urce causes these to curdle. A double boiler ...onsists of two saucepans, one slightly smal-...r than the other. The small pan fits snugly ...iside the rim of the larger pan, which is

filled with water and placed over heat. A lid fits the top pan, and both pans have handles for easy lifting. Double boiler inserts are available with two grip handles. These are less expensive and can be used to adapt an ordinary saucepan into a double boiler.

Doufeu: See Casserole.

Fish Kettle: Used for cooking whole fish, e.g. salmon. Oblong in shape, at least 50 cm/20 inches long, but can be as much as 80 cm/32 inches, they are made of metal with matching perforated steaming platform. The fish is placed on the platform, which stands proud of the water in the kettle and enables the fish to poach gently. The platform has handles for easy lifting. A worthwhile buy if whole fish are cooked frequently.

Frying Pan (Skillet): An essential piece of kitchen equipment. Choose a good quality, heavy-based pan – an inexpensive frying pan (skillet) is a false economy, since food will stick and even burn. The old-fashioned cast-iron type of frying pan is much favoured by French cooks. Deep-sided frying pans are the most versatile as they can be used to fry meat and vegetables, then liquid can be added without the food having to be transferred to a deeper pan or casserole. For most families, a 25 cm/10 inch pan is adequate. French cooks never wash a cast-iron frying pan, but simply wipe it clean with kitchen paper towels and salt after use. A little oil is then wiped over the inside to prevent rusting and sticking.

Garlic Press: A useful gadget in which whole garlic cloves can be pressed to a pulp or purée by squeezing the two handles of the press tightly together. Quicker and less messy than using a knife or mortar and pestle, as garlic can be squeezed directly onto food from the press.

Gras-maigre: A French gravy boat which, as its name suggests (literally translated *gras-maigre* means 'fat and lean'), separates the fat from the juices of a gravy or sauce. The boat has a spout at each end. The conventional spout pours both fat and juices, whereas the other spout has a funnel which takes only the juices and sediment from the bottom.

Gratin Dish: A shallow baking dish, round or oval, which traditionally has two fluted handles. To cook '*au gratin*' implies brown-ing under the grill (broiler) before serving; therefore gratin dishes should be flameproof and most are made of earthenware or cast iron. Sets of gratin dishes in different sizes are very useful, both for cooking and serving. Individual ones are perfect for starters.

Hachinette: A chopper with a curved blade, which is sold together with a wooden bowl. One of the most efficient ways to chop small amounts of herbs, garlic, onions and shallots (scallions), etc.

Hachoir: A curved chopping blade with a handle at each end which chops efficiently if 'rocked' to and fro over herbs, garlic, onions and shallots (scallions), etc. Some *hachoirs* have a double blade and are even efficient enough to chop meat very finely. Use in conjunction with a wooden chopping board.

Knives: A good set of kitchen knives is essential for French cooking. Carbon steel knives are the sharpest, but they do rust and discolour easily and need sharpening frequently, therefore stainless steel knives are probably more practical for everyday use. Apart from selecting knives of the best quality and keeping them sharp, it is also important to have the right knife for the task. A good selection should include the following:—

Boning Knife: Essential for boning out meat and poultry. It has a long, thin, slightly curved blade.

Bread Knife: Most efficient type is long (about 30 cm/12 inches) with a deep serrated edge. Use a sawing motion with this knife.

Carving Knife: Always reserve for carving cooked meat. Can have a straight or serrated edge, but the blade should be long and rigid.

Cook's Knife: Available in many sizes, but one large (about 20 cm/8 inches) and one small (about 10 cm/4 inches) should be sufficient for most jobs. Indispensable for all slicing, cutting, chopping and trimming of meat, poultry and vegetables.

Filleting Knife: With a straight-edged flexible blade and a pointed end, for boning and filleting fish.

Palette Knife: For spreading soft mixtures evenly and for lifting fragile foods. Must have a thin flexible blade. Useful to have both a large and a small one.

Serrated-edged Knife: Essential for cutting soft vegetables such as tomatoes. Always use a sawing motion for neat, thin slices. A pointed end is also useful for removing pips (seeds), etc.

Vegetable Knife: Straight-edged with a blade about 10 cm/4 inches in length. For paring, scraping and chopping small young vegetables (a large cook's knife is best for the larger, tougher vegetables).

Kugelhopf Mould: Designed for making *kugelhopf* (page 186), a sweet yeast bread similar to *brioche* with dried fruit and almonds, but also useful for making other bread and cake mixtures. The tube or funnel in the centre helps mixtures cook quickly. This mould can also be used for setting jellies and mousses, etc., so that when inverted, the hole in the centre can be filled with fruit or cream. Several sizes and different patterns are available.

Lardoire: A larding needle used for larding lean meat with strips of fat (called *lardons* – page 40). The needle is made of stainless steel with a sharp point at one end and a clip with teeth at the other to grip the fat. Used exactly like a conventional sewing needle, but with fat and meat rather than thread and material!

Madeleine Tin: Used for making French *madeleines* (page 187), not to be confused with English madeleines which are baked in dariole moulds. French *madeleines* must be cooked in these special tins, which give them a scallop shell effect.

Mandolin: Essential for very thin slicing of vegetables (carrots, cucumbers, potatoes, etc.) if you do not have a food processor. Consists of a very sharp blade on a wooden frame. Plastic and metal framed *mandolins* are also available, but are not so efficient. To slice the vegetable it is rubbed up and down against the blade, which can be altered with a screw to give different thicknesses.

Marmite: A tall, straight-sided stockpot or stew pot in which meat stews and stocks are cooked. The traditional *marmite* has two handles at the top, and is made of earthenware, cast iron or tin-lined copper. All *marmites* are flameproof because they are usually used on top of the stove. In France, a *marmite* is used to cook large quantities of meat and vegetables; for everyday use, a *marmite* is not essential – a large casserole can take its place.

Moule à manqué: A tin used for making French sponge cakes. Usually about 5 cm/2 inches deep, with sloping sides which makes it easy to turn the cake out. Some *moule à manqué* tins are fluted or funnelled on the inside. Most useful size is 20 cm/8 inches in diameter.

Mouli-grater: The famous French rotary grater is indispensable for grating cheese very finely. It is far more useful and convenien than an ordinary box, conical or flat grater because it will grate very small amounts and there is no wastage. Also good for grating nuts and chocolate.

Mouli-julienne: A hand-operated grater shredder/slicer which grips onto a work surface by means of rubber feet. Good fo preparing vegetables, if you do not have a food processor. Interchangeable discs are provided to enable different thicknesses to be cut as required.

Mouli-légumes: Also called a vegetabl mill or food press, this is a hand-operated machine with rotating discs inside a metal o plastic casing. It is used for sieving fruit and vegetables, and has several interchangeabl blades or discs which produce fine or thic purées. Blenders and food processors ar now taking the place of the *mouli-légumes* i many French kitchens.

Muslin: See Cheesecloth.

Omelette Pan: As with a *crêpe* pan, French cooks like to keep a special pan for making omelettes. The traditional omelette pan i made of steel or cast iron. It has deep curved sides, deeper than a *crêpe* pan, which make i easy to fold the omelette and slide it onto a plate. Never wash an omelette pan afte use, simply wipe clean with kitchen pape towels and salt. Always heat the pan very gently before adding oil or fat, and only us for omelettes – this way they should neve stick or burn. Several sizes are available, from individual 2-egg size, up to large 30 cm/1 inch pans.

Pancake Pan: See Crêpe pan.

Pepper Mill: To provide freshly ground pepper, which should always be used in French recipes. Always grind the pepper-corns straight from the mill onto food; never store ground pepper – like coffee, it rapidly loses its flavour.

Pestle and Mortar: Still used in many French kitchens, although blenders, food processors and grinders have now taken its place for many tasks. Can be made of wood or glass, although porcelain and solid brass are more efficient. Useful for pounding, crushing and grinding small amounts of spices and nuts, and still thought of as the best utensils for crushing garlic. Traditionally, French mayonnaise is always made with a pestle and mortar.

Pot-au-feu: A large deep earthenware casserole which is traditionally used for cooking the beef dish of the same name (page 32). A *pot-au-feu* should be straight-sided and flameproof as the beef is usually cooked on top of the stove for several hours and evaporation should be kept to a minimum. A *pot-au-feu* is similar to a *marmite* and the two are interchangeable. A large deep casserole can be used for the same purpose.

Ramekin: See *Cocotte* and Soufflé dish.

Ricer: Rather like a giant garlic press, used mostly for cooked potato. Not an essential piece of equipment, but gives an alternative thread-like effect to mashed potato. Often used for desserts made with chestnut purée.

Ring Mould: See Savarin mould.

Salt Mill: To grind coarse rock or sea salt, which should be used in all French recipes. An essential piece of equipment, both for cooking and for use at the table.

Savarin Mould: A metal ring mould with a large hole in the centre to allow maximum conduction of heat. Traditionally used for making rum babas and savarins, this mould has a rounded base which gives the cakes their characteristic shape. Also useful for making other cakes, sweet and savoury mousses and *crème caramel* (page 172) – the hole in the centre can be filled with cream, fruit, vegetables, fish, etc. Cooked rice and vegetables pressed into a savarin mould look most attractive when turned out.

Skimmer: For skimming fat and scum off the surface of liquids, especially stock, soups and casseroles. A skimmer is like a flat ladle with perforations, and is usually made of stainless steel. A slotted spoon can also be used for skimming, but is perhaps not quite so efficient as it is usually bowl-shaped.

Sorbetière: A machine for making sorbet and ice cream. Modern *sorbetières* are electric, for use in the freezer or freezing compartment of the refrigerator (the connecting wire is flat and does not affect the closing of the door). Not an essential piece of equipment, but a worthwhile investment if sorbets and ice creams are popular. Electricity drives the paddle continuously through the mixture, thus obviating the necessity for manual beating. This not only takes all the hard work out of making ices, but also ensures the final texture is not granular – a common problem with ices made by hand.

Soufflé Dish: Traditionally this is a straight-sided dish with a ridged effect on the outside, and is made of fireproof porcelain, china or earthenware. Used for both sweet and savoury soufflé mixtures, often in conjunction with a paper collar so that the mixture stands above the rim of the dish and can be decorated with chopped nuts, ratafias,

cream, etc. A set of three different sizes is most useful, from 600 ml/1 pint/2½ cups through to 1 litre/1¾ pints/4¼ cups, as they can also be used as all-purpose baking dishes and are particularly suitable for pâtés. Individual soufflé dishes, also called *cocottes* and ramekins, are perfect for entertaining, both for starters and desserts.

Terrine: An earthenware ovenproof dish which is used for cooking terrines and pâtés. (The word *terrine* has come to mean the food that is cooked in the *terrine* as well as the vessel itself.) Traditionally, French terrines are oblong in shape with a domed lid, although round terrines are also available. They are attractive for serving, but an ordinary loaf tin can be used instead, in which case the finished terrine or pâté should be turned out before serving.

Trussing Needle and Thread: For trussing poultry and game and sewing up pockets in meat which contain a stuffing. Special large trussing needles (straight or curved) make the task much easier than using a conventional sewing needle, and trussing thread is strong enough to hold during cooking.

Vegetable Mill: See *mouli-légumes*.

Zester: A useful little gadget, which quickly and easily removes the zest from citrus fruit. The sharp teeth of a zester scrape only the outer coloured part of the fruit's skin, the part that contains the flavoursome oils.

SPECIAL INGREDIENTS

Anchovies: Salted anchovies or *anchois* are used in tarts and pies, sauces and stuffings, etc., for their strong 'fishy' flavour. Years ago they were preserved by being packed in layers of salt in wooden barrels, but these days they are usually packed in large cans or jars. In some good delicatessens it is possible to buy these salted anchovies loose from the can; Italian speciality shops invariably stock them. Because of their saltiness, they should be desalted before use by soaking in milk for about 20 minutes. Small cans of anchovies in oil are readily available. The oil should be drained off before the anchovies are desalted.

Bacon: The French word for bacon is *lard*, a word that often causes confusion in French recipes, because it can be mistaken for the cooking fat we call lard which is *saindoux* in French.

Lard maigre fumé is smoked or cured belly of pork, the equivalent to English streaky bacon or American fatty bacon. Sometimes this cut is salted, in which case it is called *petit salé*. Salt pork is its nearest equivalent outside France or, failing this, unsmoked bacon. Bacon is rarely grilled (broiled) or fried in rashers in France; it is more often diced and used in casseroles, *daubes* and stews, and in pâtés and terrines, although for reasons of economy, French housewives are more likely to use dice or strips of pork fat or belly.

Bouquet Garni: A bunch of aromatic herbs tied together and used to flavour casseroles, soups, stews and stocks. Traditionally, a *bouquet garni* is made of parsley and thyme sprigs and a bay leaf, but other herbs can be used according to individual recipes, and often the herbs are tied with a leek or celery stick. The *bouquet garni* is always removed before serving – if tied together with a long piece of string which can be fastened to the pan handle, this makes for easy removal. Ready-made *bouquets garnis* of dried herbs are available in sachets and muslin bags, but these are a poor substitute for the fresh equivalent.

Calf's Foot: Often used in French casseroles and stocks, because it is one of the richest sources of natural gelatin and a dish made with a calf's foot will therefore have a rich, gelatinous gravy. Before using a calf's foot it should be boned, split lengthwise and blanched – the butcher should bone the foot and split it for you. Before use, blanch the calf's foot for a few minutes in boiling water. In France, the calf's foot is removed after cooking, then the meat is chopped into small pieces and returned to the liquid before serving. This is not necessary if you find the thought of eating calf's foot offputting – you can just use it for its gelatine and discard it before serving. Calves' feet (called cow heel in the north of England) can be difficult to obtain from the butcher unless ordered in advance. If unobtainable, use pig's trotters instead – these are more widely available.

Capers: Used in French cookery for their strong distinctive flavour in sauces, and as a seasoning in other dishes, particularly in Provence. Capers or *câpres* are preserved in vinegar and sold in jars – look for those from the Var and Bouches-du-Rhône called *non-pareilles*, as these are considered to be the best varieties by the French.

Cèpes: Found in woodlands, these are considered to have the best 'earthy' flavour and the highest nutritional value of all the wild mushrooms. The most highly prized ones come from the woodlands around Bordeaux in south-western France, and are known as *cèpes de Bordeaux*. *Cèpes* are a member of the boletus family of wild mushrooms, of which there are numerous different edible types with caps ranging in colour from light to very dark brown. The common characteristic of all *boleti* is that they have tubes underneath their caps rather than gills.

Fresh *cèpes* are available in summer and autumn and the best ones to look for should have dry, light-coloured tubes. These tubes need not be removed before cooking if they are in good condition, but if they appear wet and slimy, they should be peeled off. The caps of all *cèpes* should be wiped clean with a damp cloth, and their stalks should be peeled.

Dried *cèpes* are available all year round at continental delicatessens (they are known as *porcini* in Italian) and are well worth using if fresh *cèpes* are unavailable. They have a strong, distinctive flavour and should only be used in small quantities. Before use, soak them in lukewarm water for 30 minutes or until they have swollen to their natural size.

Chanterelles: Also known as *girolle* in France, this must be one of the prettiest of all edible wild mushrooms. It is apricot in colour and shaped like a trumpet or cornet with frilly edges. Fresh *chanterelles*, gathered in woods, are available in France in summer and autumn, and they are becoming increasingly available here in specialist greengrocers.

To prepare *chanterelles* for cooking, trim off the earthy part of the stalks, then wash the caps thoroughly under cold running water to remove all grit (the gills of *chanterelles* are like deep ribs running from the edge of the cap down to the stalk and they can harbour

pious amounts of grit). As *chanterelles* are ...gher than most other mushrooms and ...erefore take longer to cook, they are often ...ed or shredded before cooking; they ...uld then take only about 10 minutes to ...come tender, although they always have a ...ghtly chewy texture. Dried *chanterelles*, ...ailable at continental delicatessens, should ... soaked in lukewarm water for about 30 ...nutes before use until they have swollen to ...ir natural size.

...onfit d'Oie: The famous speciality of ...eserved goose from south-western France, ...ditionally used in *cassoulets* in Toulouse ...d the Languedoc. Geese are specially ...red in Toulouse, both to make *confit d'oie* ...d *pâté de foie gras*, another speciality of the ...gion. *Confit d'oie* is potted goose made by ...eping pieces of goose meat in spiced salt, ...n cooking them in melted goose fat. ...hen tender, the meat is removed from the ...nes and packed in an earthenware pot with ...e fat and some *saindoux*, which solidifies on ...oling and acts as a preservative. When the ...ose is required, the pot is placed over ...ntle heat just long enough for the fat and ...ndoux to melt so the pieces of goose can be ...moved. This process can be repeated over ...d over again until all the goose is used, ...ovided the meat remains covered in fat and ...es not become exposed to air. *Confit d'oie* is ...en made at home in France, but it can also ... bought in jars and cans. Duck and turkey ... also sometimes preserved in this way, and ...Gascony *confit de porc* (preserved pork) is a ...at delicacy.

...ie Gras: The liver of specially fattened ...ese (and sometimes ducks). *Foie gras* is a ...ciality of the regions of Alsace, Toulouse, ...asbourg and Nancy, where the geese are ...tened so their livers swell in size up to a ...ight of 2 kg (4½ lb). Locally, *foie gras* is

sliced and cooked in many different ways; it also features in many classic dishes of French *haute cuisine*, but most frequently it is made into *pâté de foie gras*, sometimes with the addition of truffles (*pâté de foie gras aux truffes*). Outside the regions in which *foie gras* is produced, it is prohibitively expensive; if specified in a recipe for a stuffing, for example, it is more economical to use *pâté de foie gras*.

Frogs' Legs: Called *cuisses de grenouilles* in French, these are the legs of a special breed of green edible frog. In France these frogs are very small, and only the back legs are eaten. They are skinned and skewered together to give just a morsel of tender flesh from each thigh, and three pairs of legs is the right amount for one serving. They are considered a great delicacy as an *hors d'oeuvre* in France. Frogs' legs are served in numerous different ways and can be fried, grilled (broiled) or served in a sauce. Frozen and canned frogs' legs are available, if fresh ones are difficult to obtain.

Garlic: Called *ail* in France, it is used extensively in French cookery, particularly in the Mediterranean and south-western regions. The amount to use is a matter of personal taste and quantities given in recipes are intended only as a guide. The fresh purple-skinned varieties of garlic are the least pungent, and raw garlic is obviously more powerful than the bulb in its cooked state – recipes with up to 40 cloves of garlic are not uncommon in French cookery.

To peel a garlic clove, place it on a board, hold the flat of the blade of a large cook's knife on top of it, then thump with the heel of your hand or fist until the skin splits – it should then come away easily. The best method to crush garlic, which the French say makes it less powerful, is to crush it with a

little salt in a mortar and pestle or with the flat of the blade of a large cook's knife. For those wary of using garlic, a peeled clove rubbed around the inside of a salad bowl or earthenware baking dish will give just a hint of its flavour without being overpowering.

Goose Fat: Used in Alsace and the regions of south-west France where geese are bred, for frying rather than dripping(s), oil or butter. The fat is rendered down in much the same way as pork fat is rendered down to make *saindoux*. Goose fat or *graisse d'oie* gives a distinctive flavour to savoury dishes and is therefore often specified in recipes from the above regions. It is also used in the making of *confit d'oie*.

Ham: See *Jambon*.

Herbs: Used to lend their aromatic scent and flavour to many French dishes. They are rarely used in large quantities, however, and care should be taken when adding herbs to a dish never to let them override the flavours of other ingredients. Whenever possible, the French prefer to use fresh *herbes*. If it is difficult to obtain fresh herbs, dried herbs can be substituted, but only half the quantity should be used because dried herbs are more pungent.

Herbs such as rosemary can be added to the dish in sprigs, and parsley and chervil can be added in the bunch, but most herbs are chopped or crumbled before adding to food. The advantage of adding a bunch of herbs is that it can be removed before serving, giving a subtle flavour. The number of herbs used in French cooking are too many to mention, but the most commonly used ones are bay leaf, chervil, chives, parsley, rosemary and tarragon. *Bouquet garni* (see opposite) is a popular way of imparting the flavour of several herbs to a dish.

Jambon: The French term for ham, it applies to both legs and shoulders of pork which have been salted, smoked and/or cured. Every region has its own recipes for ham, many of which are simply described as *jambon cru*, *jambon de campagne*, *jambon de montagne* and *jambon du pays*. These country hams are eaten raw or used in cooking, and are rarely found outside the region in which they are produced. One raw cured ham which is exported, however, is the famous *jambon de Bayonne*. It is used in cooking, but is more often served raw as an *hors d'oeuvre*, in wafer-thin slices like the Italian Parma ham. Two hams similar to this, but not so well known, are the salted and dried *jambon de Toulouse*, and *jambon d'Auvergne*.

All these hams are interchangeable in recipes. Good French delicatessens should stock at least one ham of this type, but if difficult to obtain, substitute *prosciutto* or a mildly cured gammon. Cooked ham is also popular in France and is sold under the name of *jambon glacé*, *jambon blanc*, *jambon de Paris* and *jambon de York*. These hams are ready-cooked and mild in flavour, similar to the cooked hams available in this country.

Jambonneau: The knuckle or forehock part of ham which is cured and sold as a separate cut in French *charcuteries*. A *jambonneau* is first salted, then poached in water, with vegetables and herbs added, until tender. To give the meat its characteristic rosy pink colour, saltpetre is usually added, either to the curing salt or to the poaching liquid. After cooling in the poaching liquid, the *jambonneau* is skinned and coated with toasted breadcrumbs, the meat being pushed down to expose the bone. The end result is usually cone-shaped, and often the bone is decorated with a cutlet frill. A *jambonneau* is usually sliced and served cold with other *charcuterie* as part of an *hors d'oeuvre*. If specified in a recipe it can be replaced by any mildly cured ham.

Lard: See *Saindoux*.

Marrow, Bone: A highly nutritious, tasty addition to many French beef and veal dishes – casseroles, sauces, stuffings, etc. It is also an essential ingredient in *sauce bordelaise*. The marrow in a beef leg bone is contained in the centre, and it can be extracted raw or cooked. To extract raw beef marrow, ask your butcher to saw the bones into rings about 7.5 to 10 cm/3 to 4 inches in length, then dig out the marrow from the centre with the point of a small sharp knife. Raw marrow extracted in this way can be diced or shredded and used like suet in stuffings, minced (ground) meat mixtures and dumplings. For casseroles and sauces, cooked marrow is best. Soak the pieces of bone overnight in several changes of cold water, then simmer in fresh water for about 20 minutes or until the marrow will slip out easily when the bone is shaken.

Morels: Sometimes nick-named 'sponge mushrooms' or 'poor man's truffles', these are much sought after for their delicate flavour. Fresh morels or *morilles* are available in spring. They have round or oval wrinkled caps which vary in colour from beige and grey through to black. The caps, which are sometimes longer than the stalks, are hollow and tend to collect soil and grit; they therefore need thorough washing before use. The most efficient way to clean morels is to slice them lengthways down the centre, then immerse them in a bowl of cold salted water. Morels are available dried and in cans from good delicatessens. Dried morels should be soaked in lukewarm water for about 30 minutes before use until they have swollen to their natural size.

Mushrooms: The French are very particular about their mushrooms, and many different varieties are eaten. Cultivated mushrooms, described as *champignons de couche* and *champignons de Paris*, are sold throughout France. Button mushrooms are the youngest and mildest in flavour; when they mature their caps open out and they are known as cup mushrooms. Both button and cup mushrooms can be used in any recipe calling for mushrooms; they are also used for garnishes. Fully mature mushrooms have open caps which are almost flat; these have the strongest flavour of all the cultivated mushrooms and are best reserved for stuffing whole, or for chopping and using in composite dishes. To prepare cultivated mushrooms for cooking, simply trim the ends of the stalks and wipe the caps clean with a damp cloth.

Wild mushrooms are more popular in France than the cultivated varieties for their more distinctive flavour. Varieties of fresh wild mushrooms which can be found in specialist greengrocers in this country include *cèpes*, *chanterelles* and morels or (*morilles*). In general, wild mushrooms take longer to cook than the cultivated varieties, and tend to shrink more during cooking.

Mustard: There are three main types of French mustard or *moutarde*: Dijon, Bordeaux and *Meaux*. All French mustards are sold in paste rather than powdered form, and are made from white and black mustard seeds crushed with grape must, verjuice, wine or wine vinegar, herbs and spices, etc.

Dijon mustard is a light brown, smooth-textured mustard, with a sharp rather than hot flavour. Tarragon is the predominant herb amongst its ingredients. In recipes specifying French mustard, *Dijon* is the most suitable one to use, especially in sauces. Two of the best exported varieties to look for are *Grey-Poupon* and *Maille*. Another more unusual Dijon mustard is *moutarde au poivre vert* (mustard with green peppercorns). Made from crushed green Madagascar pepper-

corns, mustard seeds, wine vinegar and salt, has a unique flavour and is well worth tryin

Bordeaux mustard is perhaps less wel known outside France than *Dijon*, but is wo worth seeking out in delicatessens speciali ing in French produce. Like *Dijon*, *Bordeau* mustard is smooth and usually flavoure with tarragon, but it is darker in colour and made with unfermented wine or wi vinegar.

Moutarde de Meaux is a whole grain mu tard made from a 17th century recipe wi black mustard seeds, wine vinegar, salt an spices. It is highly regarded in France and w even described by Brillat-Savarin as ' *moutarde des gourmets*'. *Moutarde de Meaux* best reserved for use as a condiment rath than for inclusion in made up dishes. The are many different French whole grain mu tards besides *Meaux*, simply described *moutardes en grains*. These can be made wi cider, beer or wine and are flavoured wi different herbs and spices. Contrary to wh you might expect from their appearanc they are often mild in flavour.

Oil: Generally used for cooking in France preference to other fats, such as butte dripping(s), goose fat and *saindoux*. For mo cooked dishes, the French prefer a clear o which has little taste and odour so that it do not detract from the flavour of the foo However, in southern Mediterrane regions (notably Provence) where oliv grow so prolifically, olive oil or *huile d'olive* used. It is preferred throughout France fo salad dressings and mayonnaise, when a thic fruity-tasting oil is required.

Olive oil is one of the most expensive of the oils, but if it is necessary to economize, o so on quantity rather than quality. Po quality olive oil can be as tasteless as ordina vegetable oil, and as it quickly turns ranc soon turns into a false economy. Buy a sma bottle of good-quality olive oil and reserve just for salad dressings and mayonnaise. Th best quality olive oil is green in colour, ve fruity in flavour and keeps well. Olive oil sometimes bottled with herbs and/or garlic these are very useful for incorporatir flavours quickly into salads and cooke dishes and, as long as the oil itself is of goo quality, are well worth buying.

Walnut oil is another popular oil France; it is made from dried walnuts and thick and tasty – ideal for salad dressings.

Olives: These are not only pressed for the oil in France, they are also used in cookin mostly whole as a garnish or as part of an ho d'oeuvre, but also stoned (pitted) and sliced chopped in sauces and stuffings. In Provenc where they grow so prolifically, olives are dominant feature of the local cuisine. Bo green and black varieties are eaten in Franc The olives we buy, both loose and in ja have been preserved in brine.

Onions: Used extensively in French cookery, both raw in salads, and in cooked dishes. In France, the large Spanish or Bermuda onions or *oignons* tend to be the most popular varieties, for their mild, slightly sweet flavour.

Red-skinned onions are also highly prized in France; these are usually smaller than the Spanish ones and often have red-tinted flesh. They are not always easy to find outside France, but can be obtained from time to time at specialist greengrocers and markets and are well worth trying for their distinctive flavour – their colour also makes them desirable for using raw in salads.

The French are also very fond of the small white-skinned onion, which they glaze and use for garnishes and include in dishes such as *boeuf bourguignon*, *coq au vin*, *blanquettes* and *ragoûts*. These are not so easy to obtain outside France, but the small pickling (baby) onions will do just as well, as they are also used in France. Spring onions (scallions) are used raw in salads and, because of their mild flavour, they can also be used in place of shallots in cooking.

Orange-Flower Water: A flavouring essence, used mostly in French pastries and confectionery, cakes and tea breads, although it can also be used to add an orange flavour to cream, icing (frosting) and even to salad dressings. Orange-flower water is made from the blossom of the Seville or Bigarade orange. It is available from pharmacists and delicatessens, and should be used sparingly because its flavour is highly concentrated. It can be distinctly unpleasant if used in too great a quantity.

Pig's Caul: The fatty membrane or casing which contains the intestines of the pig. When the intestines and most of the fat have been removed, the caul is cleaned and salted commercially for use in cooking as a natural casing for sausage stuffings and minced (ground) meat mixtures. Called *crépine* in French, it has given its name to the flat sausages which are wrapped in it known as *crépinettes*. Pig's caul is ideal as a casing because it naturally adheres to the mixture around which it is wrapped, and provides a protective fat coating which prevents the food from drying out.

It is available from the butcher (although it may have to be ordered in advance); check first whether it has been dry salted and therefore needs soaking before use. If soaking is necessary, place the caul in a bowl of lukewarm water to which a little lemon juice or vinegar has been added, leave for about 30 minutes, then rinse thoroughly. There is really no ideal substitute for pig's caul. Wafer-thin pieces of pork back fat can be used, but they are not so easy to wrap around food, and they need to be removed before serving.

Pine Nuts: The seeds of pine trees, called *pignons* in French. They have a distinctive flavour, reminiscent of almonds and, unlike most other nuts, their texture is soft rather than crisp. In French cooking, you are most likely to come across them in recipes from southern regions, particularly Provence; they are available ready-shelled from health food stores and some delicatessens.

Pork Rinds: Called *couennes de porc* in France, these are added to meat casseroles, *daubes* and stews to give them a rich gelatinous consistency. They are cut into thin strips and either placed in the bottom of a casserole or on the top to help keep the meat moist. After cooking, they are removed and diced or sliced thinly to make them easier to eat.

Saindoux: Rendered down pork fat which is used as a cooking fat in France, and is the closest French equivalent to our lard. It is well worth making at home because it has a much better flavour than commercial cooking fats, although the whipped *saindoux* sold in *charcuteries* and butchers in France is as good as homemade, if you can get it.

To make *saindoux*, ask your butcher for the soft fat which lies beneath the hard back fat, called the flay fat. Hard back fat can also be used but it is more difficult to melt. Dice or mince (grind) the fat, then put it in a heavy pan with a little water (about 7 tablespoons water to 450 g/1 lb fat). Cook slowly over the lowest possible heat until the fat melts and runs, stirring frequently. When the melted fat becomes clear, strain it through a very fine sieve (strainer) or thick cloth. The little pieces of crisp fat which are left, called *grattons* or *grillons* in French, are considered quite a delicacy in France where they are eaten as an *hors d'oeuvre*, and used in the making of pâtés and *rillettes*. Pour the hot clear fat into sterilized jars, filling them right

to the top, leave until completely cold and set before covering. If kept in a cool, dry place, *saindoux* will keep for several months. The fat from around ox and pig's kidneys is also rendered down to make cooking fat in the same way as *saindoux*, so too is goose fat.

Sausages: A glance in the window of any French *charcuterie* will help you understand the French appetite for sausages – the number of different shapes and sizes is almost unbelievable. Each *charcutier* has his own favourite recipes, therefore types of sausage vary considerably from town to town, region to region. Basically, however, French sausages are divided into three types:— *saucisses*, which are fresh and therefore need cooking; *saucissons*, usually the smoked frankfurter type which need to be boiled before eating; and *saucissons-secs*, which are the preserved sausages like *salame*.

Fresh sausages are made of 100 per cent pure pork by law in France; they therefore bear little resemblance to our pork sausages which contain so much cereal and preservative. They are sold in varying sizes, from small slim ones and flat *crépinettes* wrapped in pig's caul, to the large fat ones which are quite often sold by the kilo in one continuous length rather than in separate links. The flavour of these fresh pork sausages varies according to the amount and type of spices used.

One of the best known of all the French sausages is the *saucisse de Toulouse*, a coarse-textured sausage with a high proportion of fat, which is traditionally used in *cassoulet*. Both white and black puddings are popular in France; white puddings (*boudins blancs*) appear creamy white in colour because they are made from the whitest pork meat together with chicken and sometimes rabbit. Smooth-textured and relatively bland in flavour, they are highly prized in France, and one of the most expensive sausages you can buy. Black puddings (*boudins noirs*) are far

superior to their British counterparts since they are spicier in flavour and a good deal lighter in texture. Both white and black puddings are served fried or grilled (broiled).

Saucissons, or *saucissons-cervelas* as they are sometimes called, tend to be medium to large in size and look rather like saveloys with a thicker skin than the fresh pork sausages above. They are dried and sometimes smoked or cured, and should be boiled before eating – hot or cold. *Saucissons* are often made by the local *charcutier*, but many varieties are imported from other countries – often sold shrink-wrapped in polythene. Amongst these are the *saucissons* of Strasbourg, Vienna and Frankfurt. These are easily obtainable outside France in delicatessens and supermarkets, but if you can obtain genuine French *saucissons*, then so much the better – good delicatessens sometimes stock them.

Saucissons which are made in France are invariably called after their place of origin, *saucissons de Bourgogne* and *saucissons d'Arles*, for example. Perhaps the best known of these are *saucissons de Lyons*, of which there are many variations, most of them containing some beef as well as pork and a fair amount of fat. *Saucissons de Toulouse* are the best kind of sausages to use when making *saucisson en brioche*. French delicatessens should stock at least one sausage of this type.

Saucissons-secs are the *salame*-type sausages which are sliced and eaten cold with salads and/or *charcuterie* for *hors d'oeuvre*. They are sold ready-cooked by the kilo in slices, although the whole sausage can be bought and sliced at home because this type of sausage keeps well. There are hundreds of different types of *saucissons-secs*, some of them quite highly spiced and laced with garlic, some of them smoked (*saucissons fumés*).

Andouilles and *andouillettes* are tripe or chitterling sausages, considered a great delicacy in France. *Andouilles*, which are

smoked or salted, are sold by weight lik *salame* and served sliced cold; *andouillette* which are not always smoked or salted, ar small sausages usually grilled (broiled) whol and served hot.

Shallots: Frequently used in French cookin for their mild flavour. Shallots or *échalote* grow in bulbs which break into two or mor cloves when their golden brown skins ar removed. They are specified in Frenc recipes where onions would provide to strong a flavour, and are used a great deal fo sauces because they soften better than onion They are sometimes available here in the lat summer and autumn in specialist greer grocers. Shallots keep well if stored in a coo dry place, so it is well worth buying any yo see – or you can easily grow your own. I unobtainable, use spring onions or the mil Spanish onions instead.

Smoked Ham: See *Jambon*.

Snails: Although there are two types o edible snail or *escargot*, the vineyard snai (*helix pomatia*) and the garden snail (*heli aspersa*), it is the former variety which i exported from France, either canned o frozen. Canned snails are preserved in brin and are generally sold with their shel packaged separately so the snails can b returned to them for serving. Frozen snai are usually sold ready-prepared with garli butter packed into the shell with the snail.

Before fresh garden snails can be eate they must be starved to rid them of an substances they may have eaten which, al though harmless to themselves, may b poisonous to humans; as this can be a length and uncertain process it is best to cook onl those snails which you know have bee specially reared for eating. In France, snail are bred in *escargotières* on a special diet o vine leaves which makes them fat and juic and perfectly safe for eating. The best snai

are said to come from the vineyards of the Bourgogne region and are at their best at the beginning of winter because it is at this time that they hibernate by sealing themselves inside their shells.

Even specially bred fresh snails need a certain amount of preparation before using in recipes – another good reason for buying the frozen or canned ones. They must first be soaked for a few hours in a solution of water, coarse sea or rock salt, white vinegar and a pinch of flour, after which they should be rinsed and blanched in boiling water for 5 minutes. Finally, they must be poached in stock, water and/or wine, vegetables, herbs and seasonings – the poaching time can vary between 1 and 4 hours, according to the size of the snails.

Spices and Seasonings: *Epices* or spices are used in moderation in French cooking – there are very few French dishes which can be called 'spicy'. The most common use of spice is as *quatre-épices*, which is the distinctive flavouring used in nearly all French charcuterie. The exact blend of spices for *quatre-épices* varies from region to region and chef to chef, but is usually black peppercorns ground with cloves, cinnamon and nutmeg. Sometimes ginger is substituted for the cinnamon. *Quatre-épices* is available ready-ground in France, but it can easily be made at home in a grinder or mortar and pestle and kept fresh by storing in a screw-topped jar. Do not use ground mixed spice for *quatre-épices*, it is not the same.

When salt is specified in a French recipe, always use coarse sea or rock salt, and grind it straight from the mill onto food; do not use free-flowing cooking or table salt. Likewise, pepper should always be freshly ground from the mill at the time of use. Black peppercorns are used for everyday dishes, white peppercorns are reserved for delicate and light-coloured soups and sauces, such as hollandaise sauce.

Tomato Purée (Paste): Used to strengthen the flavour and colour of many cooked dishes. Some French cooks, especially those living in Provence where tomatoes grow in abundance, make their own tomato purée from fresh tomatoes in summer, and preserve or freeze it for use during the winter months. This is obviously ideal, but for those who cannot get such flavoursome tomatoes at reasonable prices, commercial tomato purée makes an acceptable substitute. Always use tomato purée sparingly as it can be bitter if too much is used. A pinch of sugar counteracts this bitterness and complements the flavour of tomatoes.

Truffles: Of all the fungi, these are the most highly prized – and highly priced! *Truffes* or truffles grow underground in the root systems of oak trees, and it is their scarcity coupled with the problem of locating them that makes them so expensive. Pigs, with their highly developed sense of smell, are the best animals to sniff out truffles, but as they tend to eat them almost as quickly as they find them, specially trained dogs are now used more frequently for truffle-hunting.

The best truffles in the world are said to be the black truffles from Perigord. The black truffle has a wizened skin and veiny flesh, but its appearance belies its excellent flavour and aroma. Even the smallest sliver of truffle will impart these qualities to other ingredients in a dish. Fresh black truffles are best simmered until tender in white wine, but it is unusual for anyone living outside the truffle-growing areas of France to be able to obtain – and afford – to cook truffles in sufficient quantities to serve on their own. Most of us have to be content with adding the shavings or peelings of truffles to other ingredients. Even these are prohibitively expensive, but they do have a particular affinity with egg dishes and poultry, and are often used in French sauces and stuffings.

Canned truffles are available from some delicatessens but they are very expensive. If a French recipe specifies truffles amongst its ingredients, they are often omitted for economy reasons. Some cooks use mushrooms as a substitute; as long as you do not compare the flavour of the two, there seems to be no harm in doing this.

Vanilla Pod/Bean: Used in preference to the synthetic flavouring of vanilla essence throughout France. They are available at good delicatessens and supermarkets in this country. Used whole, split or halved, vanilla pods are steeped in warm milk to allow the flavour to infuse, when making custards, sweet sauces, puddings and ice creams, etc.

Vanilla Sugar: Made by leaving a vanilla pod (bean) in a jar of caster sugar for a few days until it has imparted its flavour and aroma. *Sucre vanillé* or vanilla sugar is used in desserts and baking, whenever a subtle vanilla flavour is required. It will keep indefinitely in an airtight jar, and the pod can be used again. Vanilla sugar is also available in small packets (usually containing 25 g/1 oz) from good delicatessens, but homemade vanilla sugar is far superior in flavour.

Vinegar: The French word *vinaigre* means 'sour wine', which is exactly what it is. All vinegars are made from one alcohol or another, but the French favour wine vinegars, and cider vinegar to a lesser extent. They do not use malt vinegar, which is made from fermented cereals. Both red and white wine vinegars are used, and vinegars flavoured with herbs and garlic are popular.

Walnuts, Green: These are unripe walnuts, picked before their hard outer shells have formed. Green walnuts are popular in France, where they begin to appear in the markets in the autumn. In the Touraine region they are marinated and served as an *hors d'oeuvre.*

CHEESES

There is not another country in the world where cheese is loved as much as it is in France. Over 400 cheeses are listed in France, not to mention the vast number of locally produced cheeses which never find their way outside the locality in which they are made and consumed. The cheese makers may have their imitators, but true French cheeses must always bear their label of origin.

The cheeseboard is as important a part of a meal in France as any other course, and French housewives attach great importance to their selection of cheeses from the local market. In France, cheese is always served before the dessert (to finish up the last of the wine), and is often served instead of the dessert, a course the French are more than happy to dispense with. In this chapter are listed those French cheeses that are most widely available outside France. When selecting cheeses for a cheeseboard, remember that is is better to do as the French do and serve one or two very good cheeses rather than a host of inferior varieties. If you serve more than one cheese, try to choose different textures, shapes and flavours.

Banon: A Provençal cheese easily recognizable by its wrapping of chestnut leaves, tied with rafia. According to the time of year, *banon* is made of cow's or goat's milk, in dairies and on farms. It is a small round soft cheese with a mild taste and aroma when fresh, or a strong, slightly nutty flavour if cured. It has a natural, slightly sticky rind. *Poivre-d'âne* is a variety of *banon* which is covered in savory sprigs rather than chestnut leaves and sold from boxes lined with savory. *Banon* is only available at good delicatessens.

Beaufort: See *Gruyère*.

Bleu de Bresse: A blue-veined cheese made from cow's milk in the *pays de l'ain*, which lies between the Saône river and the Jura mountains in eastern France. It is a semi-hard cheese with a smooth blue rind and a creamy-blue inside. It is sometimes likened to the Italian gorgonzola, although its flavour is milder and its shape is small and cylindrical. Sold wrapped in foil and packaged in a box, *bleu de bresse* is widely available in this country.

Bonbel: See *Saint-Paulin*.

Boursin: A spiced full fat soft cheese made commercially from cow's milk in Normandy and the Ile-de-France. It is a mild cheese with a high fat content. Boursin is flavoured with herbs or garlic, or coated in crushed black peppercorns. It is always sold wrapped in foil and packed in familiar cardboard boxes. It is widely available, as are several other similar cheeses exported from different regions in France. These compare favourably with *boursin*, and are often cheaper in price.

Brie: This popular cheese derives its name from the province of La Brie in Ile-de-France. Until the last century it was always made on farms but nowadays most *brie* is produced in factories. It is a cheese with a long and celebrated history. In 1815 an international cheese competition was held at the congress of Vienna. The winner was *brie de meaux*, and ever since this occasion it has been referred to as the '*roi de fromages*' (king of cheeses).

Brie de meaux is just one of the many different varieties of *brie*, and if you inspect its label you may find that it is marked with its place of origin – *brie de coulommiers*, *brie de melun* and *brie de montereau* are just a few of the better known ones. Sadly, this practice is dying out and most exported *brie* does not bear its place of origin. What its label must state, however, is its country of origin. Brie, like many of the world's best-known cheeses, is made in other countries besides France.

Genuine French *brie* is a ripened soft cheese, made of cow's milk, and its flavour can vary from mild to strong, depending on individual varieties. It should always have a white downy rind, with a creamy, supple inside, and should never be runny or chalky white and solid in the middle.

Brie is widely available at delicatessens and supermarkets by the kilo/lb, in which case it is freshly cut for you straight from its wooden box or reed mat; it is also sold pre-wrapped in portions in cling film or cardboard boxes. Always inspect *brie* thoroughly before purchase to ensure it is in perfect condition.

Camembert: A famous soft cheese with a long history. Cheeses of the *camembert* type have been made for centuries in the *pays d'auge* in the region of Normandy, although they were probably known in the past as *augelots* rather than *camemberts*. The name *camembert* is derived from the village of that name in Orne in Normandy, and was known long before the end of the 18th century.

In those days the cheese was always made locally on farms, and packaged in straw. It wasn't until the end of the 19th century that it was put into its now familiar round wooden box, made in factories and exported. *Camembert fermier*, made from untreated cow's milk on farms in Normandy, is rarely seen outside the locality these days; the *camembert* we are most likely to buy is *camembert pasteurisé*, made in factories from pasteurised cow's milk.

A good *camembert* should have a white, downy rind and a creamy, pale yellow inside; its flavour varies from mild to fruity, usually stronger than *brie* and with a faint 'mushroomy' aroma about it. *Camembert* is stocked by most supermarkets and delicatessens in round or half-moon shaped wooden boxes (known as *demi-camembert*), and in individual portions. Never buy a *camembert* that has a runny middle which indicates it is over-ripe, or one that is chalky white and solid in the centre; this indicates an under-ripe *camembert* which often has an unpleasant bitter taste.

Cantal: A semi-hard cow's milk cheese which derives its name from the *département* in which it is made – *Cantal* in the Auvergne. *Cantal fermier* is still made by local farmers during the summer months, following the recipe that was used hundreds of years ago. It is made in tall drum shapes which can weigh as much as 45 kg/99 lb, and has a natural rind which turns from black to a reddish colour, then to the familiar greyish-white during ripening.

The flavour of *cantal* is mild and nutty. It is used in cooking as well as being served as a table cheese and is undoubtedly one of France's best-loved and most popular cheeses. To meet demand it is now not only made in the *département* of Cantal itself, but also in adjoining areas. The only stipulation is that to bear the label *cantal* it must be made at an altitude of at least 800 m/2,624 ft; if made above 850m/2,785 ft, it has the added prestige of being labelled *cantal haute montagne*.

The *cantal* produced in local factories nowadays is known as *cantal laitier* and is made from pasteurized milk. Its flavour is not quite so pronounced as that of *cantal fermier*, but it does have the advantage of being made all year round. It is also produced in smaller, more manageable cylinders weighing from 3.5 to 10 kg/8 to 22 lb, and labelled *cantalon* or *cantalet*. *Cantal* is only available from good delicatessens.

Carré de l'est: A soft cow's milk cheese made commercially in north-eastern France. It has a white bloomy rind and is packaged for export in small, square-shaped boxes. *Carré de l'est* is mild in flavour, some say similar to *camembert*. Available in good delicatessens specializing in French cheeses.

Chèvre: The generic term for goat's milk cheeses, of which there are numerous different varieties throughout France, particularly in the western regions of Anjou, Charente, Poitou and Touraine, in the mountainous areas of the Jura and French Alps, and on the island of Corsica. Since goat's milk cheeses are eaten fresh, few are exported outside the immediate locality in which they are made: to discover the different *chèvres*, you must visit these areas.

Most *chèvres* have a natural rind which is fine and often bloomy, and the texture of the cheese itself, whilst being soft, is somewhat more granular than a soft cow's milk cheese. Salt is used in the making of *chèvres*, both to make them more like cow's milk cheeses and to preserve them, and some varieties can be rather too salty and sharp for the unaccustomed palate. Varieties to look for are *banon* (opposite), *chèvre à la feuille* (also called *mothais*), *chèvre long* (or *saint-maure laitier*) and the smaller *chevret*. Apart from the difference in flavour and texture of goat's milk cheeses from cow's milk cheeses, their unusual shapes (small flat discs or cylinders) make them interesting cheeses to include on a cheeseboard. Good delicatessens specializing in French cheeses usually sell at least one *chèvre*, but supplies are not always consistent. A commonly exported brand is *Lezay*.

Comté: See *Gruyère*.

Coulommiers: A *brie*-type cheese from the town of Coulommiers in Ile-de-France. It is circular in shape and small in size – usually weighing around 450 g/1 lb. Because of its size it is an easier cheese to export than the larger *brie*, and is becoming increasingly available outside France for this reason. In France, *coulommiers* is frequently eaten fresh and salted, in which case it is very mild in flavour. Exported *coulommiers* is ripened, however, and develops a bloomy rind and a rather more pronounced flavour. Available at good delicatessens.

Crémet: A fresh, unsalted soft cheese made from cow's milk, popular throughout the western regions of France, especially in Brittany, Maine and Anjou. All *crémets* are mild in flavour, creamy in texture and pure white in colour, but their shape depends entirely on the moulds in which they have been drained. Local markets in France sell *crémets* as a dessert cheese to be served with whipped cream, fruit and compotes, or simply sprinkled with sugar. *Crémet* is also the type of cheese to use when making the famous heart-shaped dessert called *coeur à la crème*, and the moulded *crémets d'angers* with egg whites and sugar (page 173). *Petit suisse* and unsalted curd cheeses can be used as substitutes, since *crémets* are not exported.

Emmental français: Although a cheese of the *gruyère* family, connoisseurs tend to regard *emmental* as a cheese in its own right. *Emmental* originated in Switzerland, but made its way into France in the 19th century by way of immigrant Swiss cheesemakers. Today it is made in vast quantities in Franche-Comté and Savoie and, contrary to what one might expect, more *emmental* is made in France than in Switzerland.

Emmental français is easily recognized by its cartwheel shape and size – it is a giant cheese, usually weighing about 100 kg/220 lb and 1 metre/39 inches in diameter. It is a hard cow's milk cheese, manufactured solely in factories and co-operatives. It has larger holes, a softer texture, and a milder, less salty taste than *Gruyère*. French *emmental* is not available in this country but Swiss *emmental* can be used.

Fromage blanc/fromage à la pie: Fresh white cheeses made from skimmed cow's milk, on farms and some homes in country districts. These cheeses are always eaten fresh, usually with fruit and/or sugar and sometimes with the addition of milk or whipped cream. Herbs and seasonings can also be added if a savoury cheese is liked. *Petit suisse* can be used as a substitute.

Gruyère français: *Beaufort* and *gruyère de comté*, both produced along the French-Swiss border, are the main types of French *gruyère*. *Beaufort* is made high in the mountains of the Savoie region in eastern France. It is a hard cow's milk cheese with a rich creamy consistency and a full fruity flavour, made so because the grazing in these alpine pastures is excellent and the resultant milk extremely rich. The cheese is ripened in caves, where they are salted, brushed and turned at regular intervals. *Beaufort* cheeses are large (weighing up to 60 kg/132 lb) and, unlike *gruyère de comté*, have a smooth texture with just the occasional crack or small hole.

Gruyère de comté is produced in the region of Franche-Comté in the Jura mountains and, like *beaufort*, is one of France's most popular cheeses. It is a smaller cheese than *beaufort* (usually weighing around 35 kg/ 77 lb), with a fruitier flavour. During its long ripening process, the rind mould is wiped constantly with a cloth soaked in brine,

which gives the cheese a distinctive flavour and bouquet. It is easy to distinguish *comté* from *beaufort*, because *comté* has large holes.

Apart from their use as table cheeses, French *gruyères* are widely used in cooking. If either *beaufort* or *comté* are specified in a recipe, Swiss *gruyère* may be used as a substitute; French *gruyères* are made on a much smaller scale than their Swiss counterparts and the French eat so much of their own *gruyère* there is very little left over for export!

Livarot: A soft cow's milk cheese from the *pays d'auge* in Normandy, this is one of France's most celebrated cheeses. Although still made on farms surrounding the town of Livarot, factories are now taking over its production on an increasingly large scale. The two-month ripening period of *livarot* is carried out in caves; local farmers without ripening facilities have to sell their cheeses fresh to be ripened by professional *cavistes*, whereas factories now have their own caves for this purpose. During ripening, the cheese is bound with strips of marsh grass or paper to prevent it from dipping in the centre; these give the cheese a stripy effect.

Livarot is a table cheese well worth looking for in delicatessens specializing in French cheeses – its strong aroma, mild, yet spicy flavour, smooth texture and unusual appearance make it one of the more interesting cheeses to select for a cheeseboard.

Munster: A soft cow's milk cheese made in the shape of a flat disc, said to have been invented by monks in the Middle Ages in monasteries around the city of Munster in Alsace. Like many French cheeses, *munster* has been made on local farms for centuries, but with modern technology, factory production is increasing and the traditional farmhouse *munster fermier* is becoming a rarity. The *munster* you are likely to find

outside Alsace is invariably *munster laitie* produced by large commercial dairies. Bot *munsters* are interesting cheeses, ripened o beds of rye straw until they acquire a shiny reddish-coloured rind. The aroma an flavour is strong and spicy – exactly wha you would expect from a cheese made in thi part of France where the local cuisine ha something of a German flavour. Look fo both paper-wrapped and boxed *munsters* i varying sizes from *petit munster* (about 275 /10 oz) to the large *gérômé* – 'the redhead'

Neufchâtel: A soft cow's milk cheese from the *pays de bray* in Normandy, with a delicat bouquet, white bloomy rind and a mild, ye slightly salty flavour. The most interestin thing about *neufchâtel* is its shape, which ca be round (called *bonde* or *bondon*), squar (*carré*), oblong (*briquette*), or heart-shape (*coeur*). The best variety is farm-produced i summer and autumn, but exported *neufchâte* is invariably produced from pasteurized mil commercially, and is available all year round

Petit Suisse: An unsalted medium to full fa soft cheese which was first made in th farmlands north of Paris, but which is now made all over France in the Gervais chees factories. It is said that the cheese wa originally made simply from the curds o fresh cow's milk. A Swiss farmworker sug gested that fresh cream be added to th cheese, in the Swiss manner. The result wa such a success that from then on the chees was always made in this way, known as *peti suisse*. It is a very creamy cheese and becaus of its soft texture is always sold wrapped i absorbent paper or in individual plasti containers. In France it is eaten on its own sprinkled with sugar, or served with fruit as dessert. It is also useful in cooking as substitute for *fromage blanc*. *Petit suisse* i quite widely available.

Pont-l'Evêque: A soft cow's milk cheese from the *pays d'auge* in Normandy, made on farms and in commercial dairies. *Pont-l'Evêque* is one of France's most famous cheeses, protected by French law so that any imitations must state clearly their place of origin to distinguish them from the real thing. It is a small, square-shaped cheese, usually weighing around 350 g/12 oz and packaged in a box. After ripening in humid cellars, the cheeses are washed, which gives them their characteristic golden-yellow rind. The consistency of the cheese is soft and supple, and it has a fairly pronounced flavour and bouquet. *Pont-l'Evêque* is an excellent table cheese, to be found in good delicatessens specializing in French cheeses. It should be eaten when slightly runny but not over-ripe, because the flavour becomes unpleasantly strong at this stage. Dry cider is the traditional accompaniment.

Port-Salut: A cheese with a long history, it was first made under the name *port-du-salut* by Trappist monks at the beginning of the 19th century – in the abbey of Notre Dame de Port-du-Salut in southern Normandy. It is a semi-hard cow's milk cheese, still made with the same recipe today as the monks used then, but in modern factories and known simply as *port-salut*. It is a cylindrical cheese with a yellow rind, smooth texture, and mild, slightly sweet flavour. *Port-salut* is available (usually in pre-packaged portions) at most good supermarkets and delicatessens, and it has the advantage that it keeps well. See also *Saint-paulin*.

Réblochon: A small cylindrical cow's milk cheese from the Savoie mountains, usually sold on a thin wooden board. It has a creamy texture and a mild flavour, with an interesting pinkish-tinged rind. Available from good delicatessens.

Roquefort: A cheese for the connoisseur, generally rated as one of the finest cheeses in the world. *Roquefort* is one of the few great cheeses to be made from ewe's milk, and is so highly prized that to bear the *roquefort* label it must be produced in its country of origin according to the strictest regulations. The secret of *roquefort* cheese lies in its curing process, which takes place at Roquefort-sur-Soulzon in the underground caves of the Combalou mountain, south of the *massif central* in Aquitaine.

There is no doubt that *roquefort* is one of France's most ancient cheeses, some say it was even known to the early Romans. The popular legend of its invention tells of a young shepherd boy who left his parcel of bread and fresh curd cheese in one of the Roquefort caves, only to find when he returned some months later that the mould that had developed had transformed his humble snack into an exquisite blue-veined cheese.

Whether this fascinating story is true or not, *roquefort* is still made today by mixing the curds of ewe's milk cheese with a special type of breadcrumbs, and in the damp Combalou caves the fresh moist air circulates to develop the unique *penicillium roqueforti* mould which gives the cheese its characteristic blue-green veins. So special are the Combalou caves to the process of making *roquefort* that 'white' *roquefort* is sent from the Pyrenees and the island of Corsica to be ripened there.

A good *roquefort* should be creamy in consistency, evenly marbled with blue-green veins and slightly crumbly in texture. Chalky white *roquefort* should be avoided because it will be too sharp. The best *roquefort* should be freshly cut in good delicatessens specializing in French cheeses, although pre-packaged portions of *roquefort* can be obtained at supermarkets.

Saint-Paulin: A semi-hard cow's milk cheese, very similar in flavour and appearance to *port-salut*, but made by a slightly different method. It is produced commercially all over France, but mostly in Brittany. Like *port-salut*, it is cylindrical in shape, with a smooth texture and a mild flavour. It is available at most supermarkets and delicatessens, and is interchangeable with *port-salut* as a table cheese.

Tomme: There are many types of *tomme* cheese, produced in the Savoie mountains near the border with Switzerland. Depending on type, they are made with cow's or goat's milk, sometimes a mixture of these or, more rarely, with ewe's milk. Most of the farm-produced *tommes* are made only for local consumption and are therefore never exported, but the two best-known ones, *tomme de savoie* and *tomme au raisin*, are exported in large quantities.

Tomme de savoie is a semi-hard cow's milk cheese, ivory in colour, with a distinctive nutty flavour – it makes a good melting cheese, apart from its suitability for the cheeseboard. *Tomme au raisin* is a similar cheese, but has a crust made of grape pulp, and is useful on the cheeseboard for its appearance, if for nothing else. Both these cheeses are usually available at good delicatessens and supermarkets.

GLOSSARY

Bain Marie, Au: A cooking method for delicate foods (mostly sauces and egg-based dishes) which would overcook if placed over direct heat. The food is placed in a heatproof bowl or pan, which is then placed in a larger pan half-filled with water. Cooking *au bain marie* can take place either on top of the stove or in the oven, and the water can be hot or cold, depending on the food to be cooked. Most custard mixtures are placed in a cold *bain marie* so they do not curdle, but pâtés and terrines are placed in hot water to set them quickly. Food can also be kept warm *au bain marie*. The term *bain marie* also refers to the pan in which the food is cooked (see page 24).

Bake Blind: To bake a pastry case (pie shell) without its filling, usually because the filling will cause the pastry to become soggy if the two are baked together. Pastry that is baked blind without a filling tends to rise, therefore it is usually weighted down before baking. The pastry is lined with foil or greaseproof (wax) paper, then filled with baking beans – dried beans or peas, or ceramic beans. The beans and paper or foil are usually removed for the last 5 to 10 minutes.

Ballotine: From the French word *ballotin* meaning small parcel, this was originally a boned piece of meat rolled into a small bundle before cooking. Nowadays, the term is used more loosely to describe any piece of meat, poultry, game or fish that is boned and stuffed before rolling.

Bard: To cover meat, poultry and game with a layer of fat or bacon before roasting to keep it as moist as possible. The fat or bacon is usually tied around the meat or over the breast of birds which have little natural fat.

Baste: To spoon fat and cooking juices over food during cooking to keep it moist. When roasting meat and poultry, particularly those with little fat, baste at 20 minute intervals.

Beurre Manié: A mixture of flour and butter used for thickening liquids such as sauces and gravies. The proportion of flour to butter varies according to the thickness required, but is usually equal parts. Work the butter and flour together to form a paste, then whisk into the hot liquid a little at a time. Simmer for 1 to 2 minutes, whisking constantly, until the sauce has thickened and all taste of flour has been eliminated.

Bind: To combine ingredients together by adding beaten egg or a thick roux-based sauce so they do not come apart during cooking. Used for croquettes, meatballs, etc.

Blanch: To plunge into boiling water. Used mostly for vegetables to loosen skin before peeling, and to remove strong flavours. Vegetables are blanched before freezing to help preserve colour and texture. Some foods (eg, sweetbreads) are blanched to make them white and firm – literally translated *blancher* means 'to whiten'. Bacon, salt pork, pork rinds and calf's feet, etc, are blanched to remove excess salt and other strong flavours, and are often brought to the boil from cold rather than being plunged directly into boiling water. Blanching times vary according to the type of food.

Blanquette: A term used to describe a dish of white meat (usually veal or chicken), in which the cooking liquid is thickened with a *liaison* of cream and/or egg yolks.

Blister: A method of removing skins from vegetables; e.g. peppers and aubergines (eggplants). The vegetable is placed under a preheated hot grill (broiler) and turned frequently until the skin blisters and burns. After cooling, the skin of peppers can be rubbed off with a cloth. Aubergine skin needs to be peeled off with a sharp knife. Blistering over charcoal gives the flesh of vegetables a unique charred flavour.

Braise: To cook by moist heat, either on top of the stove or in the oven. Braising is the best cooking method for tough cuts of meat which cannot be dry roasted. The meat is first browned in oil or fat, then placed on a bed of vegetables with a little liquid. The lids of braising pots should be tight-fitting so no moisture can escape during cooking; casseroles with concave lids, called *doufeu* (page 25), are specially designed for braising.

Bruise: To lightly crush ingredients in a mortar and pestle, or with the flat of the blade of a large cook's knife. Garlic, root ginger and herbs are bruised to release flavour and aroma. Because the bruised ingredient is not broken into pieces, it is easily removed from the dish before serving.

Caramelize: To cook sugar and a third of its weight of water to the caramel stage. The sugar and water are heated gently until the sugar dissolves, then boiled rapidly until the liquid turns dark brown in colour. The mixture should not be stirred during boiling or it will become granular. Caramel is used to line moulds (e.g., *crème caramel* – page 172), in which case it is swirled around the inside of the mould while still hot. Caramel is also used for decorating desserts and cakes – the hot caramel is poured into a greased tray, left to harden, then cracked into small pieces.

Caramelize also applies to cooking food in butter and sugar until it becomes glazed and coated in a golden brown syrup. Onions and apples are often caramelized in this way.

Some desserts are caramelized on top by being sprinkled with sugar, then put under a preheated hot grill (broiler) until the sugar melts and forms a golden brown crust.

Carbonnade: A Flemish meat stew, usually beef, cooked in beer.

Châteaubriand: A method of preparing the middle section of fillet steak devised by one of Châteaubriand's chefs. This part of the fillet, called the heart (*coeur* in French), is twice as thick as the rest of the fillet, and serves two. The classic accompaniment is *maître d'hôtel* butter or béarnaise sauce.

Chaudfroid: Literally translated, this means 'hot and cold'. It is used to describe a cooked dish which is coated in a sauce and aspic jelly, then served cold.

Chiffonade: From the French word for rag, *chiffon*. A term used to describe salad vegetables and herbs which are shredded into fine strips. Lettuce, spinach and sorrel are most often used for *chiffonade*, which is a popular garnish for soups and egg mayonnaise.

Chine: To remove the backbone or ribs from meat, from the French word *échine*, meaning spine.

Civet: A richly flavoured *ragoût* or stew.

Clarify: To remove impurities. Clarified butter is made by melting butter over gentle heat until it foams, then skimming or straining it through cheesecloth (muslin). The strained clear liquid is clarified butter. It solidifies on cooling and must be stored in the refrigerator or it will turn rancid.

Stock is clarified with egg whites and crushed egg shells. The stock is brought to the boil from cold, then the egg whites and shells are whisked in the stock until a thick white froth or scum forms on the surface. The stock is then strained through cheesecloth (muslin) to give a clear liquid.

Compote: Fruit poached in syrup.

Confectioners' Custard: The English name for *crème pâtissière* (page 51), a thick sweet sauce enriched with eggs.

Concasser: To chop roughly or to crush to a purée. A term most usually applied to tomatoes, which should be skinned and seeded beforehand.

Consommé: A meat, poultry or game soup made from enriched stock which is clarified with egg whites (see page 61).

Coulis: A thick sauce or purée; also sometimes used to describe a soup. Shellfish *coulis* is most common.

Court-Bouillon: A stock acidulated with lemon juice or vinegar used for poaching fish and seafood. Sometimes meat and vegetables are also poached in a *court-bouillon*.

Crimp: To give a shell-like edge to pastry. Before glazing and baking, press end of thumb all around the edge of the dough, making an indentation with the back of a knife in between each thumb-print.

Croquette: A savoury mixture, often bound with a thick béchamel sauce, which is rolled into a cylindrical shape, coated with egg and breadcrumbs and deep-fried.

Croustade: A case of fried bread or pastry (puff or flaky) for hot savoury mixtures. Fried bread *croustades* can be made by stamping out thick shapes with a pastry cutter.

Croûte: A round or triangle of crustless bread which is either toasted, or fried until crisp and golden in butter, or equal parts of butter and oil. *Croûtes* are used as a base for savoury foods and as a garnish. Food baked in a pastry case is described as '*en croûte*'.

Croûtons: Small dice of crustless bread which are fried in butter or equal parts of butter and oil until crisp and golden. Used as a garnish for soups. *Croûtons* can also be cut into fancy shapes with aspic cutters.

Daube: A dish of meat (usually beef) braised in wine and herbs.

Deglaze: To dilute the sediments and cooking juices in roasting pans and frying pans (skillets) after cooking meat, poultry and game. The meat is removed, the pan placed over heat, then wine, stock or water is added and stirred to scrape up all the sediments from the bottom of the pan. This liquid is used as a sauce to serve with the meat.

Dégorger: To draw out impurities from strong-flavoured foods, usually by soaking in water and draining, or by salting (see page 41). Aubergines (eggplants) should always be *dégorged* by salting before cooking.

Degrease: To remove fat from the surface of foods to make them palatable. Liquids are degreased before serving by drawing a skimmer or slotted spoon over them, or by blotting with absorbent kitchen paper towels. If casseroles, soups and stocks, etc., are left to cool, the fat will rise to the surface of the liquid and solidify – it can then be lifted off easily. Fried foods can be degreased by draining on kitchen paper towels.

Demi-glace: A rich brown sauce which is boiled until syrupy and half-glazed (*demi-glace*), then used to coat food. A *demi-glace* sauce is usually flavoured with Madeira.

Desalt: To remove excess salt from food, usually by soaking in water. Salty ham and bacon are desalted by soaking in cold water overnight, then draining. Canned anchovies are desalted by soaking in milk (see page 28).

Dice: To cut into very small cubes. An easy way to dice food which is of uniform size and shape (e.g. bread to make croûtons), is to cut it into thin slices, then stack the slices on top of each other. Slice the stack into thin strips lengthways, then slice crossways into cubes.

Discoloration: Certain pale-fleshed fruits and vegetables discolour easily on exposure to air; i.e. they turn brown or black after peeling and/or slicing. This can be prevented by sprinkling with lemon juice or steeping in water to which lemon juice has been added immediately after cutting. Apples, pears, bananas and avocados must be treated in this way if they are not to be served immediately.

Duxelles: A mixture of very finely chopped mushrooms, onions, shallots, seasoning and herbs, which is simmered in butter, then used for flavouring sauces, soups and stuffings.

Emulsion: Describes sauces, such as mayonnaise and hollandaise, in which oil or butter is held in a thick, creamy suspension by egg yolks, i.e. the fat becomes distributed evenly throughout. When sauces curdle and separate, the globules of fat have not emulsified.

Entrée: A term with a confused meaning. Originally in French cooking, the *entrée* was the course served after the fish and before the main course of meat, but now it has come to mean the main course itself. In the USA, *entrée* means the first course.

Entremets: Originally applied to all the dishes that came after the main course, i.e. the vegetables and dessert. At one time the word was even used to describe the entertainment that came in the middle of a meal (*entremets* means 'between dishes')! Nowadays the word is used to denote the dessert course, which follows the cheese in France.

Estouffade: A dish of meat which is stewed slowly in liquid.

Farce: Stuffing or forcemeat.

Flamber: To flame or set alight. Flambé dishes are quite common in French cookery. Alcoholic spirit – usually brandy – is poured over the food, then set alight. Once the flames have died down, the alcohol has burnt off, leaving behind the concentrated flavour of the spirit. Spirit is also flamed in this way at the beginning of cooking, e.g. for *coq au vin*, so the meat absorbs the flavour during cooking. Spirits to be set alight must be warmed beforehand or they will not ignite.

Fleuron: Small crescent-shaped pieces of puff or flaky pastry. Used to garnish fish dishes and sometimes pies.

Frappé: The French word for 'iced'. Used frequently to describe iced desserts made with fruit and cream.

Fricassée: A similar dish to a *blanquette*, in which meat is cooked in a white sauce. A term most often applied to poultry, although originally it was used to describe any meat or vegetable cooked in a white sauce or stock.

Fumet: A concentrated liquid used to give flavour to sauces and stocks. A *fumet* is made by boiling bones and flavourings until reduced and concentrated in flavour, and can be made of poultry, fish, game or vegetables.

Galantine: A dish of boned and stuffed meat, poultry or game which is tightly wrapped in cheesecloth (muslin), then poached in stock until tender. When cold, and sometimes pressed, the meat is glazed with aspic and decorated. A *galantine* is always served cold.

Galette: A festive cake traditionally baked on Twelfth Night, made of flaky pastry or yeast dough. A bean is baked in the dough, and whoever takes the portion with the bean becomes 'king of the feast' for the evening.

Garbure: A thick vegetable broth or soup from the Béarn region of France. *Garbure* is always served with a thick slice of bread floating in it.

Gigot: A leg of lamb or mutton. Also often used to describe a thick slice taken from the top end of the leg.

Glaze: To give food a shiny finish. Some foods are brushed with a glaze before cooking – egg, milk and sugar being the most common glazes. Other foods are glazed after cooking, for example, sweet tarts and flans are often brushed with jam. Meat can be glazed during or after roasting with redcurrant jelly, or with a meat glaze made from brown stock and gelatine.

Goujon: A thin strip of white fish, usually sole, which is coated in egg and breadcrumbs and deep-fried until crisp and golden. *Goujons* are often served with tartare sauce.

Gratiner: To give a golden-brown crisp finish to a dish. To cook food *au gratin* means to sprinkle it with breadcrumbs and/or grated cheese, dot with butter and put under the grill (broiler) until golden brown and bubbling. *Gratin* dishes are also baked in the oven in a béchamel-type sauce, in which case the breadcrumb topping becomes crisp during baking, or is finished under the grill.

Glossary of Cooking Terms/39

Hachis: A finely chopped mixture of flavouring ingredients. The most common *hachis* is a mixture of the following: onions or shallots (scallions), garlic, mushrooms, and herbs. Breadcrumbs may also be included. A *hachis* is sprinkled over meat, poultry, vegetables and fish before cooking to give flavour. Alternatively it can be used in stuffings, mixed with minced (ground) or finely chopped meat.

Hermetical Sealing: To make the lid of a casserole or pan airtight. Many casserole dishes, pâtés and terrines are hermetically sealed in French cookery, so that moisture cannot escape during long, slow cooking. The lid of the casserole is sealed by brushing all around the edge with a luting paste made from flour and water. During cooking, this paste forms a crisp crust which must be broken to remove the lid.

Infuse: To extract flavour from an ingredient by steeping it in a hot liquid. When the liquid has absorbed the flavour it is strained. Milk for making béchamel sauce is infused in this way with onion, bay leaf, mace and peppercorns. For sweet dishes such as custards, milk is infused with a vanilla pod (bean), cinnamon stick, orange or lemon peel. Wine can be infused with mushroom or truffle peelings.

Julienne: A term used to describe foods that are shredded or cut into fine matchstick strips and used as a garnish.

Larding: To sew thin strips of pork fat, called *lardons*, into lean pieces of meat which have no natural fat of their own. Most often used for fillet of beef or veal, and for venison, which would otherwise become dry during cooking. The strips of fat are sewn or larded into the meat at regular intervals with a *lardoire* or larding needle. This not only makes the meat succulent and flavoursome, it also gives it an attractive marbled appearance when cooked.

Lardons: Thin strips of pork fat used for *larding*, also called *lardoons*. The strips can be of varying thicknesses, but are generally about 4 cm/1½ inches long and 5 mm/¼ inch wide. The term *lardon* can also apply to cooked bacon dice or strips which are used in casserole dishes to give flavour, or as a garnish.

Liason: A thickening agent for liquids, such as soups and sauces. Typical liasons include butter and flour mixtures, used as *roux* and *beurre manié*, cornflour (cornstarch), arrowroot, egg yolks and cream.

Luting Paste: A paste of flour and water used for hermetically sealing casseroles, pâtés and terrines (see above).

Macédoine: A mixture of diced fruit or vegetables, raw or cooked. A vegetable *macédoine* should be colourful and varied – e.g. a combination of carrots, peas, turnips and potatoes – and is often served hot in a béchamel or cream sauce, or cold in mayonnaise. Fruit *macédoines* are often poached and served in a sugar syrup.

Macerate: To soak fruit in a liquid to soften and flavour it. Sugar syrup is often used for macerating, but more frequently brandy, rum or liqueur is used.

Marinate: To soak or steep food in a spiced liquid called a marinade. The term originally only applied to fish (hence the name), but nowadays it more often applies to meat. The purpose of marinating is to impart flavour to food and, in the case of tough sinewy cuts of meat, to help tenderize it. For the latter reason a meat marinade usually includes an acid ingredient, such as wine, lemon juice or vinegar, to help break down tough fibres. Oil is often included in a marinade, as are herbs, spices and vegetables such as onions, garlic, shallots (scallions) and sometimes carrots. Marinating times vary from a few hours up to several days, depending on the type of meat and temperature. During the marinating time, the marinade should be frequently spooned over the meat.

Medaillon: Round or oval medallion-shaped cuts of meat, poultry and fish, and sometimes vegetables. See also *Tournedos*.

Mirepoix: A mixture of diced vegetables used in sauces, braised dishes and pot roasts to give flavour. Root vegetables are most often used in a *mirepoix*, which may or may not include raw ham or blanched belly pork. In braised dishes and pot roasts the meat is placed on a bed of *mirepoix*.

Mousseline: A term used to describe a mixture that has whipped cream added to it. Sauces in particular are described in this way, *hollandaise mousseline* being perhaps the best known. *Mousseline* can also refer to small moulds made from a paste or purée of fish, poultry or game – enriched with cream.

Navarin: A mutton stew which should always have onions and potatoes amongst its ingredients. Other root vegetables, such as carrots and turnips, are also usually included.

Noisette: A 'nut' or round of meat which is boned, rolled and tied into an individual portion. The fillet or leg of lamb is normally used for *noisettes*, although beef and veal fillet can also be prepared in this way. *Noisette* is also used to describe dishes that are flavoured with hazelnuts, and *noisette* butter is so described because it is cooked until it turns a dark hazelnut colour.

Panada: A thick paste for thickening or binding mixtures. The most common *panadas* are the béchamel-type sauces used as thickening bases for soufflés. Choux pastry is made of a *panada* of water, butter and flour. Breadcrumbs soaked in milk or water are another kind of *panada*.

Papillote, En: To bake food, usually fish or poultry, in a parcel made of buttered or oiled greaseproof (waxed) paper. This parcel was traditionally heart-shaped, but nowadays a *papillote* can be any shape so long as it seals in the fish or poultry and its juices. *Papillote* is also the term applied to the paper frills placed on the bone ends of crown roast of lamb.

Parboil: To boil until partially cooked, to tenderize before continuing cooking in some other way. Potatoes should be parboiled before roasting to ensure thorough cooking.

Paring: To shave or cut off the thin outer peel of fruits and vegetables. A vegetable parer is the best piece of equipment for this.

Paupiette: A thin slice of meat, usually beef fillet or veal escalope, which is spread with a stuffing, then rolled and tied up before cooking. Fillets of fish, such as plaice and sole, can also be made into *paupiettes*.

Persillade: By strict definition, this is a sprinkling of finely chopped parsley, but it is often used to describe a mixture of parsley and garlic, or parsley and shallots (scallions). A *persillade* can be sprinkled over meat before cooking, or used as a garnish.

Piquant: Used to describe a dish with a strong, sharp flavour. Piquant dishes often contain vinegar or some other acid ingredient. *Sauce piquante*, for example, is a brown sauce sharpened by the addition of gherkins (small sweet dill pickles).

Pit: To remove the stones or seeds (pits) from fruit and vegetables. Special pitting gadgets are available to make the task easier.

Plumping: To soak an ingredient in a liquid until it becomes soft and swollen. Dried fruits, such as prunes and raisins, are usually plumped in hot water, tea, brandy or rum.

Poach: To cook food gently in liquid on top of the stove. The poaching liquid should not exceed simmering point. A popular method of cooking for eggs, fish and fruit.

Pot Roast: To cook meat slowly and gently with liquid, vegetables and herbs. The ideal cooking method for the cheaper, tougher cuts of meat to ensure maximum tenderness and flavour. The meat is usually browned in fat first, then vegetables and liquid are added and the pot covered tightly during cooking.

Pound: To crush an ingredient, to break it into small pieces or even a paste. Pounding releases flavours and, in the case of meat and fish, tenderizes tough fibres.

Praline: A mixture of blanched almonds and sugar which is cooked until brown and caramelized. When cool, it is pounded until very fine, then used in many French desserts. (See recipe on page 52.)

Purée: A mixture with a paste-like consistency which is obtained by pounding, crushing, mashing or sieving (straining). The most efficient way to purée is to use a *mouli-légumes* (vegetable mill), electric blender or food processor, although rubbing through a sieve (strainer) is also effective.

Quenelle: A kind of dumpling, traditionally oval in shape, made from minced (ground) chicken, fish or veal. The mixture is bound with eggs and poached or steamed in special individual moulds. *Quenelles* are served on their own in a creamy sauce, or used as a garnish for certain savoury dishes.

Quiche: An open flan or tart with a savoury custard filling.

Ragoût: A meat stew, usually lamb, mutton or beef, although poultry and fish *ragoûts* are known. The meat is generally browned in fat, sprinkled with flour for thickening, then cooked in liquid, slowly in the oven.

Ramekin: Small individual tartlets made of pastry with a savoury filling. The term ramekin also applies to individual *cocottes* and soufflé dishes (see page 27).

Rechauffé: The French word for 'reheated'. A term used to describe a dish that is made from previously cooked food.

Reduce: To boil a liquid rapidly in order to reduce its volume and therefore thicken and concentrate its flavour. The pan should always be left uncovered to allow evaporation. Liquids can be reduced down to a mere spoonful in the bottom of the pan.

Relax: A term used in pastry making to describe resting the dough before it is rolled. This allows the gluten in the flour to contract and the pastry is therefore less likely to shrink during baking. Always relax dough in a cool place for at least 30 minutes before using.

Render: To melt fat until it becomes dripping(s). Small pieces of fat from meat are placed in a roasting pan and cooked in a cool oven until the dripping runs – the dripping is then strained and the residue discarded. Fat can also be rendered by simmering with a little water in an uncovered pan until the water has evaporated. Strain before use.

Roux: A *liaison* or mixture of butter, or margarine, and flour which forms the base of a sauce and thickens it. After melting the butter for a *roux*, the flour should be sprinkled in over gentle heat, then cooked for 1 to 2 minutes to eliminate the taste of the flour. A *roux* should be stirred constantly during cooking.

Salmis: A dish of game or duck in which a whole bird is roasted, then cut into serving pieces and finished off in a rich brown or *demi-glace* sauce flavoured with red wine. A *salmis* is traditionally served garnished with *croûtons*.

Salpicon: A mixture of finely diced or shredded meat, poultry, game, mushrooms, etc., bound together with a thick sauce and used as a filling for *vol-au-vent* cases and *croustades*.

Salting: Salt is not only used as a seasoning to bring out the flavour of foods, it can also be used to draw out water – by osmosis. Watery vegetables, such as cucumber, are often salted and drained before cooking to draw out excess moisture which would otherwise interfere with any future cooking process. Salting aubergines (eggplants) draws out their bitter and unpalatable juices – these should be rinsed off after about 30 minutes and the aubergine dried thoroughly before cooking.

Sauté: From the French *sauter*, 'to jump'. To fry foods quickly in butter or oil or a mixture of both, shaking the pan constantly so that the food literally 'jumps' in the pan. A sauté pan or frying pan (skillet) with straight sides is most suitable. A dish called a sauté is first sautéed in fat, then cooked rapidly in a sauce.

Scald: To plunge – usually fruit and vegetables – into boiling water so that the skins become easy to peel. The term can also mean to bring milk to just below boiling point when making infusions for custards and sauces, etc.

Scoring: To make shallow cuts in the surface of certain foods to improve their appearance and, in some cases, make cooking time shorter. Skins of fruit, such as apples, are scored around the middle to prevent bursting during baking, and pork rind is scored to help crackling become crisp and facilitate carving.

Sear: A method of frying over high heat that seals in the juices and nutrients. Frequently used for meat that is to be cooked slowly for a long time. The fat must be very hot before the meat is added to the pan or the juices will run. After the meat has become browned and seared, the heat can be lowered without fear of this happening.

Simmering: To keep a liquid at just below boiling point so that the water trembles or shivers at a temperature of 85 to 88°C/185 to 190°F.

Skimming: To degrease a liquid by drawing a skimmer or slotted spoon across its surface to remove globules of fat and/or scum. See also Degreasing.

Soaking: To steep in liquid before cooking or serving, to eliminate strong flavours and impurities, and to help soften the ingredient. For example, anchovies need to be soaked in milk to make them less salty; dried pulses need to be soaked overnight in water or they will not become tender when boiled; and sweetbreads need to be soaked to remove impurities.

Steaming: A method of cooking by moist heat, popular for vegetables. Food is placed in the top half of a steamer, boiling water in the bottom. Steam passes from the bottom to the top via perforations.

Suprêmes: The breasts and wings of poultry and game birds which are removed in one piece when raw. *Suprême* is also a term used to describe a dish that is made of the finest ingredients and prepared in a special way.

Sweating: To cook very gently in oil, butter or other fat to draw out the juices of a food prior to cooking it with other ingredients. Finely diced or sliced vegetables are often sweated in this way when making soups and casseroles. The pan must be covered during sweating, and the heat kept as low as possible.

Tournedos: A thick slice from the centre or 'eye' of a fillet of beef. Usually grilled (broiled) or sautéed and served with a classic garnish.

Truss: To secure the wings and legs of poultry and game with trussing thread and/or skewers. Also to enclose stuffing in the cavity of birds. Trussing ensures a neat shape for serving and carving.

Vandyke: To cut the rind of citrus fruit and the skin of melons and tomatoes into zigzag shapes to make them look more attractive. Fish tails which are cut into 'V' shapes are also described as *vandyked*.

Zesting: To remove the zest from citrus fruit with a special tool called a zester (see page 27), or with the finest side of a box or conical grater. The zest is the oil in the rind which gives the fruit its colour, aroma and flavour. For sweet dishes the zest can be removed by rubbing a sugar lump against the rind, then crushing it into a mixture or dissolving it over heat.

BASIC RECIPES

BOUILLON DE VIANDE
Meat Stock

This basic meat stock can be used in any recipe calling for 'beef stock'. For a richer 'brown' stock, a must for classic sauces such as demi-glace and espagnole, the meat and bones should first be browned in the pan in a little hot dripping, or roasted in a hot oven (220°C/425°F/Gas Mark 7) for 30 to 40 minutes. After browning, proceed with the recipe as below. Some recipes which are both delicate in flavour and colour call for 'light' or veal stock. This is made in exactly the same way as beef stock, but using a knuckle of veal and pieces of shin, breast or shoulder of veal instead of the beef. After straining meat stocks, do not discard the meat – it can be chopped or minced (ground) and used for making meatballs and stuffings, etc.

Metric/Imperial	American
2 carrots, peeled and roughly chopped	2 carrots, peeled and roughly chopped
2 celery sticks, roughly chopped	2 celery stalks, roughly chopped
2 leeks, roughly chopped	2 leeks, roughly chopped
750 g/1½ lb flank or shin of beef, cut into large chunks	1½ lb flank or shin of beef, cut into large chunks
450 g/1 lb knuckle of veal, cut into large chunks	1 lb knuckle of veal, cut into large chunks
1 calf's foot★, chopped (optional)	1 calf's foot★, chopped (optional)
1 onion, peeled and stuck with 2 whole cloves	1 onion, peeled and stuck with 2 whole cloves
1 bouquet garni★	1 bouquet garni★
6 black peppercorns	6 black peppercorns
salt	salt
3 litres/5½ pints water	6½ pints/13 cups water

Put the vegetables, except the onion, in the bottom of a large pan. Place the beef, veal and calf's foot (if using) on top. Add the onion, bouquet garni, peppercorns and salt to taste.

Pour in the water and bring slowly to the boil. Lower the heat, skim off the scum with a slotted spoon, then half-cover with a lid. Simmer for 3 hours, skimming off the scum again after the first 15 minutes and topping up the water during cooking if the liquid falls below the level of the meats.

Leave to cool, then remove the beef, veal and calf's foot (if used). Tip the vegetables and liquid into a sieve or fine colander lined with muslin (cheesecloth) wrung out in hot water. Press firmly to extract as much stock as possible.

Leave the stock until completely cold, then remove the fat that has risen to the surface. Store covered in the refrigerator for up to 4 days, or in the freezer for up to 3 months. Bring to the boil before using as required.
MAKES ABOUT 1.5 litres/2½ pints/6¼ cups

BOUILLON DE VOLAILLE
Chicken Stock

Eat the chicken from this stock hot as a main course with vegetables, or leave until cold, then slice, chop or mince (grind) and use in salads or made-up dishes.

Metric/Imperial	American
2 carrots, peeled and roughly chopped	2 carrots, peeled and roughly chopped
2 celery sticks, roughly chopped	2 celery stalks, roughly chopped
2 leeks, roughly chopped	2 leeks, roughly chopped
1 × 1.5 kg/3–3½ lb chicken, with giblets	1 × 3–3½ lb chicken, with giblets
1 calf's foot★, chopped (optional)	1 calf's foot★, chopped (optional)
1 onion, peeled and stuck with 2 whole cloves	1 onion, peeled and stuck with 2 whole cloves
1 bouquet garni★	1 bouquet garni★
6 black peppercorns	6 black peppercorns
salt	salt
3 litres/5½ pints water	6½ pints/13 cups water

Put the vegetables, except the onion, in the bottom of a large pan. Place the chicken on top of the vegetables with the giblets, calf's foot (if using), onion, bouquet garni, peppercorns and salt to taste.

Pour in the water and bring slowly to the boil. Skim off the scum with a slotted spoon, then lower the heat and half-cover with a lid. Simmer for 3 hours, skimming off the scum again after the first 15 minutes and topping up the water during the cooking time if it falls below the level of the chicken.

Leave to cool, then remove the chicken, giblets and calf's foot (if used). Tip the vegetables and liquid into a sieve or fine colander lined with muslin (cheesecloth) wrung out in hot water. Press firmly to extract as much stock as possible.

Leave the stock until completely cold, then remove the fat that has risen to the surface. Store covered in the refrigerator for up to 4 days, or in the freezer for up to 3 months. Bring to the boil before using as required.
MAKES ABOUT 1.5 litres/2½ pints/6¼ cups

FUMET DE POISSON
Fish Stock

Do not use oily fish for making this stock or it will have too strong a flavour. Cod, halibut and plaice are ideal, so too are turbot and sole, which will make the stock rich and gelatinous. Dry white wine, if available, can be used to replace some of the water to give the stock extra flavour.

Metric/Imperial	American
1 kg/2 lb white fish trimmings (including heads and bones)	2 lb white fish trimmings (including heads and bones)
1 large onion, peeled and sliced	1 large onion, peeled and sliced
1 large carrot, peeled and sliced	1 large carrot, peeled and sliced
2 celery sticks, roughly chopped	2 celery stalks, roughly chopped
1.75 litres/3 pints water	$3\frac{3}{4}$ pints/$7\frac{1}{2}$ cups water
2 tablespoons lemon juice	2 tablespoons lemon juice
1 bouquet garni★	1 bouquet garni★
6 white peppercorns	6 white peppercorns
1 teaspoon salt	1 teaspoon salt

Put all the ingredients in a large pan and bring slowly to the boil. Lower the heat and skim off the scum with a slotted spoon. Simmer uncovered for 30 minutes, skimming off the scum again during this time, if necessary.

Tip the contents of the pan into a sieve or fine colander lined with muslin (cheesecloth) wrung out in hot water. Press firmly to extract as much stock as possible.

Leave the stock until completely cold. Cover and store in the refrigerator for up to 2 days. Use as required.

MAKES ABOUT 1.5 litres/$2\frac{1}{2}$ pints/$6\frac{1}{4}$ cups

BOUILLON DE LEGUMES
Vegetable Stock

For use in vegetarian dishes and in delicately flavoured sauces and vegetable cream soups, etc., when the flavour of meat or poultry stock would be too strong.

Metric/Imperial	American
25 g/1 oz butter	2 tablespoons butter
450 g/1 lb onions, peeled and sliced	1 lb onions, peeled and sliced
450 g/1 lb carrots, peeled and sliced	1 lb carrots, peeled and sliced
1 head celery, with the leaves, roughly chopped	1 head celery, with the leaves, roughly chopped
1.75 litres/3 pints water	$3\frac{3}{4}$ pints/$7\frac{1}{2}$ cups water
1 bouquet garni★	1 bouquet garni★
6 white peppercorns	6 white peppercorns
$\frac{1}{2}$ teaspoon salt	$\frac{1}{2}$ teaspoon salt

Melt the butter in a large pan, add the vegetables and fry gently until softened, stirring frequently. Do not allow the vegetables to become browned or this will spoil the colour of the finished stock.

Stir in the water, then add the remaining ingredients and bring slowly to the boil. Lower the heat, skim off any scum with a slotted spoon, then half-cover with a lid. Simmer for 1 to 2 hours. Top up the water during the cooking time if the liquid reduces in the pan.

Tip the contents of the pan into a sieve or fine colander lined with muslin (cheesecloth) wrung out in hot water. Press firmly to extract as much stock as possible.

Leave the stock until completely cold. Cover and store in the refrigerator for up to 5 days, or in the freezer for up to 3 months. Bring to the boil before using as required.

MAKES ABOUT 1.5 litres/$2\frac{1}{2}$ pints/$6\frac{1}{4}$ cups

SAUCE BÉCHAMEL

This basic white coating sauce is used in numerous different ways – on its own, as a base for other sauces, in gratin dishes and quiches, etc.

Metric/Imperial	American
50 g/2 oz butter	¼ cup butter
50 g/2 oz plain flour	½ cup all-purpose flour
500 ml/18 fl oz hot milk	2¼ cups hot milk
salt	salt
freshly ground white pepper	freshly ground white pepper
freshly grated nutmeg	freshly grated nutmeg

Melt the butter in a heavy pan, sprinkle in the flour and cook, stirring constantly, for 1 minute to obtain a smooth *roux* (paste). Remove from the heat.

Pour the milk into the pan a little at a time, stirring vigorously after each addition to allow the *roux* to absorb the milk without forming lumps.

Bring slowly to the boil, stirring constantly, then lower the heat and simmer for 5 to 6 minutes until the sauce thickens, stirring frequently.

Add salt, pepper and nutmeg to taste, then remove from the heat. Use immediately.
MAKES ABOUT 600 ml/1 pint/2½ cups

NOTE: For extra flavour, add chopped parsley, chervil or tarragon to taste.

Sauce crème: After making the béchamel sauce, whisk in 25 g/1 oz/2 tablespoons softened butter, 200 ml/⅓ pint/1 cup double (heavy) cream and 1 teaspoon lemon juice. Serve with plain-boiled vegetables or roast chicken.

SAUCE MORNAY
Cheese Sauce

This sauce has a pouring consistency, and is most often served with vegetables and fish.

Metric/Imperial	American
25 g/1 oz butter	2 tablespoons butter
25 g/1 oz plain flour	¼ cup all-purpose flour
500 ml/18 fl oz hot milk	2¼ cups hot milk
salt	salt
freshly ground white pepper	freshly ground white pepper
freshly grated nutmeg	freshly grated nutmeg
100 g/4 oz Gruyère cheese★, grated	1 cup grated Gruyère cheese★
1 egg yolk	1 egg yolk
4 tablespoons double cream	¼ cup heavy cream

Make a béchamel sauce (as above) with the butter, flour, milk and salt, pepper and nutmeg to taste.

Add the cheese a little at a time, over the lowest possible heat, stirring vigorously with a wooden spoon until the cheese melts.

Put the egg yolk in a bowl and whisk with a fork. Whisk in the cream gradually, then stir into the sauce a little at a time.

Reheat very gently whisking all the time; do not allow the sauce to boil at this stage or it will separate and become lumpy. Use immediately.
MAKES ABOUT 600 ml/1 pint/2½ cups

SAUCE SOUBISE
Onion Sauce

This onion sauce is used for coating fish and meat dishes. It is also a classic accompaniment to gigot à la bretonne (leg of lamb with haricot (navy) beans – page 141).

Metric/Imperial	American
75 g/3 oz butter, softened	⅓ cup softened butter
225 g/8 oz onions, peeled and thinly sliced	½ lb onions, peeled and thinly sliced
7 tablespoons double cream	7 tablespoons heavy cream
BÉCHAMEL SAUCE:	BÉCHAMEL SAUCE:
50 g/2 oz butter	¼ cup butter
50 g/2 oz plain flour	½ cup all-purpose flour
500 ml/18 fl oz hot milk	2¼ cups hot milk
salt	salt
freshly ground white pepper	freshly ground white pepper
freshly grated nutmeg	freshly grated nutmeg

Melt 25 g/1 oz/2 tablespoons butter in a heavy pan, add the onions and fry very gently for 30 minutes until soft and golden, stirring frequently.

Meanwhile, make a béchamel sauce (see opposite) with the butter, flour, milk, and salt, pepper and nutmeg to taste.

Stir the béchamel sauce into the onions, cover the pan and simmer very gently for 15 minutes, stirring from time to time.

Work the onion sauce through a fine sieve (strainer) into a clean pan, rubbing vigorously. Bring slowly to just below boiling point, stirring constantly, then remove from the heat.

Stir the cream into the sauce, then whisk in the remaining softened butter a little at a time. Taste and adjust seasoning. Serve immediately.
MAKES ABOUT 600 ml/1 pint/2½ cups

SAUCE MOUTARDE
Mustard Sauce

A coating sauce to serve with veal escalopes, pork and veal chops and vegetables.

Metric/Imperial	American
50 g/2 oz butter	¼ cup butter
50 g/2 oz plain flour	½ cup all-purpose flour
500 ml/18 fl oz hot milk	2¼ cups hot milk
salt	salt
freshly ground white pepper	freshly ground white pepper
1 onion, peeled and stuck with 1 clove (optional)	1 onion, peeled and stuck with 1 clove (optional)
150 ml/¼ pint double cream	⅔ cup heavy cream
3 tablespoons prepared French mustard★	3 tablespoons prepared French mustard★
dash of red wine vinegar	dash of red wine vinegar

Make a béchamel sauce (see opposite) with the butter, flour, milk, and salt and pepper to taste.

Add the onion (if using) and simmer very gently for 30 minutes, stirring frequently.

Remove the onion from the sauce, then stir in the cream, mustard and wine vinegar. Bring back to the boil, stirring constantly, then taste and adjust seasoning. Use immediately.
MAKES ABOUT 750 ml/1¼ pints/3 cups

SAUCE HOLLANDAISE

To accompany cooked fish dishes and vegetables, particularly asparagus and boiled new potatoes. In this recipe the finished sauce is passed through a strainer before serving, to remove any particles of pepper and make the sauce extra smooth. This process is not absolutely necessary if time is short.

Metric/Imperial	American
225 g/8 oz butter, cut into small pieces	1 cup butter, cut into small pieces
2 tablespoons white wine vinegar	2 tablespoons white wine vinegar
4 tablespoons water	$\frac{1}{4}$ cup water
$\frac{1}{4}$–$\frac{1}{2}$ teaspoon freshly ground white pepper, according to taste	$\frac{1}{4}$–$\frac{1}{2}$ teaspoon freshly ground white pepper, according to taste
3 egg yolks	3 egg yolks
1–2 tablespoons lemon juice	1–2 tablespoons lemon juice
salt	salt

To clarify the butter: put the butter in a heavy pan and melt over very low heat. Skim off the white foam that rises to the surface, then strain the clear yellow liquid into a bowl, leaving behind the milky residue.

Put the vinegar in a heavy pan with 2 tablespoons water, and pepper to taste. Boil rapidly until the liquid has reduced to 1 teaspoon. Remove from the heat, then stand the pan in a hot *bain marie*★.

Stir 1 tablespoon water into the reduced liquid, then add the egg yolks one at a time, whisking vigorously after each addition.

Whisk in the clarified butter a little at a time, then whisk in the remaining water. The consistency of the sauce should be like thick cream at this stage.

Pass the sauce through a *chinois* then whisk in the lemon juice and salt to taste. Serve immediately.

4 SERVINGS

Sauce mousseline: Fold 2 tablespoons lightly whipped cream into the hollandaise sauce just before serving.

SAUCE BÉARNAISE

To accompany all grilled (broiled) steaks and roast beef.

Metric/Imperial	American
225 g/8 oz butter, cut into small pieces	1 cup butter, cut into small pieces
7 tablespoons white wine vinegar	7 tablespoons white wine vinegar
2 shallots, peeled and very finely chopped	2 scallions, peeled and very finely chopped
$\frac{1}{4}$–$\frac{1}{2}$ teaspoon freshly ground white pepper, according to taste	$\frac{1}{4}$–$\frac{1}{2}$ teaspoon freshly ground white pepper, according to taste
2 tablespoons chopped tarragon	2 tablespoons chopped tarragon
3 egg yolks	3 egg yolks
2 tablespoons water	2 tablespoons water
salt	salt

To clarify the butter: put the butter in a heavy pan and melt over very low heat. Skim off the white foam that rises to the surface, then strain the clear yellow liquid into a bowl, leaving behind the milky residue.

Put the vinegar in a heavy pan with the shallots (scallions), pepper to taste and half the tarragon. Boil rapidly until the liquid has reduced to 1 tablespoon.

Rub the reduced liquid through a fine sieve (strainer) into a clean pan, then stand the pan in a hot *bain marie*★.

Add the egg yolks to the strained liquid one at a time, whisking vigorously after each addition. Whisk in the water.

Whisk in the clarified butter a little at a time until the consistency of the sauce is like thick cream. Add the remaining tarragon and salt to taste. Serve immediately.

4 SERVINGS

Sauce choron: Substitute tomato purée (paste) for the 2 tablespoons of tarragon and whisk it in at the end of making the béarnaise sauce. The quantity can vary from 1 to 4 tablespoons, according to taste.

SAUCE VELOUTÉ

One of the classic French sauces, which can be served on its own like béchamel sauce, or used as a base for other classic sauces.

Metric/Imperial	American
100 g/4 oz butter	$\frac{1}{2}$ cup butter
25 g/1 oz plain flour	$\frac{1}{4}$ cup all-purpose flour
500 ml/18 fl oz hot chicken stock (page 42)	$2\frac{1}{4}$ cups hot chicken stock (page 42)
salt	salt
freshly ground white pepper	freshly ground white pepper

To clarify the butter: put half of the butter in a heavy pan and melt over very low heat. Skim off the white foam that rises to the surface, then strain the clear yellow liquid into a clean pan, leaving behind the milky residue.

Place over low heat again, sprinkle in the flour and cook, stirring constantly, for 2 minutes.

Stir in the hot stock a little at a time, whisking vigorously after each addition. Bring slowly to the boil, stirring constantly, then stand over the lowest possible heat and simmer very gently for 1 hour, stirring occasionally. Skim the sauce with a slotted spoon from time to time to remove any impurities and fat that rise to the surface.

Remove from the heat, then work through a fine sieve (strainer) into a clean pan. Reheat very gently, then remove from the heat and whisk in the remaining butter a little at a time until thoroughly incorporated. Add salt and pepper to taste. Serve immediately.
MAKES ABOUT 600 ml/1 pint/2$\frac{1}{2}$ cups

NOTE: If the sauce is not to be served immediately, make it up to the sieving stage, then leave to cool. Reheat and add the butter just before serving – once the butter is added the sauce will not keep.

SAUCE VERTE
Piquant Green Sauce

This 'green sauce' is served as an accompaniment to grilled (broiled) fish and meat, the meat from a pot-au-feu (page 132) and boiled salt pork.

Metric/Imperial	American
1 tablespoon wine vinegar	1 tablespoon wine vinegar
salt	salt
freshly ground black pepper	freshly ground black pepper
2 tablespoons chopped parsley	2 tablespoons chopped parsley
1 tablespoon chopped chervil	1 tablespoon chopped chervil
1 tablespoon snipped chives	1 tablespoon snipped chives
1 tablespoon very finely chopped capers	1 tablespoon very finely chopped capers
6 small gherkins, very finely chopped	6 small sweet dill pickles, very finely chopped
2 shallots, peeled and very finely chopped	2 scallions, peeled and very finely chopped
4 tablespoons olive oil	$\frac{1}{4}$ cup olive oil

Put the vinegar in a bowl with salt and pepper to taste. Add the remaining ingredients, except the oil; stir well.

Pour in the oil in a steady stream, whisking vigorously with a fork until all the oil is incorporated. Pour into a sauceboat and serve cold.
4 SERVINGS

VARIATIONS: Other ingredients can be added to this sauce, according to taste – very finely chopped canned anchovies (drained and desalted★), very finely chopped hard-boiled (cooked) egg and crushed garlic are just a few suggestions. Mint, tarragon or basil can be substituted for some of the herbs, or mixed with them according to availability. If a thicker sauce is liked, whisk in a few tablespoons of fresh breadcrumbs.

SAUCE TOMATE

This is just one of the many variations of tomato sauce to be found in French cooking – each region has its own favourite.

Metric/Imperial	American
0 g/2 oz goose fat★, or 4 tablespoons olive oil	¼ cup goose fat★ or olive oil
large onions, peeled and finely chopped	2 large onions, peeled and finely chopped
garlic cloves, peeled and crushed	4 garlic cloves, peeled and crushed
kg/2 lb ripe tomatoes, skinned, seeded and crushed	4 cups skinned, seeded and crushed tomatoes
tablespoon tomato purée	1 tablespoon tomato paste
–½ teaspoon sugar	¼–½ teaspoon sugar
bouquet garni★	1 bouquet garni★
lt	salt
eshly ground black pepper	freshly ground black pepper
eshly grated nutmeg	freshly grated nutmeg
opped parsley	chopped parsley

Heat the fat or oil in a heavy pan, add the onions and garlic and fry gently for 15 minutes, stirring often.

Add the tomatoes, tomato purée (paste), sugar, bouquet garni, and salt, pepper and nutmeg to taste. Bring to the boil, then lower the heat, cover and simmer gently for 45 minutes, stirring occasionally.

Remove from the heat and discard the bouquet garni. Taste and adjust seasoning, then add parsley to taste. Serve hot.
MAKES ABOUT 450 ml/¾ pint/2 cups

SAUCE POULETTE
Mushroom Sauce

This sauce is the traditional accompaniment to tripe, although it is also sometimes served with shellfish.

Metric/Imperial	American
5 g/1 oz butter	2 tablespoons butter
25 g/8 oz mushrooms, finely sliced	2–2½ cups finely sliced mushrooms
juice of 1 lemon	juice of 1 lemon
tablespoons double cream	7 tablespoons heavy cream
egg yolks	3 egg yolks
00 ml/18 fl oz chicken stock (page 42)	2¼ cups chicken stock (page 42)
tablespoon cornflour	1 tablespoon cornstarch
tablespoons water	2 tablespoons water
tablespoon chopped parsley	1 tablespoon chopped parsley
lt	salt
eshly ground white pepper	freshly ground white pepper

Melt the butter in a pan, add the mushrooms and lemon juice and cook over moderate heat for 15 minutes.

Meanwhile, put the cream in a bowl, add the egg yolks and whisk to combine

Bring the stock to the boil in a pan. Mix the cornflour (cornstarch) to a paste with the water, then stir into the stock and cook until beginning to thicken.

Whisk 3 tablespoons of the hot stock into the cream and egg yolk mixture, then pour this mixture gradu-ally into the stock in the pan, whisking vigorously all the time. Add the mushrooms and their cooking juices, the parsley and salt and pepper to taste.

Heat through gently over very low heat, whisking constantly; do not allow the sauce to boil or it will curdle. Serve immediately.
MAKES ABOUT 600 ml/1 pint/2½ cups

ROUILLE
Chilli Pepper and Garlic Sauce

This is the fiery hot sauce that is traditionally served with Bouillabaisse (page 92) in the Midi. Sometimes the breadcrumbs are replaced with a mashed or puréed boiled potato, and sometimes an egg yolk is used which makes the rouille more like a mayonnaise. Guests help themselves to rouille, which they stir into their bouillabaisse according to taste. It can be served with other fish soups, and is often spread like a paste on dried or toasted bread, then placed in the bottom of soup bowls before the soup is poured over. Rouille also makes an excellent accompaniment to grilled (broiled) fish, in which case, use water or milk in place of the fish stock.

Metric/Imperial	American
3 garlic cloves, peeled and halved	3 garlic cloves, peeled and halved
3 red chilli peppers, halved, cored and seeded	3 red chili peppers, halved, cored and seeded
1 thick slice bread, crust removed and crumbled	1 thick slice bread, crust removed and crumbled
1 tablespoon hot bouillabaisse stock or fish stock (page 43)	1 tablespoon hot bouillabaisse stock or fish stock
200 ml/⅓ pint olive oil	1 cup olive oil
salt	salt

Put the garlic and chilli peppers in a mortar and pound to a paste with a pestle. Add the breadcrumbs and hot stock, then leave to stand for 1 minute.

Pound the mixture again until well mixed, then add the oil a drop at a time as when making mayonnaise. Pound constantly until all the oil is added and the sauce has become emulsified. Taste and add salt if necessary. Serve at room temperature, straight from the mortar.
6 SERVINGS

VINAIGRETTE
Oil and Vinegar Dressing

This is the basic recipe for vinaigrette, but there are many regional variations. For example, garlic and chopped fresh herbs are added in the south, fresh cream in Normandy.

Metric/Imperial	American
2 tablespoons wine vinegar	2 tablespoons wine vinegar
salt	salt
freshly ground black pepper	freshly ground black pepper
6 tablespoons olive oil	6 tablespoons olive oil

Put the vinegar in a bowl with salt and pepper to taste. Whisk with a fork, then add the oil and continue whisking until the dressing is thick. Taste and adjust seasoning.
MAKES ABOUT 120 ml/4 fl oz/½ cup

MAYONNAISE

This recipe is for the classic French mayonnaise made in a mortar and pestle, without mustard or other flavourings. If the flavour of mustard is liked, add ½ teaspoon prepared French mustard to the egg yolk before adding the oil; if left for 1 minute, this will also help the egg yolk and oil emulsify. A rotary beater or electric whisk can be used instead of the mortar and pestle, if this seems easier.

Metric/Imperial	American
1 egg yolk	1 egg yolk
120–150 ml/4–5 fl oz groundnut, corn or olive oil	½–⅓ cup groundnut, corn or olive oil
pinch of salt	pinch of salt
3–4 teaspoons white wine vinegar or lemon juice	3–4 teaspoons white wine vinegar or lemon juice

Have all equipment and ingredients at room temperature.

Put the egg yolk in a mortar and work with a pestle to break up the yolk.

Add the oil to the egg yolk a drop at a time, working together thoroughly before adding more oil.

When the mayonnaise begins to emulsify, add the oil faster and use the pestle more vigorously. The mayonnaise should be thick within 5 to 8 minutes.

Add salt to taste, then blend in the vinegar or lemon juice. Serve at room temperature, straight from the mortar.
MAKES ABOUT 150 ml/¼ pint/⅔ cup

AÏOLI

Garlic Mayonnaise

This is the very thick mayonnaise from Provence which is heavily laced with garlic (ail). It is often served with raw vegetables (crudités) at the start of a meal, but it also lends its name to le grand aïoli, an array of mixed meats, fish and vegetables served around a bowl of garlic mayonnaise, which is used as a dipping sauce. Aillade is a similar kind of provençal mayonnaise used to flavour the fish soups of the area – sometimes with chopped nuts added.

Metric/Imperial	American
5 garlic cloves, peeled and halved	5 garlic cloves, peeled and halved
1 thick slice white bread, soaked in milk	1 thick slice white bread, soaked in milk
2 egg yolks	2 egg yolks
pinch of salt	pinch of salt
250 ml/8 fl oz olive oil	1 cup olive oil
2 tablespoons lemon juice, or to taste	2 tablespoons lemon juice, or to taste
1–2 tablespoons boiling water	1–2 tablespoons boiling water

Pound the garlic in a mortar and pestle until well crushed. Squeeze the bread to extract as much milk as possible, then add to the garlic and pound again until a smooth purée is formed.

Add the egg yolks and salt and continue pounding until thoroughly incorporated and beginning to thicken.

Add the olive oil a drop at a time, as when making

mayonnaise, adding it in a thin, steady stream as t mixture thickens. Continue pounding all the time make a thick, smooth mayonnaise.

Stir in lemon juice to taste, then whisk in the boili water to help 'set' the sauce – it should be very thi and heavy. Serve at room temperature.
MAKES ABOUT 450 ml/¾ pint/2 cups

SAUCE TARTARE

To accompany any cooked fish, meat or poultry dish. It particularly good with 'spatch-cocked' chicken – the bird usually a small poussin, is split down the back, secured w skewers, then grilled (broiled) or spit-roasted with melte butter.

Metric/Imperial	American
2 hard-boiled eggs	2 hard-cooked eggs
250 ml/8 fl oz olive oil	1 cup olive oil
1 tablespoon mayonnaise (opposite)	1 tablespoon mayonnaise (opposite)
1 teaspoon wine vinegar	1 teaspoon wine vinegar
1 tablespoon very finely chopped capers	1 tablespoon very finely chopped capers
6 small gherkins, very finely chopped	6 small sweet dill pickles, very finely chopped
1 tablespoon snipped chives	1 tablespoon snipped chive
salt	salt
freshly ground black pepper	freshly ground black pepp

Put the egg yolks in a bowl and mash with a fork t smooth paste. Add the oil a drop at a time, whiski vigorously after each addition as for mayonna (opposite).

When all the oil is incorporated and the mixture thick and creamy, whisk in the mayonnaise a vinegar, then the remaining ingredients with salt a pepper to taste. Serve cold.
6 SERVINGS

NOTE: For a sauce with more body, sieve the leftov egg whites and whisk into the sauce just before servir

BEURRE BLANC

This butter sauce is the classic accompaniment to cooked fi dishes. The recipe is from Brittany, where more salted o slightly salted (semisweet) butter is used than in other regions of France. Most French cooks tend to use unsalte (sweet) butter in cooking, then add salt to taste before serving.

Metric/Imperial	American
4 medium shallots, peeled and very finely chopped	4 medium scallions, peele and very finely choppe
150 ml/¼ pint dry white wine	⅔ cup dry white wine
7 tablespoons white wine vinegar	7 tablespoons white wine vinegar
225 g/8 oz slightly salted butter, chilled and diced	1 cup semisweet butter, chilled and diced
freshly ground white pepper	freshly ground white pepp

Put the shallots (scallions) in a heavy pan with the wi and wine vinegar. Boil rapidly until the liquid h reduced to about 1 tablespoon.

Transfer the liquid to a heatproof bowl and stat

over a pan of hot water. Add the chilled butter to the liquid, a piece at a time, whisking vigorously after each addition until the consistency of the mixture is like thick cream. Add pepper to taste.

Pour directly onto food or hand separately in a warmed sauceboat. Serve immediately.

5 TO 6 SERVINGS

NOTE: If a smooth sauce is liked, pour the sauce through a fine sieve (strainer) before serving.

BEURRE ROUGE

The classic red butter sauce to accompany grilled (broiled) steaks or roast beef. If roasting beef, make beurre rouge in the roasting pan: pour off any excess fat after roasting, then add the shallots (scallions) and wine etc. to the cooking juices and sediment in the pan and follow the recipe below.

Metric/Imperial	American
4 medium shallots, peeled and very finely chopped	4 medium scallions, peeled and very finely chopped
250 ml/8 fl oz red wine	1 cup red wine
1 tablespoon red wine vinegar	1 tablespoon red wine vinegar
salt	salt
freshly ground black pepper	freshly ground black pepper
225 g/8 oz unsalted butter, chilled and diced	1 cup sweet butter, chilled and diced

Put the shallots (scallions) in a heavy pan with the wine and wine vinegar, and salt and pepper to taste. Boil rapidly until the liquid has reduced to about 1 tablespoon.

Transfer the liquid to a heatproof bowl and stand over a pan of hot water. Add the chilled butter to the liquid, a piece at a time, whisking vigorously after each addition until the mixture is the consistency of thick cream. Taste and adjust seasoning.

Pour directly onto food or hand separately in a warmed sauceboat. Serve immediately.

5 TO 6 SERVINGS

NOTE: If a smooth sauce is liked, pour the sauce through a fine sieve (strainer) before serving.

BEURRE BERCY

This white butter with beef marrow is the classic accompaniment to grilled (broiled) steaks and roast beef.

Metric/Imperial	American
1 beef marrow bone★ (about 225 g/8 oz in weight)	1 beef marrow bone★ (about ½ lb in weight)
salt	salt
2 shallots, peeled and very finely chopped	2 scallions, peeled and very finely chopped
200 ml/⅓ pint dry white wine	1 cup dry white wine
150 g/5 oz butter, softened	⅔ cup butter, softened
1 tablespoon lemon juice	1 tablespoon lemon juice
1 tablespoon chopped parsley	1 tablespoon chopped parsley
freshly ground black pepper	freshly ground black pepper

Split the marrow bone down the centre and take out the marrow. Chop it as finely as possible, using a knife dipped in hot water.

Drop the chopped marrow into a pan of boiling salted water, then lower the heat and simmer for 5 minutes until soft. Drain thoroughly.

Put the shallots (scallions) in a heavy pan with the wine and boil rapidly until reduced by half. Leave to cool.

Add the butter a little at a time to the reduced liquid, whisking vigorously after each addition, then whisk in the softened marrow a piece at a time. Add the lemon juice, parsley, and salt and pepper to taste, then whisk thoroughly to combine. The consistency of the butter should be like whipped cream. Serve cold on top of meat or hand separately in a serving bowl.
6 SERVINGS

BEURRE MARCHAND DE VIN

This butter is the classic accompaniment to entrecôte steak, but it can be served with any grilled (broiled) beef.

Metric/Imperial	American
3 shallots, peeled and very finely chopped	3 scallions, peeled and very finely chopped
200 ml/⅓ pint red wine	1 cup red wine
200 g/7 oz butter, softened	1 cup butter, softened
1 tablespoon lemon juice	1 tablespoon lemon juice
1 tablespoon chopped parsley	1 tablespoon chopped parsley
salt	salt
freshly ground black pepper	freshly ground black pepper

Put the shallots (scallions) in a heavy pan with the wine and boil rapidly until reduced by half. Leave to cool.

Add the butter a little at a time to the reduced liquid, whisking vigorously after each addition.

Add the lemon juice, parsley, and salt and pepper to taste, then whisk thoroughly to combine. The consistency of the butter should be like whipped cream.

Serve cold on top of meat or hand separately in a serving bowl.
6 SERVINGS

CRÈME ANGLAISE
Custard Sauce

This is the basic recipe for a custard sauce without flavourings, used either hot or cold for coating puddings and desserts when something a little less rich than fresh cream is required. If liked, infuse the milk with a vanilla pod (bean) before use, or add 1 teaspoon vanilla essence (extract) once the custard is cooked. 1 tablespoon liqueur can also be added for extra flavour, and melted chocolate can be stirred in to make a chocolate custard sauce for coating chocolate puddings.

Metric/Imperial	American
4 large egg yolks	4 large egg yolks
50–75 g/2–3 oz sugar, according to taste	¼–⅓ cup sugar, according to taste
1 teaspoon cornflour	1 teaspoon cornstarch
450 ml/¾ pint milk	2 cups milk

Put the egg yolks in a bowl with sugar to taste and whisk together until pale and thick. Whisk in the cornflour (cornstarch).

Bring the milk to just below boiling point, then gradually whisk into the egg yolk and sugar mixture.

Pour the custard into a heavy-based pan and stir over gentle heat with a wooden spoon until the custard begins to thicken and just coats the back of the spoon. Do not allow to boil or the custard will separate.

Remove from the heat, continue stirring for 1 to 2 minutes, then pour into a jug and serve immediately. To serve cold, cool quickly by transferring the sauce to a cold bowl, standing in a larger bowl of iced water. Stir continually until cold, then press a piece of cling film or greaseproof (wax) paper onto the surface of the sauce and chill in the refrigeratOr. Whisk vigorously before serving.
MAKES ABOUT 450 ml/¾ pint/2 cups

CRÈME CHANTILLY
Chantilly Cream

Serve this cream either separately in a small bowl or pipe it attractively on desserts.

Metric/Imperial	American
250 ml/8 fl oz double cream, chilled	1 cup heavy cream, chilled
3 teaspoons caster sugar	3 teaspoons sugar

Whisk the cream in a cold basin until fluffy. Gradually add the sugar and continue to whisk slowly until the cream just holds its shape. Serve immediately.
MAKES ABOUT 250 ml/8 fl oz/1 cup

Crème chantilly aux Fruits can be made by doubling the basic recipe above and then adding 200 ml/⅓ pint/1 cup fresh strawberry or raspberry purée.

CRÈME FRAÎCHE

This cream is often used in France instead of sweet cream, especially in soups and fish and poultry dishes etc. as it adds more of a piquant flavour than ordinary double (heavy) cream. When first made, crème fraîche is sweet but on keeping it gradually acquires a tart flavour.

Metric/Imperial	American
250 ml/8 fl oz double cream	1 cup heavy cream
120 ml/4 fl oz soured cream	½ cup sour cream

Put both creams in a pan and stir well. Heat gently to 25°C/77°F (lukewarm). Pour cream into a jug and partly cover. Keep the cream at this warm temperature for 6 to 8 hours until thickened. Stir the cream then cover and refrigerate for up to 2 weeks.
MAKES ABOUT 350 ml/12 fl oz/1½ cups

CRÈME PÂTISSÌERE

Confectioner's Custard

So-called because of its use as a filling for all kinds of pâtisserie, crème patissière is a thick rich custard which sets on cooling to become quite firm. It is a popular filling for fruit flans and sweet tarts, and is also often used in choux buns and profiteroles. When crème pâtissière has beaten egg whites added to it, it is called crème Saint-Honoré.

Metric/Imperial	American
450 ml/¾ pint milk	2 cups milk
1 vanilla pod	1 vanilla bean
4 large egg yolks	4 large egg yolks
100 g/4 oz sugar	½ cup sugar
50 g/2 oz plain flour	½ cup all-purpose flour
knob of butter, to finish	knob of butter, to finish

Bring the milk to just below boiling point with the vanilla, then cover the pan and leave to infuse for 15 minutes. Strain, then bring to boiling point again.

Put the egg yolks in a bowl with the sugar and whisk together until pale and thick. Add the flour and whisk again until thoroughly incorporated, then gradually whisk in the boiling hot milk.

Pour the custard into a heavy-based pan and whisk over moderate heat until boiling. The mixture may be lumpy, in which case, remove from the heat and whisk vigorously until smooth. Return to the heat and bring to the boil again, then simmer for 1 to 2 minutes to cook the flour, whisking constantly.

Remove the custard from the heat, then rub the surface with the knob of butter to prevent a skin forming. Leave to cool before use.
MAKES ABOUT 450 ml/¾ pint/2 cups

PRALIN

Praline or Caramelized Almonds

*In France, pralin is available ready-made from most
pâtisseries, but if it is difficult for you to obtain, then it is
quite easy to make at home and will keep for weeks in a
screw-topped jar. Use it to sprinkle over ice cream and
cream desserts and in icings, fillings and sauces.*

Metric/Imperial	American
100 g/4 oz whole unblanched almonds	*¾ cup whole unblanced almonds*
100 g/4 oz sugar	*½ cup sugar*

Put the almonds and sugar in a heavy-based pan and
stir over gentle heat until the sugar melts and cara-
melizes and the almonds are toasted.

Pour the mixture onto an oiled marble slab or
baking sheet, then leave until completely cold and
crisp.

Break the praline into pieces, then work in an
electric grinder until pulverized to a fine powder, or
pound in a mortar and pestle. Store in a screw-topped
jar.

MAKES ABOUT 225 g/½ lb

PÂTE BRISÉE

Shortcrust Pastry (Basic Pie Dough)

*A general-purpose pastry used for most savoury tarts and
quiches, etc. For a richer pastry, add 2 egg yolks after cutting
in the butter, then add less iced water to mix.*

Metric/Imperial	American
225 g/8 oz plain flour	*2 cups all-purpose flour*
½ teaspoon salt	*½ teaspoon salt*
112 g/4 oz butter	*½ cup butter*
about 4 tablespoons iced water	*about ¼ cup iced water*

Sift the flour and salt into a bowl. Cut the butter into
small pieces over the bowl then, with a round-bladed
knife, cut it into the flour.

With the fingertips, rub the butter into the flour
until the mixture resembles fine breadcrumbs. Work
lightly, with hands held above the rim of the bowl to
aerate the flour as much as possible to keep it light and
short.

Stir in the water with the knife, adding it gradually
until the mixture begins to draw together. With one
hand, gather the dough together and form into a ball.
Knead lightly until the dough is smooth and supple and
free from cracks. Wrap in cling film or foil, then leave
to relax in a cool place for 1 hour before use. In warm
weather, chill in the refrigerator for 30 minutes, but
allow to come to room temperature again before
rolling out.

MAKES A '225 g/½ lb QUANTITY'

Pâte sucrée, or sweet shortcrust pastry (pie dough) is
made exactly as for *pâte brisée* above, except that caster
sugar is added to the flour before cutting in the butter.
Pâte sucrée is used for sweet tarts and flans, and the
amount of sugar varies according to individual recipes,
from 25 g/1 oz/2 tablespoons to 100 g/4 oz/½ cup sugar
for every 225 g/8 oz/2 cups flour.

Pâte sablée, commonly called French flan pastry, is a
rich sweetened pastry used for flans and tarts which
contain juicy fruits. It is made with the same ingredients as *pâte sucrée*, but enriched with egg yolks
(2 to 4 egg yolks per 225 g/8 oz/2 cups flour according
to individual recipes). It is more difficult to work than
other less rich pastries, and is therefore usually mixed
on a marble slab or other cold surface rather than in a
bowl. It is easier to press it into the flan ring or pan
rather than to roll it out on a floured board.

PÂTE À CHOUX

Choux Pastry

*This is the basic recipe for choux pastry, used mostly in the
making of choux buns, profiteroles and éclairs, but also in
such recipes as the savoury cheese gougère de Bourgogne
(page 74) and the sumptuous gâteau Saint-Honoré (page
185). Quantities of ingredients for making choux pastry
vary considerably from one recipe to another, but you will
notice that the proportions are always the same. It is
therefore quite simple to use this basic method for recipes
with different quantities.*

Metric/Imperial	American
275 ml/½ pint water	*scant 1¼ cups water*
100 g/4 oz butter	*½ cup butter*
¾ teaspoon salt	*¾ teaspoon salt*
150 g/5 oz plain flour	*1¼ cups all-purpose flour*
about 4 large eggs	*about 4 large eggs*

eat the water in a large pan with the butter and salt.
'hen the butter has melted, bring the liquid to the boil
d remove from the heat.

Immediately add the flour all at once, then beat
gorously with a wooden spoon. Return the pan to a
w heat and continue beating until the mixture draws
gether and leaves the sides of the pan. Do not
erbeat – the dough should be smooth and shiny, but
t oily.

Remove the pan from the heat, then add the eggs
e at a time, beating vigorously after each addition
d making sure the egg is thoroughly incorporated
fore adding the next. Add the last egg a little at a
ne, beating to make a shiny dough that just falls from
e spoon – if the dough will not absorb all the last egg,
en do not add it.

For best results, use choux dough immediately,
hile still warm. If this is impossible, brush lightly
th butter while still warm (to prevent a crust
rming on its surface), leave until cool, then cover
sely with greaseproof (wax) paper. Store in the
frigerator for up to 8 hours. To use, warm through in
e pan on top of the stove, beating vigorously until
100th and shiny again.
AKES A '4 EGG QUANTITY'

PÂTE FEUILLETÉE
Puff Pastry

*Homemade puff pastry is far superior to its commercial
frozen counterpart, but although not difficult to make, it is
time-consuming. Remember always to work in the coolest
conditions, with both cool hands and cool utensils, or the
finished pastry will not be satisfactory. Puff pastry is very
rich, with its equal weights of butter and flour. Similar but
less rich pastries are rough puff and flaky, which use three-
quarters fat to flour. Rough puff is the easiest of the three to
make because the butter is simply stirred into the flour in
pieces; in flaky pastry the butter is 'flaked' over the dough.
All three pastries use the same rolling, folding and turning
technique. For a puff pastry which is less rich, use only two-
thirds of the butter specified here; this will also make it
easier to handle.*

Metric/Imperial	American
450 g/1 lb strong white flour	4 cups strong white (bread) flour
½ teaspoon salt	½ teaspoon salt
450 g/1 lb unsalted butter, chilled but not hard	2 cups sweet butter, chilled but not hard
2 teaspoons lemon juice (optional)	2 teaspoons lemon juice (optional)
about 250 ml/8 fl oz iced water	about 1 cup iced water

Sift the flour and salt onto a marble slab or other cold
surface and make a well in the centre. Soften 25 g/
1 oz/2 tablespoons butter by working with a wooden
spoon (keeping the remaining butter chilled).

Put the softened butter into the well in the centre of
the flour with the lemon juice (if using) and almost all
the water. Work the ingredients with the fingertips
until a soft elastic dough is formed, adding more water
if the dough is crumbly or dry. Knead lightly, wrap in
cling film or foil, then chill in the refrigerator for
15 minutes.

Sprinkle the chilled butter with a little flour or cover
with greaseproof (wax) paper, then flatten it with a
rolling pin to make a pliable 18 cm/6 inch square, the
same consistency as the dough.

Roll out the dough on a floured cold surface to a
30 cm/12 inch square. Place the square of butter in the
centre of the dough. Fold the sides of the dough over
the butter, then the ends, to enclose it like a parcel.
Wrap in cling film or foil, then chill in the refrigerator
for 15 minutes.

Unwrap the dough and place on the floured surface,
join facing downwards. Flatten it with the rolling pin,
then roll it out to a rectangle three times as long as it is
wide. Fold this rectangle into three by folding the top
third down and the bottom third up. Seal the edges by
pressing lightly with the rolling pin, keeping the edges
as straight as possible.

Turn the pastry so that one of the open edges is
facing towards you, then roll out into a rectangle
again. Fold into three, then wrap the dough as before
and chill in the refrigerator for 15 minutes.

Continue turning and rolling the dough in this way
until the dough has been turned six times altogether,
chilling it in the refrigerator after every two turns.
After the final turn, return to the refrigerator to chill
before using.
MAKES A '450 g/1 lb QUANTITY'

SOUPS

When you are served soup (potage) in France, almost without exception it will be homemade. The reason for this is very simple: in France, soup is regarded as an essential part of the meal (if not the whole part in some cases), and therefore as much care and attention goes into making the soup as it does into any other course. A perfect soup at the beginning of a meal gives a good impression of what is to follow, but remember that a soup is intended to whet the appetite, not to satiate or dull it.

The custom of eating soup in France varies enormously, not only from region to region, but also between the cities and provincial towns and rural districts. In Paris and the larger provincial towns where the main meal of the day is usually eaten in the evening, soup is served as a first course and is likely to be a clear or purée soup with a light texture. In the provinces and country districts where the main meal is more often eaten in the middle of the day, soup is served on its own in the evening, in which case it will be more substantial – a meal in itself, such as a broth with meat and vegetables.

No soup which calls for stock (bouillon or fond) will ever taste good unless it is made with a well-flavoured homemade stock, whether it be beef or veal, chicken, fish or vegetable. Recipes for stocks are given on page 42–3, and it is well worth taking the extra time to make these yourself. If you skimp by using a stock cube, the flavour of the finished soup will be disappointing, no matter how good the other ingredients are. Soups made with stock cubes will always have a 'samey' flavour.

French soups can be divided into three categories. Broths are simple soups made from meat or fish and vegetables in the same way as stock – the French use the same word bouillon for both broth and stock. Meat or fish and vegetables are simmered in water with herbs and seasonings for several hours, then the liquid is strained off and the meat or fish and vegetables left behind. Broths are usually more flavoursome than stocks. In France, broths are usually poured over a thick slice of bread in the soup bowl. In some cases (as in pot-au-feu, page 132), the meat or fish from the broth is eaten afterwards as a main course.

Clear soups and consommés are made from meat and vegetables in the same way as broths, except that stock is used for the simmering liquid rather than water. After straining, the liquid is clarified with egg whites which attract all the fat and impurities. A consommé should be clear and sparkling and completely free from grease. Sometimes finely diced meat and vegetables are added.

Purée soups are made from fresh vegetables gently simmered in stock or water with flavourings and seasonings. After simmering, both vegetables and liquid are puréed until smooth. A mouli-légumes is mostly used for this purpose in France, although electric blenders and processors are now taking its place. Many purée soups are thickened – with rice, potatoes, flour or bread, for example. A soup thickened with bread is called a panade (from the French word pain meaning bread), whereas a soup thickened with cream is known as a crème. Velouté soups are thickened with flour, then enriched with a liaison of egg yolks and cream.

ALSACE-LORRAINE

SOUPE À LA BIÈRE
Beer Soup

Metric/Imperial	American
25 g/1 oz butter	2 tablespoons butter
1 large onion, peeled and thinly sliced	1 large onion, peeled and thinly sliced
1 litre/1¾ pints hot well-flavoured chicken stock (page 42)	4¼ cups hot well-flavored chicken stock (page 42)
500 ml/18 fl oz light ale	2¼ cups beer
250 g/9 oz toasted fresh breadcrumbs	4½ cups toasted fresh bread crumbs
freshly grated nutmeg	freshly grated nutmeg
salt	salt
freshly ground black pepper	freshly ground black pepp
120 ml/4 fl oz double cream	½ cup heavy cream
6 slices hot toast (optional)	6 slices hot toast (optiona

Melt the butter in a pan, add the onion and fry gen for about 5 minutes. Stir in the stock and beer, then t breadcrumbs. Stir well to combine, then add nutme salt and pepper to taste. Bring to the boil, then lov the heat and simmer gently for 30 minutes, stirri occasionally.

Remove from the heat, then work through the fi blade of a *mouli-légumes* (vegetable mill) or purée in electric blender. Return to the rinsed-out pan, then s in the cream and heat through very gently for a fe minutes, stirring constantly. Taste and adjust t seasoning.

Pour the hot soup into a warmed soup tureen a serve immediately with slices of toast, if liked.
SERVES 6

Soupe à l'oignon
gratinée; Potage Saint-
Germain

SOUPE À L'OIGNON GRATINÉE

Onion Soup au Gratin

Metric/Imperial	American
100 g/4 oz butter	½ cup butter
450 g/1 lb onions, peeled and thinly sliced	1 lb onions, peeled and thinly sliced
1 litre/1¾ pints well-flavoured beef stock (page 42)	4¼ cups well-flavored beef stock (page 42)
salt	salt
freshly ground black pepper	freshly ground black pepper
12 slices French bread (baguette), toasted	12 slices French bread (baguette), toasted
150 g/5 oz Gruyère cheese★, grated	1¼ cups grated Gruyère cheese★

Melt the butter in a heavy pan. Add the onions and fry very gently for about 15 minutes or until golden, stirring frequently with a wooden spoon to prevent sticking.

Stir in the stock a little at a time, then bring to the boil. Add salt and pepper to taste, lower the heat, cover and cook gently for 30 minutes.

Taste and adjust the seasoning, then pour the soup into 4 individual heatproof soup bowls. Float 3 slices of bread in each bowl, then sprinkle over the grated cheese.

Put the bowls under a preheated hot grill (broiler) until the cheese melts and is bubbling. Serve immediately.

SERVES 4

POTAGE SAINT-GERMAIN

Split Pea Soup

Metric/Imperial	American
450 g/1 lb dried split peas	2 cups dried split peas
100 g/4 oz boned salt pork, blanched★ and cut into strips	¼ lb boneless salt pork, blanched★ and cut into strips
25 g/1 oz butter	2 tablespoons butter
1 carrot, peeled and diced	1 carrot, peeled and diced
1 onion, peeled and chopped	1 onion, peeled and chopped
2 litres/3½ pints water	4½ pints/9 cups water
1 bay leaf	1 bay leaf
1 celery stick	1 celery stalk
1 garlic clove, peeled and bruised★	1 garlic clove, peeled and bruised★
salt	salt
freshly ground black pepper	freshly ground black pepper
120 ml/4 fl oz double cream	½ cup heavy cream
croûtons, to serve (optional)	croûtons, to serve (optional)

Rinse the split peas thoroughly under cold running water, add to a pan of boiling water and boil for 5 minutes, then drain. Pat the strips of pork dry with kitchen paper towels.

Melt the butter in a large heavy pan, add the strips of pork and fry over brisk heat for 5 minutes until browned on all sides. Add the carrot and onion and continue frying for a further 2 minutes, stirring constantly.

Stir in the water and split peas, then bring to the boil. Tie the bay leaf and celery together, then add to the pan with the garlic. Add a little salt and pepper, lower the heat, cover and simmer very gently for 2 hours.

Discard the bay leaf, celery and garlic. Remove the strips of pork from the pan and reserve. Work the soup through the fine blade of a *mouli-légumes* (vegetable mill) or purée in an electric blender.

Return to the rinsed-out pan, then stir in the cream and the reserved strips of pork. Heat through very gently for a few minutes, stirring constantly. Taste and adjust seasoning.

Pour the hot soup into a warmed soup tureen and serve immediately with *croûtons* handed separately, if liked.

SERVES 6

CRÈME DE CÈPES

Cream of Mushroom Soup

If cèpes are difficult to obtain, use field mushrooms instead for this soup.

Metric/Imperial	American
25 g/1 oz butter	2 tablespoons butter
225 g/8 oz cèpe mushrooms★, trimmed and thinly sliced	½ lb cèpe mushrooms★, trimmed and thinly sliced
1 tablespoon plain flour	1 tablespoon all-purpose flour
1 litre/1¾ pints chicken stock (page 42)	4¼ cups chicken stock (page 42)
salt	salt
freshly ground black pepper	freshly ground black pepper
120 ml/4 fl oz double cream	½ cup heavy cream

Melt the butter in a heavy pan, add the mushrooms and fry gently for a few minutes until soft. Sprinkle the flour over the mushrooms and cook for 1 minute, stirring constantly with a wooden spoon.

Stir in the stock a little at a time, then bring to the boil. Lower the heat, add salt and pepper to taste, then cover and simmer gently for 30 minutes, stirring occasionally.

Work the soup through the fine blade of a *mouli-légumes* (vegetable mill) or purée in an electric blender. Return the soup to the rinsed-out pan. Stir in the cream, then reheat gently for a few minutes. Taste and adjust seasoning.

Pour the hot soup into a warmed soup tureen and serve immediately.

SERVES 4

SOUPE TOURANGELLE

Touraine Mixed Vegetable Soup

Metric/Imperial	American
1 small white cabbage, quartered, cored and shredded	1 small white cabbage, cored and shredded
50 g/2 oz butter	¼ cup butter
3 turnips, peeled and diced	3 turnips, peeled and diced
3 leeks (white part only), sliced into rings	3 leeks (white part only), sliced into rings
450 g/1 lb boned belly pork, diced	1 lb boneless belly pork, diced
2 litres/3½ pints chicken stock (page 42)	4½ pints/9 cups chicken stock (page 42)
salt	salt
freshly ground black pepper	freshly ground black pepper
450 g/1 lb fresh young peas, shelled	1 lb fresh young peas, podded

Blanch the cabbage in boiling water for 5 minutes, then drain.

Melt the butter in a large heavy pan, add the turnips, leeks and pork. Fry gently for 5 minutes, stirring frequently.

Add the cabbage and stock, and salt and pepper to taste. Bring to the boil, then lower the heat, cover and simmer gently for 1 hour. Add the peas and simmer for a further 30 minutes or until tender. Taste and adjust seasoning.

Pour the hot soup into a warmed soup tureen and serve immediately.

SERVES 6

Crème de cèpes; Soupe savoyarde; Soupe aux châtaignes de l'ardèche

SOUPE AUX CHÂTAIGNES DE L'ARDÈCHE

Ardèche Chestnut Soup

Metric/Imperial	American
225 g/8 oz chestnuts	½ lb chestnuts
2 tablespoons olive oil	2 tablespoons olive oil
2 large onions, peeled and thinly sliced	2 large onions, peeled and thinly sliced
1 litre/1¾ pints chicken stock (page 42)	4¼ cups chicken stock (page 42)
salt	salt
freshly ground black pepper	freshly ground black pepper
croûtons fried in olive oil (optional)	croûtons fried in olive oil (optional)

Plunge the chestnuts into a pan of boiling water and simmer for 15 minutes. Remove a few at a time with a slotted spoon, then split the outer shells with a sharp knife while the chestnuts are still hot. Remove both outer and inner skins.

Heat the oil in a heavy pan, add the onions and fry gently for 5 minutes until soft. Add the stock and chestnuts, and salt and pepper to taste, then bring to the boil. Lower the heat, cover and simmer for 45 minutes to 1 hour or until the chestnuts are soft.

Work the chestnuts and liquid through the fine blade of a *mouli-légumes* (vegetable mill) or purée in an electric blender. Return the soup to the rinsed-out pan and reheat gently. Taste and adjust seasoning.

Pour the hot soup into a warmed soup tureen and serve immediately, with *croûtons* if liked.

SERVES 4

SOUPE SAVOYARDE

Savoie Vegetable and Cheese Soup

Metric/Imperial	American
50 g/2 oz butter	¼ cup butter
2 turnips, peeled and cut into thick chunks	2 turnips, peeled and cut into thick chunks
2 leeks (white part only), sliced into thick rings	2 leeks (white part only), sliced into thick rings
1 head celeriac, peeled and cut into thick chunks	1 head celeriac, peeled and cut into thick chunks
4 potatoes, peeled and sliced into rounds	4 potatoes, peeled and sliced into rounds
1 litre/1¾ pints chicken stock (page 42)	4¼ cups chicken stock (page 42)
salt	salt
freshly ground black pepper	freshly ground black pepper
croûtons fried in butter	croûtons fried in butter
100 g/4 oz Gruyère cheese★, coarsely grated	1 cup coarsely grated Gruyère cheese★
500 ml/18 fl oz milk	2¼ cups milk

Melt the butter in a heavy pan, add the turnips, leeks and celeriac. Fry gently for 10 minutes, stirring frequently.

Add the potatoes and stock and bring to the boil. Lower the heat, add salt and pepper to taste, then simmer gently for 30 minutes or until the vegetables are tender.

Put the *croûtons* in the bottom of a warmed soup tureen and sprinkle over the grated cheese.

Stir the milk into the soup in the pan and bring to the boil. Taste and adjust seasoning, then pour into the tureen. Serve immediately.

SERVES 4

Chestnuts, fresh, dried and canned, are used extensively in French cookery, in both savoury and sweet dishes. Normandy and Brittany are the regions where chestnut trees abound, but the best French chestnuts are said to come from the *Ardèche* in the Lyonnais. The largest of these are used to make *marrons glacés* – candied chestnuts which are preserved and glazed in a thick sugar syrup.

TOURAIN TOULOUSAIN

Toulouse Egg and Cheese Soup

Metric/Imperial	American
50 g/2 oz goose fat★, dripping or butter	¼ cup goose fat★, drippings or butter
6 garlic cloves, peeled and crushed	6 garlic cloves, peeled and crushed
2 litres/3½ pints boiling chicken stock (page 42)	4½ pints/9 cups boiling chicken stock (page 42)
1 bouquet garni★	1 bouquet garni★
salt	salt
freshly ground black pepper	freshly ground black pepper
3 eggs, separated	3 eggs, separated
6 slices hot toast	6 slices hot toast
100 g/4 oz Gruyère cheese★, grated	1 cup grated Gruyère cheese★

Melt the fat in a heavy pan (preferably earthenware). Add the garlic and fry gently for 3 minutes. Add the boiling stock, bouquet garni, and salt and pepper to taste, and boil for 30 minutes.

Meanwhile, beat the egg whites lightly with a fork to break them up; do not let them become too frothy. In a separate bowl, beat the yolks together in the same way.

Whisk the egg whites into the soup with a balloon whisk. Stir a little of the hot soup into the yolks, whisking vigorously until thoroughly incorporated.

Simmer the soup for 3 minutes, then remove from the heat and discard the bouquet garni. Gradually add the egg yolk mixture, whisking vigorously all the time.

Put the slices of toast in the bottom of a warmed soup tureen, then sprinkle over the grated cheese. Pour over the hot soup and serve immediately.
SERVES 6

TOUR À LA TOMATE

Tomato and Onion Soup

Metric/Imperial	American
1 tablespoon goose fat★, dripping or butter	1 tablespoon goose fat★, drippings or butter
225 g/8 oz onions, peeled and thinly sliced	½ lb onions, peeled and thinly sliced
1 garlic clove, peeled and crushed	1 garlic clove, peeled and crushed
450 g/1 lb ripe tomatoes, quartered	1 lb ripe tomatoes, quartered
1 litre/1¾ pints chicken stock (page 42) or water	4¼ cups chicken stock (page 42) or water
1 teaspoon sugar	1 teaspoon sugar
salt	salt
freshly ground black pepper	freshly ground black pepper
2 tablespoons broken vermicelli	2 tablespoons broken vermicelli

Melt the fat in a heavy pan, add the onions and garlic and fry gently for 5 minutes until golden. Add the tomatoes, stock or water and sugar, with salt and pepper to taste. Bring to the boil, stirring, then lower the heat and simmer, uncovered, for 20 minutes.

Work the soup through the medium blade of a *mouli-légumes* (vegetable mill). Alternatively, purée in an electric blender, then work through a fine sieve (strainer).

Return the soup to the rinsed-out pan and bring to the boil again. Add the vermicelli and cook for 10 minutes until *al dente* (tender yet firm to the bite). Taste and adjust seasoning.

Pour the hot soup into a warmed soup tureen and serve immediately.
SERVES 4

The traditional *tourin* **from the Aquitaine region of south-western France is French onion soup with a difference. Onions and garlic are cooked in goose fat, then simmered gently in stock and thickened with eggs.**

Cheese is not usually included in a traditional *tourin*, **but the soup is always poured over slices of bread in individual soup bowls – known in France as 'tremper la soupe' or 'to soak the soup'.**

SOUPE FROIDE À LA TOMATE

Chilled Tomato Soup

Metric/Imperial	American
2 tablespoons olive oil	2 tablespoons olive oil
2 onions, peeled and chopped	2 onions, peeled and chopped
2 garlic cloves, peeled and crushed	2 garlic cloves, peeled and crushed
1 kg/2 lb ripe tomatoes, quartered	2 lb ripe tomatoes, quartered
1 bay leaf	1 bay leaf
1 thyme sprig	1 thyme sprig
1 teaspoon sugar	1 teaspoon sugar
salt	salt
freshly ground black pepper	freshly ground black pepper

Heat the oil in a heavy pan, add the onions and garlic and fry gently for 5 minutes until soft. Add the tomatoes, bay leaf, thyme, sugar, and salt and pepper to taste. Cook over moderate heat, uncovered, for 25 minutes.

Discard the bay leaf and thyme, then work the soup through the medium blade of a *mouli-légumes* (vegetable mill). Alternatively, purée in an electric blender, then work through a fine sieve (strainer).

Leave until cool, then chill in the refrigerator for at least 3 hours. Taste and adjust seasoning. Serve in a chilled soup tureen.

SERVES 4

Potage au cresson; Soupe froide à la tomate

POTAGE AU CRESSON

Cream of Watercress Soup

Metric/Imperial	American
50 g/2 oz butter	$\frac{1}{4}$ cup butter
2 leeks (white part only), roughly chopped	2 leeks (white part only), roughly chopped
1 bunch watercress, leaves and stalks separated	1 bunch watercress, leaves and stalks separated
2 litres/3½ pints chicken stock (page 42)	4½ pints/9 cups chicken stock (page 42)
225 g/8 oz potatoes, peeled and diced	1⅓ cups peeled and diced potatoes
salt	salt
freshly ground black pepper	freshly ground black pepper
120 ml/4 fl oz double cream	½ cup heavy cream
croûtons fried in butter (optional)	croûtons fried in butter (optional)

Melt half the butter in a heavy pan, add the leeks and watercress stalks and fry gently for 5 minutes.

Add the stock and potatoes, and salt and pepper to taste, then bring to the boil. Lower the heat and simmer for 45 minutes, stirring occasionally.

Work the soup through the fine blade of a *mouli-légumes* (vegetable mill) or purée in an electric blender. Return to the rinsed-out pan and reheat gently.

Chop the watercress leaves. Melt the remaining butter in a separate pan, add the watercress leaves and cook gently for a few minutes. Add to the soup with the cream and bring to the boil, stirring constantly. Taste and adjust seasoning.

Pour the hot soup into a warmed soup tureen. Serve immediately with *croûtons*, if liked.

SERVES 6

Soupe aux poissons de
Marseille; Potage Crécy

ILE DE FRANCE

POTAGE CRÉCY
Cream of Carrot Soup

Metric/Imperial	American
50 g/2 oz butter	1/4 cup butter
2 onions, peeled and thinly sliced	2 onions, peeled and thinly sliced
2 litres/3½ pints chicken stock (page 42)	4½ pints/9 cups chicken stock (page 42)
1 kg/2 lb small young carrots, peeled and sliced into thin rounds	2 lb small young carrots, peeled and sliced into thin rounds
salt	salt
freshly ground black pepper	freshly ground black pepper
3 tablespoons long-grain rice	3 tablespoons long-grain rice
120 ml/4 fl oz double cream	½ cup heavy cream

Melt half the butter in a heavy pan, add the onions and fry gently for 5 minutes until soft. Add the stock and carrots and bring to the boil. Lower the heat, add salt and pepper to taste, then simmer for 1½ hours.

Stir in the rice and simmer for a further 30 minutes or until the rice is tender. Work the soup through the medium blade of a *mouli-légumes* (vegetable mill) or purée in an electric blender.

Return the soup to the rinsed-out pan, add the cream and the remaining butter and reheat gently, stirring constantly. Taste and adjust seasoning.

Pour the hot soup into a warmed soup tureen and serve immediately.

SERVES 6

Note: 450 g/1 lb peeled and diced potatoes can be used instead of the rice.

CONSOMMÉ
Beef Consommé

Many cooks are hesitant about making their own consommé, but it is quite simple to make provided the basic stock is completely free of grease from the start. All pans and utensils should be scrupulously clean. Consommé can be served plain as in this recipe, or garnished with finely shredded beef or vegetables. Chicken and game consommé are made in exactly the same way as below, using chicken or game stock instead of beef.

Metric/Imperial	American
1.5 litres/2½ pints well-flavoured beef stock (page 42)	6¼ cups well-flavored beef stock (page 42)
450 g/1 lb shin of beef, finely shredded	1 lb shin of beef, finely shredded
1 onion, peeled and finely chopped	1 onion, peeled and finely chopped
1 carrot, peeled and finely chopped	1 carrot, peeled and finely chopped
2 egg whites, with crushed shells	2 egg whites, with crushed shells
4–6 tablespoons Madeira, port or dry sherry, to taste	4–6 tablespoons Madeira, port or dry sherry, to taste
salt	salt
freshly ground black pepper	freshly ground black pepper

Pour the cold stock into a clean enamel saucepan, then add the beef and vegetables. Whisk the egg whites to a light froth, then add to the pan with the crushed shells.

Bring the stock slowly to the boil, whisking constantly with a wire whisk. As the stock reaches boiling point, a thick white froth will form on the surface of the stock. Remove the pan from the heat immediately at this point to allow the froth to settle, then return to the lowest possible heat and simmer very gently for 40 minutes. Do not whisk or stir throughout this stage – the froth should remain completely undisturbed or the finished consommé will be cloudy.

Pour the stock carefully through a scalded cloth into a clean bowl, holding the froth back at first, then letting it slide onto the cloth at the end. Pour the stock again through the cloth to 'filter' it for the second time.

Reheat the consommé gently with Madeira, port or sherry to taste; do not allow to boil. Taste and adjust seasoning. Serve hot.
SERVES 4

Any French dish with the word *crécy* in its title will always have carrots as an ingredient or garnish. There are conflicting views on why this should be so. The town of Crécy in Seine-et-Maine does produce high quality carrots, but its best known association is with the Battle of Crécy, fought on the Somme in 1346.

SOUPE AUX POISSONS DE MARSEILLE
Marseille Fish Soup

*The rock fish normally used in this recipe are commonplace in the Mediterranean. If they are impossible to obtain at your local fish market use whatever fresh fish is available to you. John Dory, red mullet, whiting, brill, sea bass and conger eel are all perfectly acceptable substitutes.
Rouille, grated Parmesan and toasted baguette are traditionally served with this soup. Each slice of toast is spread with rouille, then sprinkled with Parmesan and placed in the soup before eating.*

Metric/Imperial	American
7 tablespoons oil	7 tablespoons oil
2 onions, peeled and thinly sliced	2 onions, peeled and thinly sliced
2 leeks (white part only), thinly sliced	2 leeks (white part only), thinly sliced
3 tomatoes, quartered and seeded	3 tomatoes, quartered and seeded
salt	salt
freshly ground black pepper	freshly ground black pepper
6 garlic cloves, peeled and crushed	6 garlic cloves, peeled and crushed
pinch of powdered saffron	pinch of powdered saffron
3 parsley sprigs	3 parsley sprigs
1 fennel sprig	1 fennel sprig
1 thyme sprig	1 thyme sprig
1 bay leaf	1 bay leaf
1 strip fresh or dried orange peel (optional)	1 strip fresh or dried orange peel (optional)
1.5 kg/3 lb mixed fresh fish (see above), scaled, gutted and cleaned	3 lb mixed fresh fish (see above), scaled, gutted and cleaned
2 litres/3½ pints boiling water	4½ pints/9 cups boiling water
TO SERVE (optional):	TO SERVE (optional):
rouille (page 47)	rouille (page 47)
12 slices baguette, or other French bread, toasted	12 slices baguette or other French bread, toasted
50 g/2 oz Parmesan cheese, freshly grated	½ cup freshly grated Parmesan cheese

Heat the oil in a large flameproof casserole, add the onions and leeks and fry gently until soft. Add the tomatoes and fry for a further 6 to 8 minutes, stirring and pressing constantly with a wooden spoon to reduce them to a purée. Add salt and pepper to taste.

Stir in the garlic, saffron, herbs and orange peel, if using, then add the prepared whole fish. Stir well, then cover and cook over moderate heat for 10 minutes or until the fish begin to disintegrate. Pour in the boiling water and stir well. Boil rapidly for 15 minutes until the liquid has reduced by one quarter.

Pass the soup through a fine sieve (strainer), pressing firmly to work through as much of the flesh from the fish as possible, leaving behind only the bones.

Return the puréed soup to the rinsed-out casserole and reheat. Taste and adjust seasoning. Serve hot, with the *rouille*, toast and cheese handed separately, if liked.
SERVES 6

HORS D'OEUVRE & SALADS

The French term hors d'oeuvre often causes confusion amongst those who are not acquainted with the French style of eating. Literally translated, hors d'oeuvre means 'outside the work' and the term originated in the 18th century when it was the custom to eat certain dishes away from the dining table, before sitting down to the actual meal. The idea was to provide your guests with an appetizer or foretaste of what was to come, both to stave off hunger pains and to stimulate the gastric juices. Nowadays, of course, the hors d'oeuvre is always eaten at the table, usually as a first course or alternative to soup. Sometimes soup is served after the hors d'oeuvre, but in most French homes the hors d'oeuvre is eaten as a first course.

When serving hors d'oeuvre it is important to observe a few basic rules. The food should look attractive and colourful, to please the eye and stimulate the appetite, but at the same time it should not be too substantial. For this reason, portions should be kept small and are often better served on individual plates rather than on one large platter. Whether you decide to offer a selection of different hors d'oeuvre (hors d'oeuvre variés) or simply one, is a matter of personal choice. For an everyday meal in France, for example, a simple salad or a dish of vegetables tossed in a well-flavoured vinaigrette dressing is considered more than adequate as an hors d'oeuvre.

French cooks are spoilt in their choice of hors d'oeuvre by the excellence of their charcuteries. Many of the delicious salads and pâtés which you are served as hors d'oeuvre in France will have come from the local charcuterie. If you have a good local delicatessen nearby, look for Bayonne ham, cured or smoked sausages, rillettes or pâtés. Ready-made salads are expensive to buy and will always taste fresher if made at home.

If you are making up a mixed hors d'oeuvre, choose dishes which provide contrast in texture and colour, and remember to include both sweet and savoury flavours. One or two salads, together with a selection of cold cooked meats and/or pâté, hard-boiled eggs coated in a thick homemade mayonnaise, some pickled or smoked fish, and side dishes of olives or gherkins make a typical hors d'oeuvre variés.

Some of the recipes in this chapter, such as the quiches and savoury tarts, the egg and cheese dishes and the crêpes, may seem too substantial to serve as an hors d'oeuvre. These dishes were originally served as entrées, ie after the soup and the fish, but before the meat course. Although such entrées are still served on special occasions, for informal meals they are served as a first course. You will also find that many of these dishes make quite substantial lunch or supper dishes on their own or served with a salad, and many French families treat them as such.

PICARDIE

FLAMICHE AUX POIREAUX

Leek Pie

If preferred, this pie can be made with pâte feuilletée (page 53), in which case it should be baked at 220°C/425°F/Gas Mark 7.

Metric/Imperial	American
PÂTE BRISÉE:	PÂTE BRISÉE:
250 g/9 oz plain flour	2¼ cups all-purpose flour
pinch of salt	pinch of salt
125 g/4½ oz butter	½ cup + 1 tablespoon butter
1 egg yolk	1 egg yolk
2–3 tablespoons iced water	2–3 tablespoons iced water
FILLING:	FILLING:
50 g/2 oz butter	¼ cup butter
450 g/1 lb leeks (white part only), thinly sliced	1 lb leeks (white part only), thinly sliced
pinch of freshly grated nutmeg	pinch of freshly grated nutmeg
salt	salt
freshly ground white pepper	freshly ground white pepper
3 egg yolks	3 egg yolks
120 ml/4 fl oz double cream	½ cup heavy cream
GLAZE:	GLAZE:
1 egg yolk	1 egg yolk
1 tablespoon water	1 tablespoon water

PISSALADIÈRE

Provençal Onion and Anchovy Pie

There are many versions of pissaladière, many of them with a pastry base. This version, with its base of bread dough, is not unlike the pizzas of neighbouring Italy. The name pissaladière does not come from the Italian word pizza, however, but from the French pissalat, a purée of tiny fish preserved in brine and spices which was originally used as a topping for pissaladière. If you do not have a pan or mould large enough to hold the pissaladière, it can be baked on its own on a dampened baking sheet – simply make the edges a little thicker and higher than the middle to prevent the topping spilling over during baking.

Metric/Imperial	American
DOUGH:	DOUGH:
25 g/1 oz fresh yeast	1 cake compressed yeast
4 tablespoons lukewarm water	$\frac{1}{4}$ cup lukewarm water
350 g/12 oz plain flour	3 cups all-purpose flour
pinch of salt	pinch of salt
50 g/2 oz butter, cut into small pieces	$\frac{1}{4}$ cup butter, cut into small pieces
2 eggs, beaten	2 eggs, beaten
TOPPING:	TOPPING:
6 tablespoons olive oil	6 tablespoons olive oil
1 kg/2 lb onions, peeled and thinly sliced	2 lb onions, peeled and thinly sliced
12 canned anchovies, drained and desalted★	12 canned anchovies, drained and desalted★
50 g/2 oz black olives, halved and stoned	$\frac{1}{2}$ cup halved and pitted ripe olives
freshly ground black pepper	freshly ground black pepper

Flamiche aux poireaux

Make the *pâte brisée* according to the method on page 2. Leave in a cool place for 1 hour.

Meanwhile, prepare the filling: melt the butter in a heavy pan, add the leeks and cook very gently for 10 minutes, stirring occasionally.

Remove from the heat, add the nutmeg and salt and pepper to taste, then leave to cool. Put the egg yolks and cream in a bowl and whisk together with salt and pepper to taste. Stir into the cooled leeks.

Cut off two thirds of the pastry (dough) and roll out on a floured surface. Use to line a buttered 20 to 23 cm/8 to 9 inch flan tin (pie pan) or flan ring placed on a buttered baking sheet.

Spread the filling in the pastry shell, then roll out the remaining pastry to make a lid and place over the filling. Moisten the edges of the pastry and pinch together to seal. If liked, decorate the top of the pie with shapes cut from the pastry trimmings, or mark the pastry with the prongs of a fork.

Beat the egg yolk and water together, then brush over the pastry lid to glaze. Bake in a preheated moderately hot oven (200°C/400°F/Gas Mark 6) for 35 to 40 minutes. Serve warm.
SERVES 6

Make the dough: dissolve the yeast in the water and set aside. Sift the flour and salt into a bowl, rub in the butter, then make a well in the centre. Add the eggs and yeast liquid, then mix together, gradually drawing in the flour from the sides of the bowl. Turn out onto a floured surface and knead well until the dough is smooth, then form into a ball and cover with a damp cloth. Leave to rise in a warm place for about 2 hours or until doubled in bulk.

Meanwhile make the topping: heat 4 tablespoons/$\frac{1}{4}$ cup oil in a heavy pan, then add the onions. Cover and simmer very gently for about 30 minutes until the onions are soft and lightly coloured but not browned. Stir from time to time.

Knock down the dough, then knead again for a few minutes. Roll out to a circle to fit an oiled deep 25 cm/10 inch round baking pan or mould, then press into the pan to line the base and sides.

Spread the onions over the dough, then decorate with the anchovies and olives, making a lattice pattern if liked. Sprinkle liberally with pepper, then with the remaining oil. Leave to rise in a warm place for about 15 minutes.

Bake in a preheated hot oven (230°C/450°F/Gas Mark 8) for 30 minutes. Serve warm.
SERVES 6 TO 8

QUICHE TOURANGELLE

Touraine Quiche with Pork Rillettes

In France, rillettes can be bought at every charcuterie, although some cooks make their own (see page 66), from pork, duck, goose or rabbit. If you do not want to go to the trouble of making rillettes especially for this quiche, they can be bought in jars and cans from good delicatessens and supermarkets.

Metric/Imperial	American
PÂTE BRISÉE:	PÂTE BRISÉE:
250 g/9 oz plain flour	2¼ cups all-purpose flour
pinch of salt	pinch of salt
125 g/4½ oz butter	½ cup + 1 tablespoon butter
1 egg yolk	1 egg yolk
2–3 tablespoons iced water	2–3 tablespoons iced water
FILLING:	FILLING:
225 g/8 oz pork rillettes	½ lb pork rillettes
1 bunch fresh parsley, finely chopped	1 bunch fresh parsley, finely chopped
4 eggs	4 eggs
200 ml/⅓ pint milk	1 cup milk
120 ml/4 fl oz double cream	½ cup heavy cream
salt	salt
freshly ground black pepper	freshly ground black pepper

Make the *pâte brisée* according to the method on page 52. Leave in a cool place for 1 hour.

Roll out the pastry (dough) on a floured surface and use to line a buttered 20 to 23 cm/8 to 9 inch flan tin (pie pan) or flan ring placed on a buttered baking sheet.

Spread the pork over the pastry, then sprinkle with the parsley. Put the eggs, milk and cream in a bowl and whisk together with salt and pepper to taste. Pour into the pastry shell.

Bake in a preheated moderately hot oven (200°C/400°F/Gas Mark 6) for 35 minutes or until just set. Serve warm.

SERVES 4 TO 6

RIGHT: **Tarte à l'oignon; Quiche Lorraine**
BELOW: **Quiche tourangelle**

TARTE À L'OIGNON

Creamy Onion Quiche

Metric/Imperial	American
PÂTE BRISÉE:	PÂTE BRISÉE:
250 g/9 oz plain flour	2¼ cups all-purpose flour
pinch of salt	pinch of salt
125 g/4½ oz butter	½ cup + 1 tablespoon butter
1 egg yolk	1 egg yolk
2–3 tablespoons iced water	2–3 tablespoons iced water
FILLING:	FILLING:
50 g/2 oz butter	¼ cup butter
1 kg/2 lb onions, peeled and thinly sliced	2 lb onions, peeled and thinly sliced
salt	salt
freshly ground white pepper	freshly ground white pepper
200 ml/⅓ pint milk	1 cup milk
200 ml/⅓ pint double cream	1 cup heavy cream
2 eggs	2 eggs
2 egg yolks	2 egg yolks
freshly grated nutmeg (optional)	freshly grated nutmeg (optional)

Make the *pâte brisée* according to the method on page 52. Leave in a cool place for 1 hour.

Meanwhile, prepare the filling: melt the butter in a heavy pan, add the onions and cook gently for 20 minutes, stirring occasionally. Take care not to let the onions become brown; they should be soft and light golden. Add salt and pepper to taste.

Put the milk, cream, eggs and egg yolks in a bowl and whisk together with salt and pepper to taste, and nutmeg if using.

Roll out the pastry (dough) on a floured surface and use to line a buttered 20 to 23 cm/8 to 9 inch flan tin (pie pan) or flan ring placed on a buttered baking sheet. Spread the onions over the pastry base, then pour in the milk, cream and egg mixture.

Bake in a preheated moderately hot oven (200°C/400°F/Gas Mark 6) for 35 to 40 minutes or until just set. Serve warm.

SERVES 4 TO 6

TOURTE AUX ANCHOIS

Anchovy and Cheese Pie

Metric/Imperial	American
PASTRY:	PIE DOUGH:
300 g/11 oz plain flour	2¾ cups all-purpose flour
pinch of salt	pinch of salt
pinch of dried yeast	pinch of active dry yeast
7 tablespoons olive oil	7 tablespoons olive oil
about 50 ml/2 fl oz water	about ¼ cup water
FILLING:	FILLING:
225 g/8 oz Gruyère cheese★, thinly sliced	½ lb Gruyère cheese★, thinly sliced
10 canned anchovy fillets, drained and desalted★	10 canned anchovy fillets, drained and desalted★
GLAZE:	GLAZE:
1 egg yolk	1 egg yolk
1 tablespoon water or milk	1 tablespoon water or milk

QUICHE LORRAINE

Cheese is never included in the traditional quiche lorraine from the Alsace-Lorraine region of north-east France.

Metric/Imperial	American
PÂTE BRISÉE:	PÂTE BRISÉE:
250 g/9 oz plain flour	2¼ cups all-purpose flour
pinch of salt	pinch of salt
125 g/4½ oz butter	½ cup + 1 tablespoon butter
1 egg yolk	1 egg yolk
2–3 tablespoons iced water	2–3 tablespoons iced water
FILLING:	FILLING:
150 g/5 oz smoked bacon, rinds removed and cut into small pieces	5 oz smoked bacon, cut into small pieces
50 g/2 oz butter	¼ cup butter
250 ml/8 fl oz double cream	1 cup heavy cream
2 eggs	2 eggs
¼ teaspoon freshly grated nutmeg	¼ teaspoon freshly grated nutmeg
salt	salt
freshly ground white pepper	freshly ground white pepper

Make the *pâte brisée* according to the method on page 52. Leave in a cool place for 1 hour.

Meanwhile, prepare the filling: plunge the bacon pieces into a pan of boiling water for 2 minutes, then drain. Melt half the butter in a heavy pan, add the bacon pieces and cook gently until lightly coloured. Remove from the pan with a slotted spoon.

Put the cream and eggs in a bowl and whisk together with the nutmeg and salt and pepper to taste.

Roll out the pastry (dough) on a floured surface and use to line a buttered 20 to 23 cm/8 to 9 inch flan tin (pie pan) or flan ring placed on a buttered baking sheet. Sprinkle the bacon pieces over the pastry base, then dot with the remaining butter. Pour in the cream and egg mixture.

Bake in a preheated moderately hot oven (200°C/400°F/Gas Mark 6) for about 30 minutes or until just set. If the filling rises rapidly during baking, simply prick it in the centre with the point of a sharp knife. Serve warm.
SERVES 4 TO 6

ake the pastry (pie dough): sift the flour and salt into bowl and make a well in the centre. Add the yeast and l, then mix into the flour. Mix in just enough water make a soft dough. Knead lightly until smooth. ave in a cool place for 30 minutes.

Roll out half the dough on a floured surface, then se to line an oiled 20 to 23 cm/8 to 9 inch flan tin (pie n) or flan ring placed on an oiled baking sheet. Place lf the cheese in the pastry shell, cover with the nchovies, then top with the remaining cheese.

Roll out the remaining pastry and use to cover the lling. Moisten the edges of the pastry and pinch gether to seal. Mix the egg yolk and water or milk gether, then brush over the pastry to glaze. Bake in a eheated hot oven (220°C/425°F/Gas Mark 7) for minutes until the pastry is golden. Serve warm.
ERVES 6

The French words *tarte*, *tourte* and *quiche* all mean an open, single-crust pie. Originally these were made with a base of bread dough, but nowadays they are usually made with shortcrust pastry (pie dough).

GÂTEAU DE FOIES BLONDS DE VOLAILLE

Chicken Liver Terrine

Metric/Imperial	American
450 g/1 lb chicken livers	1 lb chicken livers
50 g/2 oz plain flour, sifted	½ cup all-purpose flour, sifted
3 whole eggs	3 whole eggs
3 egg yolks	3 egg yolks
120 ml/4 fl oz double cream	·3 egg yolks
450 ml/¾ pint milk	½ cup heavy cream
1 garlic clove, peeled and crushed	2 cups milk
1–2 tablespoons chopped parsley	1 garlic clove, peeled and crushed
freshly grated nutmeg	1–2 tablespoons chopped parsley
salt	freshly grated nutmeg
freshly ground black pepper	salt
	freshly ground black pepper

Work the chicken livers in an electric blender or twice through the fine blade of a *Mouli-légumes* (vegetable mill). Stir in the flour, then the eggs and egg yolks one at a time.

Whip the cream until it just holds its shape, then add to the liver mixture with the milk, garlic and parsley. Add nutmeg, salt and pepper to taste, then mix well until thoroughly combined.

Pour the mixture into a well-buttered 1.2 litre/2 pt/ 5 cup mould and place in a hot *bain marie*. Bake in a preheated moderate oven (180°C/350°F/Gas Mark 4) for 1¼ hours or until a skewer inserted into the centre comes out clean.

Leave to cool, then place a weight on top of the pâté and chill in the refrigerator overnight.

Unmould onto a serving platter and serve with hot toast.

SERVES 8 TO 10

RILLETTES DE PORC D'ANJOU

Anjou Pork Rillettes

Pork rillettes are best described as 'potted pork'. They are usually made in large quantities such as this because they keep fresh for 2 months in a refrigerator. Use equal quantities of lean and fatty pork – fillet (tenderloin), loin, belly, neck, etc.

Metric/Imperial	American
450 g/1 lb pork back fat, cut into small pieces	1 lb pork back fat, cut into small pieces
2 kg/4 lb boned pork (see above)	4 lb boneless pork (see above)
7 tablespoons water	7 tablespoons water
1 bouquet garni★	1 bouquet garni★
salt	salt
freshly ground black pepper	freshly ground black pepper
ground mixed spice	ground allspice
	ground cinnamon

Put the back fat in a heavy pan and heat very gently for about 30 minutes until melted.

Meanwhile, cut the pork into small cubes, mixing the lean and fat together. Add the pork to the pan with the water, bouquet garni and salt, pepper and spice(s) to taste.

Cover the pan and cook very gently for 4 hours, stirring occasionally. At the end of the cooking time the pork should have rendered down and become extremely soft. Any large pieces of meat can be removed at this stage with a slotted spoon and eaten separately, either hot or cold.

Pour the remaining meat and fat into small earthenware pots and leave to cool. The fat will rise to the surface of the pots and solidify, thus sealing the *rillettes*.

Cover the pots with lids, then store in the refrigerator for up to 2 months.

MAKES ABOUT 2.5 kg/5 lb

VARIATIONS
1. Add 2 to 3 cloves to the pan before cooking the pork, for added flavour.
2. For *rillettes du Mans*: use 450 g/1 lb pork back fat, 1 kg/2 lb pork and 2 kg/4 lb boned goose and make as above.

TERRINE DE LAPIN AUX PRUNEAUX

Rabbit Terrine with Prunes

Metric/Imperial	American
MARINADE:	MARINADE:
1 litre/1¾ pints dry red wine (e.g. Vouvray)	4¼ cups dry red wine (e.g. Vouvray)
2–3 tablespoons brandy	2–3 tablespoons brandy
2 tablespoons oil	2 tablespoons oil
1 carrot, peeled and finely chopped	1 carrot, peeled and finely chopped
1 onion, peeled and finely chopped	1 onion, peeled and finely chopped
1 garlic clove, peeled and finely chopped	1 garlic clove, peeled and finely chopped
6 whole cloves	6 whole cloves
1 thyme sprig	1 thyme sprig
1 tarragon sprig	1 tarragon sprig
1 bay leaf	1 bay leaf
salt	salt
freshly ground black pepper	freshly ground black pepper
TERRINE:	TERRINE:
2 small rabbits (about 1.5 kg/3–3½ lb)	2 small rabbits (about 3–3½ lb)
20 prunes	20 prunes
50 g/2 oz streaky or fatty bacon, rind removed and diced	¼ cup diced fatty bacon
225 g/8 oz sausagemeat	1 cup sausagemeat
1 egg, beaten	1 egg, beaten
ground mixed spice	ground allspice
2–3 tablespoons brandy	ground cinnamon
TO FINISH:	2–3 tablespoons brandy
6 streaky bacon rashers	TO FINISH:
a few bay leaves (optional)	6 fatty bacon slices
a few thyme leaves (optional)	a few bay leaves (optional)
2 tablespoons plain flour	a few thyme leaves (optional)
	2 tablespoons all-purpose flour

Rillettes de porc d'Anjou; Terrine de lapin aux pruneaux

Mix together the ingredients for the marinade, reserving 2 glasses wine. Cut the rabbits into small pieces, but keep the backbones intact so that the fillets can be removed whole after marinating.

Put the rabbit pieces (including the livers) in a bowl, then pour over the marinade. Cover and leave to marinate for 24 hours, turning the meat from time to time.

Put the prunes in a separate bowl and cover with the reserved 2 glasses wine. Cover and leave for 24 hours until plump.

The next day, drain the rabbit. Strain the marinade and reserve 1 glass. Remove the whole fillets from the backbones and set aside. Using a sharp pointed knife, scrape all meat from the other bones, then mince (grind) this meat with the livers.

Put the minced (ground) meat and livers in a bowl with the diced bacon, sausagemeat, beaten egg, spice(s), salt and pepper to taste and the brandy. Knead thoroughly with the hands until well mixed. Drain the prunes and remove the stones (pits).

Line a greased 2 litre/3½ pint/9 cup terrine with the bacon rashers (slices), reserving 2 rashers for the top. Press a layer of the minced meat mixture in the bottom of the terrine, arrange a few whole fillets on top, then a few prunes. Repeat these layers until all the ingredients are used up, finishing with a layer of the minced meat mixture.

Prick the top of the terrine with a skewer or fork, then slowly pour over the reserved marinade. Cover the top of the terrine with the reserved bacon rashers, pressing bay and thyme leaves in between them if liked.

Cover the terrine with a lid, then seal around the edge of the lid with a paste made from the flour and a few drops of water. Bake in a hot *bain marie* in a preheated moderate oven (180°C/350°F/Gas Mark 4) for 2 hours.

Break the pastry seal, remove the lid and leave the terrine to cool for a few minutes. Cover with a board or plate, then place heavy weights on top. Leave until completely cold, then chill in the refrigerator for 24 hours before serving.
SERVES 8 TO 10

***Saucisson en brioche* takes a certain amount of skill and practise to make, because the brioche dough can be difficult for those unused to working with it.**

One method which makes the sausage and dough easier to handle is to cut the sausage in half and place the two halves side by side in the pastry, making the finished roll wider but shorter. This also makes the brioche a more manageable size for most ovens, and the finished roll looks more attractive when sliced.

PAYS DE LA LOIRE

TERRINE DE CANETON

Duckling Terrine

Metric/Imperial

1 duckling (about 1 kg/2–2$\frac{1}{2}$ lb)
225 g/8 oz pork back fat
100 g/4 oz streaky or fatty bacon, rinds removed
few thyme leaves, chopped or crumbled
ground mixed spice
salt
freshly ground black pepper
about 200 ml/$\frac{1}{3}$ pint Vouvray or other white wine
TO FINISH:
175 g/6 oz pork back fat, thinly sliced
a few bay leaves (optional)
a few thyme leaves (optional)
2 tablespoons plain flour

American

1 duckling (about 2–2$\frac{1}{2}$ lb)
$\frac{1}{2}$ lb pork back fat
$\frac{1}{4}$ lb fatty bacon
few thyme leaves, chopped or crumbled
ground allspice
ground cinnamon
salt
freshly ground black pepper
about 1 cup Vouvray or other white wine
TO FINISH:
6 oz pork back fat, thinly sliced
a few bay leaves (optional)
a few thyme leaves (optional)
2 tablespoons all-purpose flour

Bone the duckling. Cut off as many whole strips of meat as possible and reserve.

Scrape the remaining meat away from the bones with a sharp pointed knife, then mince (grind) together with the pork back fat, bacon and the liver from the duckling. Add the thyme and spice(s), salt and pepper to taste, then mix together with the wine until thoroughly combined.

Line a greased 1.2 litre/2 pint/5 cup terrine with the sliced pork back fat, reserving 2 slices for the tops. Press half the minced (ground) mixture in the bottom of the terrine, then arrange the strips of duckling on top. Cover with the remaining minced mixture, pressing down firmly.

Cover the top of the terrine with the reserved pork back fat, pressing bay and thyme leaves in between them if liked. Cover the terrine with a lid, then seal around the edge of the lid with a paste made from the flour and a few drops of water.

Bake in a preheated moderate oven (160°C/325°F/Gas Mark 3) for 2 hours. Break the pastry seal, remove the lid and leave the terrine until completely cold. Chill in the refrigerator for 24 hours before serving.

SERVES 8

VARIATIONS

1. Mince or finely chop 225 g/8 oz/2$\frac{1}{2}$ cups mushrooms, cook in olive oil and garlic, then add to the minced meat mixture with freshly chopped parsley to taste.
2. Substitute 3 tablespoons wine with brandy.

LYONNAIS

SAUCISSON EN BRIOCHE

Hot Sausage in Pastry

In simple terms this recipe is best likened to a large sausage roll, although the different types of spicy French cooking sausage make it far more unusual – and far more tasty.

Metric/Imperial

BRIOCHE DOUGH:
15 g/$\frac{1}{2}$ oz fresh yeast
3 tablespoons lukewarm water
275 g/10 oz plain flour, sifted
2 eggs, beaten
pinch of salt
50 g/2 oz butter, softened
FILLING:
1 × 750 g/1$\frac{1}{2}$ lb Lyon or other French cooking sausage★
GLAZE:
1 egg yolk
2 teaspoons milk

American

BRIOCHE DOUGH:
$\frac{1}{2}$ cake compressed yeast
3 tablespoons lukewarm water
2$\frac{1}{2}$ cups all-purpose flour, sifted
2 eggs, beaten
pinch of salt
$\frac{1}{4}$ cup softened butter
FILLING:
1 × 1$\frac{1}{2}$ lb Lyon or other French cooking sausage★
GLAZE:
1 egg yolk
2 teaspoons milk

To make the brioche dough: mix the yeast to a paste with the lukewarm water, then gradually work in 25 g/1 oz/$\frac{1}{4}$ cup flour. Cover with a damp cloth and leave to rise in a warm place for 1 hour.

Put the remaining flour in a separate bowl and make a well in the centre. Put the yeast mixture in the well with the eggs, salt and softened butter.

Mix the wet ingredients together with a wooden spoon, then gradually draw in the flour from the sides of the bowl until thoroughly incorporated. Cover and leave to rise in a warm place for 1 hour or until doubled in bulk.

Meanwhile, prick the sausage skin with a fork to prevent it bursting during cooking. Plunge the sausage into a pan of boiling water, then lower the heat and poach gently for 20 minutes. Drain and leave until cool enough to handle.

Turn the dough out onto a well floured surface and knead lightly with floured hands (it will be quite sticky at this stage). Put the dough on a buttered baking sheet then press out lightly with the hands to a 1 to 2 cm/$\frac{1}{2}$ to $\frac{3}{4}$ inch thick rectangle, slightly longer than the sausage and about 15 cm/6 inches wide.

Remove the skin from the sausage while still warm then place the sausage in the centre of the dough. Brush the edges of the dough lightly with water, then fold the dough over the sausage to enclose it, pressing the edges firmly together to seal.

Turn the roll over on the baking sheet so that the join in the dough is underneath; this will prevent the dough coming open during baking. Leave to rise in a warm place for 30 to 45 minutes.

Mix the egg yolk and milk together, then brush all over the dough to glaze. Bake in a preheated hot oven (220°C/425°F/Gas Mark 7) for 30 minutes until golden brown.

Remove from the oven and cut into 1 cm/$\frac{1}{2}$ inch thick slices, Serve immediately.

SERVES 6 TO 8

Saucisson en brioche; Terrine de caneton

OEUFS EN MEURETTE

Poached Eggs with Red Wine and Bacon

If liked, sautéed or grilled (broiled) mushrooms can be added to the sauce before pouring over the eggs and bacon.

Metric/Imperial	American
125 g/4½ oz butter	9 tablespoons butter
150 g/5 oz streaky bacon, rinds removed and diced	7–8 slices fatty bacon, diced
1 onion, peeled and finely chopped	1 onion, peeled and finely chopped
1 shallot, peeled and finely chopped	1 scallion, peeled and finely chopped
1 garlic clove, peeled and crushed	1 garlic clove, peeled and crushed
500 ml/18 fl oz Bourgogne or other red wine	2¼ cups Bourgogne or other red wine
1 small bouquet garni★	1 small bouquet garni★
1 whole clove	1 whole clove
pinch of sugar	pinch of sugar
salt	salt
freshly ground black pepper	freshly ground black pepper
4 slices bread, crusts removed	4 slices bread, crusts removed
4 eggs	4 eggs
1 tablespoon plain flour	1 tablespoon all-purpose flour

Melt 50 g/2 oz/4 tablespoons butter in a heavy pan. Add the bacon and fry until lightly coloured, then add the onion, shallot (scallion) and garlic and fry gently until soft.

Stir in the wine, then add the bouquet garni, clove, sugar, and salt and pepper to taste. Simmer gently for 10 minutes.

Meanwhile, trim the bread to fit in the bottom of 4 individual *cocottes* or *ramekins*. Melt 40 g/1½ oz/3 tablespoons butter in a small frying pan (skillet), add the bread and fry gently until golden on both sides. Place in the bottom of the *cocottes* and keep hot.

Strain the liquid from the bacon pan into a large casserole, reserving the pieces of bacon. Bring the liquid to a gentle simmer, then break in the eggs one at a time. Poach gently for 3 minutes.

Remove the eggs from the liquid with a slotted spoon, drain thoroughly, then place one on top of each piece of bread. Sprinkle the reserved bacon over the eggs. Keep hot.

Boil the liquid in the casserole for about 10 minutes until reduced to about 300 ml/½ pint/1¼ cups. Meanwhile, work 1 tablespoon butter and the flour together to make a *beurre manié*. Whisk into the liquid and cook, stirring, until thickened. Whisk in the remaining butter, then taste and adjust seasoning.

Pour the hot sauce over the eggs and bacon and serve immediately.

SERVES 4

Oeufs frits aux aubergines; Omelette brayaude

OEUFS FRITS AUX AUBERGINES

Eggs with Aubergines (Eggplant) and Ham

Bayonne ham can dry out very quickly, so keep well wrapped and do not cut into strips until the last possible moment.

Metric/Imperial	American
large or 2 small aubergines, peeled and sliced into thin rounds	1 large or 2 small eggplant, peeled and sliced into thin rounds
salt	salt
tablespoons oil	6 tablespoons oil
ripe tomatoes, quartered	4 ripe tomatoes, quartered
garlic cloves, peeled and crushed	2 garlic cloves, peeled and crushed
bouquet garni★	1 bouquet garni★
freshly ground black pepper	freshly ground black pepper
eggs	6 eggs
thick slices raw Bayonne ham★, cut into thick strips	2 thick slices raw Bayonne ham★, cut into thick strips
chopped parsley, to garnish	chopped parsley, for garnish

Place the aubergine (eggplant) slices in a single layer on a plate and sprinkle with salt. Leave to *dégorge* for about 20 minutes.

Meanwhile, heat 2 tablespoons oil in a heavy pan, add the tomatoes, garlic and bouquet garni, and salt and pepper to taste. Cover the pan and cook gently for 10 minutes, crushing the tomatoes from time to time by pressing them firmly with a wooden spoon. Work through a fine sieve (strainer), return to the rinsed-out pan and keep hot.

Rinse the aubergines, then dry thoroughly with kitchen paper towels. Heat 2 tablespoons oil in a frying pan (skillet), add the aubergines and fry until golden brown on both sides. Remove from the pan with a slotted spoon and keep hot.

Heat the remaining oil in the frying pan (skillet), break in the eggs one at a time and fry until cooked to your liking. Add the strips of ham and heat through.

Arrange the aubergine slices on a warmed serving platter, then top with the fried eggs interspersed with the strips of ham. Cover with the tomato sauce and garnish with parsley. Serve immediately.
SERVES 6

OMELETTE BRAYAUDE

Potato and Ham Omelette

Metric/Imperial	American
25 g/1 oz pork dripping or lard	2 tablespoons pork drippings or lard
225 g/8 oz potatoes, peeled and diced	1⅓ cups peeled and diced potatoes
225 g/8 oz raw Auvergne ham★, diced	1 cup diced raw Auvergne ham★
9 eggs	9 eggs
25 g/1 oz butter, cut into thin slivers	2 tablespoons butter, cut into thin slivers
freshly ground black pepper	freshly ground black pepper
3 tablespoons double cream	3 tablespoons thick cream
100 g/4 oz Cantal cheese★, grated	1 cup grated Cantal cheese★

Melt the dripping(s) or lard in a large omelette pan, add the potatoes and fry over brisk heat for 5 minutes, shaking the pan constantly. Lower the heat, cover the pan and cook gently for 10 to 15 minutes until the potatoes are almost tender, shaking the pan occasionally. Add the ham and mix very gently, taking great care not to break the potatoes.

Whisk the eggs together lightly, add the slivers of butter with pepper to taste, then pour over the potatoes and ham. Increase the heat, cook the omelette until the underside is golden, then turn the omelette over and cook the other side.

Slide the omelette out of the pan onto a warmed serving platter without folding it over, then sprinkle with the cream and cheese. Serve immediately.
SERVES 6

Most cooks have their own individual way of making a classic French omelette. A good-quality, heavy-based pan is a must and it is best to reserve this pan just for omelette making.

To make an omelette: heat the pan over moderate heat and, at the same time, lightly mix the eggs together with a fork. Do not beat or whisk them as this will spoil the texture. The maximum practical number of eggs to cook at one time is six.

Drop a knob of butter into the heated pan and, when foaming, pour in all the eggs. Stir briskly with a fork, in a figure of eight pattern, adding chopped herbs and seasonings to taste. Lift up the edge of the mixture so that the uncooked egg runs onto the base of the pan. Cook until most of the egg is set but the centre is still runny (or *baveuse* as the French say), then slide the omelette out of the pan onto the plate, folding it as you do so.

Any filling ingredients, such as grated cheese, mushrooms or diced ham, should be sprinkled over the omelette in the pan just before folding.

Hors d'oeuvre & Salads/71

MATAFAM

Savoury Thick Crêpe

The name matafam is derived from the Spanish, meaning literally 'to deaden hunger'. It is such a filling dish that it is quite easy to see how it came by its name.

Metric/Imperial	American
100 g/4 oz plain flour	*1 cup all-purpose flour*
200 ml/⅓ pint milk	*1 cup milk*
4 eggs, beaten	*4 eggs, beaten*
2 shallots, peeled and finely chopped	*2 scallions, peeled and finely chopped*
salt	*salt*
freshly ground white pepper	*freshly ground white pepper*
100 g/4 oz butter	*½ cup butter*

Sift the flour into a bowl, then stir in the milk a little at a time. Add the eggs and shallots (scallions), and salt and pepper to taste. Stir well until thoroughly incorporated, then leave to stand for 25 minutes.

Melt half the butter in a shallow flameproof baking dish, then pour in the crêpe mixture – it should be about 2 cm/¾ inch thick. Fry until set and golden on the underside, shaking the dish constantly to prevent the mixture from sticking.

Slide the crêpe out of the dish onto a plate, then melt the remaining butter in the dish. Invert the crêpe into the dish, cooked side uppermost, then transfer to a preheated moderate oven (180°C/350°F/Gas Mark 4) and bake for about 12 minutes. Serve immediately.
SERVES 4

VARIATIONS:

1. Add 100 g/4 oz/1 cup grated *Gruyère* cheese to the mixture with the eggs. Freshly grated nutmeg can also be added if liked.
2. In Savoie, 225 g/8oz/ 2 cups grated raw potato and strips of bacon or ham are added to the mixture with the eggs.

OMELETTE AUX CÈPES

Cèpe Omelette

If cèpes are difficult to obtain, replace with field mushrooms or button mushrooms.

Metric/Imperial	American
50 g/2 oz goose fat★, dripping or butter	*¼ cup goose fat★, drippings or butter*
450 g/1 lb cèpe mushrooms★, thinly sliced	*1 lb cèpe mushrooms★, thinly sliced*
salt	*salt*
freshly ground black pepper	*freshly ground black pepper*
2 garlic cloves, peeled and crushed	*2 garlic cloves, peeled and crushed*
1 small bunch parsley, finely chopped	*1 small bunch parsley, finely chopped*
8 eggs	*8 eggs*
40 g/1½ oz butter	*3 tablespoons butter*

Melt the fat in a heavy pan, add the mushrooms and fry until light golden in colour. Lower the heat, cover the pan and cook gently for 30 minutes if using cèpes; 5 to 10 minutes for field or button mushrooms.

Add salt and pepper to taste, then the garlic and parsley. Cover again and cook gently for a further minute.

Whisk the eggs together lightly, adding salt and pepper to taste. Add the mushrooms, reserving a few for garnish. Melt 25 g/1 oz/2 tablespoons butter in a large omelette pan, increase the heat, then pour in the egg mixture, tilting the pan to spread it evenly. Push the cooked mixture into the centre with a spatula so that the unset egg can run onto the bottom of the pan. Cook only until the underneath is set – the top of the omelette should still be soft.

Slide the omelette onto a warmed serving platter and quickly fold one half over the other. Melt the remaining butter, brush over the omelette and sprinkle with the reserved mushrooms. Serve immediately.
SERVES 4

ESCARGOTS À LA BOURGUIGNONNE

Snails with Garlic and Parsley Butter from Bourgogne

Fresh snails are time-consuming to prepare and less easily obtainable in this country than in France. If you prefer to use canned ones, omit the cleansing and boiling in the court-bouillon, and simply follow the stuffing and baking instructions.

Metric/Imperial	American
4 dozen snails	*4 dozen snails*
FOR CLEANSING:	FOR CLEANSING:
3 tablespoons coarse sea salt	*3 tablespoons coarse sea salt*
about 200 ml/⅓ pint vinegar	*about 1 cup vinegar*
pinch of plain flour	*pinch of all-purpose flour*
soda crystals	*soda crystals*
COURT-BOUILLON:	COURT-BOUILLON:
500 ml/18 fl oz dry white wine	*2¼ cups dry white wine*
500 ml/18 fl oz water	*2¼ cups water*
1 carrot, peeled and chopped	*1 carrot, peeled and chopped*
1 onion, peeled and chopped	*1 onion, peeled and chopped*
1 shallot, peeled and chopped	*1 scallion, peeled and chopped*
1 bouquet garni★	*1 bouquet garni★*
salt	*salt*
5 peppercorns	*5 peppercorns*
SNAIL BUTTER:	SNAIL BUTTER:
400 g/14 oz unsalted butter	*1¾ cups sweet butter*
2 garlic cloves, peeled and crushed	*2 garlic cloves, peeled and crushed*
20 g/¾ oz parsley, finely chopped	*1 cup finely chopped parsley*
salt	*salt*
freshly ground black pepper	*freshly ground black pepper*

Escargots à la bourguignonne;
Omelette aux cèpes

Put the fresh snails in a bowl and cover with the salt, vinegar and flour. Leave for 2 hours.

Rinse the snails thoroughly under cold running water, then plunge into a pan of boiling water for 5 minutes. Drain, rinse under cold running water, then remove the shells, discarding the black intestines.

To make the *court-bouillon*: put all the ingredients, except the peppercorns, in a large pan. Add the snails, then bring to the boil. Skim off the scum with a skimmer or slotted spoon, then lower the heat and simmer very gently for 3 to 4 hours.

Add the peppercorns, simmer for a further 5 minutes, then remove the pan from the heat. Leave the snails to cool in the *court-bouillon*.

Meanwhile, wash the empty snail shells under cold running water, plunge them into a pan of boiling water to which a handful of soda crystals has been added, then boil for 30 minutes. Drain and wash the snail shells again under cold running water, then leave to dry in a sieve (strainer).

To make the snail butter: put the butter in a bowl and beat with a wooden spoon to soften. Add the garlic and parsley and beat together until creamy. Season with salt and pepper to taste.

Replace the snails in their shells, then fill each shell with the prepared snail butter. Place the snails in a special snail dish or a shallow baking dish, open ends uppermost to prevent the butter spilling out when hot. Bake in a preheated moderately hot oven (200°C/ 400°F/Gas Mark 6) for a few minutes, just until the butter begins to melt. Serve immediately, taking great care not to spill the butter when removing the snails from the baking dish.

SERVES 6 TO 8

VARIATIONS:

1. Substitute a little finely chopped shallot (scallion) for half the garlic in the snail butter.
2. Add a few breadcrumbs to the snail butter, with a drop or two of brandy.

The most highly prized snails to come from France are those from the vineyards of Burgundy (Bourgogne), called *helix pomatia*. These are the largest of all the snails, fattened in special snail farms on local vine leaves. They are almost always served stuffed with the classic garlic and parsley butter – known as *beurre à la bourguignonne* – from the region where snails are most bountiful.

CORNIOTTES
Cheese Tricorns

If Saint-Florentin or other soft white cheese is difficult to obtain, grated Gruyère makes an acceptable substitute in this recipe.

Metric/Imperial	American
PÂTE BRISÉE:	PÂTE BRISÉE:
200 g/7 oz plain flour	1¾ cups all-purpose flour
pinch of salt	pinch of salt
100 g/3½ oz butter	7 tablespoons butter
2–3 tablespoons iced water	2–3 tablespoons iced water
FILLING:	FILLING:
1 × 200 g/7 oz Saint-Florentin, well drained	1 × 7 oz Saint-Florentin, well drained
3 eggs, beaten	3 eggs, beaten
3 tablespoons double cream	3 tablespoons heavy cream
salt	salt
freshly ground white pepper	freshly ground white pepper

Make the *pâte brisée* according to the method on page 52. Leave in a cool place for 1 hour.

Roll out the pastry (dough) on a floured surface and cut into 12 circles about 10 cm/4 inches in diameter. Place on a buttered and floured baking sheet, spacing them slightly apart. Lift up the edges of the circles.

To make the filling: mash the cheese lightly with a fork, add the eggs and cream, and beat until smooth. Add salt and pepper to taste.

Divide the filling equally between the pastry rounds, placing it in the centre of each one. Brush the edges of the dough with water and fold over the filling to make tricorn shapes. Press the edges together to seal, then bake in a preheated moderately hot oven (200°C/400°F/Gas Mark 6) for about 30 minutes or until golden. Serve warm or cold.

SERVES 6 OR 12

GOUGÈRE

Like all choux pastries, gougère must be baked immediately after the dough is made. If you do not have a large enough baking dish, place the dough directly on a baking sheet.
This quantity is ideal for a party dish; for a smaller gougère to serve 4 people, use 100 g/4 oz/½ cup butter, 300 ml/½ pint/1¼ cups water, 150 g/5 oz/1¼ cups flour, 4 eggs and 175 g/6 oz/1 cup cheese.

Metric/Imperial	American
750 ml/1¼ pints water	3 cups water
175 g/6 oz butter, cut into small pieces	¾ cup butter, cut into small pieces
salt	salt
215 g/7½ oz plain flour, sifted	scant 2 cups all-purpose flour, sifted
5–6 eggs, beaten	5–6 eggs, beaten
225 g/8 oz Gruyère cheese★, diced	1⅓ cups diced Gruyère cheese★
½–1 teaspoon mustard powder	½–1 teaspoon mustard powder
freshly ground black pepper	freshly ground black pepper

Put the water, butter and a pinch of salt in a large heavy pan and bring to the boil. Add the flour all at once, taking care not to splash the boiling water. Beat vigorously with a wooden spoon over gentle heat until the mixture forms a smooth dough which leaves the sides of the pan clean.

Remove the pan from the heat, then beat in the eggs a little at a time, making sure that each addition is thoroughly incorporated before adding the next. Add as many eggs as the dough will absorb; it should be thick and shiny, not liquid. Reserve a little beaten egg for the glaze. Beat in the diced cheese, and mustard, salt and pepper to taste.

Place tablespoonfuls of the dough in a well-buttered 25 to 28 cm/10 to 11 inch circular baking dish, arranging them side by side to fill the dish completely, or leaving a hole in the centre to make a crown shape. Beat the reserved egg with 1 tablespoon water for the glaze, then brush all over the dough. Bake in a preheated moderately hot oven (200°C/400°C/Gas Mark 6) for 40 to 45 minutes until golden brown. Serve warm or cold.

SERVES 6 TO 8

FONDUE SAVOYARDE
Savoie Three-Cheese Fondue

It isn't absolutely essential to make such a large quantity of fondue as suggested here. Simply allow 150 g/5 oz cheese and 1 wine glass (about 7 tablespoons) dry white wine per person and make up the exact quantity required. For the best flavour, try to use all three different cheeses, but if this isn't possible, you can use only one or two.

Metric/Imperial	American
1 garlic clove, peeled	1 garlic clove, peeled
300 g/11 oz Gruyère cheese★, thinly sliced	11 oz Gruyère cheese★, thinly sliced
300 g/11 oz Emmental cheese★, thinly sliced	11 oz Emmental cheese★, thinly sliced
300 g/11 oz Beaufort cheese★, thinly sliced	11 oz Beaufort cheese★, thinly sliced
about 6 wine glasses dry white wine (e.g. Crécy or Apremont)	about 6 wine glasses dry white wine (e.g. Crécy or Apremont)
2 tablespoons kirsch	2 tablespoons kirsch
salt	salt
freshly ground white pepper	freshly ground white pepper
1 large loaf crusty bread, cut into small cubes	1 large loaf crusty bread, cut into small cubes

Rub the inside of a glazed earthenware fondue pot with the garlic. Place the cheeses in the pot, then pour in the wine – it should just cover the cheese.

Cook the fondue over moderate heat until the cheeses have melted, stirring gently all the time with a wooden spoon.

Stir in the liqueur, a little salt and plenty of pepper. Transfer the fondue pot to the centre of the dining table, standing it firmly over its burner to keep hot.

Divide the bread cubes equally between individual plates and let guests help themselves by dipping the cubes into the pot with fondue forks.

SERVES 6

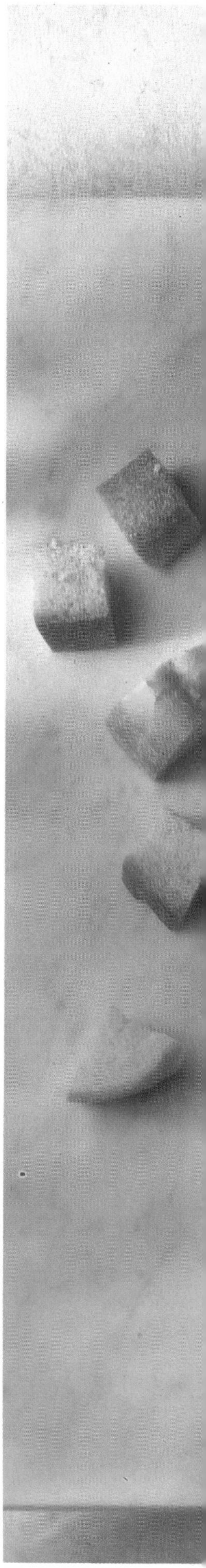

FONDUE FRANC-COMTOISE

Gruyère Fondue with Eggs

If you do not have a special fondue set, cook the fondue in a flameproof casserole on top of the stove, then transfer to a hot oven for 10 minutes. Serve straight from the casserole, allowing guests to help themselves to a few spoonfuls each.

Metric/Imperial	American
2 garlic cloves, peeled	2 garlic cloves, peeled
500 ml/18 fl oz dry white wine (e.g. Lavigny)	$2\frac{1}{4}$ cups dry white wine (e.g. Lavigny)
450 g/1 lb Gruyère cheese★, thinly sliced	1 lb Gruyère cheese★, thinly sliced
pinch of cayenne pepper	pinch of cayenne pepper
salt	salt
freshly ground white pepper	freshly ground white pepper
3 tablespoons cornflour	3 tablespoons cornstarch
4 tablespoons kirsch	$\frac{1}{4}$ cup kirsch
4 eggs, beaten	4 eggs, beaten
75 g/3 oz butter, softened	$\frac{1}{3}$ cup softened butter
1 large loaf crusty bread, cut into small cubes	1 large loaf crusty bread, cut into small cubes

Rub the inside of a glazed earthenware fondue pot with the garlic. Pour in the wine, then heat gently until just bubbling.

Add the cheese and cayenne, and salt and pepper to taste, then cook gently until the cheese has melted, stirring constantly with a wooden spoon.

Mix the cornflour (cornstarch) to a paste with the kirsch. Stir into the melted cheese, then remove the pot from the heat.

Stir in the beaten eggs and the butter and keep stirring gently until the butter has melted.

Transfer the fondue pot to the centre of the dining table, standing it firmly over its burner to keep hot.

Divide the bread cubes equally between individual plates and let guests help themselves by dipping the cubes into the pot with fondue forks.

SERVES 6

Fondue savoyarde; Corniottes

Cheese or Swiss fondue sets should not be confused with the type used for meat. Cheese fondue sets are usually made of ceramic with a thick, heavy base. Meat fondue pots are metal and not heavy enough for cheese fondue.

A certain mystiq e surrounds soufflés, yet there are no special secrets to making them. Basically, a hot savoury soufflé is a sauce (usually béchamel), enriched with egg yolks, then lightened with egg whites and baked in the oven.

The sauce which forms the base of the soufflé should have a soft dropping consistency. If the sauce is too thin it will not hold the egg whites, if too thick, the finished soufflé will not rise properly.

The egg whites should be whisked to a volume twice that of the basic sauce mixture. For maximum volume, French chefs always use at least one more egg white than yolks, and a copper bowl and wire balloon whisk.

Adding the egg whites is possibly the most tricky part of soufflé making. The whites should be folded in with a large metal spoon, quickly, yet gently, to ensure that air is not lost from the mixture. Bake and serve immediately – a hot soufflé waits for no-one!

SOUFFLÉ AU FROMAGE

Cheese Soufflé

Metric/Imperial	American
50 g/2 oz butter	$\frac{1}{4}$ cup butter
25 g/1 oz plain flour	$\frac{1}{4}$ cup all-purpose flour
250 ml/8 fl oz milk	1 cup milk
2 tablespoons cream (optional)	2 tablespoons cream (optional)
4 egg yolks	4 egg yolks
150 g/5 oz Gruyère cheese★, grated	1$\frac{1}{4}$ cups grated Gruyère cheese★
salt	salt
freshly ground white pepper	freshly ground white pepper
freshly grated nutmeg	freshly grated nutmeg
5 egg whites	5 egg whites

Make a béchamel sauce with the butter, flour and milk according to the method on page 44. Cook very gently for 15 minutes, stirring constantly with a wooden spoon. Remove from the heat and stir in the cream, if using.

Stir the egg yolks into the béchamel sauce one at a time, then add the cheese and salt, pepper and nutmeg to taste. Beat well, then leave to cool slightly. Whisk the egg whites until stiff, then fold gently into the sauce mixture.

Transfer the mixture to a well-buttered 1.2 litre/ 2 pint/5 cup soufflé dish, then bake in a preheated moderate oven (180°C/350°F/Gas Mark 4) for 15 minutes. Increase the heat to moderately hot (200°C/400°F/Gas Mark 6) and bake for a further 15 to 20 minutes until the soufflé is well-risen and golden. Serve immediately.
SERVES 4

BETTERAVES ROUGES

Beetroot (Beets) with Salt Pork

Metric/Imperial	American
100 g/4 oz salt pork, diced	$\frac{1}{2}$ cup diced salt pork
2 large onions, peeled and chopped	2 large onions, peeled and chopped
1 teaspoon plain flour	1 teaspoon all-purpose flour
7 tablespoons chicken stock (page 42)	7 tablespoons chicken stock (page 42)
450 g/1 lb cooked beetroot, skinned and chopped into large pieces	1 lb cooked beets, skinned and chopped into large pieces
TO FINISH:	TO FINISH:
dash of vinegar	dash of vinegar
1 tablespoon chopped herbs (e.g. chives and parsley)	1 tablespoon chopped herbs (e.g. chives and parsley)

Put the pork in a heavy pan and cook over moderat heat until the fat runs. Add the onions and fry until sof but not coloured.

Sprinkle in the flour, cook for 3 minutes, stirrin constantly, then stir in the stock. Cook gently fo about 10 minutes, then add the beetroot (beets) Simmer for a few minutes, then remove from the hea and sprinkle with the vinegar and chopped herbs Serve immediately.
SERVES 4

SALADE DE MOULES AUX HARICOTS BLANCS

Mussel and Bean Salad

Metric/Imperial	American
3 litres/5$\frac{1}{2}$ pints fresh mussels	6$\frac{1}{2}$ pints/13 cups fresh mussels
150 ml/$\frac{1}{4}$ pint dry white wine	$\frac{2}{3}$ cup dry white wine
1 clove garlic, crushed	1 clove garlic, crushed
3 tablespoons double cream	3 tablespoons heavy cream
3 tablespoons oil	3 tablespoons oil
1 tablespoon vinegar	1 tablespoon vinegar
freshly ground black pepper	freshly ground black pepper
225 g/8 oz cooked dried white haricot beans	$\frac{1}{2}$ lb cooked navy beans
salt	salt
2 tomatoes, sliced, to garnish	2 tomatoes, sliced, for garnish

Scrub the mussel shells clean and discard any that are open. Place in a large pan with the wine and garlic. Cover and cook over high heat for 5 to 7 minutes, until the shells open; discard any that do not. Drain and discard the mu sel shells.

Put the cream in a bowl with the oil and vinegar. Add pepper to taste, then whisk with a fork until thick.

Put the beans and mussels in a deep serving dish, pour over the sauce and mix well. Season with salt to taste. Garnish with the tomato slices to serve.
SERVES 5 TO 6

SAUCISSON CHAUD, POMMES À L'HUILE

Hot Sausage and Potato Salad

This is a simple dish of spicy sausage surrounded with a hot potato salad. It is usually served as an hors d'oeuvre in France, but can equally well be served as a lunch dish. If you like the flavour of shallots (scallions), add about four of these, finely chopped, to the wine and vinegar dressing.

Metric/Imperial	American
1 kg/2 lb waxy potatoes	2 lb waxy potatoes
salt	salt
1 × 750 g/1½ lb French cooking sausage★	1 × 1½ lb French cooking sausage★
6 tablespoons dry white wine	7 tablespoons dry white wine
2 tablespoons cider vinegar	2 tablespoons cider vinegar
6 tablespoons oil	7 tablespoons oil
1 tablespoon chopped parsley	1 tablespoon chopped parsley
1 tablespoon snipped chives	1 tablespoon snipped chives
freshly ground black pepper	freshly ground black pepper

Cook the potatoes in their skins in boiling salted water for about 20 minutes until just tender.

Meanwhile, prick the sausage skin with a fork to prevent it bursting during cooking. Plunge the sausage into a pan of boiling water, lower the heat and cook gently for 20 minutes.

Drain the potatoes and remove their skins while still hot. Cut them into 1 cm/½ thick slices, then place in a heavy pan. Sprinkle over the wine, vinegar and oil, then shake the pan gently to mix the potatoes and dressing together. Place the pan over very gentle heat and reheat the potatoes.

Meanwhile, drain the sausage, leave until cool enough to handle, then remove the skin. Cut the sausage into 1 cm/½ inch thick slices and arrange in the centre of a serving platter.

When the potatoes and dressing are fairly hot, remove from the heat and sprinkle with the parsley and chives, and salt and pepper to taste. Toss gently to mix, then pile around the sausage on the platter. Serve warm.

SERVES 6

LEFT: **Soufflé au fromage**
BELOW: **Saucisson chaud, pommes à l'huile; Salade de moules aux haricots blancs**

FONDS D'ARTICHAUTS AU FOIE GRAS

Artichoke Hearts with Foie Gras

Sauce béarnaise (page 45) can be poured over the artichoke hearts just before serving, if liked.

Metric/Imperial	American
6 young globe artichokes	6 young globe artichokes
2 lemons	2 lemons
1 litre/1¾ pints water	4¼ cups water
2 tablespoons oil	2 tablespoons oil
salt	salt
25 g/1 oz butter	2 tablespoons butter
7 tablespoons Madeira	7 tablespoons Madeira
freshly ground black pepper	freshly ground black pepper
GARNISH:	GARNISH:
6 small slices foie gras★	6 small slices foie gras★
6 thin slices truffle★	6 thin slices truffle★
(optional)	(optional)

Cut away the hard outer leaves of the artichokes to expose the hearts. Scoop out the chokes with a sharp-edged teaspoon and discard. Cut one of the lemons in half and rub the cut surface against the artichoke hearts to prevent discoloration.

Put the water in a pan with the oil, the juice of the remaining lemon and a little salt. Bring to the boil, add the artichoke hearts and simmer for 20 minutes; drain.

Melt the butter in a frying pan (skillet), then place the artichoke hearts in the pan in a single layer. Sprinkle with the Madeira and pepper to taste, then cover and cook very gently for 10 minutes.

Remove the artichokes from the pan with a slotted spoon and arrange on a warmed serving platter. Add the *foie gras* to the pan and heat through very gently.

Garnish the artichokes with the *foie gras* and the truffle, if using, and serve immediately.
SERVES 6

SALADE FÉCAMPOISE

Smoked Herring, Potato and Egg Salad

A little cream can be added to the oil and vinegar dressing if liked, and this dressing handed separately.

Metric/Imperial	American
1 kg/2 lb waxy potatoes	2 lb waxy potatoes
salt	salt
3 hard-boiled eggs, thinly sliced	3 hard-cooked eggs, thinly sliced
1 onion, peeled and very thinly sliced	1 onion, peeled and very thinly sliced
1 shallot, peeled and very thinly sliced	1 scallion, peeled and very thinly sliced
few sprigs each parsley, tarragon and chervil, finely chopped	few sprigs each parsley, tarragon and chervil, finely chopped
freshly ground black pepper	freshly ground black pepper
2–3 smoked herrings	2–3 smoked herrings
3 tablespoons oil	3 tablespoons oil
1½ tablespoons vinegar	1½ tablespoons vinegar

Cook the potatoes in their skins in boiling salted water for about 20 minutes until just tender. Drain, then remove the skins while still hot. Slice thinly.

Place the potatoes in a salad bowl with the eggs, onion, shallot (scallion), herbs, and salt and pepper to taste. Fold gently to mix, taking care not to break the potatoes and eggs.

Grill (broil) the herrings, skin and bone them, then cut the flesh into small strips. Arrange the herring strips on top of the salad.

Whisk the oil and vinegar together with a fork and sprinkle over the salad before serving. Serve immediately.
SERVES 6

Fonds d'artichauts au foie gras; Salade cauchoise; Salade Fécampoise

SALADE CAUCHOISE

Potato, Celery and Ham Salad

This salad looks most attractive with its colourful sprinkling of ham and chervil. If you prefer the ham to be coated in the dressing, however, it can be mixed in with the vegetables and just the chervil sprinkled on top.

Metric/Imperial	American
1 kg/2 lb waxy potatoes	*2 lb waxy potatoes*
salt	*salt*
200 ml/⅓ pint double cream	*1 cup heavy cream*
1 tablespoon cider vinegar or lemon juice	*1 tablespoon cider vinegar or lemon juice*
freshly ground black pepper	*freshly ground black pepper*
2 heads celery, trimmed and cut into julienne (matchstick strips)★	*2 heads celery, trimmed and cut into julienne (matchstick strips)★*
225 g/8 oz lean smoked ham★, diced	*1–1⅓ cups diced lean smoked ham★*
1 truffle★, finely chopped (optional)	*1 truffle★, finely chopped (optional)*
chopped chervil, to garnish	*chopped chervil, for garnish*

Cook the potatoes in their skins in boiling salted water for about 20 minutes until just tender. Drain, then remove the skins while still hot. Slice thinly.

Whip the cream lightly until just fluffy, then whip in the vinegar or lemon juice, and salt and pepper to taste.

Place the potatoes and celery in a bowl. Pour over the cream dressing and fold gently to mix. Sprinkle the ham and truffle, if using, over the top. Garnish with chervil and serve as soon as possible.

SERVES 6

SALADE DE MOULES ET POMMES DE TERRE

Mussel and Potato Salad

Metric/Imperial	American
3 litres/5½ pints fresh mussels	*6½ pints/13 cups fresh mussels*
1 onion, peeled and chopped	*1 onion, peeled and chopped*
1 bouquet garni★	*1 bouquet garni★*
150 ml/¼ pint water	*⅔ cup water*
1 kg/2 lb waxy potatoes	*2 lb waxy potatoes*
250 ml/8 fl oz dry white wine	*1 cup dry white wine*
juice of 1 lemon	*juice of 1 lemon*
200 ml/7 fl oz single cream	*⅔ cup light cream*
salt	*salt*
4 tablespoons olive oil	*¼ cup olive oil*
few chives, snipped	*few chives, snipped*
5 chervil sprigs, chopped	*5 chervil sprigs, chopped*
5 gherkins, thinly sliced	*5 small sweet dill pickles, thinly sliced*
freshly ground black pepper	*freshly ground black pepper*

Scrub the mussel shells clean and discard any that are open. Put them in a large heavy pan with the onion, bouquet garni and water. Cover and cook over high heat for 5 to 7 minutes until the shells open, shaking the pan from time to time; discard any that do not open. Remove the mussels from their shells and reserve.

Cook the potatoes in their skins in boiling salted water for about 20 minutes until just tender. Remove the skins while still hot, cut the potatoes into 1 cm/½ inch thick slices and place in a bowl. Sprinkle over the wine.

Put the lemon juice in a separate bowl, add the cream and salt to taste, then gradually stir in the oil. Add the herbs and gherkins (dill pickles), and pepper to taste. Mix well.

Alternate the potatoes, mussels and sauce in layers in a salad bowl. Serve immediately.

SERVES 4

Salade Niçoise; Salade de
poivrons grillés; Salade
verte au bresse bleu

SALADE DE POIVRONS GRILLÉS

Pepper Salad

This is a good salad to serve with grilled (broiled) fish and steaks.

Metric/Imperial	American
1 kg/2 lb mixed green and red peppers	*2 lb mixed green and red peppers*
2 garlic cloves, peeled and finely chopped	*2 garlic cloves, peeled and finely chopped*
4 tablespoons olive oil	*¼ cup olive oil*
1 tablespoon vinegar	*1 tablespoon vinegar*
salt	*salt*
freshly ground black pepper	*freshly ground black pepper*

Grill (broil) the peppers for about 10 minutes, turning frequently, until the skin is charred on all sides. Transfer to a bowl, cover and leave to stand for 30 minutes.

Remove the skin from the peppers, halve and remove the seeds. Slice the flesh into thin strips.

Put the strips of pepper in a salad bowl with the remaining ingredients, and salt and pepper to taste. Fold gently to mix.

SERVES 4

SALADE VERTE AU BRESSE BLEU

Green Salad with Blue Cheese Dressing

Metric/Imperial	American
50 g/2 oz Bleu de Bresse cheese★	*¼ cup Bleu de Bresse cheese★*
250 ml/8 fl oz double cream	*1 cup heavy cream*
pinch of cayenne pepper	*pinch of cayenne pepper*
salt	*salt*
freshly ground white pepper	*freshly ground white pepper*
2 lettuces	*2 lettuces*

Work the cheese and cream together until soft and well mixed, then work through a fine sieve (strainer). Stir in the cayenne, and salt and pepper to taste.

Separate the lettuce leaves and place in a salad bowl. Pour over the cheese dressing and toss gently to coat the lettuce. Serve immediately.

SERVES 5 TO 6

SALADE NIÇOISE

Niçoise Salad

A true salade niçoise should never include vinegar in its dressing – the juice from the tomatoes should provide enoug acid. Neither should any of the vegetables be cooked: they should be sufficiently fresh, young and tender to be eaten raw.

Metric/Imperial	American
1 garlic clove, peeled and bruised★	*1 garlic clove, peeled and bruised★*
1 lettuce	*1 lettuce*
100 g/4 oz celery hearts, thinly sliced	*1 cup thinly sliced celery hearts*
100 g/4 oz cucumber, peeled and thinly sliced	*1 cup thinly sliced peeled cucumber*
225 g/8 oz small French beans, topped and tailed (optional)	*½ lb small green beans, topped and tailed (optional)*
225 g/8 oz young tender artichoke hearts, thinly sliced (optional)	*½ lb young tender artichoke hearts, thinly sliced (optional)*
450 g/1 lb tomatoes, skinned, quartered and seeded	*1 lb tomatoes, skinned, quartered and seeded*
1 large green pepper, cored, seeded and sliced into rings	*1 large green pepper, cored, seeded and sliced into rings*
1 onion, peeled and sliced into rings	*1 onion, peeled and sliced into rings*
4 hard-boiled eggs, halved	*4 hard-cooked eggs, halved*
50 g/2 oz black olives	*½ cup ripe olives*
8 canned anchovy fillets, drained and desalted★	*8 canned anchovy fillets, drained and desalted★*
1 × 225 g/8 oz can tuna fish in oil, drained and separated into chunks	*1 × ½ lb can tuna fish in oil, drained and separated into chunks*
DRESSING:	DRESSING:
7 tablespoons olive oil	*7 tablespoons olive oil*
4 basil leaves, finely chopped	*4 basil leaves, finely chopped*
salt	*salt*
freshly ground white pepper	*freshly ground white peppe*

Rub the inside of a large salad bowl with the bruise garlic, then line the bowl with lettuce leaves. Chop th remaining lettuce leaves and arrange in the bottom o the bowl.

Mix together the celery and cucumber, with th French (green) beans and artichoke hearts, if using Place in the salad bowl. Arrange the tomatoes, peppe onion, eggs, olives, anchovies and tuna decoratively o top.

Mix together the ingredients for the dressing wit salt and pepper to taste. Pour over the salad just befor serving. Serve immediately.

SERVES 4

Sweet basil is a very popular herb for flavouring salads in France, particularly in Provence where the herb grows so prolifically. Window sills, garden tubs and pots filled with flourishing basil plants are a common sight throughout this region, and a handful of chopped fresh basil gives an unmistakably 'provençal' flavour to many savoury dishes, apart from salads.

Tomatoes have a special affinity with this herb. Eggs, mushrooms and all salad dressings made with olive oil also combine well with basil.

It is however one of the stronger-tasting herbs and should always be used sparingly, especially in cooked dishes, since cooking seems to increase its potency.

CRUDITÉS

Raw Vegetable Hors d'Oeuvre

Crudités is a platter of prepared raw vegetables served with a simple dressing of olive oil, vinegar and salt and pepper, or with a variety of other sauces (see opposite), or a thick homemade mayonnaise (page 48). Guests help themselves to the vegetables, which are then coated in dressing or dipped into a sauce and eaten raw. The choice of vegetables for crudités is a personal one, governed by seasonal availability. As long as the vegetables are young and tender, fresh and crisp, that is all that matters.

Crudités; Anchoïade; Tapénade; Bagna caudo

Metric/Imperial	American
6 small green peppers, cored, seeded and sliced into rings	*6 small green peppers, cored, seeded and sliced into rings*
1 large red pepper, cored, seeded and sliced into rings	*1 large red pepper, cored, seeded and sliced into rings*
1 large yellow pepper, cored, seeded and sliced into rings	*1 large yellow pepper, cored, seeded and sliced into rings*
1 bunch celery (white part only), separated into sticks and halved	*1 bunch celery (white part only), separated into sticks and halved*
2 fennel bulbs (white part only), quartered	*2 fennel bulbs (white part only) quartered*
8 small pickling onions, peeled	*8 small button onions, peeled*
2 cucumbers, thinly sliced	*2 cucumbers, thinly sliced*
1 bunch radishes, topped and tailed	*1 bunch radishes, topped and tailed*
450 g/1 lb young, tender broad beans	*1 lb young, tender fava or lima beans*
8 small violet-coloured artichokes, stalks, outer leaves and chokes removed	*8 small violet-coloured artichokes, stalks, outer leaves and chokes removed*

Arrange the prepared vegetables attractively on a large platter or in a basket, mixing the colours as much as possible – they look pretty arranged in the shape of a flower. The artichokes must be immersed in a bowl of water to which a few drops of lemon juice have been added or they will discolour. Serve as soon as possible after preparing the vegetables, with an oil and vinegar dressing, thick homemade mayonnaise or the sauces opposite.
SERVES 8

ANCHOÏADE
Hot Anchovy Spread

Serve as a dip for crudités, or spread while still warm on slices of hot toast.

Metric/Imperial	American
12 whole anchovies in brine, drained, skinned and boned	12 whole anchovies in brine, drained, skinned and boned
500 ml/18 fl oz olive oil	2¼ cups olive oil
6 garlic cloves, peeled and crushed	6 garlic cloves, peeled and crushed
3 shallots, peeled and finely chopped	3 scallions, peeled and finely chopped
1 tablespoon red wine vinegar	1 tablespoon red wine vinegar
chopped parsley	chopped parsley
chopped thyme	chopped thyme

Rinse the anchovies thoroughly under cold running water to remove the salt. Divide them into fillets.

Crush the anchovies in a mortar, then add the oil a little at a time, as for making mayonnaise, working it into the anchovies with the pestle. Work in the garlic and shallots (scallions). Alternatively the ingredients can be worked in an electric blender.

Transfer the paste to a heatproof bowl, then stand in a hot *bain-marie* until warm, stirring constantly. Stir in the vinegar, and parsley and thyme to taste. Serve warm.

6 SERVINGS

VARIATION: Use 225 g/8 oz canned anchovies in oil instead of the anchovies in brine. Drain and desalt★ them, then mix as above with 1 garlic clove, peeled and crushed, 1 onion, peeled and finely chopped, 6 chopped basil leaves and 500 ml/18 fl oz/2¼ cups olive oil.

Provence has a style of cuisine all of its own, more Mediterranean in character than that of the other French regions and not dissimilar from the cooking of neighbouring Liguria on the Italian Mediterranean coast.

Olive trees grow all along this coastline and black and green olives are used in many dishes. Green olives are also pressed into thick, fruity olive oil, used for cooking in preference to butter, and an essential ingredient of all local salads and salad dressings.

Freshly picked, sun-ripened vegetables – tomatoes, onions, peppers, artichokes, courgettes (zucchini) and aubergines (eggplant) – are also a dominant feature of Provençal cuisine, and the locally grown garlic lends its pungent aroma and flavour to almost every savoury dish. Fresh herbs (predominantly basil) are used in abundance. Strong salty anchovies are also popular and help to give the Provençal cuisine a truly Mediterranean flavour.

BAGNA CAUDO
Hot Sauce with Anchovies

Serve hot as a dip with small croutôns or crudités.

Metric/Imperial	American
15 whole anchovies in brine, drained, skinned and boned	15 whole anchovies in brine, drained, skinned and boned
75 g/3 oz butter	⅓ cup butter
3 tablespoons olive oil	3 tablespoons olive oil
5 garlic cloves, peeled and quartered	5 garlic cloves, peeled and quartered

Rinse the anchovies thoroughly under cold running water to remove salt. Divide into fillets, then slice thinly.

Melt the butter in a heavy pan, add the oil, anchovies and garlic. Heat gently, pressing the anchovies and garlic with the back of a wooden spoon until a smooth paste is formed. Serve hot.

6 SERVINGS

VARIATION: Pound the anchovies, oil and garlic to a paste with a mortar and pestle, then transfer to a heavy pan and heat through gently with half the above quantity of butter.

TAPÉNADE
Olive, Anchovy and Caper Sauce

Tapénade can be served as a dip for crudités, or it can be spread on bread. It can also be used as a stuffing for halved hard-boiled (-cooked) eggs, mixed with the mashed yolks.

Metric/Imperial	American
200 g/7 oz stoned black olives	1⅓ cups pitted ripe olives
100 g/4 oz canned anchovy fillets, drained and desalted★	¼ lb canned anchovy fillets, drained and desalted★
2 tablespoons capers	2 tablespoons capers
2 tablespoons brandy	2 tablespoons brandy
½ teaspoon prepared mustard	½ teaspoon prepared mustard
freshly ground black pepper	freshly ground black pepper
7 tablespoons olive oil	7 tablespoons olive oil

Work all the ingredients, except the oil, in an electric blender or pound with a mortar and pestle. Add the oil a little at a time, as when making mayonnaise, until a thick paste is formed. Taste and adjust seasoning, then transfer to a serving bowl.

6 SERVINGS

FISH & SHELLFISH

Not surprisingly, fish plays an important part in the cuisine of France, bordered as it is by the Atlantic and the Mediterranean. The vast network of rivers and streams provide an additional supply of freshwater fish.

Some of France's most celebrated dishes feature fish – classics like Sole Colbert (sole with maître d'hôtel butter) and Homard à l'américaine (lobster with tomatoes, white wine and brandy) are found on menus of top international restaurants and hotels all over the world. However, the French do not always treat their fish in such a complicated manner. Most visitors to France are pleasantly surprised to find that contrary to what they might expect, fish is usually cooked and served in the simplest of manners. It is grilled (broiled) or poached rather than fried, and more often than not is served simply with melted butter and lemon. Most fish is bought fresh from the market within hours of being landed, and is eaten on the same day, long before it has a chance to lose any of its freshness.

For poaching fish, the French use a poaching liquid called court-bouillon, made from water, vegetables, herbs and seasonings. Sometimes wine is added to, or used instead of water, especially if the fish to be poached has a strong flavour such as mackerel. Shellfish too are often poached in a wine court-bouillon. Sometimes wine vinegar is used instead of wine, although in smaller quantities, for freshwater fish which tend to have a more piquant flavour than seawater fish. A fish that is described as 'au bleu' has been poached in a vinegar court-bouillon – the acid quite literally turns the skin of the fish blue.

For delicately-flavoured fish such as whiting and turbot, and for fish steaks and fillets that need to retain their whiteness during cooking, a milk and lemon juice court-bouillon is more suitable than one made with wine or wine vinegar. There is another more concentrated liquid for poaching fish known as a fumet (page 43), but this is best reserved for mildly-flavoured fish which will benefit from its extra 'fishy' flavour.

There are literally hundreds of different varieties of fish to be found in France, and the French waste none of them, from the tiniest morsels which are no more than a mouthful, to the largest and most ugly – all are turned into delectable fish dishes. Along the Mediterranean coastline, but particularly in Provence, the custom of simple grilling and poaching is broken. Here, obscure varieties of fish are used in the traditional and unique fish stews of the area. Every fishing port from the smallest village jetty to the vast quay at Marseille, has its individual way of turning locally-caught varieties of fish – such as wrasse, rascasse and gurnard and the lobster-like petite cigale – into a fish stew of some kind. Bouillabaisse (page 92) and Bourride (page 95) are the most celebrated of these, and are best described as a cross between a stew and a soup, but there are numerous different local versions. Usually these stews are served in two parts – the broth or cooking liquid being served first as a soup, then the fish eaten separately as a main course.

FILETS DE SOLE À LA NORMANDE

Sole with Mussels, Prawns (Shrimp) and Mushrooms

This recipe is a much simplified version of the original, which included oysters and crayfish amongst its ingredients.

Metric/Imperial	American
4 sole (about 300 g/11 oz each)	4 sole (about 11 oz each)
1 onion, peeled and thinly sliced	1 onion, peeled and thinly sliced
2 carrots, peeled and thinly sliced	2 carrots, peeled and thinly sliced
1 bouquet garni★	1 bouquet garni★
400 ml/14 fl oz water	1¾ cups water
300 ml/½ pint dry white wine	1¼ cups dry white wine
salt	salt
freshly ground black pepper	freshly ground black pepper
150 g/5 oz butter	⅔ cup butter
100 g/4 oz mushrooms, stalks removed	1 cup mushrooms, stalks removed
1 tablespoon lemon juice	1 tablespoon lemon juice
1.2 litres/2 pints fresh mussels	5 cups fresh mussels
4 shallots, peeled and finely chopped	4 scallions, peeled and finely chopped
100 g/4 oz uncooked prawns	1 cup uncooked shrimp
2 egg yolks	2 egg yolks
200 ml/⅓ pint double cream	1 cup heavy cream
croûtons★ fried in butter, to garnish (optional)	croûtons★ fried in butter, for garnish (optional)

Filets de sole à la normande

kin the sole and separate into fillets, reserving the
eads and bones. Put the heads and bones in a large pan
vith the onion, carrots, bouquet garni, water and
oo ml/⅓ pint/1 cup wine. Bring to the boil, then
ower the heat, cover and simmer for 20 minutes.

Sprinkle the sole fillets with salt and pepper. Melt
5 g/1 oz/2 tablespoons butter in a flameproof casserole,
dd the sole fillets, then strain the fish stock over them.
Cover with foil and bake in a preheated moderate oven
180°C/350°F/Gas Mark 4) for 12 to 15 minutes, until
ender.

Meanwhile, place the mushrooms in a small pan
vith a little water, then add the lemon juice and salt to
aste. Simmer gently for 10 minutes or until cooked;
rain.

Scrub the mussels and discard any that are open. Put
hem in a pan with the shallots (scallions) and the
emaining wine. Cook over high heat until the shells
pen, then remove the mussels from their shells.
Discard any that do not open. Reserve the cooking
uices. Cook the prawns (shrimp) in boiling water for
minutes, then drain and shell them.

Transfer the sole to a warmed serving platter,
eserving the cooking juices. Surround with the
nussels, prawns (shrimp) and mushrooms. Keep hot.

Strain the cooking juices from the mussels and sole
nto a pan and boil steadily until reduced by three
uarters. Remove from the heat. Mix together the egg
olks and cream, then stir into the reduced cooking
uices. Return the pan to the heat and cook very gently
or 3 to 4 minutes, stirring constantly; do not allow the
auce to boil or it will separate.

Remove from the heat and whisk the remaining
utter into the sauce a little at a time. Taste and adjust
easoning. Pour the sauce over the sole and garnish
vith *croûtons*, if liked. Serve immediately.
ERVES 6

ANGUILLES AU VERT
Eel with Herbs

*If it is difficult to obtain all the fresh herbs in this recipe,
simply increase the quantity of those available to make up
the same total amount. Sorrel can be replaced by spinach in
this way.*

Metric/Imperial	American
40 g/1½ oz butter	3 tablespoons butter
1 kg/2 lb eel, skinned, boned and cut into 4 cm/1½ inch thick pieces	2 lb eel, skinned, boned and cut into 1½ inch thick slices
3 shallots, peeled and finely chopped	3 scallions, peeled and finely chopped
120 ml/4 fl oz dry white wine	½ cup dry white wine
1 bay leaf	1 bay leaf
1 thyme sprig	1 thyme sprig
100 g/4 oz sorrel, hard stalks removed, cut into thin strips	¼ lb sorrel, hard stalks removed, cut into thin strips
100 g/4 oz spinach, hard stalks removed, cut into thin strips	¼ lb spinach, hard stalks removed, cut into thin strips
10 parsley sprigs, finely chopped	10 parsley sprigs, finely chopped
6 chive stems, snipped	6 chive stems, snipped
3 chervil sprigs, finely chopped	3 chervil sprigs, finely chopped
2 sage leaves, finely chopped	2 sage leaves, finely chopped
2 mint leaves, finely chopped	2 mint leaves, finely chopped
1 tarragon sprig, finely chopped	1 tarragon sprig, finely chopped
salt	salt
freshly ground black pepper	freshly ground black pepper
120 ml/4 fl oz double cream	½ cup heavy cream
2 egg yolks	2 egg yolks

Melt the butter in a heavy frying pan (skillet), then add
the eel and shallots (scallions). Cook gently for about
5 minutes until the eel is lightly coloured on all sides.

Remove the pan from the heat and drain off the
butter and cooking juices. Return the pan to the heat,
add the wine, bay leaf and thyme, then cover and cook
gently for 5 minutes.

Discard the bay leaf and thyme, then add the sorrel,
spinach, herbs, and salt and pepper to taste. Cover
again and cook gently for a further 5 minutes, or until
the eel is tender.

Mix together the cream and egg yolks, then pour
into the pan off the heat. Stir gently with a wooden
spoon to mix the cream with the cooking juices and
coat the pieces of fish.

Taste and adjust the seasoning of the sauce, then
transfer the pieces of fish to a warmed serving platter.
Pour the sauce over the fish. Serve immediately.
SERVES 4 TO 6

ROUGETS À LA BONIFACIENNE

Corsican Red Mullet

The red mullet should be left whole for this dish. Simply remove the scales and rinse thoroughly.

Metric/Imperial	American
6 canned anchovy fillets, drained and desalted★	6 canned anchovy fillets, drained and desalted★
3 garlic cloves, peeled and crushed	3 garlic cloves, peeled and crushed
1 tablespoon chopped parsley	1 tablespoon chopped parsley
3 tablespoons tomato purée	3 tablespoons tomato paste
2 tablespoons oil	2 tablespoons oil
freshly ground black pepper	freshly ground black pepper
6 red mullet (about 175 g/ 6 oz each)	6 red mullet (about 6 oz each)
2 tablespoons dried breadcrumbs	2 tablespoons dry bread crumbs

Pound the anchovies to a paste using a mortar and pestle. Add the garlic, parsley, tomato purée (paste), oil, and pepper to taste. Stir well to mix.

Spread this mixture in the bottom of a buttered baking dish and place the fish on top. Sprinkle the fish with the breadcrumbs, then cover the dish with foil. Bake in a preheated moderately hot oven (200°C/ 400°F/Gas Mark 6) for 20 minutes. Serve hot.

SERVES 3 TO 6

TURBOT POCHÉ SAUCE HOLLANDAISE

Poached Turbot with Hollandaise Sauce

If you do not have a fish kettle or a large enough casserole to cook the turbot whole, cut into thick slices and poach for 15 to 20 minutes only.

Metric/Imperial	American
1 × 2 kg/4 lb turbot, cleaned and split open	1 × 4 lb turbot, cleaned and split open
1 lemon, thinly sliced	1 lemon, thinly sliced
300 ml/½ pint milk	1¼ cups milk
salt	salt
20 g/¾ oz butter, melted	1½ tablespoons butter, melted
HOLLANDAISE SAUCE:	HOLLANDAISE SAUCE:
300 g/11 oz butter	1⅓ cups butter
2 tablespoons white wine vinegar	2 tablespoons white wine vinegar
5 tablespoons water	5 tablespoons water
freshly ground white pepper	freshly ground white pepper
5 egg yolks	5 egg yolks
salt	salt
juice of ½ lemon	juice of ½ lemon
GARNISH:	GARNISH:
1 small bunch parsley, finely chopped	1 small bunch parsley, finely chopped
4 lemons, halved and vandyked★	4 lemons, halved and vandyked★

Place the turbot in a fish kettle or large flameproof casserole with the sliced lemon and milk. Add salt to taste, then pour in enough water to just cover the fish. Bring to the boil, then lower the heat and simmer gently for about 25 minutes until tender.

Meanwhile, make the hollandaise sauce (see page 45).

Drain the turbot and place on a napkin on a serving platter, dark skin uppermost. Remove the dark skin. Brush the melted butter over the fish, then garnish with the parsley and vandyked lemons.

Serve immediately, with the hollandaise sauce handed separately in a sauceboat.

SERVES 8

SARDINES FARCIES AU VERT

Sardines Stuffed with Spinach

Although cottage cheese is specified in this recipe, the correct cheese to use is fromage de brousse, a sheep's milk cheese unique to the Vésubie region and unavailable outside France. The Italian ricotta cheese and cottage cheese are the best substitutes.

Metric/Imperial	American
750 g/1½ lb fresh spinach, chopped	1½ lb fresh spinach, chopped
salt	salt
3 tablespoons oil	3 tablespoons oil
1 onion, peeled and finely chopped	1 onion, peeled and finely chopped
1 garlic clove, peeled and crushed	1 garlic clove, peeled and crushed
1 tablespoon plain flour	1 tablespoon all-purpose flour
6 tablespoons milk	6 tablespoons milk
25 g/1 oz ricotta or sieved cottage cheese	2 tablespoons ricotta or sieved cottage cheese
pinch of freshly grated nutmeg	pinch of freshly grated nutmeg
freshly ground black pepper	freshly ground black pepper
18 fresh sardines, split, cleaned and backbone removed	18 fresh sardines, split, cleaned and backbone removed
2 tablespoons dried breadcrumbs	2 tablespoons dry bread crumbs

Cook the spinach in a pan of boiling salted water for 5 minutes, then drain thoroughly.

Heat 2 tablespoons oil in a heavy pan, add the onion and garlic and fry gently for a few minutes. Add the spinach, then sprinkle in the flour and stir well to mix. Stir in the milk, then the cheese, nutmeg, and salt and pepper to taste. Cook gently for 15 minutes, stirring frequently.

Fill each sardine cavity with 1 tablespoon of the spinach mixture, closing the fish firmly around it. Place the remaining spinach in the bottom of a baking dish and arrange the stuffed sardines in a single layer on top. Sprinkle with the breadcrumbs and remaining oil.

Bake in a preheated moderately hot oven (200°C/ 400°F/Gas Mark 6) for 15 minutes. Serve hot, straight from the baking dish.

SERVES 6

Outside the Mediterranean, the sardine is best known in its canned form, but fresh sardines, which take their name from the Italian island of Sardinia, are a sorely neglected fish. Best eaten while still small and young, they are much loved by the French as an *hors d'oeuvre* or appetizer served simply grilled (broiled) or fried, with a sprinkling of lemon juice and freshly ground black pepper.

MERLAN À LA L'ORIENTAISE

Whiting with Wine and Mustard Sauce

Metric/Imperial	American
1 bunch parsley	1 bunch parsley
75 g/3 oz butter	⅓ cup butter
4 shallots, peeled and finely chopped	4 scallions, peeled and finely chopped
salt	salt
freshly ground black pepper	freshly ground black pepper
750 g/1½ lb whiting fillets	1½ lb whiting fillets
1 tablespoon prepared hot mustard	1 tablespoon prepared hot mustard
7 tablespoons dry white wine (e.g. Muscadet)	7 tablespoons dry white wine (e.g. Muscadet)
2 tablespoons double cream	2 tablespoons heavy cream
juice of 1 lemon	juice of 1 lemon

Remove the stalks from the parsley and chop the leaves finely.

Melt 25 g/1 oz/2 tablespoons butter in a flameproof casserole, then add the shallots (scallions), parsley, and salt and pepper to taste. Place the whiting on top and sprinkle with more salt and pepper.

Mix the mustard and wine together, pour over the whiting and dot with 25 g/1 oz/2 tablespoons butter. Cover with greaseproof (waxed) paper, then bake in a preheated moderately hot oven (200°C/400°F/Gas Mark 6) for 10 minutes or until the fish is tender.

Transfer the fish to a warmed serving platter and keep hot. Boil the cooking juices on top of the stove until reduced to about 3 tablespoons, then stir in the remaining butter, the cream and lemon juice. Taste and adjust seasoning.

Pour the sauce over the fish, then place under a preheated hot grill (broiler) for 5 minutes. Serve immediately.
SERVES 4

Sardines farcies au vert;
Rougets à la bonifacienne

SAUMON DE L'AVEN

Salmon Brittany Style

The salmon steaks look most attractive if grilled (broiled) on a hot metal grid or barbecue. Turn them a quarter-turn every 3 minutes, then the bars of the grid will leave scorch marks on the surface of the fish.

Metric/Imperial	American
4 Dublin Bay prawns, uncooked	4 Pacific prawns, uncooked
3 tablespoons oil	3 tablespoons oil
1 carrot, peeled and finely chopped	1 carrot, peeled and finely chopped
1 onion, peeled and finely chopped	1 onion, peeled and finely chopped
2–3 tablespoons brandy	2–3 tablespoons brandy
300 ml/½ pint dry white wine (e.g. Muscadet)	1¼ cups dry white wine (e.g. Muscadet)
300 ml/½ pint water	1¼ cups water
1 bouquet garni★	1 bouquet garni★
1 garlic clove, peeled and crushed	1 garlic clove, peeled and crushed
300 g/11 oz tomatoes, skinned, chopped and seeded	1½ cups skinned, chopped and seeded tomatoes
salt	salt
freshly ground black pepper	freshly ground black pepper
100 g/4 oz butter	½ cup butter
25 g/1 oz plain flour	¼ cup all-purpose flour
4 fresh salmon steaks (about 2.5 cm/1 inch thick)	4 fresh salmon steaks (about 1 inch thick)
pinch of cayenne pepper	pinch of cayenne pepper
25 g/1 oz butter, melted	2 tablespoons butter, melted
few parsley sprigs, to garnish	few parsley sprigs, for garnish

Plunge the prawns into a pan of boiling water and cook for about 8 minutes. Drain and shell them, reserving the shells.

Heat 2 tablespoons oil in a heavy pan, add the carrot and onion and fry gently for 5 minutes. Add the prawn shells and stir vigorously over high heat. Pour in the brandy, flame it, then pour in the wine and water. Add the bouquet garni, garlic, tomatoes, and salt and pepper to taste. Cover and cook for about 1 hour.

Work the mixture through a fine sieve (strainer), pressing firmly to extract as much of the juice as possible.

Melt 25 g/1 oz/2 tablespoons butter in a heavy flameproof casserole. Sprinkle in the flour and cook for 1 minute, stirring constantly. Stir in the sieved mixture a little at a time, stirring vigorously after each addition. Bring slowly to the boil, stirring constantly, then lower the heat and simmer gently until quite thick.

Brush the salmon on both sides with the remaining oil and sprinkle with salt and pepper. Grill (broil) the steaks under a preheated moderate grill (broiler) or on a barbecue for 7 to 8 minutes on each side, until tender.

Meanwhile, add the cayenne pepper to the sauce, then taste and adjust seasoning. Remove the sauce from the heat and whisk in the remaining butter a little at a time.

When the salmon is cooked, carefully remove the skin around each steak. Place the steaks on a warmed serving platter and keep hot. Reheat the prawns by tossing them in the melted butter in a small pan over moderate heat. Garnish the salmon with the parsley sprigs and prawns. Hand the sauce separately in a sauceboat. Serve immediately.

SERVES 4

RAIE À LA NORMANDE

Skate with Cream Sauce

*aumon de l'Aven; Loup
n fenouil*

*There are two main types of skate, the most common one
being raie batis. The original French for this recipe specifies
raie bouclée or thornback skate, but this is the rarer of the
two outside French waters. Use whatever skate is available
to you, it will make little or no difference to the finished
dish.*

Metric/Imperial	American
1 large onion, peeled and sliced into rings	*1 large onion, peeled and sliced into rings*
2 litres/3½ pints water	*4½ pints/9 cups water*
200 ml/⅓ pint vinegar	*1 cup vinegar*
1 bouquet garni★	*1 bouquet garni★*
1 whole clove	*1 whole clove*
salt	*salt*
freshly ground black pepper	*freshly ground black pepper*
1 kg/2 lb skate	*2 lb skate*
150 ml/¼ pint double cream	*⅔ cup heavy cream*
1 tablespoon drained capers	*1 tablespoon drained capers*
1 tablespoon chopped parsley	*1 tablespoon chopped parsley*
1 tablespoon cider vinegar	*1 tablespoon cider vinegar*

Put the onion in a fish kettle or large pan with the water, vinegar, bouquet garni, clove, and salt and pepper to taste. Boil steadily for 30 minutes, then leave the *court-bouillon* to cool.

Cut the skate into serving portions, then place in the cold *court-bouillon*. Bring slowly to the boil and simmer gently for 15 to 20 minutes. Remove the skate with a slotted spoon and drain thoroughly. Remove the skin, then place the pieces of skate on a warmed serving platter and keep hot.

Heat the cream gently in a heavy pan, then add the capers, parsley, and salt and pepper to taste. Pour this sauce over the skate, then sprinkle the cider vinegar over the top. Serve immediately.

SERVES 4

LOUP EN FENOUIL

Charcoal-Grilled (–Broiled) Bass with Fennel

*A summer fish dish which must be cooked outside over
charcoal for an authentic flavour.*

Metric/Imperial	American
1 × 1 kg/2 lb sea bass, cleaned	*1 × 2 lb sea bass, cleaned*
4 tablespoons olive oil	*¼ cup olive oil*
salt	*salt*
freshly ground black pepper	*freshly ground black pepper*
few dried fennel stalks	*few dried fennel stalks*
SAUCE:	SAUCE:
2 egg yolks	*2 egg yolks*
1 teaspoon prepared French mustard	*1 teaspoon prepared French mustard*
300 ml/½ pint oil	*1¼ cups oil*
2 tablespoons vinegar	*2 tablespoons vinegar*
2 gherkins, well drained and finely chopped	*2 small sweet dill pickles, well drained and finely chopped*
1 tablespoon drained capers, finely chopped	*1 tablespoon drained capers, finely chopped*
1 tablespoon chopped parsley	*1 tablespoon chopped parsley*
1 tablespoon snipped chives	*1 tablespoon snipped chives*

Sprinkle the fish with the olive oil and salt and pepper to taste, then wrap in the fennel. Place on a grid over charcoal or under a preheated moderate grill (broiler) and cook for 25 to 30 minutes, turning the fish over carefully halfway through cooking.

Meanwhile, make the sauce: put the egg yolks in a bowl with the mustard and salt and pepper to taste and mix well. Add the oil a drop at a time, as when making mayonnaise, then pour in a steady stream once the sauce begins to emulsify, whisking vigorously all the time.

When the sauce is thick, whisk in the vinegar until thoroughly incorporated, then stir in the gherkins (dill pickles), capers, herbs, and salt and pepper to taste.

Arrange the cooked fish on a warmed serving platter. Serve immediately, removing the fennel as the fish is cut into serving pieces. Hand the sauce separately in a sauceboat.

SERVES 4

TRUITES AU RIESLING

Trout with Riesling

Use a dry Riesling for this recipe, preferably from the Alsace region of northern France.

Metric/Imperial	American
75 g/3 oz butter	⅓ cup butter
150 g/5 oz mushrooms, finely chopped	1½ cups finely chopped mushrooms
salt	salt
freshly ground black pepper	freshly ground black pepper
4 trout, gutted and cleaned through the gills	4 trout, gutted and cleaned through the gills
4 shallots, peeled and finely chopped	4 scallions, peeled and finely chopped
½ bottle (about 350 ml/ 12 fl oz) Riesling	½ bottle (about 1½ cups) Riesling
120 ml/4 fl oz double cream	½ cup heavy cream

Mix 25 g/1 oz/2 tablespoons butter in a pan and add two thirds of the mushrooms and salt and pepper to taste. Stuff the trout with this mixture.

Sprinkle the shallots (scallions) and remaining mushrooms in the bottom of a well-buttered baking dish. Place the trout on top and pour over the wine. Sprinkle with salt and pepper to taste.

Cover the dish with greaseproof (waxed) paper and bake in a preheated moderately hot oven (200°C/400°F/Gas Mark 6) for 20 minutes. Remove the trout from the dish, then carefully remove the skin. Arrange the trout on a warmed serving platter and keep hot.

Strain the cooking juices from the trout into a small heavy pan. Boil rapidly until reduced by two thirds, then stir in the cream. Heat gently for 2 to 3 minutes, stirring constantly, then remove from the heat and whisk in the remaining butter a little at a time. Taste and adjust seasoning. Pour the sauce over the fish and serve immediately.

SERVES 4

In France, river trout are always cooked and served simply. To smother a trout in a rich complex sauce detracts from the delicate flavour of the fish.

Truite aux amandes is one of the simplest and best-loved ways of serving trout in France. But the most famous of all French trout dishes is undoubtedly *truite au bleu*, for which the fish is plunged into a vinegar *court-bouillon* straight after killing, then served with melted butter or Hollandaise sauce and parsley.

ALSACE-LORRAINE

MATELOTE À L'ALSACIENNE
Alsatian Fish Stew

This fish stew is traditionally garnished with croûtons and eaten with freshly cooked noodles, although neither of these is necessary as the dish is substantial enough to be served on its own.

Metric/Imperial	American
carrots, peeled and chopped	3 carrots, peeled and chopped
leeks, chopped	3 leeks, chopped
onions, peeled and chopped	2 onions, peeled and chopped
litres/3½ pints water	4½ pints/9 cups water
thyme sprig	1 thyme sprig
bay leaf	1 bay leaf
few parsley stalks	few parsley stalks
pinch of freshly grated nutmeg	pinch of freshly grated nutmeg
salt	salt
freshly ground black pepper	freshly ground black pepper
600 ml/1 pint dry white wine	2½ cups dry white wine
kg/4 lb freshwater fish (e.g. eel, tench, perch, etc.), cleaned and cut into serving pieces	4 lb freshwater fish (e.g. eel, tench, perch, etc.), cleaned and cut into serving pieces
150 g/5 oz butter	⅔ cup butter
0 g/2 oz plain flour	½ cup all-purpose flour
00 ml/⅓ pint double cream	1 cup heavy cream
egg yolks	3 egg yolks

Put the carrots, leeks and onions in a large pan with the water, thyme, bay leaf, parsley, nutmeg, and salt and pepper to taste. Bring to the boil, then lower the heat and simmer for 1 hour.

Strain the liquid into a clean pan, add the wine and bring to the boil again. Lower the heat, add the fish and simmer gently for about 15 minutes or until the fish flakes when tested with a fork.

Remove the fish from the pan with a slotted spoon and keep hot in a warmed serving bowl. Boil the cooking liquid rapidly until reduced to about 1.2 litres/2 pints/5 cups, then strain.

Melt 75 g/3 oz/⅓ cup butter in a separate pan, sprinkle in the flour and cook, stirring constantly, for 1 minute to obtain a smooth *roux*. Add the strained liquid a little at a time, stirring vigorously after each addition. Bring slowly to the boil, stirring constantly, then lower the heat and simmer until thick, stirring frequently. Mix the cream and egg yolks together in a bowl, then stir in a little of the hot sauce. Stir this mixture back into the pan and heat gently without boiling, stirring constantly.

Remove the pan from the heat and whisk in the remaining butter a little at a time. Taste and adjust seasoning. Pour the sauce over the fish and serve immediately.

SERVES 6 TO 8

VARIATION: Sautéed small pickling (baby) onions, diced bacon and mushrooms can be added if liked.

CHAMPAGNE

TRUITES AUX AMANDES
Trout with Almonds

Metric/Imperial	American
4 trout (about 225 g/8 oz each), cleaned, with heads and tails left on	4 trout (about ½ lb each), cleaned, with heads and tails left on
200 ml/⅓ pint milk	1 cup milk
1 tablespoon plain flour	1 tablespoon all-purpose flour
1 tablespoon oil	1 tablespoon oil
150 g/5 oz butter	⅔ cup butter
salt	salt
freshly ground black pepper	freshly ground black pepper
100 g/4 oz blanched almonds	1 cup blanched almonds
lemon quarters, to garnish (optional)	lemon quarters, for garnish (optional)

Dip the trout in the milk, then coat in the flour. Shake to remove excess flour. Heat the oil and 100 g/4 oz/½ cup butter in a heavy frying pan (skillet). Add the trout and cook gently for 5 minutes on each side, taking care that the butter does not burn.

Remove the trout from the pan and place on a warmed serving platter. Sprinkle with salt and pepper to taste. Keep hot.

Melt the remaining butter in the rinsed-out pan. Add the almonds and cook over moderate heat for about 2 minutes, stirring constantly, until golden on all sides. Sprinkle the almonds and butter over the trout and garnish with lemon quarters, if liked. Serve immediately.

SERVES 4

ABOVE: **Truites aux amandes**
LEFT: **Matelote à l'alsacienne; Truites au Riesling**

Fish & Shellfish/91

BOUILLABAISSE

Fish Stew from Marseille

Bouillabaisse is served in different ways along the coast of Provence: sometimes the fish and broth are served separately, sometimes together in the same tureen, as in this recipe. Guests should place a few slices of hot toast in individual soup plates, pour over enough broth to moisten generously, then help themselves to a few pieces of fish of their choice.

Metric/Imperial	American
200 ml/⅓ pint olive oil	1 cup olive oil
2 onions, peeled and thinly sliced	2 onions, peeled and thinly sliced
2 leeks (white part only), sliced into thin rings	2 leeks (white part only), sliced into thin rings
3 tomatoes, skinned, crushed and seeded	3 tomatoes, skinned, crushed and seeded
4 garlic cloves, peeled and crushed	4 garlic cloves, peeled and crushed
1 fennel sprig	1 fennel sprig
1 thyme sprig	1 thyme sprig
1 bay leaf	1 bay leaf
1 sliver fresh or dried orange peel	1 sliver fresh or dried orange peel
750 g/1½ lb small shellfish (e.g. crabs, cigales)	1½ lb small shellfish (e.g. crabs, cigales)
2 litres/3½ pints boiling water	4 pints boiling water
salt	salt
freshly ground black pepper	freshly ground black pepper
2.5 kg/5 lb fish (e.g. rascasse, John Dory, weaver, angler fish, whiting, sea bass, wrasse, etc.), cleaned and cut into serving pieces	5 lb fish (e.g. rascasse, John Dory, weaver, angler fish, whiting, sea bass, wrasse, etc.), cleaned and cut into serving pieces
4 pinches of saffron powder	4 pinches of saffron powder
24 small slices hot toast, to serve	24 small slices hot toast, to serve
ROUILLE:	ROUILLE:
2 small red peppers, cored, seeded and chopped	2 small red peppers, cored, seeded and chopped
2 garlic cloves, peeled and chopped	2 garlic cloves, peeled and chopped
pinch of saffron powder	pinch of saffron powder
50 g/2 oz crustless white bread	2 slices crustless white bread
250 ml/8 fl oz olive oil	1 cup olive oil

Heat the oil in a large pan, add the onions, leeks, tomatoes and garlic, then the fennel, thyme, bay leaf and orange peel. Stir well and cook gently for about 10 minutes.

Add the shellfish, boiling water, and salt and pepper to taste. Boil for 3 minutes to allow the oil and water to amalgamate.

Add those fish that take longest to cook first (e.g. *rascasse*, angler fish) and those with shorter cooking times (e.g. John Dory, sea bass) 5 minutes later. Cook by boiling rapidly over high heat for 12 to 15 minutes.

Meanwhile, make the *rouille*: crush the peppers and garlic to a paste using a mortar and pestle. Add the saffron and salt and pepper to taste. Moisten the bread with a little of the cooking liquid from the *bouillabaisse*, then work into the peppers and garlic until thoroughly incorporated. Add the oil a little at a time, as when making mayonnaise, then pour it in a thin steady stream as the *rouille* becomes thick.

When all the fish are cooked, taste and adjust the seasoning of the *bouillabaisse*, then stir in the saffron. Pour into a warmed soup tureen and serve immediately with the slices of hot toast. Hand the *rouille* separately in a sauceboat.

SERVES 6 TO 8

FILETS DE MAQUEREAU À LA FÉCAMPOISE

Mackerel Fillets with Mussels in Cider Sauce

Metric/Imperial	American
2 shallots, peeled and finely chopped	2 scallions, peeled and finely chopped
4 mackerel, filleted	4 mackerel, filleted
salt	salt
freshly ground black pepper	freshly ground black pepper
about 400 ml/14 fl oz dry cider	about 1¾ cups hard cider
1.2 litres/2 pints fresh mussels	5 cups fresh mussels
50 g/2 oz butter	¼ cup butter
25 g/1 oz plain flour	¼ cup all-purpose flour
1 tablespoon lemon juice	1 tablespoon lemon juice
1 tablespoon chopped parsley, to garnish	1 tablespoon chopped parsley, for garnish

Spread the shallots (scallions) in the bottom of a well-buttered baking dish. Place the mackerel fillets on top and sprinkle with salt and pepper to taste. Pour over half the cider. Cover the dish with greaseproof (waxed) paper and bake in a preheated moderately hot oven (200°C/400°F/Gas Mark 6) for 10 to 15 minutes.

Meanwhile, scrub the mussels and discard any that are open. Put them in a pan with the remaining cider and cook over high heat until the shells open. Discard any that do not open. Remove the mussels from their shells, strain the cooking juices and reserve.

Remove the mackerel from the dish, reserving the cooking liquid, and drain thoroughly. Arrange on a warmed serving platter with the mussels and keep hot. Strain the cooking juices.

Melt half the butter in a heavy pan, sprinkle in the flour and cook, stirring constantly, for 1 minute to obtain a smooth *roux*. Add the strained juices from the mussels and mackerel a little at a time, stirring after each addition. Bring slowly to the boil, stirring constantly, then simmer until thick, stirring frequently. Stir in the lemon juice, then remove from the heat and whisk in the remaining butter a little at a time. Taste and adjust seasoning.

Pour the sauce over the mackerel and mussels and sprinkle with parsley. Serve immediately.

SERVES 4

It is impossible to make a truly authentic *bouillabaisse* outside the Mediterranean waters around Marseille, for the fish used there are virtually unknown outside local waters.

In making a *bouillabaisse*, many different kinds of fish are used. *Rascasse*, unique to this part of the Mediterranean, is considered essential, but failing this some other white fish with firm flesh can be used. John Dory, angler fish (monkfish) and weaver all make acceptable substitutes.

In contrast, small delicate fish must also be included, such as *wrasse* and whiting, and a shellfish or two completes the selection. In the Mediterranean, *petites cigales* (tiny lobster-like creatures) are added, but small pieces of lobster (*langouste*) may be used, and even mussels, since these are widely available.

Apart from the choice of fish for *bouillabaisse*, there are other necessary ingredients. Olive oil and boiling water should form the essential part of the broth. Onions, garlic and tomatoes are used for flavouring; colour is provided by saffron.

COTRIADE

Fish and Potato Stew with Vinaigrette

The custom with this kind of fish stew is to serve the fish and potatoes on their own as a first course with a vinaigrette dressing, then to follow with the cooking liquid served as a soup in a tureen. Slices of crusty bread, sometimes fried in butter, are placed in the bottom of the tureen and the liquid is poured on top.

Metric/Imperial	American
100 g/4 oz slightly salted butter	*½ cup semisweet butter*
4 onions, peeled and very thinly sliced	*4 onions, peeled and very thinly sliced*
2 leeks (white part only), sliced into very thin rings	*2 leeks (white part only), sliced into very thin rings*
2 litres/3½ pints water	*4 pints water*
2 kg/4 lb fish (e.g. conger eel, wrasse, bream, angler fish, whiting, sardines, etc.), cleaned and cut into serving pieces, heads reserved	*4 lb fish (e.g. conger eel, wrasse, bream, angler fish, whiting, sardines, etc), cleaned and cut into serving pieces, heads reserved*
salt	*salt*
freshly ground black pepper	*freshly ground black pepper*
1 kg/2 lb small new potatoes, scrubbed	*2 lb small new potatoes, scrubbed*
VINAIGRETTE:	VINAIGRETTE:
2 shallots, peeled and finely chopped	*2 scallions, peeled and finely chopped*
3 tablespoons cider vinegar	*3 tablespoons cider vinegar*
150 ml/¼ pint oil	*⅔ cup oil*
1 tablespoon finely chopped parsley	*1 tablespoon finely chopped parsley*

Melt the butter in a large pan, add the onions and leeks and cook very gently for 10 minutes until soft but not coloured.

Add the water, fish heads and a little salt and pepper. Increase the heat and boil rapidly for about 20 minutes. Add the potatoes and bring back to the boil.

Add those fish that take longest to cook first and those with shorter cooking times (e.g. whiting) 5 minutes later. Boil rapidly for 15 minutes or until the fish is tender.

Meanwhile, make the *vinaigrette*: put the shallots (scallions) in a bowl with the vinegar and salt and pepper to taste. Add the oil in a thin steady stream, whisking vigorously with a fork until thick. Whisk in the parsley, then taste and adjust seasoning.

When all the fish are cooked, remove the pieces carefully from the liquid with the potatoes, using a slotted spoon. Place both the fish and potatoes in a warmed serving bowl. Strain the cooking liquid and sprinkle a little over the fish and potatoes. Serve immediately, with the vinaigrette dressing handed separately.

Return the remaining cooking liquid to the rinsed-out pan and reheat. Taste and adjust seasoning. Serve piping hot, after the fish and potatoes.
SERVES 6

Bourride provençale

BRANDADE DE MORUE

Creamed Salt Cod

Metric/Imperial	American
600 g/1¼ lb salt cod	*1¼ lb salt cod*
2 garlic cloves, peeled and crushed	*2 garlic cloves, peeled and crushed*
about 150 ml/¼ pint olive oil	*about ⅔ cup olive oil*
about 150 ml/¼ pint warm milk	*about ⅔ cup warm milk*
salt	*salt*
freshly ground black pepper	*freshly ground black peppe*[r]
fried croûtons, to serve	*fried croûtons, to serve*

Soak the salt cod in cold water for at least 12 hours (24 [if] possible), to remove excess salt.

The next day, drain the fish and rinse thorough[ly] under cold running water. Remove any skin an[d] bones, then flake the flesh and place in a heavy pan wi[th] the garlic. Cook very gently, pounding and crushi[ng] the mixture with a wooden spoon or pestle.

Add the oil a drop at a time, as when maki[ng] mayonnaise, gradually increasing the oil to a stead[y] stream until about 7 tablespoons is incorporated.

Add about 7 tablespoons of warm milk in exact[ly] the same way as the oil, until the paste will absorb n[o] more, then add oil and milk alternately until the paste [is] really thick, like double (heavy) cream. Stir in salt an[d] pepper to taste. Serve hot, with fried *croûtons*.
SERVES 4

BOURRIDE PROVENÇALE

Fish Soup with Aïoli

Brandade de morue is one of the less well known fish dishes outside France and, to unaccustomed palates, can taste unusually strong. It is much loved by the French, however, who traditionally eat it on Fridays, either as a light lunch or as a first course at dinner with toast or croûtons to dip into it.

If you are unfamiliar with making brandade, it may take a while to get the right consistency. It is impossible to give the exact quantities for the oil and milk to be added to the salt cod, they are simply added until the brandade has the right texture and 'feel' about it — this comes with practise and a great deal of pounding and crushing.

If you find using a pestle and mortar too time-consuming and laborious, an electric mixer, blender or food processor may be used instead.

Metric/Imperial	American
2 tablespoons olive oil	2 tablespoons olive oil
2 leeks (white part only), thinly sliced	2 leeks (white part only), thinly sliced
2 onions, peeled and thinly sliced	2 onions, peeled and thinly sliced
1 carrot, peeled and thinly sliced	1 carrot, peeled and thinly sliced
1 celery stick, thinly sliced	1 celery stalk, thinly sliced
2 kg/4 lb fish (e.g. whiting, angler fish, turbot, eel, John Dory, etc.), cleaned and cut into serving pieces, heads reserved	4 lb fish (e.g. whiting, angler fish, turbot, eel, John Dory, etc.), cleaned and cut into serving pieces, heads reserved
1 litre/1¾ pints water	4¼ cups water
750 ml/1¼ pints dry white wine	3 cups dry white wine
1 bay leaf	1 bay leaf
1 fennel sprig	1 fennel sprig
1 sliver fresh or dried orange peel	1 sliver fresh or dried orange peel
salt	salt
6 slices hot toast, to serve	6 slices hot toast, to serve
AÏOLI:	AÏOLI:
10 garlic cloves, peeled	10 garlic cloves, peeled
6 egg yolks	6 egg yolks
400 ml/14 fl oz olive oil	1¾ cups olive oil

Heat the oil in a large pan, add the vegetables and fish heads and cook gently for 5 minutes.

Add the water, wine, bay leaf, fennel and orange peel, and salt to taste. Bring to the boil, then lower the heat and simmer uncovered for 20 minutes.

Meanwhile, make the aïoli: crush the garlic and 4 pinches of salt to a paste using a mortar and pestle. Add 2 egg yolks and mix well.

Add the oil a little at a time, as when making mayonnaise, then pour it in a thin steady stream as the aïoli becomes thick. Divide the aïoli in half and whisk the remaining egg yolks into one half.

Strain the fish and vegetable mixture through a fine sieve (strainer), pressing firmly to extract as much of the juice as possible. Return to the rinsed-out pan and reheat gently.

Add the fish to the stock, putting in those that take longest to cook first (e.g. angler fish, turbot, eel), and those with shorter cooking times (e.g. whiting, John Dory) after about 5 minutes. Cook over moderate heat for 15 to 20 minutes until all the fish are tender.

Remove the fish from the stock with a slotted spoon and arrange on a warmed serving platter. Keep hot.

Strain the stock again through a fine sieve (strainer) and return to the rinsed-out pan. Reheat gently, then stir 1 tablespoon into the aïoli and egg yolk mixture. Whisk this mixture back into the stock and reheat gently, whisking vigorously all the time. Do not allow the stock to boil or it will separate. Taste and adjust seasoning, then pour into a warmed soup tureen.

Serve the soup hot as a first course, followed by the fish. Hand the remaining aïoli separately.

SERVES 6

HOMARD À L'AMÉRICAINE

Lobster à l'Américaine

It is traditional, although not essential, to cook and serve this very special dish in a copper pan. To add extra flavour to the sauce, use homemade fish stock instead of water.

Metric/Imperial	American
450 g/1 lb ripe tomatoes, skinned, chopped and seeded	1 lb ripe tomatoes, skinned, chopped and seeded
salt	salt
1 live lobster (about 750 g/ 1¾ lb)	1 live lobster (about 1¾ lb in weight)
100 g/4 oz butter	½ cup butter
1 tablespoon oil	1 tablespoon oil
freshly ground black pepper	freshly ground black pepper
8 shallots, peeled and finely chopped	8 scallions, peeled and finely chopped
1 carrot, peeled and cut into julienne★	1 carrot, peeled and cut into julienne★
1 turnip, peeled and cut into julienne★	1 turnip, peeled and cut into julienne★
1 celery stick, cut into julienne★	1 celery stalk, cut into julienne★
3 garlic cloves, peeled and crushed	3 garlic cloves, peeled and crushed
3 tablespoons champagne or dry white wine	3 tablespoons champagne or dry white wine
1 bouquet garni★	1 bouquet garni★
300 ml/½ pint dry white wine	1¼ cups dry white wine
120 ml/4 fl oz water	½ cup water
2 pinches of cayenne pepper	2 pinches of cayenne pepper
GARNISH:	GARNISH:
1 tablespoon chopped parsley	1 tablespoon chopped parsley
1 tablespoon chopped tarragon	1 tablespoon chopped tarragon

Put the tomatoes in a sieve (strainer). Sprinkle with salt, stir well, then leave to drain.

Meanwhile, split the lobster down the centre from head to tail. Cut off the head and discard the gritty sac, but reserve the creamy coral and greenish parts and place in a bowl with three quarters of the butter.

Sever the claws from the body of the lobster and crack them open. Slice the body of the lobster into small pieces, following the marks on the shell. Pour all the liquid that runs from the lobster into the bowl containing the coral and butter.

Heat the oil and remaining butter in a deep frying pan (skillet). Add the lobster pieces and cook for 3 to 4 minutes until they turn red, stirring constantly.

Add salt and pepper to taste, then the vegetables and garlic, and cook gently for 3 to 4 more minutes, stirring all the time. Pour in the champagne or wine and cook until it has completely evaporated, then remove the lobster pieces with a slotted spoon and reserve.

Add the bouquet garni to the pan with the wine and water. Boil rapidly until reduced by two thirds, then add the drained tomatoes and boil again until reduced by half, stirring constantly and vigorously. Sprinkle with the cayenne, then return the lobster pieces to the pan. Lower the heat and cook gently for 5 minutes.

Put the coral and butter mixture in a heavy pan and cook over low heat until the butter has melted. Whisk vigorously all the time until the mixture becomes creamy.

Remove the bouquet garni from the frying pan (skillet), then gradually stir in the creamy mixture, being careful not to allow the liquid to boil. Remove from the heat, taste and adjust seasoning, then sprinkle with the herbs. Serve immediately, straight from the pan.

SERVES 2

Homard à l'américaine; Crabe farci

CRABE FARÇI

Stuffed Crab

If you prefer not to deal with a live crab, buy a dressed crab from the fishmonger – the recipe can be followed in exactly the same way.

Metric/Imperial	American
1 large live crab (about 1 kg/2 lb)	1 large live crab (about 2 lb)
2 tablespoons vinegar	2 tablespoons vinegar
1 bouquet garni★	1 bouquet garni★
salt	salt
60 g/2½ oz butter	5 tablespoons butter
2 shallots, peeled and finely chopped	2 scallions, peeled and finely chopped
1 onion, peeled and finely chopped	1 onion, peeled and finely chopped
1 tablespoon chopped parsley	1 tablespoon chopped parsley
2 garlic cloves, peeled and crushed	2 garlic cloves, peeled and crushed
100 g/4 oz fresh white breadcrumbs	2 cups soft white bread crumbs
freshly ground black pepper	freshly ground black pepper
120 ml/4 fl oz dry white wine	½ cup dry white wine
2–3 tablespoons calvados	2–3 tablespoons calvados

Scrub the crab shell thoroughly with a stiff brush under cold running water, then plunge into a pan of boiling water to which the vinegar, bouquet garni and a pinch of salt have been added. Bring back to the boil and boil for 20 minutes.

Drain the crab and leave to cool. Twist off the legs and claws, crack them open with nutcrackers and extract the meat with pincers or a skewer.

Pull the body of the crab away from its shell and take out all the meat, discarding the stomach sac, the pale grey fronds or 'dead men's fingers', and any greenish matter. Scoop out the dark meat from the shell with a sharp teaspoon. Flake all the extracted crabmeat and remove any cartilage. Scrub inside the shell thoroughly and reserve.

Melt 40 g/1½ oz/3 tablespoons butter in a heavy pan, add the shallots (scallions) and onion and fry gently until soft but not coloured. Add the crabmeat, parsley, garlic, 75 g/3 oz/1½ cups breadcrumbs and salt and pepper to taste. Sprinkle with the wine, then cook gently for 10 minutes.

Add the calvados, ignite it, then stuff the mixture inside the cleaned crab shell. Sprinkle with the remaining breadcrumbs and dot with the remaining butter.

Bake in a preheated hot oven (220°C/425°F/Gas Mark 7) for 10 minutes. Serve hot, straight from the shell.
SERVES 2

QUEUES DE LANGOUSTINES GRATINÉES

Dublin Bay (Pacific) Prawns au Gratin

Metric/Imperial	American
24 Dublin Bay prawns	24 Pacific prawns
1 bouquet garni★	1 bouquet garni★
salt	salt
freshly ground black pepper	freshly ground black pepper
150 ml/¼ pint Sauce mornay (page 44)	⅔ cup Sauce mornay (page 44)
4–5 tablespoons dry white wine	4–5 tablespoons dry white wine
225 g/8 oz mushrooms, chopped	2 cups chopped mushrooms
50 g/2 oz Gruyère cheese★, grated	½ cup grated Gruyère cheese★
25 g/1 oz butter	2 tablespoons butter

Plunge the prawns into a pan of boiling water to which the bouquet garni and a pinch each of salt and pepper have been added. Bring back to the boil and boil for 7 to 8 minutes, then drain the prawns and remove their shells.

Mix the *Sauce mornay* with the wine. Put the prawns in a gratin dish and sprinkle with the mushrooms. Spoon the sauce over the top and sprinkle with the cheese. Dot with the butter and bake in a preheated moderately hot oven (200°C/400°F/Gas Mark 6) for 15 minutes. Serve immediately, from the gratin dish.
SERVES 6

CREVETTES AU CIDRE

Shrimp(s) or Prawns in Cider

Cooking raw shrimp(s) or prawns in cider gives them more flavour. Serve them in their shells and let guests remove the shells themselves. Be sure to provide finger bowls, napkins and a bowl for the discarded shells.

Metric/Imperial	American
750 ml/1¼ pints dry cider	3 cups hard cider
2 litres/3½ pints water	4½ pints/9 cups water
pinch of salt	pinch of salt
1 teaspoon freshly ground black pepper	1 teaspoon freshly ground black pepper
1 kg/2 lb uncooked shrimps or prawns	2 lb uncooked shrimp
thinly sliced brown bread, buttered, to serve	thinly sliced brown bread, buttered, to serve

Pour the cider and water into a large pan, add the salt and pepper and bring to the boil.

Plunge the shrimp(s) or prawns into the water, bring back to the boil and boil for 5 minutes. Drain thoroughly, then arrange on a warmed serving platter. Serve immediately with brown bread and butter.

SERVES 6

MOULES MARINIÈRE

Mussels Marinière

Metric/Imperial	American
4 litres/7 pints fresh mussels	8 pints/16 cups fresh mussels
60 g/2½ oz butter	5 tablespoons butter
6 shallots, peeled and finely chopped	6 scallions, peeled and finely chopped
1 garlic clove, peeled and crushed	1 garlic clove, peeled and crushed
600 ml/1 pint dry white wine (e.g. Muscadet)	2½ cups dry white wine (e.g. Muscadet)
1 bouquet garni★	1 bouquet garni★
freshly ground black pepper	freshly ground black pepper
2 tablespoons chopped parsley	2 tablespoons chopped parsley

Scrub the mussels and discard any that are open.

Melt the butter in a large pan, add the shallots (scallions) and garlic and fry gently until soft but not coloured.

Stir in the wine, then add the bouquet garni and bring to the boil. Boil for 2 minutes, then add pepper to taste and the mussels.

Shake or stir the mussels vigorously over high heat until the shells open, then remove from the pan with a slotted spoon and set aside, discarding any that have not opened.

Boil the liquid rapidly until reduced by half, then return the mussels to the pan and heat through for 1 minute, shaking the pan constantly.

Sprinkle with the parsley, then shake the pan again. Pile the mussels in a warmed deep serving dish, discarding the bouquet garni. Serve immediately.

SERVES 6

ÉCREVISSES À LA CHAMPENOISE

Crayfish in Champagne and Cream Sauce

A recipe to reserve for very special occasions.

Metric/Imperial	American
36 crayfish	36 crayfish
50 g/2 oz butter	¼ cup butter
4 shallots, peeled and finely chopped	4 scallions, peeled and finely chopped
½ bottle champagne	½ bottle champagne
salt	salt
freshly ground black pepper	freshly ground black pepper
300 ml/½ pint double cream	1¼ cups heavy cream
pinch of cayenne pepper	pinch of cayenne pepper
2 teaspoons chopped tarragon, to garnish	2 teaspoons chopped tarragon, for garnish

Gut the crayfish by pulling the middle fin on the tail. Twist sharply to remove black thread, stomach and intestines. Wash the crayfish thoroughly under cold running water.

Melt the butter in a flameproof casserole, add the shallots (scallions) and fry gently for 5 minutes until soft but not coloured. Pour in the champagne, add salt and pepper to taste, then bring to the boil and boil for 4 minutes.

Add the crayfish, cover and cook for 10 minutes, stirring occasionally. Remove the crayfish with a slotted spoon, drain and arrange on a warmed serving platter. Keep hot.

Boil the cooking liquid rapidly until reduced by half. Stir in the cream, then cook until the sauce is thick, stirring constantly. Add the cayenne, taste and adjust seasoning, then pour through a fine sieve (strainer) over the crayfish. Sprinkle with the tarragon and serve immediately.

SERVES 6

MOUCLADE

Mussels with White Wine and Cream Sauce

A more ritzy version of the classic moules marinière.

Metric/Imperial	American
3 litres/5½ pints fresh mussels	6½ pints/13 cups fresh mussels
400 ml/14 fl oz dry white wine (e.g. Muscadet)	1¾ cups dry white wine (e.g. Muscadet)
1 bay leaf	1 bay leaf
1 thyme sprig	1 thyme sprig
3 parsley stalks, bruised	3 parsley stalks, bruised
25 g/1 oz butter	2 tablespoons butter
3 shallots, peeled and finely chopped	3 scallions, peeled and finely chopped
150 ml/¼ pint double cream	⅔ cup heavy cream
pinch of cayenne pepper	pinch of cayenne pepper
3 egg yolks	3 egg yolks
1 teaspoon curry powder	1 teaspoon curry powder

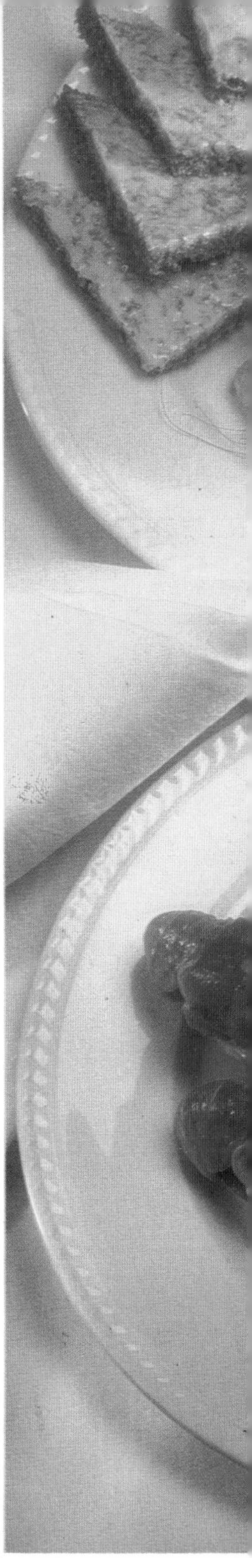

This version of *mouclade* is spiced with cayenne pepper and curry powder which may seem unusual ingredients in French cookery. However, in the days of the slave trade, spices were brought to the French ports on the Atlantic coast. African slaves employed by the wealthy French often used these spices in cooking. Recipes like this one retain the flavour of those times.

rub the mussels and discard any that are open. Bring
e wine to the boil in a large pan with the bay leaf,
yme and parsley. Add the mussels and shake the pan
ver high heat until the shells open. Remove the
ussels from the pan with a slotted spoon, discarding
y that have not opened, and set aside.

Continue boiling the liquid in the pan. Meanwhile,
elt the butter in a separate pan, add the shallots
allions) and fry gently for 1 to 2 minutes. Stir the
ine and mussel liquid slowly into the pan (taking care
ot to add any sediment from the bottom), then boil
pidly until reduced by half.

Pour the reduced liquid through a fine sieve
rainer) into a clean pan. Stir in two thirds of the
eam and the cayenne and bring to the boil. Boil to
duce for 1 minute.

Meanwhile, put the egg yolks in a bowl with the
remaining cream and the curry powder. Whisk with a
fork, then gradually whisk in 2 tablespoons of the hot
liquid. Whisk this mixture slowly back into the pan
over the lowest possible heat and heat through very
gently, stirring constantly. Do not allow the liquid to
boil or it will separate. Taste and adjust seasoning.

Add the mussels to the sauce and heat through for
1 minute, shaking the pan constantly to coat each
mussel in sauce. Divide the mussels and sauce equally
between 4 warmed individual serving bowls. Serve
immediately.
SERVES 4 TO 6

VARIATION: Brandy can be added to the sauce for extra
flavour, also crushed garlic and/or finely chopped
parsley.

**Crevettes au cidre;
Ecrevisses à la
champenoise; Moules
marinière**

CHIPIRONES À L'AMÉRICAINE

Squid in Tomato Sauce

*Chipirones is the word used in the Basque district for squid.
Boiled rice is the usual accompaniment to this dish.*

Squid, otherwise known as inkfish and calamares, belong to the same family as the octopus and cuttlefish. The long thin body of the squid has ten tentacles, two long and eight short, and a sac of black ink which is squirted out whenever the squid is attacked.

When buying squid for cooking, select the smallest possible creatures, no longer than 15 cm/6 inches in length. Squid that are larger than this can be tough and rubbery, even after lengthy cooking. Preliminary blanching in boiling water for 3 minutes will help tenderize tough squid.

Metric/Imperial	American
1 kg/2 lb squid	2 lb squid
5 tablespoons olive oil	5 tablespoons olive oil
4 onions, peeled and chopped	4 onions, peeled and chopped
50 ml/2 fl oz armagnac or brandy	$\frac{1}{4}$ cup armagnac or brandy
3 garlic cloves, peeled and crushed	3 garlic cloves, peeled and crushed
350 g/12 oz ripe tomatoes, skinned and roughly chopped	$1\frac{1}{2}$ cups skinned and chopped ripe tomatoes
300 ml/$\frac{1}{2}$ pint dry white wine	$1\frac{1}{4}$ cups dry white wine
1 bouquet garni★	1 bouquet garni★
$\frac{1}{2}$ teaspoon paprika pepper	$\frac{1}{2}$ teaspoon paprika pepper
pinch of cayenne pepper	pinch of cayenne pepper
salt	salt
freshly ground black pepper	freshly ground black pepper

Cut off the head and tentacles of the squid and disca the intestines, transparent spine bone and ink sacs. Tu the fish inside out and wash thoroughly under co running water. Dry on kitchen paper towels, then sli thinly.

Heat the oil in a frying pan (skillet), add the squ and fry gently for 15 minutes. Remove from the p with a slotted spoon and set aside.

Add the onions to the pan and fry gently until s but not coloured. Add the armagnac and let evaporate, then add the remaining ingredients with s and pepper to taste. Bring to the boil, then lower t heat and simmer for 20 minutes, stirring occasionally

Work the sauce through a fine sieve (strainer), the return to the rinsed-out pan. Add the squid to the sau and simmer gently for 45 minutes or until the squid tender. Taste and adjust seasoning. Serve hot.
SERVES 4

HUÎTRES FARCIES

Stuffed Oysters

Metric/Imperial	American
24 oysters, shelled, with juice and shells reserved	24 oysters, shucked, with juice and shells reserved
100 g/4 oz blanched almonds	1 cup blanched almonds
25 g/1 oz butter, softened	2 tablespoons softened butt
freshly ground black pepper	freshly ground black peppe

ut the oysters and their juice in a pan. Poach very ently for 2 to 3 minutes, without allowing the juice to oil, then remove with a slotted spoon. Replace the ysters in their shells, then place in a flameproof gratin ish. Reserve the juice in the pan.

Pound or crush the almonds, reserving 1 tablespoon whole. Mix the crushed almonds with the butter and epper to taste. Whisk this mixture into the reserved yster juice, then pour over the oysters in the gratin ish.

Sprinkle the oysters with the reserved almonds, then ut under a preheated hot grill (broiler) for 2 to 3 ninutes until golden. Serve immediately.

ERVES 4

ARIATION: A more traditional way of stuffing oysters s to use breadcrumbs, garlic and parsley instead of lmonds. Combine these with the oyster juice, sprinkle ver the poached oysters in their shells and dot with utter. Grill (broil) as above.

NORMANDIE

COQUILLES SAINT-JACQUES AU CIDRE

Scallops with Cider and Cream

Metric/Imperial	American
2 scallops	12 scallops
o g/2½ oz butter	5 tablespoons butter
shallots, peeled and finely chopped	3 scallions, peeled and finely chopped
50 ml/8 fl oz dry cider	1 cup hard cider
alt	salt
reshly ground black pepper	freshly ground black pepper
tablespoons double cream	¼ cup heavy cream

Detach the white scallop meat from the shells and eparate the red coral. Cut away the muscular skin on he outside of the white meat. Wash and drain well. Scrub 4 shells and dry thoroughly.

Melt 25 g/1 oz/2 tablespoons butter in a heavy pan, idd the shallots (scallions) and fry gently for 1 to 2 ninutes, until soft but not coloured. Pour in the cider, oring to the boil, then turn off the heat. Add the callops and coral with salt and pepper to taste, then immer gently for 15 minutes.

Remove the scallops and coral from the liquid with slotted spoon and divide equally between the cleaned shells. Keep hot.

Boil the cooking liquid rapidly until reduced to bout 7 tablespoons. Stir in the cream, then simmer gently for about 10 minutes until the sauce is thick, stirring frequently.

Remove the pan from the heat and add the remaining butter a little at a time, whisking vigorously until dissolved. Taste and adjust seasoning. Pour over the scallops and serve immediately.

SERVES 4

LANDES

COQUILLES SAINT-JACQUES À LA LANDAISE

Scallops with Pine Nuts

Metric/Imperial	American
16 scallops	16 scallops
about 300 ml/½ pint light ale	about 1¼ cups beer
salt	salt
freshly ground black pepper	freshly ground black pepper
50 g/2 oz plain flour	½ cup all-purpose flour
4 tablespoons oil	¼ cup oil
50 g/2 oz pine nuts	½ cup pine nuts
1 tablespoon vinegar	1 tablespoon vinegar
50 g/2 oz butter, softened	¼ cup softened butter
1 tablespoon chopped parsley, to garnish	1 tablespoon chopped parsley, for garnish

Detach the white scallop meat from the shells and separate the red coral. Cut away the muscular skin on the outside of the white meat. Wash and drain well, then place in a bowl and add enough beer to cover. Add salt and pepper to taste, cover and leave to marinate for 15 minutes.

Drain the scallops and coat with the flour, shaking off the excess. Heat the oil in a frying pan (skillet), add the scallops and fry gently until golden. Add the pine nuts, cover and cook gently for 15 minutes.

Stir the vinegar into the pan, then remove the scallops with a slotted spoon and arrange in a warmed serving dish. Keep hot.

Add the butter to the sauce a little at a time off the heat, whisking vigorously until dissolved. Taste and adjust seasoning, then pour over the scallops and sprinkle with the parsley. Serve immediately.

SERVES 4

ABOVE: **Coquilles Saint-Jacques à la landaise**
LEFT: **Chipirones à l'américaine; Huîtres farcies**

Fish & Shellfish/101

POULTRY & GAME

Poultry is cooked and served in all manner of ways in France, from stuffing and roasting a whole bird, poaching it with vegetables and liquid, to grilling, sautéeing, and frying it in butter. From the simple methods of regional cookery to the classic dishes of la haute cuisine, the French have a way with chicken.

Not for the French housewife the deep-frozen chickens and chicken portions that are so popular in other countries; poultry is invariably brought fresh and free-range – and in country districts still with its feathers on and clucking! If chickens from the Bresse region are available then so much the better, for these are the most highly prized for quality, tenderness, succulence and flavour. Local markets throughout France are ideal places to select poussin, chicken, plump capon or freshly killed turkey. Even cockerels and old hens are not scorned in France, for the right amount of long, slow simmering in stock or wine, with herbs and seasonings, or with a succulent stuffing, turn these birds into tasty dishes. For good quality chickens, simple methods – like roasting in butter and tarragon, or sautéeing in butter then serving with a sprinkling of lemon juice and parsley – are just as popular as stuffing and roasting.

Although not so widely available as chicken, duck and geese are immensely popular in France, for their richness of flavour. Ducks from Nantes and Rouen are the most highly prized, and the region of Languedoc is famous for its geese. The whole of south-western France is dedicated to the rearing of geese, not only for their specially fattened livers, (foie gras) but also for their fat and the famous delicacy – confit d'oie or preserved goose (page 29).

Guinea fowl, pigeon, partridge and pheasant are also very popular in France, both domesticated and wild, particularly in country districts where shooting is a common pastime, for the French game laws are not so restrictive as they are in this country. Recipes for game birds and animals are therefore prolific in France, and it is well worth experimenting with them as a welcome change from poultry.

BOURGOGNE

COQ AU VIN

Chicken in Red Wine

Metric/Imperial	American
2 tablespoons oil	2 tablespoons oil
50 g/2 oz butter	¼ cup butter
1 × 2.5 kg/5 lb chicken, cut into 12 serving pieces	1 × 5 lb chicken, cut into 12 serving pieces
24 small pickling onions, peeled	24 baby onions, peeled
100 g/4 oz smoked bacon, rind removed and diced	½ cup diced smoked bacon
1 tablespoon plain flour	1 tablespoon all-purpose flour
1 bottle good red wine (e.g. Burgundy, Champigny or Pomerol)	1 bottle good red wine (e.g. Burgundy, Champigny or Pomerol)
1 bouquet garni★	1 bouquet garni★
2 garlic cloves	2 garlic cloves
pinch of sugar	pinch of sugar
freshly grated nutmeg	freshly grated nutmeg
salt	salt
freshly ground black pepper	freshly ground black pepper
24 button mushrooms	24 button mushrooms
1 tablespoon brandy	1 tablespoon brandy
12 large croûtes★	12 large croûtes★

Coq au vin

Heat the oil and butter in a large flameproof casserole, add the chicken pieces and fry gently until golden on all sides. Remove from the casserole with a slotted spoon and set aside.

Pour off half the fat from the casserole, then add the onions and bacon. Fry over moderate heat until lightly coloured, then sprinkle in the flour and stir well.

Pour in the wine and bring to the boil, then add the bouquet garni, garlic cloves (unpeeled), sugar, and nutmeg, salt and pepper to taste. Return the chicken to the casserole, lower the heat, cover and simmer for 15 minutes.

Add the mushrooms, then continue cooking gently for a further 45 minutes or until the chicken is tender. Remove the chicken with a slotted spoon and arrange on a warmed serving platter. Keep hot.

Pour the brandy into the sauce and boil, uncovered, for 5 minutes until reduced to about 300 ml/½ pint/ 1¼ cups. Remove the bouquet garni and garlic cloves. Taste and adjust seasoning.

Pour the sauce over the chicken, then surround with the *croûtes*. Serve immediately.
SERVES 6 TO 8

POULE AU POT À LA TOULOUSAINE
Stuffed Chicken with Vegetables

Ideally, this chicken casserole should be cooked over the lowest possible heat for the longest possible time – to ensure the flavour of the stock is very rich. Years ago it would be cooked in a cast iron pot over the fire and left overnight. These days it is best cooked gently on top of the stove or in the oven on a very low setting.

Metric/Imperial	American
STUFFING:	STUFFING:
150 g/5 oz fresh breadcrumbs	2½ cups fresh bread crumbs
225 g/8 oz fatty ham, finely chopped	1 cup finely chopped fatty ham
8 garlic cloves, peeled and crushed	8 garlic cloves, peeled and crushed
1 tablespoon chopped parsley	1 tablespoon chopped parsley
freshly grated nutmeg	freshly grated nutmeg
salt	salt
freshly ground black pepper	freshly ground black pepper
liver and gizzard from chicken, finely chopped (optional)	liver and gizzard from chicken, finely chopped (optional)
2 eggs, beaten	2 eggs, beaten
	1 × 4–4½ lb chicken
1 × 2 kg/4–4½ lb chicken	6½ pints/13 cups water
3 litres/5½ pints water	3 carrots, peeled
3 carrots, peeled	2 turnips, peeled
2 turnips, peeled	4 leeks (white part only)
4 leeks (white part only)	2 onions, peeled and stuck with 5 whole cloves
2 onions, peeled and stuck with 5 whole cloves	1 bouquet garni★
1 bouquet garni★	¼ lb vermicelli or 6 slices hot toast, to serve (optional)
100 g/4 oz vermicelli or 6 slices hot toast, to serve (optional)	

Prepare the stuffing: put the breadcrumbs in a bowl with the ham, 2 garlic cloves, parsley and nutmeg, salt and pepper to taste. Stir well to mix. If liked, add the chopped liver and gizzard from the chicken. Bind with the beaten eggs.

Put the stuffing in the chicken cavity, then truss with thread or fine string. Bring the water to the boil in a large flameproof casserole with the vegetables, bouquet garni and salt and pepper to taste.

Place the chicken in the casserole, cover and cook gently for 3 to 3½ hours until the chicken is very tender and the stock rich with flavour.

To serve, remove the chicken from the stock and cut into serving pieces. Slice the stuffing. Keep the chicken and stuffing hot.

Discard the bouquet garni from the stock and cut the vegetables into bite-sized pieces. Reheat, adding the vermicelli if serving. Taste and adjust seasoning. Serve hot as a soup for a first course. If serving with toast rather than vermicelli, pour over slices of hot toast in individual soup bowls. Serve the chicken and stuffing separately as a main course.
SERVES 6

POULET VALLÉE D'AUGE

Chicken with Mushrooms, Cider and Cream

There are numerous recipes for poulet vallée d'auge. Madeira may be used instead of the cider, and the chicken can also be flambéed in calvados. Small pickling onions sometimes replace mushrooms. The usual accompaniments are sautéed potatoes and a julienne★ of mixed vegetables such as carrots, onions, turnips and leeks.

Metric/Imperial	American
75 g/3 oz butter	⅓ cup butter
1 × 1.5 kg/3¼–3½ lb chicken, cut into 4–6 serving pieces	1 × 3¼–3½ lb chicken, cut into 4–6 serving pieces
salt	salt
freshly ground black pepper	freshly ground black pepper
450 g/1 lb mushrooms, finely chopped	4 cups finely chopped mushrooms
200 ml/⅓ pint dry cider	1 cup hard cider
120 ml/4 fl oz double cream	½ cup heavy cream

Melt 50 g/2 oz/¼ cup butter in a large flameproof casserole, add the chicken pieces and fry gently until golden on all sides. Sprinkle with salt and pepper to taste, cover and cook gently for 10 minutes.

Melt the remaining butter in a separate pan, add the mushrooms and cook gently until their juices run into the butter. Pour off the liquid into the casserole, draining the mushrooms thoroughly. Pour in the cider, add salt and pepper to taste, then cover and simmer gently for 45 minutes or until the chicken is tender.

Remove the chicken and set aside. Stir the cream into the casserole and simmer until thick, stirring constantly. Return the chicken to the casserole, add the mushrooms and simmer for a few minutes to reheat. Taste and adjust the seasoning. Serve immediately.
SERVES 4 TO 6

POULET AU FROMAGE

Chicken with Gruyère, White Wine and Cream

Metric/Imperial	American
50 g/2 oz butter	¼ cup butter
4 chicken portions	4 chicken portions
1 shallot, peeled and finely chopped	1 scallion, peeled and finely chopped
300 ml/½ pint dry white wine	1¼ cups dry white wine
300 ml/½ pint double cream	1¼ cups heavy cream
freshly grated nutmeg	freshly grated nutmeg
salt	salt
freshly ground black pepper	freshly ground black pepper
1 tablespoon prepared French mustard	1 tablespoon prepared French mustard
100 g/4 oz Gruyère cheese★, grated	1 cup grated Gruyère cheese★

Melt 40 g/1½ oz/3 tablespoons butter in a large flameproof casserole, add the chicken and shallot (scallion) and fry over moderate heat until the chicken is lightly coloured on all sides.

Pour in the wine and cream. Add nutmeg, salt and pepper to taste, then bring to the boil. Stir in the mustard, then half of the cheese. Stir well, then cover and cook very gently for 1 hour or until the chicken is tender.

Taste and adjust the seasoning of the sauce, then transfer the chicken and sauce to a flameproof serving dish. Sprinkle with the reserved cheese and dot with the remaining butter. Put under a preheated hot grill (broiler) for a few minutes until golden brown. Serve immediately.
SERVES 4

POULET AU VERJUS

Chicken with Grapes

Verjus or verjuice was used extensively in cooking as a flavouring or condiment hundreds of years ago, but it is little used today. Originally it was the juice of a special variety of unripe grapes of the same name, preserved by evaporation which gave it a concentrated flavour. These days we have to use fresh green grapes to provide a similar, less strong flavour.

Metric/Imperial	American
2 tablespoons goose fat★ or butter	2 tablespoons goose fat★ or butter
6 small pickling onions, peeled	6 baby onions, peeled
1 × 1.5 kg/3¼–3½ lb chicken, cut into 8 serving pieces with the liver reserved and chopped	1 × 3¼–3½ lb chicken, cut into 8 serving pieces with the liver reserved and chopped
2 garlic cloves, peeled and crushed	2 garlic cloves, peeled and crushed
120 ml/4 fl oz chicken stock (page 42)	½ cup chicken stock (page 42)
salt	salt
freshly ground black pepper	freshly ground black pepper
about 225 g/8 oz ripe green grapes, skinned and seeded	about ½ cup ripe green grapes, skinned and seeded
chopped parsley	chopped parsley

Melt the fat or butter in a large flameproof casserole, add the onions and fry over moderate heat until lightly coloured. Remove with a slotted spoon, then place the chicken pieces in the casserole and fry gently until golden on all sides.

Return the onions to the casserole, then add the garlic and stock, and salt and pepper to taste. Cook gently for 30 minutes.

Add the grapes to the chicken, with the chopped liver and parsley to taste. Boil rapidly for 15 minutes to thicken the sauce. Taste and adjust seasoning, then transfer to a warmed serving dish. Serve immediately.
SERVES 4

Although frozen and chilled chickens are available in France, freshly killed birds, available at the local market, are still more popular. Maize is the favourite cereal for feeding poultry in France, and it is this which gives the birds their appetizing golden-yellow colour.

Poulets de Bresse are the most highly prized chickens throughout the whole of France; fed on maize and dairy products, their breeding is strictly controlled to 1 million birds each year, and regulations are laid down as to the number of birds reared together.

Anyone who has ever had the good fortune to eat *poulet de Bresse* will appreciate the true meaning of the term 'free-range'.

COQ EN PÂTE

Stuffed Chicken in Pastry

Truffles are very expensive to use in a stuffing like this, where they may not be fully appreciated. Use button mushrooms for a more economical stuffing. Sausagemeat can replace the foie gras for the same reason. Alternatively, paté de foie gras aux truffes, makes a good substitute for both. In Périgord where truffles are prolific, this would be served with the classic Sauce périgueux. Outside Périgord, where they are prohibitively expensive, sauce poulette (page 47) would make an acceptable alternative.

Metric/Imperial	American
STUFFING:	STUFFING:
liver from chicken, finely chopped	liver from chicken, finely chopped
100 g/4 oz sausagemeat	½ cup sausagemeat
225 g/8 oz foie gras★	½ lb foie gras★
50 g/2 oz canned truffles★, drained and thinly sliced, juice reserved (optional)	2 oz canned truffles★, drained and thinly sliced, juice reserved (optional)
1 tablespoon brandy	1 tablespoon brandy
salt	salt
freshly ground black pepper	freshly ground black pepper
1 × 1.5 kg/3¼–3½ lb chicken	1 × 3¼–3½ lb chicken
50 g/2 oz butter, softened	¼ cup softened butter
400 g/14 oz pâte feuilletée (page 53)	14 oz pâte feuilletée (page 53)
1 egg yolk mixed with a little milk, to glaze	1 egg yolk mixed with a little milk, to glaze

Prepare the stuffing: put the chicken liver in a bowl with the sausagemeat, foie gras and truffles (if using). Mix well, add the brandy, juice from the truffles (if using) and salt and pepper to taste. Mix well again.

Put the stuffing in the chicken cavity, then truss with thread or fine string. Place the chicken in a roasting pan, brush with the softened butter and sprinkle with salt and pepper. Roast in a preheated hot oven (220°C/425°F/Gas Mark 7) for 20 minutes, then reduce the temperature to moderately hot (200°C/400°F/Gas Mark 6) and cook for another 20 minutes.

Meanwhile, roll out the pastry on a floured surface until large enough to wrap around the whole chicken.

Remove the chicken from the oven, leave until cool enough to handle, then remove the thread or string. Place the chicken in the centre of the pastry, then wrap the pastry around the chicken to enclose it completely. Moisten the edges with water and seal firmly. Make a small hole in the top of the pastry, and decorate with pastry trimmings, if liked.

Stand the chicken parcel on a dampened baking sheet and brush all over with the egg yolk mixture. Bake in the moderately hot oven for 45 minutes until the pastry is golden brown and crisp.

To serve, remove the pastry, then cut the chicken into serving pieces, scooping out the stuffing. Let guests help themselves to slices of pastry, chicken and stuffing. Serve *sauce poulette* separately in a sauceboat.
SERVES 4 TO 6

Coq en pâte; Poulet vallée d'Auge

POULET SAUTÉ BASQUAISE

Sautéed Chicken with Peppers, Tomatoes, Ham and Sausage

In the Basque country, this dish would be garnished with the small spicy sausages known as louquenkas, which are peculiar to the region. They are not unlike the Spanish chorizos, which may be used as a substitute.

Metric/Imperial

2 tablespoons oil
50 g/2 oz butter
1 × 1.5 kg/3¾–3½ lb chicken, cut into 8 serving pieces
1 onion, peeled and finely chopped
2 garlic cloves, peeled and crushed
6 green peppers, cored, seeded and thinly sliced
4 tomatoes, skinned, chopped and seeded
salt
freshly ground black pepper
120 ml/4 fl oz dry white wine
GARNISH:
225 g/8 oz cooked ham★, diced
6 small spicy sausages★, thickly sliced
chopped parsley

American

2 tablespoons oil
¼ cup butter
1 × 3¾–3½ lb chicken, cut into 8 serving pieces
1 onion, peeled and finely chopped
2 garlic cloves, peeled and crushed
6 green peppers, cored, seeded and thinly sliced
4 tomatoes, skinned, chopped and seeded
salt
freshly ground black pepper
½ cup dry white wine
GARNISH:
1 cup diced cooked ham★
6 small spicy sausages★, thickly sliced
chopped parsley

Heat the oil and butter in a large flameproof casserole, add the chicken pieces and fry over moderate heat until lightly coloured on all sides. Remove from the casserole with a slotted spoon and set aside.

Add the onion to the casserole with the garlic, peppers, tomatoes, and salt and pepper to taste. Cook over brisk heat for about 10 minutes, stirring constantly, then pour in the wine. Bring to the boil, then lower the heat and add the chicken pieces. Cook gently for 45 minutes to 1 hour or until the chicken is tender.

Just before the end of the cooking time, put the ham and sausage in a separate pan and toss gently over moderate heat until hot, taking care not to overcook and toughen the meat.

Taste and adjust the seasoning of the sauce, then arrange the chicken and sauce in the centre of a warmed serving platter. Sprinkle with chopped parsley to taste. Alternate the ham and sausage around the edge of the platter. Serve immediately.
SERVES 4

POULET AUX QUARANTE GOUSSES D'AIL

Chicken with Forty Garlic Cloves

It is customary to serve this dish with slices of hot toast. Divide the cooked garlic cloves equally amongst your guests, who should then spread the garlic over the toast themselves. The garlic will be so soft from the long cooking, that it will mash to a purée (paste) and the garlic skins will come away easily.

Poulet sauté basquaise;
Poulet aux quarante
gousses d'ail

Metric/Imperial	American
1 × 1.75 kg/4 lb chicken	1 × 4 lb chicken
salt	salt
1 bouquet garni★	1 bouquet garni★
40 garlic cloves	40 garlic cloves
200 ml/⅓ pint oil	1 cup oil
few rosemary, thyme, sage and parsley leaves	few rosemary, thyme, sage and parsley leaves
1 celery stick, chopped	1 celery stalk, chopped
freshly ground black pepper	freshly ground black pepper
2 tablespoons plain flour, for sealing	2 tablespoons all-purpose flour, for sealing
6 slices hot toast, to serve	6 slices hot toast, to serve

Sprinkle the inside of the chicken with salt, then place the bouquet garni in the cavity. Truss the chicken with thread or fine string.

Separate the garlic cloves, but do not peel them. Heat the oil in a large flameproof casserole, add the garlic, herbs and celery, then the chicken. Turn the chicken over to coat in the oil and herbs, then sprinkle with salt and pepper to taste.

Cover the casserole with a lid, then seal around the edge of the lid with a paste made from the flour and a few drops of water.

Bake in a preheated moderate oven (180°C/350°F/Gas Mark 4) for 1½ hours, without opening the lid.

Break the seal and transfer the chicken and garlic to a warmed serving platter. Serve immediately, with the toast.

SERVES 6

DINDE AUX MARRONS

Turkey with Chestnut and Sausagemeat Stuffing

Metric/Imperial	American
450 g/1 lb chestnuts	1 lb chestnuts
450 g/1 lb sausagemeat	2 cups sausagemeat
1 tablespoon chopped herbs (e.g. chives, parsley, tarragon)	1 tablespoon chopped herbs (e.g. chives, parsley, tarragon)
7 tablespoons brandy	7 tablespoons brandy
freshly grated nutmeg	freshly grated nutmeg
salt	salt
freshly ground black pepper	freshly ground black pepper
1 egg, beaten	1 egg, beaten
1 × 4 kg/9 lb turkey	1 × 9 lb turkey
chestnuts to garnish (optional)	chestnuts to garnish (optional)

Plunge the chestnuts into boiling water and simmer for 10 minutes. Drain and peel, then simmer in fresh water for about 30 minutes or until tender.

Drain the chestnuts thoroughly, then crumble them roughly in a bowl. Add the sausagemeat, herbs and brandy, with nutmeg, salt and pepper to taste. Mix well until thoroughly combined, then add enough egg to bind the mixture. Mince (grind) or finely chop the liver from the turkey, then mix into the stuffing until evenly distributed.

Put the stuffing inside the cavity of the turkey, then truss with thread or fine string. Place on a rack in a roasting pan and roast in a preheated moderately hot oven (200°C/400°F/Gas Mark 6) for 15 minutes. Lower the temperature to moderate (180°C/350°F/Gas Mark 4) and cook for a further 2¼ hours or until the turkey is tender. (To test if the turkey is cooked, pierce the thickest part of the thigh with a skewer – the juices should run clear.) Baste the turkey occasionally during cooking.

Serve the turkey hot on a warmed serving platter. Surround with whole peeled chestnuts, poached until tender as for the stuffing above, if liked.

SERVES 8 TO 10

NOTE: This stuffing can also be used for goose.

OIE FARCIE
Stuffed Goose

*Although the calf's (veal) foot is traditional in this recipe, it
can be omitted if difficult to obtain. Braised cabbage is the
usual accompaniment to this dish.*

Metric/Imperial	American
STUFFING:	STUFFING:
25 g/1 oz butter	*2 tablespoons butter*
2 shallots, peeled and finely chopped	*2 scallions, peeled and finely chopped*
1 onion, peeled and finely chopped	*1 onion, peeled and finely chopped*
1 garlic clove, peeled and crushed	*1 garlic clove, peeled and crushed*
250 ml/8 fl oz dry white wine	*1 cup dry white wine*
liver from goose	*liver from goose*
450 g/1 lb sausagemeat	*2 cups sausagemeat*
2 tablespoons chopped parsley	*2 tablespoons chopped parsley*
ground mixed spice	*ground allspice*
salt	*ground cinnamon*
freshly ground black pepper	*salt*
	freshly ground black pepper
1 × 2.5 kg/5½–5¾ lb goose	*1 × 5½–5¾ lb goose*
4 rashers streaky bacon, rinds removed and cut into strips	*4 slices fatty bacon, cut into strips*
2 carrots, peeled and sliced into rings	*2 carrots, peeled and sliced into rings*
2 onions, peeled and sliced into rings	*2 onions, peeled and sliced into rings*
½ calf's foot★, split and chopped	*½ veal foot★, split and chopped*
750 ml/1¼ pints dry white wine	*3 cups dry white wine*
250 ml/8 fl oz chicken stock (page 42)	*1 cup chicken stock (page 42)*

Prepare the stuffing: melt the butter in a pan, add the
shallots (scallions), onion and garlic and fry gently until
soft. Remove with a slotted spoon, drain on kitchen
paper towels, then place in a large pan with the wine.
Boil until reduced to one third of the original volume.

Meanwhile, poach the goose liver in a little water
until soft. Drain and pound to a smooth paste, using a
mortar and pestle. Place in a bowl with the sausagemeat and reduced wine, then add the parsley, and
spice(s), salt and pepper to taste. Mix thoroughly.

Put the stuffing in the goose cavity, then truss with
thread or fine string. Place the bacon strips, carrot and
onion rings in the bottom of a large casserole. Place the
goose on top, then surround with the pieces of calf's
(veal) foot. Pour in the wine and stock, then cover and
cook in a preheated moderately hot oven (200°C/
400°F/Gas Mark 6) for 15 minutes. Lower the temperature to moderate (180°C/350°F/Gas Mark 4) and
cook for a further 2 to 2¼ hours. Baste the goose
occasionally during the cooking time.

Remove the goose from the cooking liquid and
discard the thread or string. Place the goose on a
warmed serving platter and keep hot. Strain the
cooking liquid, pressing the vegetables firmly in the
sieve (strainer) to extract all their juices. Skim off the fat
from the surface of the liquid, then boil rapidly on top
of the stove until thick and reduced. Taste and adjust
seasoning. Serve the goose hot, with the sauce handed
separately.
SERVES 6

CANARD À LA MONTMORENCY
Duck with Montmorency Cherries

*Use bright red bitter cherries for this dish. If Montmorency
are difficult to obtain, morello cherries are equally as good.*

Metric/Imperial	American
2 carrots, peeled and sliced into thin rings	*2 carrots, peeled and sliced into thin rings*
1 onion, peeled and sliced into thin rings	*1 onion, peeled and sliced into thin rings*
1 × 1.75 kg/4 lb duck, trussed with thread or fine string	*1 × 4 lb duck, trussed with thread or fine string*
1 bouquet garni★	*1 bouquet garni★*
salt	*salt*
freshly ground black pepper	*freshly ground black pepper*
75 g/3 oz butter	*⅓ cup butter*
3 tablespoons cherry brandy	*3 tablespoons cherry brandy*
1 tablespoon brandy	*1 tablespoon brandy*
250 ml/8 fl oz duck or chicken stock (page 42)	*1 cup duck or chicken stock (page 42)*
225 g/8 oz bitter cherries	*1½–2 cups bitter cherries*
2 tablespoons red wine	*2 tablespoons red wine*

Put the carrots and onion in the bottom of a large
flameproof casserole. Place the duck on top, then add
the bouquet garni and salt and pepper to taste. Dot
with the butter, then cover and cook gently for 1½
hours or until the duck is tender. Baste occasionally
during the cooking time.

Remove the duck from the casserole and cut into
serving pieces (wings, legs and thin slivers of breast
meat). Place the duck on a plate, cover tightly, then
stand the plate over a pan of hot water to keep the
duck moist and hot.

Remove the bouquet garni from the casserole and
pour off the excess fat. Stir in the cherry brandy and
brandy, then scrape all the sediment from the bottom
of the pan and mix with the vegetables and juices. Stir
in the stock, bring to the boil and boil rapidly until
reduced by half.

Meanwhile, put the cherries and wine in a separate
pan and poach for a few minutes until the cherries are
just tender.

Work the cooking liquid through a fine sieve
(strainer), then return to the rinsed-out pan and reheat.
Taste and adjust seasoning.

Arrange the duck in the centre of a warmed serving
platter. Remove the cherries from their liquid with a
slotted spoon and arrange around the duck. Pour the
sauce over the duck and serve immediately.
SERVES 4 TO 6

Canard à la montmorency
takes its name from the
Montmorency variety of
cooking cherry. This
fruit, grown in and
around Montmorency
north of Paris, is tart and
acidic in flavour, unlike
the sweet eating cherries,
known in France as
bigarreaux.

Montmorency cherries
are bright crimson red in
colour and give their
name to any dish, sweet
or savoury, which has
cherries amongst its
ingredients. Despite the
name, there is no need to
seek out this special
variety for cooking.
They are not easy to
obtain outside France and
any other tart or bitter
variety of cherry may be
used as a substitute –
morello cherries are
ideal.

Meanwhile, heat half the calvados in a small pan, flame it, then pour over the duck. When the flames have died down, transfer the duck to a board and cut into serving pieces (legs, wings and thin slivers of breast meat). Discard the bacon and threads.

Place the duck on a plate, cover tightly, then stand the plate over a pan of hot water to keep the duck moist and hot.

Pour the cider into a heavy pan and boil vigorously until reduced by half. Stir in the cream, a little at a time, then simmer until reduced and glossy, stirring constantly. Taste and adjust seasoning.

Arrange the duck in the centre of a warmed serving platter. Remove the potatoes from the roasting pan, with a slotted spoon, then arrange around the duck. Sprinkle with the remaining calvados. Pour a little of the sauce over the duck. Serve hot, with the remaining sauce handed separately in a sauceboat.
SERVES 4 TO 6

ALSACE-LORRAINE

CANARD AUX HERBES

Duck with Herbs

If sorrel is difficult to obtain, use double the quantity of spinach. The herbs can be varied according to taste and availability. Steamed or boiled potatoes are the usual accompaniment to this dish.

Metric/Imperial	American
100 g/4 oz streaky bacon, diced	*½ cup diced fatty bacon*
1 × 2–2.5 kg/4–5 lb duck, cut into 6 serving pieces	*1 × 4–5 lb duck, cut into 6 serving pieces*
100 g/4 oz sorrel, shredded	*1½ cups shredded sorrel*
100 g/4 oz spinach, shredded	*1½ cups shredded spinach*
100 g/4 oz lettuce, shredded	*1½ cups shredded lettuce*
2 leeks (white part only), thinly sliced	*2 leeks (white part only), thinly sliced*
3 celery sticks, thinly sliced	*3 celery stalks, thinly sliced*
3 tarragon sprigs, finely chopped	*3 tarragon sprigs, finely chopped*
3 parsley sprigs, finely chopped	*3 parsley sprigs, finely chopped*
3 mint sprigs, finely chopped	*3 mint sprigs, finely chopped*
1 bunch chives, snipped	*1 bunch chives, snipped*
1 tablespoon plain flour	*1 tablespoon all-purpose flour*
200 ml/⅓ pint dry white wine	*1 cup dry white wine*
120 ml/4 fl oz double cream	*½ cup heavy cream*
salt	*salt*
freshly ground black pepper	*freshly ground black pepper*

Put the bacon in a heavy flameproof casserole and heat gently until the fat runs. Add the duck pieces and sauté for 15 to 20 minutes until well browned. Drain off all but 2 tablespoons of the fat.

Add the vegetables and herbs to the casserole, then sprinkle in the flour and cook, stirring for 1 minute. Add the wine and cream, then continue cooking gently for a further 30 minutes or until the duck is tender. Add salt and pepper to taste. Serve hot.
SERVES 6

Cider, cream and calvados, the three ingredients for which Normandy is famous, are all included in this recipe for *bonhomme normand*. What Normandy lacks in the way of vineyards, it more than compensates for in prolific orchards.

Cider and calvados are both produced from local apples, and apples are used extensively in the regional cooking of Normandy. Cider, combined with local butter and cream, makes wonderfully rich sauces to complement pork, veal and chicken, as well as the duck dishes of the region.

Calvados, unique to this region, is a fiery brandy made from the same apples as the cider. It is used both as a digestif, and in the cooking of many regional dishes.

NORMANDIE

BONHOMME NORMAND

Duck with Cider and Cream

This recipe can also be used for pheasant or woodcock.

Metric/Imperial	American
1 × 1.75 kg/4 lb duck, trussed with thread or fine string	*1 × 4 lb duck, trussed with thread or fine string*
salt	*salt*
freshly ground black pepper	*freshly ground black pepper*
2 large rashers streaky bacon	*2 large slices fatty bacon*
100 g/4 oz butter	*½ cup butter*
750 g/1½ lb potatoes, peeled and quartered	*1½ lb potatoes, peeled and quartered*
2 tablespoons calvados, warmed	*2 tablespoons calvados, warmed*
200 ml/⅓ cup dry cider	*1 cup hard cider*
450 ml/¾ pint double cream	*2 cups heavy cream*

Sprinkle the inside of the duck lightly with salt and pepper. Put the bacon over the breast of the duck and tie in position with trussing thread or fine string.

Melt half the butter in a large flameproof roasting pan, add the duck and brown on all sides for about 10 minutes.

Cook, uncovered, in a preheated hot oven (220°C/425°F/Gas Mark 7) for 15 minutes. Lower the temperature to moderate (180°C/350°F/Gas Mark 4) and roast for a further 1 hour or until tender, basting occasionally.

Remove the duck from the pan and keep hot. Transfer the pan to the top of the stove, add the remaining butter and heat until melted. Add the potatoes and sauté for about 20 minutes until tender and golden, turning frequently.

CANARD À L'ORANGE

Duck with Orange

Metric/Imperial	American
75 g/3 oz butter	⅓ cup butter
1 × 2 kg/4 lb duck, trussed with thread or fine string	1 × 4 lb duck, trussed with thread or fine string
onions, peeled and sliced into thin rings	4 onions, peeled and sliced into thin rings
carrots, peeled and sliced into thin rings	4 carrots, peeled and sliced into thin rings
750 ml/1¼ pints dry white wine	3 cups dry white wine
bouquet garni★	1 bouquet garni★
salt	salt
freshly ground black pepper	freshly ground black pepper
oranges	2 oranges
teaspoon arrowroot	1 teaspoon arrowroot
juice of 2 oranges	juice of 2 oranges
teaspoon caster sugar	1 teaspoon sugar

Melt the butter in a large flameproof casserole, add the duck, onions and carrots and fry until the duck is golden brown on all sides, turning frequently.

Pour in the wine, bring to the boil and simmer for a few minutes until reduced slightly. Add the bouquet garni and salt and pepper to taste. Lower the heat, cover the casserole and simmer gently for 1½ hours or until the duck is tender, basting occasionally during cooking.

Meanwhile, finely pare the rind from the oranges, using a canelle knife or vegetable peeler to ensure none of the white pith is included. Cut the rind into fine strips, then plunge into a small pan of boiling water and blanch for 5 minutes. Drain, dry thoroughly on kitchen paper towels and set aside.

Cut the pared oranges into segments, removing the pith and skin which surrounds the segments. Set aside.

Remove the duck from the casserole and cut into serving pieces (wings, legs and thin slivers of breast meat). Place the duck on a plate, cover tightly, then stand the plate over a pan of hot water to keep the duck moist and hot.

Skim off excess fat from the cooking liquid, then strain. Pour 2 tablespoons of the liquid into a bowl, leave to cool, then mix to a paste with the arrowroot.

Pour the remaining cooking liquid into a heavy pan and reheat. Stir in the arrowroot paste, then simmer until the sauce thickens, stirring constantly. Remove from the heat, stir in the orange juice, sugar and blanched orange rind. Taste and adjust seasoning. Arrange the duck in the centre of a warmed serving platter and surround with the orange segments. Spoon the sauce over the duck and serve immediately.
SERVES 6

ABOVE: **Canard aux herbes; Canard à l'orange**
LEFT: **Bonhomme normand**

CIVET DE LIÈVRE

Jugged Hare

Steamed or boiled potatoes are the classic accompaniment to jugged hare. It is such a rich dish that it is best served with only the plainest of vegetables.

Metric/Imperial	American
MARINADE:	MARINADE:
4 carrots, peeled and roughly chopped	4 carrots, peeled and roughly chopped
2 onions, peeled and roughly chopped	2 onions, peeled and roughly chopped
1 garlic clove, peeled and crushed	1 garlic clove, peeled and crushed
1 bay leaf	1 bay leaf
2 parsley sprigs	2 parsley sprigs
1 thyme sprig	1 thyme sprig
1 rosemary sprig	1 rosemary sprig
1 litre/1$\frac{3}{4}$ pints full-bodied red wine	4$\frac{1}{4}$ cups full-bodied red wine
freshly ground black pepper	freshly ground black pepper
1 × 2$\frac{1}{2}$ kg/5 lb hare, cut into serving pieces, blood and liver reserved	1 × 5 lb hare, cut into serving pieces, blood and liver reserved
2 tablespoons red wine vinegar	2 tablespoons red wine vinegar
60 g/2$\frac{1}{2}$ oz butter	5 tablespoons butter
2 tablespoons oil	2 tablespoons oil
100 g/4 oz smoked bacon, rind removed and diced	$\frac{1}{2}$ cup diced smoked bacon
18 small pickling onions, peeled	18 baby onions, peeled
225 g/8 oz button mushrooms, thinly sliced	2 cups thinly sliced button mushrooms
2 tablespoons brandy	2 tablespoons brandy
2 tablespoons plain flour	2 tablespoons all-purpose flour
salt	salt
ground mixed spice	ground allspice
6 croûtes★, to serve	ground cinnamon
	6 croûtes★, to serve

Prepare the marinade: put all the ingredients in a large bowl with pepper to taste and stir well. Add the pieces of hare and mix well. Put the hare's blood in a separate bowl with the wine vinegar. Leave the hare and blood in a cool place (not in the refrigerator) for 24 hours. Turn the hare over in the marinade from time to time.

The next day, remove the pieces of hare from the marinade and dry thoroughly on kitchen paper towels. Reserve the marinade. Melt the butter in a large flameproof casserole, add the oil, then the bacon and whole onions. Fry gently until lightly coloured on all sides, then remove with a slotted spoon and drain on kitchen paper towels. Add the mushrooms to the casserole, fry gently for 1 to 2 minutes, then remove and drain with the bacon and onions.

Pour off half the fat from the casserole, then add the pieces of hare and fry briskly until lightly coloured on all sides. Sprinkle in the brandy, then the flour, and stir until the fat is absorbed.

Strain the reserved marinade over the hare, pouring in just enough to cover. Add salt, pepper and spice(s) to taste, then the drained onions, bacon and mushrooms. Bring to the boil, then lower the heat, cover and simmer gently for 1 hour or until the hare is tender. Stir occasionally during cooking.

Chop the hare liver roughly, then stir into the blood and vinegar mixture. Stir about 4 tablespoons ($\frac{1}{4}$ cup) of the cooking liquid from the hare into the blood, adding only a little at a time to prevent coagulation. Pour this mixture slowly back into the casserole, stirring constantly. Simmer gently without boiling for 2 minutes.

Taste and adjust the seasoning of the sauce, then transfer the hare and sauce to a warmed deep serving dish. Surround with *croûtes* and serve immediately.
SERVES 6

LAPIN AUX PRUNEAUX

Rabbit with Prunes

This dish is extremely popular throughout northern France, and has many different variations. It is particularly good served with potatoes which have been roasted with a spoonful or two of redcurrant jelly.

Metric/Imperial	American
1 × 2 kg/4 lb rabbit, skinned and cut into serving pieces, liver reserved	1 × 4 lb rabbit, skinned and cut into serving pieces, liver reserved
250 ml/8 fl oz red wine vinegar	1 cup red wine vinegar
4 onions, peeled and sliced into rings	4 onions, peeled and sliced into rings
2 carrots, peeled and sliced into rings	2 carrots, peeled and sliced into rings
few black peppercorns	few black peppercorns
1.25 litres/2$\frac{1}{4}$ pints red wine	5$\frac{3}{4}$ cups red wine
1 bay leaf	1 bay leaf
1 thyme sprig	1 thyme sprig
few parsley sprigs	few parsley sprigs
750 g/1$\frac{1}{2}$ lb prunes	1$\frac{1}{2}$ lb prunes
75 g/3 oz butter	$\frac{1}{3}$ cup butter
3 tablespoons oil	3 tablespoons oil
150 g/5 oz boned belly pork, rind removed and diced	$\frac{2}{3}$ cup diced boneless belly pork
12 small pickling onions, peeled	12 baby onions, peeled
2 tablespoons plain flour	2 tablespoons all-purpose flour
2 garlic cloves, peeled and halved	2 garlic cloves, peeled and halved
few thyme, parsley and sage leaves	few thyme, parsley and sage leaves
salt	salt
freshly ground black pepper	freshly ground black pepper
3 tablespoons redcurrant jelly, to finish	3 tablespoons redcurrant jelly, to finish

Put the rabbit liver in a bowl and cover with 1 tablespoon wine vinegar.

Put the rabbit pieces in a separate bowl with the sliced onions, carrots, remaining wine vinegar, peppercorns, half the wine, the bay leaf, thyme and parsley sprigs. Stir well to mix.

Put the prunes in a separate bowl and cover with the remaining wine. Leave the liver, rabbit and prunes to marinate overnight.

The next day, remove the rabbit pieces from the

Wine and wine vinegar are used in marinades for meat because their acid content helps break down tough fibres and thus tenderizes the meat. For this reason, game is frequently marinated before cooking, since it tends to be more sinewy than other meats. Marinating game also helps to reduce its strong or 'high' flavour.

marinade and dry thoroughly with kitchen paper towels. Reserve the marinade. Melt the butter in a large flameproof casserole, add 1 tablespoon oil, then add the rabbit pieces and fry gently until lightly coloured on all sides. Remove the rabbit with a slotted spoon and set aside. Pour off all the fat from the casserole.

Heat the remaining oil in the casserole, add the belly pork and whole onions, then fry over moderate heat until golden brown, shaking the pan constantly. Return the rabbit to the casserole, sprinkle in the flour and stir for a few minutes until all the fat has been absorbed.

Drain the wine from the prunes into the casserole, add the garlic, herbs, reserved marinade from the rabbit, and salt and pepper to taste. Stir well to mix and bring to the boil.

Lower the heat, cover and simmer gently for 30 minutes. Add the prunes and simmer for a further 30 minutes. A few minutes before the end of the cooking time, drain and mash the rabbit liver, then stir into the sauce.

Remove the rabbit pieces from the sauce with a slotted spoon and place in a warmed serving dish. Keep hot. Stir the redcurrant jelly into the sauce and heat through, stirring constantly. Taste and adjust seasoning, then pour over the rabbit. Serve immediately.
SERVES 6

**Lapin aux pruneaux;
Civet de lièvre**

FAISANS EN BARBOUILLE

Pheasant Casserole with Mushrooms and Onions

Metric/Imperial	American
100 g/4 oz butter	*½ cup butter*
4 carrots, peeled and thinly sliced	*4 carrots, peeled and thinly sliced*
4 onions, peeled and thinly sliced	*4 onions, peeled and thinly sliced*
2 pheasants (about 2 kg/4 lb total weight), drawn and cut into 8 serving pieces	*2 pheasants (about 4 lb total weight), drawn and cut into 8 serving pieces*
1 tablespoon plain flour	*1 tablespoon all-purpose flour*
350 ml/12 fl oz good red wine	*1½ cups good red wine*
3 tablespoons brandy	*3 tablespoons brandy*
7 tablespoons chicken stock (page 42)	*7 tablespoons chicken stock (page 42)*
salt	*salt*
freshly ground black pepper	*freshly ground black pepper*
10 button mushrooms, thickly sliced	*10 button mushrooms, thickly sliced*

100 g/4 oz streaky bacon, rinds removed and cut into thin strips	*¼ lb fatty bacon, sliced into thin strips*
10 small pickling onions, peeled	*10 baby onions, peeled*

Melt half the butter in a large flameproof casserole, add the carrots and onions and fry gently for a few minutes. Add the pieces of pheasant and fry until lightly coloured on all sides, then sprinkle in the flour and cook, stirring, until all the fat has been absorbed.

Pour in the wine, brandy, stock and a little salt and pepper to taste, then bring to the boil. Lower the heat, cover and simmer gently for 20 minutes.

Meanwhile, melt the remaining butter in a separate flameproof casserole. Add the mushrooms, bacon and onions and fry over brisk heat until lightly coloured. Remove the pheasant from its cooking liquid with a slotted spoon, then place in the casserole with the mushrooms, bacon and onions.

Strain the pheasant cooking liquid over the pheasant, stir well, then cover and simmer gently for a further 45 minutes or until the pheasants are tender. Taste and adjust the seasoning of the sauce. Serve immediately, straight from the casserole.
SERVES 8

LAPIN À L'AIL

Rabbit with Twenty Garlic Cloves

This recipe is a speciality of the Haut-Languedoc district, where it is also sometimes made with pork or tournedos steaks instead of the rabbit. If a whole rabbit is difficult to obtain, use fresh or frozen rabbit portions. For a milder garlic flavour, use only 12 garlic cloves.

Metric/Imperial	American
3 tablespoons oil	3 tablespoons oil
1 × 1.5 kg/3–3½ lb rabbit, trussed with thread or fine string, liver reserved	1 × 3–3½ lb rabbit, trussed with thread or fine string, liver reserved
225 g/8 oz piece smoked bacon	½ lb piece smoked bacon
20 garlic cloves	20 garlic cloves
salt	salt
freshly ground black pepper	freshly ground black pepper
150 ml/¼ pint well-flavoured chicken stock (page 42)	⅔ cup well-flavored chicken stock (page 42)

Heat the oil in a large flameproof casserole, then put in the rabbit with the whole piece of bacon. Fry over brisk heat for about 10 minutes until lightly coloured on all sides.

Separate 10 garlic cloves, but do not peel them. Add them to the casserole, cover and cook over moderate heat for 10 minutes. Turn the rabbit over, sprinkle with salt and pepper to taste, then cover and cook for a further 10 minutes.

Peel the remaining garlic cloves and cut them in half lengthways. Remove the rabbit and bacon from the casserole, then add the halved garlic cloves and fry gently for a few minutes.

Return the rabbit and bacon to the casserole and cook over moderate heat for 10 minutes. Add the reserved rabbit liver and continue cooking for a further 10 to 20 minutes or until the rabbit is tender – the flesh should be white and fall away easily from the bones.

Remove the rabbit, bacon and liver. Cut the rabbit into serving pieces, the bacon and liver into thin strips. Keep hot.

Crush the garlic in the casserole with a wooden spoon, removing all the garlic skins which should come away easily. The garlic should be so soft that it mashes to a purée (paste). Stir the stock into this purée gradually, then simmer gently. Taste and adjust seasoning.

Place the rabbit in the centre of a warmed serving platter and surround with the strips of bacon and liver. Pour the sauce over the rabbit and serve immediately.
SERVES 4

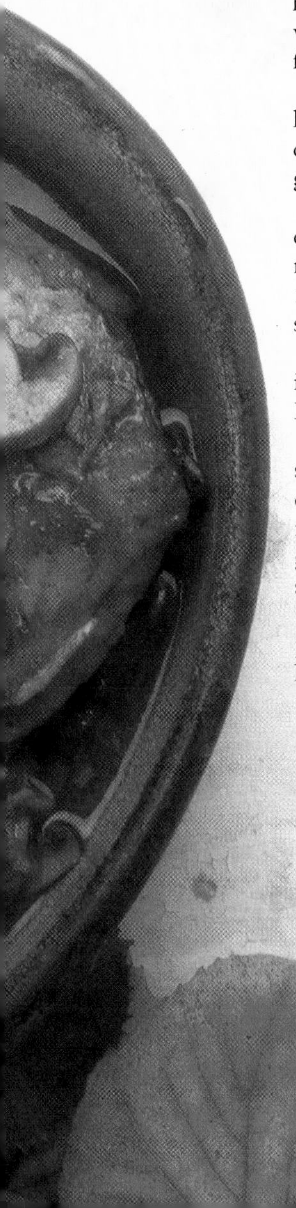

Faisans en barbouille

GIGUE DE CHEVREUIL

Pot-Roasted Venison

Metric/Imperial	American
1 × 1.5 kg/3–3½ lb leg of venison	1 × 3–3½ lb leg venison
5 tablespoons olive oil	5 tablespoons olive oil
leaves of 1 large rosemary sprig	leaves of 1 large rosemary sprig
6 shallots, peeled and sliced	6 scallions, peeled and sliced
2 carrots, peeled and sliced	2 carrots, peeled and sliced
2 onions, peeled and sliced	2 onions, peeled and sliced
1 litre/1¾ pints dry white wine	4¼ cups dry white wine
400 ml/14 fl oz red wine vinegar	1¾ cups red wine vinegar
1 bouquet garni★	1 bouquet garni★
few juniper berries	few juniper berries
salt	salt
freshly ground black pepper	freshly ground black pepper
ground mixed spice	ground allspice
150 g/5 oz smoked fatty bacon, rind removed and cut into strips	ground cinnamon
100 g/4 oz butter	5 oz smoked fatty bacon, cut into strips
7 tablespoons hot water	½ cup butter
40 g/1½ oz plain flour	7 tablespoons hot water
2 teaspoons redcurrant jelly, to finish	⅓ cup all-purpose flour
	2 teaspoons redcurrant jelly, to finish

Remove the outer membrane from the venison and any visible sinews and tendons. Rub the meat with 2 tablespoons oil, then roll it over the rosemary leaves so that they adhere to the meat.

Put half the shallots (scallions) in a large bowl with the carrots, onions, wine, half the wine vinegar, the remaining oil, the bouquet garni, juniper berries, and salt, pepper and spice(s) to taste.

Add the venison to this marinade, then leave in a cool place (not in the refrigerator) for 24 hours, turning the venison over from time to time.

The next day, remove the venison from the marinade and dry thoroughly on kitchen paper towels. Strain the marinade and reserve. Sew or lard the strips of fatty bacon into the venison.

Place the venison in a roasting pan and spread with two thirds of the butter. Roast in a preheated moderately hot oven (190°C/375°F/ Gas Mark 5) for 1½ to 1¾ hours, basting the venison occasionally during cooking with the reserved marinade.

Halfway through the cooking time, sprinkle the meat with salt and pepper. Put the remaining shallots in a small heavy pan with the remaining wine vinegar. Boil rapidly until reduced by half, then add about 200 ml/⅓ pint/1 cup reserved marinade and the hot water. Stir well and simmer gently.

Meanwhile, melt the remaining butter in a separate pan, sprinkle in the flour and cook for 1 minute, stirring constantly. Stir in the shallot liquid gradually, stirring after each addition. Simmer until thick, then stir in the redcurrant jelly. Taste and adjust seasoning.

Transfer the venison to a warmed serving platter. Serve hot, with the sauce handed separately.
SERVES 6

Wild quail have become so scarce in Britain that they are now protected, but frozen oven-ready quail, many of which are bred in Japan, are available. Whilst the flavour of these tame birds will never be quite as rich as their wild counterparts in France, they make acceptable substitutes. Since quail look and taste very similar to partridges, the two birds are interchangeable.

Check the weight before buying quail. Whereas one wild quail may be sufficient to serve one person, it may be necessary to serve two purchased quail, because they normally weigh only about 150 g/5 oz each.

Quails quickly become dry during cooking; it is therefore essential to wrap them to keep them moist. Vine leaves are popular in France for wrapping around quails, but if the birds are to be simply grilled, fried or roasted, they can be protected with a piece of barding fat or fatty bacon.

CAILLES À LA VIGNEROLLE

Quails in White Wine with Vine Leaves

Fresh vine leaves are not easy to obtain outside France, but vine leaves preserved in brine are available at Middle Eastern stores and some good supermarkets. Soak preserved vine leaves in hot water for 30 minutes before use to extract the strong flavour of brine, then dry thoroughly.

Metric/Imperial	American
6 oven-ready quail	6 oven-ready quail
18 vine leaves	18 vine leaves
6 streaky bacon rashers, rinds removed	6 fatty bacon slices
75 g/3 oz butter	$\frac{1}{3}$ cup butter
salt	salt
freshly ground black pepper	freshly ground black pepper
about 200 ml/$\frac{1}{3}$ pint dry white wine, or half wine and half chicken stock	about 1 cup dry white wine, or half wine and half chicken stock
6 slices bread, crusts removed and cut into triangles	6 slices bread, crusts removed and cut into triangles

Wrap each quail in three vine leaves, leaving the heads of the birds protruding. Tie a rasher (slice) of bacon on top of each bird with trussing thread or string.

Melt a little butter in the bottom of a flameproof casserole large enough to hold the quail in a single layer. Add the quail and fry gently on all sides for a few minutes, then sprinkle with salt and pepper to taste.

Pour in enough wine, or wine and stock, to come halfway up the sides of the quail, then bring to the boil. Lower the heat, cover and poach very gently for 25 to 30 minutes or until the quail are tender when pierced with a skewer.

Remove the quail from the casserole, then untie and discard the vine leaves. Keep the quail and bacon hot. Boil the cooking liquid vigorously until reduced by half, then return the quail and bacon to the casserole and heat through for a few minutes.

Melt the remaining butter in a frying pan (skillet), add the bread triangles and fry until golden brown on both sides. Place these *croûtes* on a warmed serving platter and arrange one quail and one piece of bacon on top of each. Taste and adjust the seasoning of the cooking juices, then sprinkle over the quail. Serve immediately.
SERVES 3

VARIATIONS: Sometimes this dish is garnished with thinly sliced apples. Toss them in melted butter, then dip them in the quail cooking juices just before serving.

Young partridge can be substituted for the quail, in which case the cooking time should be at least 30 minutes. Allow one partridge per person.

Cailles à la vignerolle; Salmis de bécasses

SALMIS DE BÉCASSES

Woodcock Ragoût

Metric/Imperial	American
2 woodcock	2 woodcock
8 slices bread, crusts removed	8 slices bread, crusts removed
40 g/1$\frac{1}{2}$ oz butter	3 tablespoons butter
salt	salt
400 ml/14 fl oz chicken stock (page 42)	1$\frac{3}{4}$ cups chicken stock (page 42)
7 tablespoons champagne (optional)	7 tablespoons champagne (optional)
6 shallots, peeled and finely chopped	6 scallions, peeled and finely chopped
1 garlic clove, peeled and halved	1 garlic clove, peeled and halved
2 whole cloves	2 whole cloves
few thyme leaves	few thyme leaves
few parsley leaves	few parsley leaves
freshly ground black pepper	freshly ground black pepper
7 tablespoons full-bodied red wine	7 tablespoons full-bodied red wine
1 tablespoon olive oil	1 tablespoon olive oil
juice of $\frac{1}{2}$ lemon	juice of $\frac{1}{2}$ lemon

Truss the woodcock with thread or fine string, but do not draw them. Thread each woodcock on a skewer.

Spread the bread with the butter and place in the bottom of a buttered roasting pan. Place the woodcock on top. Roast in a preheated moderate oven (180°C/350°F/Gas Mark 4) for 30 minutes sprinkling the bird with salt halfway through cooking.

Meanwhile, pour half the stock into a heavy pan, add the champagne (if using), shallots (scallions) garlic, cloves, thyme, parsley, and salt and pepper to taste. Bring to the boil, then lower the heat and simmer gently.

When the woodcock are cooked, remove the skewers and thread, then cut the birds into serving pieces. Discard the gizzard. Mash the entrails and mix with the red wine. Stir this mixture into the simmering stock. Cover and simmer for 10 minutes.

Place the pieces of woodcock in a frying pan (skillet). Strain the sauce into the pan, then stir in the remaining stock and the oil and lemon juice. Place the bread slices on top of the woodcock, taking care they do not dip into the juice. Cover the pan and simmer gently for 10 minutes. The bread will become soft in the steam from the cooking juices.

Place the bread slices on a warmed serving platter, then place the woodcock on top. Boil the sauce to reduce slightly if not already thick, then taste and adjust seasoning. Pour over the woodcock and serve immediately.
SERVES 4

MEATS

To understand meat cookery in France, it is almost essential to take a look in the window or chilling cabinet of a French butcher. To see the neatly trimmed steaks, escalopes and cutlets; the beautifully boned, rolled and larded joints, some with flavoursome stuffings; trays piled high with finely minced beef and veal; strings of white and black puddings, and bowls of creamy-white whipped lard.

Meat is expensive in France, but it is also of exceptionally high quality; thanks to the skill of the butcher, there is very little wastage. The French like to buy their meat ready-boned, trimmed and free from gristle and fat, and cut to the exact size for the dish that is to be cooked. These rules apply to both the prime and cheaper cuts of meat.

In France, braising, casseroling and stewing are popular cooking methods for the cheaper cuts. The meat is often marinated in wine or wine vinegar before cooking to help tenderize it; onions, garlic, herbs and seasonings are added for extra flavour. Before slow-cooking, the meat is usually fried quickly in hot fat or oil, to seal in the juices and give extra flavour to the finished dish. The choice of cooking vessel for casseroles and stews is also important. Cast iron and earthenware casserole dishes with tight-fitting lids are suitable, but a traditional French doufeu with an inverted lid is even better (see page 25). Water is poured into the top of the lid to create steam, so that the coarser, drier cuts of meat become moist during long, slow cooking in the oven.

Long, gentle cooking may be the preferred method for cooking cheaper cuts, but for roasting cuts the French prefer shorter cooking times. Often these times will seem incredibly short to those unused to French cooking – lamb in particular is always served pink. But taking into consideration that the meat is always of the highest quality, it is not surprising that the French prefer to appreciate its full flavour and succulence when underdone.

The French have their own very individual way of dividing a carcass and this sometimes makes it awkward or difficult to adapt French recipes. For this reason, the cuts of meat used in the recipes in this chapter have been adapted to the more usual cuts found in this country.

ARTOIS/NORD

CAGHUSE
Pork with Onions

This simple dish is also called Kakusse in some regions of northern France. Although it is traditionally served cold, it is also excellent served hot.

Metric/Imperial	American
2 tablespoons saindoux★, pork dripping or butter	2 tablespoons saindoux★, pork drippings or butter
1.5 kg/3 lb leg of pork (fillet end)	3 lb leg of pork (fillet end)
6 medium onions, peeled and thickly sliced	6 medium onions, peeled and thickly sliced
salt	salt
freshly ground black pepper	freshly ground black pepper
2 tablespoons white wine vinegar	2 tablespoons white wine vinegar

Brush a baking dish or roasting pan with half the fat, then put in the pork. Sprinkle the onions around the pork, then sprinkle with salt and pepper to taste. Dot the pork and onions with the remaining fat.

Roast in a preheated moderate oven (160°C/325°F/Gas Mark 3) for $2\frac{1}{4}$ to $2\frac{1}{2}$ hours or until the pork is tender, basting the pork with the cooking juices frequently during cooking.

Pour the wine vinegar into the onions and stir well to combine. Leave until cold before serving.
SERVES 4 TO 6

RÔTI DE PORC AUX QUETSCHES

Roast Pork with Plums

Plums grow prolifically in Alsace–Lorraine, and the purple-skinned quetsch plums are the correct variety to use for this recipe. Golden mirabelle or any other variety of plum can be used instead of quetsch, but they may not need such a long cooking time. Braised cabbage is the traditional accompaniment.

Metric/Imperial	American
2 tablespoons saindoux★, pork dripping or butter	2 tablespoons saindoux★, pork drippings or butter
6 sage leaves, halved	6 sage leaves, halved
1.5 kg/3 lb boned and rolled loin or shoulder of pork	3 lb boned and rolled loin or shoulder of pork
salt	salt
freshly ground black pepper	freshly ground black pepper
2 tablespoons soft brown sugar	2 tablespoons soft brown sugar
7 tablespoons water	7 tablespoons water
1 kg/2 lb quetsch plums	2 lb quetsch plums

Brush a roasting pan with 1 tablespoon fat, then sprinkle with half the sage leaves. Put the pork in the pan, brush with the remaining fat, then sprinkle with salt and pepper and the remaining sage. Roast in a preheated moderately hot oven (190°C/375°F/Gas Mark 5) for 2 to 2¼ hours or until the pork is tender.

Fifteen minutes before the end of the cooking, put the sugar in a separate heavy pan with the water. Bring to the boil, add the plums and simmer gently for about 15 minutes, until tender but still whole.

Slice the pork neatly, then place in the centre of a warmed serving platter. Remove the plums from their cooking liquid with a slotted spoon and arrange around the edge of the platter. Drizzle a few spoons of the plum cooking liquid over the pork. Keep hot.

Boil the remaining plum cooking liquid for a few minutes, stirring constantly. Pour over the pork and plums or hand separately in a sauceboat. Serve immediately.

SERVES 4 TO 6

Porc au lait

PORC AU LAIT

Pork Cooked in Milk

Metric/Imperial	American
1.5 kg/3 lb boned and rolled loin or shoulder of pork	3 lb boned and rolled loin or shoulder of pork
2 garlic cloves, peeled and cut into thin slivers	2 garlic cloves, peeled and cut into thin slivers
salt	salt
freshly ground black pepper	freshly ground black pepper
25 g/1 oz butter	2 tablespoons butter
1 thyme sprig	1 thyme sprig
1 bay leaf	1 bay leaf
1 litre/1¾ pints milk	4¼ cups milk

Make a few incisions in the pork with a sharp knife, then insert the slivers of garlic. Sprinkle with salt and pepper.

Melt the butter in a large flameproof casserole, add the pork and fry over moderate heat until browned on all sides. Add the thyme and bay leaf, then pour in the milk and bring slowly to the boil.

Cover and cook in a preheated moderate oven (160°C/325°F/Gas Mark 3) for 2¼ to 2½ hours or until the pork is tender, turning it over halfway during cooking.

Transfer the pork to a warmed serving dish. Discard the thyme and bay leaf and boil the milk rapidly for a few minutes to reduce slightly, then taste and adjust seasoning. Serve immediately, with the sauce handed separately in a sauceboat.

SERVES 4 TO 6

VARIATION: Add 150 ml/¼ pint/⅔ cup double (heavy) cream and 1 tablespoon prepared French mustard to the milk at the end of the cooking, then cook until reduced and thickened.

Blanquette de porc;
Fleischknepfle

FLEISCHKNEPFLE

Pork and Veal Meatballs with Caper Sauce

*If liked, use minced (ground) beef instead of the veal, and
add a little grated horseradish to the sauce for extra flavour.*

Metric/Imperial	American
150 g/5 oz crustless bread	5 slices bread, crusts removed
120 ml/4 fl oz milk	½ cup milk
2 onions, peeled	2 onions, peeled
50 g/2 oz butter	¼ cup butter
350 g/12 oz boned loin of pork, minced	¾ lb boneless loin of pork, ground
350 g/12 oz boned shoulder of veal, minced	¾ lb boneless shoulder of veal, ground
1 egg, beaten	1 egg, beaten
2 tablespoons chopped parsley	2 tablespoons chopped parsley
freshly grated nutmeg	freshly grated nutmeg
salt	salt
freshly ground black pepper	freshly ground black pepper
2 litres/3½ pints water	4½ pints/9 cups water
1 whole clove	1 whole clove
1 veal bone	1 veal bone
1 bouquet garni★	1 bouquet garni★
25 g/1 oz plain flour	¼ cup all-purpose flour
2 tablespoons double cream	2 tablespoons heavy cream
2 tablespoons capers	2 tablespoons capers

Crumble the bread into a bowl, stir in the milk and leave to soak. Meanwhile, chop 1 onion finely. Melt half the butter in a small pan, add the chopped onion and fry gently until soft.

Squeeze the bread firmly to extract the excess milk, then place in a bowl with the minced (ground) meats, egg, fried onion, half the parsley and nutmeg, salt and pepper to taste. Mix together with the hands. Leave to stand.

Bring the water to the boil in a large pan. Add the remaining whole onion stuck with the clove, the veal bone, bouquet garni and salt and pepper to taste. Boil for 30 minutes.

Meanwhile, form the meat mixture into small balls, about the size of an egg. Remove the onion, veal bone and bouquet garni from the stock and lower the heat. Add the meatballs to the stock and simmer gently for 10 to 15 minutes until cooked through. Transfer to a warmed serving dish, using a slotted spoon; keep hot.

Measure 750 ml/1¼ pints/3 cups of the cooking liquid. Melt the remaining butter in a large heavy pan, sprinkle in the flour and cook, stirring, for 1 minute to obtain a smooth *roux* (paste). Pour in the measured stock a little at a time, stirring vigorously after each addition. Bring slowly to the boil, stirring constantly, then lower the heat and simmer for 5 to 6 minutes until the sauce thickens, stirring frequently.

Stir the cream and capers into the sauce, then taste and adjust seasoning. Pour the sauce over the meatballs, then sprinkle with the remaining parsley. Serve immediately.

SERVES 6

SAVOIE

FRICASSÉE DE CAÏON

Pork Fricassée with Red Wine and Cream

The original French recipe for this fricassée includes 120 ml/4 fl oz/½ cup pig's blood, which is mixed with the cream and added at the end of the cooking time. The blood undoubtedly enriches the sauce, both in colour and flavour, but it may not be to everyone's taste!

Metric/Imperial	American
1 kg/2 lb boned loin of pork, cut into 2.5 cm/1 inch cubes	*2 lb boned loin of pork, cut into 1 inch cubes*
2 large onions, peeled and sliced into rings	*2 large onions, peeled and sliced into rings*
2 carrots, peeled and sliced into thin rings	*2 carrots, peeled and sliced into thin rings*
3 garlic cloves, peeled and crushed	*3 garlic cloves, peeled and crushed*
2 thyme sprigs	*2 thyme sprigs*
1 bay leaf	*1 bay leaf*
400 ml/14 fl oz dry white wine	*1¾ cups dry white wine*
2 tablespoons oil	*2 tablespoons oil*
6 black peppercorns	*6 black peppercorns*
salt	*salt*
1 tablespoon saindoux★, pork dripping or butter	*1 tablespoon saindoux★, pork drippings or butter*
1 tablespoon plain flour	*1 tablespoon all-purpose flour*
200 ml/⅓ pint red wine	*1 cup red wine*
200 ml/⅓ pint chicken stock (page 42)	*1 cup chicken stock (page 42)*
120 ml/4 fl oz double cream	*½ cup heavy cream*
freshly ground black pepper	*freshly ground black pepper*
croûtons★, to serve (optional)	*croûtons★, to serve (optional)*

Put the pork in a large bowl with the onions, carrots, garlic, thyme, bay leaf, white wine, oil, peppercorns, and salt to taste. Stir well, then cover and leave to marinate for 12 hours.

The next day, remove the pork from the marinade, drain and dry thoroughly on kitchen paper towels. Strain the marinade and reserve. Melt the fat in a large flameproof casserole, add the pork and fry over brisk heat until browned on all sides.

Sprinkle the flour over the pork and cook for 1 minute, stirring constantly. Pour in the red wine and stock gradually. (If the meat is not covered by the liquid, add just enough of the strained marinade to cover the meat.)

Bring to the boil, then lower the heat, cover and cook gently for 1¼ to 1½ hours until the pork is tender.

Stir the cream slowly into the casserole. Simmer gently for 10 minutes without boiling, stirring constantly, then taste and adjust seasoning. Serve immediately, with *croûtons*, if liked.
SERVES 4

ORLÉANAIS

BLANQUETTE DE PORC

Blanquette of Pork

If you prefer the Normandy version of blanquette de porc, use cider instead of the wine and stock in this recipe. Strictly speaking, sucking pig should also be used, but this is rarely available and is not essential.

Metric/Imperial	American
1 tablespoon saindoux★, pork dripping or butter	*1 tablespoon saindoux★, pork drippings or butter*
225 g/8 oz small pickling onions, peeled	*½ lb baby onions, peeled*
1.5 kg/3 lb boned loin of pork, cut into 2.5 cm/1 inch cubes, bone reserved	*3 lb boned loin of pork, cut into 1 inch cubes, bone reserved*
2 tablespoons plain flour	*2 tablespoons all-purpose flour*
200 ml/⅓ pint chicken stock (page 42)	*1 cup chicken stock (page 42)*
200 ml/⅓ pint dry white wine	*1 cup dry white wine*
1 bouquet garni★	*1 bouquet garni★*
3 garlic cloves, peeled	*3 garlic cloves, peeled*
salt	*salt*
freshly ground black pepper	*freshly ground black pepper*
25 g/1 oz butter	*2 tablespoons butter*
450 g/1 lb button mushrooms, sliced	*4 cups sliced button mushrooms*
120 ml/4 fl oz double cream	*½ cup heavy cream*
1 egg yolk	*1 egg yolk*
juice of 1 lemon	*juice of 1 lemon*
croûtons★, to serve	*croûtons★, to serve*

Melt the fat in a large flameproof casserole, add the onions and fry over moderate heat until lightly coloured. Remove with a slotted spoon and set aside.

Add the pork and bone to the casserole and fry gently until lightly coloured on all sides. Sprinkle in the flour and cook, stirring, for 1 minute. Stir in the stock and wine gradually, then add the bouquet garni, 2 whole garlic cloves, and salt and pepper to taste. Cover and cook gently for 1 hour.

Meanwhile, crush the remaining garlic. Melt the butter in a frying pan (skillet), add the mushrooms and garlic and fry over brisk heat for 5 minutes. Remove from the heat and add salt and pepper to taste.

Add the onions to the casserole and cook gently for a further 30 minutes or until the pork is tender, adding the mushrooms and their cooking juices 5 minutes before the end of the cooking time.

Transfer the pork, onions and mushrooms to a warmed deep serving dish, using a slotted spoon; keep hot. Discard the bone, bouquet garni and whole garlic cloves from the sauce.

Mix together the cream, egg yolk and lemon juice in a small bowl. Stir in a few spoons of the hot sauce, then pour this mixture back into the casserole on top of the stove. Heat gently without boiling, stirring vigorously all the time. Taste and adjust seasoning, then pour over the meat and vegetables. Serve immediately, garnished with *croûtons*.
SERVES 6

CAILLETTES

Pork and Spinach Patties

Caillettes are very similar to the better known crépinettes, often seen on French menus. Here they are served hot with a tomato sauce, but they are equally good served cold, in which case omit the tomato sauce and serve a tossed green salad instead.

Metric/Imperial	American
450 g/1 lb spinach, roughly chopped	1 lb spinach, roughly chopped
salt	salt
750 g/12 oz boned pork, minced	¾ lb boneless pork, ground
175 g/6 oz streaky bacon, rinds removed and minced	9 slices fatty bacon, ground
2 garlic cloves, peeled and crushed	2 garlic cloves, peeled and crushed
1 teaspoon dried thyme	1 teaspoon dried thyme
½ teaspoon dried marjoram	½ teaspoon dried marjoram
3 sage leaves, finely chopped	3 sage leaves, finely chopped
freshly ground black pepper	freshly ground black pepper
150 g/5 oz long-grain rice, boiled and drained	⅔ cup long-grain rice, boiled and drained
pig's caul casing★, soaked and drained	pig's caul casing★ soaked and drained
2 tablespoons olive oil	2 tablespoons olive oil
600 ml/1 pint tomato sauce (page 47), to serve	2½ cups tomato sauce (page 47), to serve

Put the spinach in a pan with just the water clinging to the leaves after washing, and a little salt. Cover and cook over brisk heat for 5 minutes until tender. Drain thoroughly and chop very finely.

Put the spinach in a bowl with the minced (ground) meat, bacon, garlic, herbs, and salt and pepper to taste. Mix well with the hands, then add the rice and mix until thoroughly combined.

Stretch out the pig's caul on a flat surface, then cut into six 15 cm/6 inch squares. Divide the meat and spinach mixture equally between the squares, placing it in the centre. Press the mixture flat and wrap the caul carefully around it.

Heat the oil in a frying pan (skillet). Place the *caillettes* in the pan and cook very gently for 1 hour, turning them over halfway during the cooking time. Serve hot, with the tomato sauce handed separately in a sauceboat.

SERVES 4 TO 6

PORC AUX POMMES

Pork with Apples

Metric/Imperial	American
1.5 kg/2 lb boned and rolled loin of pork	2 lb boned and rolled loin of pork
salt	salt
freshly ground black pepper	freshly ground black pepper
2 tablespoons water	2 tablespoons water
1 kg/2 lb cooking apples	2 lb tart apples
4 tablespoons dry cider	¼ cup hard cider
25 g/1 oz butter	2 tablespoons butter
2 tablespoons double cream	2 tablespoons heavy cream

Place the pork in a buttered roasting pan and sprinkle with salt and pepper. Add the water, then roast in a preheated moderately hot oven (190°C/375°F/Gas Mark 5) for 1¾ hours, basting frequently.

Peel and core the apples and slice into quarters. Remove the pork from the pan and drain off the cooking juices. Pour the cider into the pan, add the pork, then surround with the apples. Sprinkle with salt and pepper, then dot with the butter. Return to the moderately hot oven and roast for a further 20 minutes or until the pork is tender.

Transfer the pork to a warmed serving platter and surround with the apples. Stir the cream into the juices in the pan, then cook on top of the stove for 2 minutes, stirring constantly. Taste and adjust seasoning, then pour over the apples. Serve immediately.

SERVES 4 TO 6

Porc aux pommes; Côtes de porc aux lentilles

CÔTES DE PORC AUX LENTILLES

Pork Chops with Lentils

Metric/Imperial	American
450 g/1 lb green lentils	2 cups green lentils
1 bay leaf	1 bay leaf
2 onions, peeled	2 onions, peeled
1 whole clove	1 whole clove
salt	salt
freshly ground black pepper	freshly ground black pepper
6 pork chops, trimmed of fat	6 pork chops, trimmed of fat
4 sage leaves, chopped	4 sage leaves, chopped
50 g/2 oz saindoux★, pork dripping or butter	¼ cup saindoux★, pork drippings or butter
6 small sausages★	6 small sausages★
2 carrots, peeled and diced	2 carrots, peeled and diced
about 600 ml/1 pint chicken stock (page 42)	about 2½ cups chicken stock (page 42)

Rinse the lentils under cold running water and pick them over to remove any grit. Place in a large pan with the bay leaf and 1 onion stuck with the clove. Cover with water, bring to the boil and simmer for 1 hour. Add salt and pepper to taste halfway through the cooking time.

Meanwhile, sprinkle the chops with the sage and salt and pepper to taste. Melt the fat in a large flameproof casserole, add the chops and fry over brisk heat for 10 minutes until browned on all sides. Remove with a slotted spoon and set aside.

Prick the sausage skins with a fork. Chop the remaining onion. Add to the casserole with the carrots and fry over brisk heat for 10 minutes until lightly coloured, stirring constantly.

Drain the lentils, then add to the casserole with the chops. Cover with the stock and bring to the boil. Lower the heat, cover and cook gently for 1 hour or until the chops are tender.

Taste and adjust seasoning. Remove the chops and sausages from the casserole and arrange around the edge of a warmed serving platter. Pile the lentils in the centre. Serve immediately.

SERVES 6

ABOVE: **Echine de porc au raisin**

RIGHT: **Entrecôte Bercy**

ÉCHINE DE PORC AU RAISIN

Loin of Pork with Grapes

If you prefer a thick sauce to serve with the pork and grap mix 10 g/¼ oz/1½ teaspoons butter with 10 g/¼ oz/ 1 tablespoon plain (all-purpose) flour to make a beurre manie★. Whisk this into the sauce after adding the cream Simmer until thick, whisking constantly.

Metric/Imperial	American
2 onions, peeled and sliced into rings	2 onions, peeled and slice into rings
1 garlic clove, peeled and crushed	1 garlic clove, peeled and crushed
3 thyme sprigs	3 thyme sprigs
few rosemary leaves	few rosemary leaves
1 bay leaf	1 bay leaf
salt	salt
freshly ground black pepper	freshly ground black pepp
2 tablespoons oil	2 tablespoons oil
4 tablespoons marc or brandy	¼ cup marc or brandy
1.5 kg/3 lb boned and rolled loin of pork	3 lb boned and rolled loin pork
25 g/1 oz butter	2 tablespoons butter
200 ml/⅓ pint dry white wine	1 cup dry white wine
1 kg/2 lb green grapes, peeled and seeded	2 lb green grapes, peeled a seeded
120 ml/4 fl oz double cream	½ cup heavy cream

Put the onions, garlic, thyme, rosemary and bay leaf i large bowl with salt and pepper to taste. Stir in half t oil and the *marc* or brandy, then place the pork in t bowl. Turn the pork over several times in the marina then cover and leave to marinate for 2 to 3 hours.

Remove the pork from the marinade, drain and d thoroughly on kitchen paper towels. Strain the ma nade and reserve. Heat the remaining oil in a lar flameproof casserole with the butter. Add the pork a fry over brisk heat until browned on all sides. Add t reserved marinade and the white wine and bring to t boil.

Lower the heat, cover and cook gently for 1½ to hours or until the pork is tender. Add the grap 5 minutes before the end of the cooking time.

Remove the pork from the casserole and slice neat Arrange on a warmed serving platter and keep hot. S the cream into the cooking liquid and simmer fo minutes, stirring constantly. Taste and adjust seasoni then pour over the pork. Serve immediately.
SERVES 6

CÔTES DE PORC VIGNERONNE

Pork Chops with Tomatoes and White Wine

The most suitable wine for this dish is Mâcon Blanc.

Metric/Imperial	American
6 pork chops, trimmed of fat	6 pork chops, trimmed of fat
salt	salt
freshly ground black pepper	freshly ground black pepper
2 tablespoons saindoux★, pork dripping or butter	2 tablespoons saindoux★, pork drippings or butter
4 ripe tomatoes, skinned and chopped	4 ripe tomatoes, skinned and chopped
200 ml/⅓ pint dry white wine	1 cup dry white wine
2 tablespoons Dijon-style mustard★	2 tablespoons Dijon-style mustard★
1 tablespoon snipped chives	1 tablespoon snipped chives
25 g/1 oz butter, softened	2 tablespoons butter

Sprinkle the chops with salt and pepper to taste. Melt the fat in a large frying pan (skillet), add the chops and fry over brisk heat until browned on all sides. Lower the heat, cover and cook gently for 45 minutes or until tender.

Meanwhile, purée the tomatoes in an electric blender or *Mouli-légumes* (vegetable mill).

Transfer the chops to a warmed serving platter and keep hot. Pour the wine into the pan and stir to mix with the cooking juices and sediment. Add the puréed tomatoes, cook for 2 minutes, then remove from the heat and stir in the mustard and chives, and salt and pepper to taste. Whisk the butter into the sauce a little at a time, then pour over the chops. Serve immediately.
SERVES 6

STEAK AUX OIGNONS

Rump Steak with Onions

*If you like the flavour of fresh herbs with steak, they can be
finely chopped and sprinkled over the dish just before
serving. Parsley, chervil and tarragon go well with steak.*

Metric/Imperial	American
5 g/1 oz butter	2 tablespoons butter
2 onions, peeled and thinly sliced	2 onions, peeled and thinly sliced
50 g/1 lb rump steak	1 lb top round steak
salt	salt
freshly ground black pepper	freshly ground black pepper
7 tablespoons dry white wine	7 tablespoons dry white wine
0 g/4 oz mushrooms, thinly sliced	1 cup thinly sliced mushrooms

Melt half the butter in a frying pan (skillet), add the
onions and fry gently for 10 minutes.

Meanwhile, melt the remaining butter in a separate
pan. Add the steak and cook over moderate heat for 3 to
5 minutes on each side, according to taste. Transfer to a
warmed serving platter, sprinkle with salt and pepper
and keep hot.

Stir the wine into the meat juices in the pan and scrape
up any sediment. Add the mushrooms, increase the heat
and cook rapidly until the liquid is glazed and reduced.
Add salt and pepper to taste.

Sprinkle the steak with the onions, mushrooms and
the juices. Serve immediately.

SERVES 2 TO 3

ENTRECÔTE BERCY

Entrecôte (Sirloin) Steaks with Beurre Bercy

Metric/Imperial	American
BEURRE BERCY:	BEURRE BERCY:
1 beef marrow bone★ (about 175 g/6 oz in weight)	1 beef marrow bone★ (about 6 oz in weight)
salt	salt
120 ml/4 fl oz dry white wine	½ cup dry white wine
1 shallot, peeled and finely chopped	1 scallion, peeled and finely chopped
100 g/4 oz butter, softened	½ cup butter, softened
1 teaspoon lemon juice	1 teaspoon lemon juice
1 teaspoon chopped parsley	1 teaspoon chopped parsley
freshly ground black pepper	freshly ground black pepper
25 g/1 oz butter	2 tablespoons butter
1 tablespoon oil	1 tablespoon oil
4 entrecôte (sirloin) steaks, about 1 cm/½ inch thick	4 entrecôte (sirloin) steaks, about ½ inch thick

Make the *beurre Bercy* according to the method on page
50. Leave to cool.

Meanwhile, cook the steaks: Melt the butter in a
heavy frying pan (skillet) with the oil. Add the steaks
and fry for 3 to 5 minutes on each side, according to taste.

Sprinkle the steaks with salt and pepper, then transfer
to a warmed serving platter. Top with the butter and
serve immediately.

SERVES 4

In France, steaks are often
cooked over a charcoal
fire or barbecue, in which
case they are brushed
with 50 ml/2 fl oz/⅓ cup
oil before cooking. They
are usually served with
pommes frites (French
fries).

DAUBE LANGUEDOCIENNE
Beef in Red Wine Languedoc-Style

If possible, use red wine from the Languedoc region to get the authentic flavour of this dish. Pork rinds★ add richness and flavour but they are not an essential ingredient and can therefore be omitted if difficult to obtain.

Metric/Imperial	American
150 g/5 oz pork back fat, cut into thin strips (lardons★)	*⅔ cup pork back fat, cut into thin strips (lardons★)*
5 tablespoons armagnac or brandy	*⅓ cup armagnac or brandy*
6 garlic cloves, peeled and crushed	*6 garlic cloves, peeled and crushed*
1.5 kg/3–3½ lb topside or top rump of beef	*3–3½ lb top round of beef*
salt	*salt*
freshly ground black pepper	*freshly ground black pepper*
ground mixed spice	*ground allspice*
150 g/5 oz fresh pork rinds★	*ground cinnamon*
75 g/3 oz saindoux★, dripping or butter	*5 oz fresh pork rinds★*
2 leeks (white part only), sliced	*⅓ cup saindoux★, drippings or butter*
3 onions, peeled	*2 leeks (white part only), sliced*
3 carrots, peeled and diced	*3 onions, peeled*
25 g/1 oz dried mushrooms★, soaked and drained (optional)	*3 carrots, peeled and diced*
450 g/1 lb tomatoes, skinned, quartered and seeded	*1 oz dried mushrooms★, soaked and drained (optional)*
2 bouquet garni★	*1 lb tomatoes, skinned, quartered and seeded*
1 bottle dry red wine	*2 bouquet garni★*
2 tablespoons plain flour, for sealing	*1 bottle dry red wine*
450 g/1 lb dried haricot beans, soaked overnight in cold water	*2 tablespoons all-purpose flour, for sealing*
1 whole clove	*2⅓ cups dried navy beans, soaked overnight in cold water*
1 × 350 g/12 oz Toulouse sausage★, cut into 6 pieces	*1 whole clove*
	1 × ¾ lb Toulouse sausage★, cut into 6 pieces

Macerate the pork fat with 2 tablespoons *armagnac* or brandy and a quarter of the crushed garlic. Using a *lardoire★*, insert the strips of fat into the piece of beef (see Larding – page 26). Rub the meat with salt, pepper and spice(s) to taste.

Plunge the pork rinds into a pan of boiling water to blanch them, then drain.

Melt 50 g/2 oz/¼ cup fat in a very large flameproof casserole, add the beef, then fry over brisk heat until browned on all sides. Add the leeks, pork rinds, 2 chopped onions, the carrots, the remaining garlic, mushrooms (if using), tomatoes, 1 bouquet garni and the wine.

Bring to the boil, cover the casserole with a lid, then seal around the edge of the lid with a paste made from the flour and a few drops of water. Transfer to a preheated moderate oven (160°C/325°F/Gas Mark 3) and cook for 2½ hours.

Meanwhile, drain the haricots, rinse under cold running water, then place in a large pan. Cover with fresh cold water and add the remaining bouquet garni and the remaining whole onion stuck with the clove. Bring to the boil, lower the heat, cover and simmer for 45 minutes or until just tender. Add salt and pepper to taste halfway through cooking. Drain, discarding the bouquet garni, onion and clove.

Melt the remaining fat in a frying pan (skillet). Prick the sausage skin, then add the sausage pieces to the pan and fry until lightly coloured.

Transfer the casserole to the top of the stove and break the pastry seal. Discard the bouquet garni, then skim off any fat on the surface of the cooking liquid, or blot with kitchen paper towels. Add the haricots and sausage, mix well, then cover and simmer gently for a further 30 minutes.

A few minutes before serving time, stir in the remaining *armagnac* or brandy and heat through. Taste and adjust seasoning. Remove the meat carefully from the cooking liquid and slice neatly. Remove the pork rinds and cut into very thin strips. Return the beef and rinds to the cooking liquid and heat through. Serve immediately.
SERVES 6

NOTE: The beef can be cut into serving pieces before cooking rather than being cooked as a whole piece. Coat the pieces lightly with flour seasoned with salt, pepper and spice(s), and omit the larding with pork fat, then fry in the fat as for the whole piece. Cook for 2 hours before adding the beans and sausage.

MIROTON LYONNAIS
Sauté of Beef with Onions

A tasty way to use up beef leftovers from the Sunday roast

Metric/Imperial	American
2 tablespoons saindoux★, dripping or butter	*2 tablespoons saindoux★, drippings or butter*
1 kg/2 lb onions, peeled and finely chopped	*2 lb onions, peeled and finely chopped*
1 kg/2 lb cooked beef, thinly sliced	*2 lb cooked beef, thinly sliced*
salt	*salt*
freshly ground black pepper	*freshly ground black pepper*
2 tablespoons red wine vinegar	*2 tablespoons red wine vinegar*
PERSILLADE:	PERSILLADE:
1 bunch parsley, finely chopped	*1 bunch parsley, finely chopped*
3 garlic cloves, peeled and finely chopped	*3 garlic cloves, peeled and finely chopped*

Melt the fat in a large flameproof casserole. Add the onions and fry gently until soft and lightly coloured, stirring frequently.

Add the beef, stir well to mix with the onions, then cook until heated through and browned on all sides. Add salt and pepper to taste.

Mix together the parsley and garlic for the *persillade*, then sprinkle over the beef and onions with the vinegar. Mix well. Serve hot, straight from the casserole.
SERVES 6

The term *miroton* is used to describe a certain Lyonnais dish made with leftover beef. Originally called a *mironton*, the dish is always composed of slices of cold beef mixed with a large quantity of onions which have been fried in butter. The original *mironton* was cooked in the oven with a Lyonnais (onion) sauce poured over, but this is not usual nowadays. The finished dish is always sprinkled with chopped parsley before serving.

BOEUF BOURGUIGNON

Boeuf Bourguignon is excellent reheated, some say even better than when served the first time.

Metric/Imperial	American
1 large onion, peeled and thinly sliced	1 large onion, peeled and thinly sliced
1 parsley sprig	1 parsley sprig
1 thyme sprig, crumbled	1 thyme sprig, crumbled
1 bay leaf, crushed	1 bay leaf, crushed
1 kg/2 lb chuck steak or top rump, cut into large pieces	2 lb chuck steak or top round of beef, cut into large pieces
2 tablespoons marc or brandy	2 tablespoons marc or brandy
400 ml/14 fl oz red wine (preferably Bourgogne)	1¾ cups red wine (preferably Bourgogne)
2 tablespoons oil	2 tablespoons oil
50 g/2 oz butter	¼ cup butter
150 g/5 oz lean bacon, rind removed and cut into thin strips	⅔ cup lean bacon, cut into thin strips
24 small pickling onions, peeled	24 baby onions, peeled
450 g/1 lb button mushrooms, sliced	4 cups sliced button mushrooms
25 g/1 oz plain flour	¼ cup all-purpose flour
300 ml/½ pint beef stock (page 42)	1¼ cups beef stock (page 42)
1 garlic clove, peeled and crushed	1 garlic clove, peeled and crushed
1 bouquet garni★	1 bouquet garni★
salt	salt
freshly ground black pepper	freshly ground black pepper

Put a few onion slices in the bottom of a deep bowl with the parsley and a little of the thyme and bay leaf. Place a few pieces of beef on top. Continue with these layers until all the beef and herbs are used. Mix together the *marc* or brandy, wine and oil and pour over the beef. Cover and leave to marinate for at least 4 hours, stirring occasionally.

Melt the butter in a flameproof casserole, add the bacon and fry over moderate heat until golden brown. Remove with a slotted spoon and set aside. Add the small onions to the casserole and fry until lightly coloured on all sides, then remove with a slotted spoon and set aside. Add the mushrooms and fry, stirring, for 1 minute; drain.

Remove the pieces of beef from the marinade, then strain the marinade and set aside. Dry the beef thoroughly on kitchen paper towels, then add to the casserole and fry over brisk heat until browned on all sides. Sprinkle in the flour and cook, stirring, for 1 minute. Stir in the strained marinade gradually, then add the stock, garlic and bouquet garni. Add salt and pepper to taste, cover and simmer gently for 2 hours.

Skim off any fat on the surface of the cooking liquid. Add the bacon, onions and mushrooms, cover and simmer for 30 minutes or until the beef is tender.

Discard the bouquet garni, then taste and adjust seasoning. Transfer to a warmed serving dish and serve immediately.

SERVES 4 TO 6

CARBONNADES FLAMANDES

Flemish Carbonnade of Beef

Belgian beer is ideal for this recipe, but other beers may be used instead. Stout and dark beers are often used in carbonnades because they impart a rich flavour and dark colour. Half beer and half beef stock gives a lighter gravy.

Metric/Imperial	American
1 tablespoon saindoux★, dripping or butter	1 tablespoon saindoux★, drippings or butter
1 kg/2 lb chuck steak, cut into chunks	2 lb chuck steak, cut into chunks
450 g/1 lb onions, peeled and chopped	1 lb onions, peeled and chopped
1 tablespoon brown sugar	1 tablespoon brown sugar
2 tablespoons wine vinegar	2 tablespoons wine vinegar
salt	salt
freshly ground black pepper	freshly ground black pepper
1 bouquet garni★	1 bouquet garni★
1 large slice fresh bread, crust removed	1 large slice fresh bread, crust removed
2 tablespoons hot mustard★	2 tablespoons hot mustard★
about 600 ml/1 pint beer	about 2½ cups beer
2 tablespoons plain flour, for sealing	2 tablespoons all-purpose flour, for sealing
chopped parsley, to garnish	chopped parsley, for garnish

The secret of making a successful casserole lies in the choice of top quality ingredients. Prime beef suitable for long, slow cooking is obviously the essential ingredient, neither too fat and sinewy, nor too lean (chuck steak is the best cut to buy outside France). Use fresh vegetables and freshly picked herbs when available.

If stock is called for, use homemade stock. Stock cubes and boiling water will never impart the same richness of flavour. Good quality wine or beer should also be used.

ESTOUFFAT D'ARMAGNAC

Beef Casseroled in Wine with Armagnac

This dish is best made the day before required, so that the cooking liquid can become jellied and rich before reheating. No self-respecting French cook would make an estouffat without calf's (veal) foot★ and pork rinds★, since these are the ingredients that make the finished dish so rich in flavour. If you find they are difficult to obtain, omit them, but the end result will not be quite the same.

Metric/Imperial	American
1 calf's foot★, split	1 veal foot★, split
12 strips fresh pork rind★	12 strips fresh pork rind★
2 tablespoons saindoux★, dripping or butter	2 tablespoons saindoux★, drippings or butter
1 kg/2 lb stewing beef, cut into large pieces	2 lb stewing beef, cut into large pieces
225 g/8 oz shallots, peeled and chopped	2 cups chopped scallions
450 g/1 lb carrots, peeled and sliced into rings	1 lb carrots, peeled and sliced into rings
5 garlic cloves, peeled	5 garlic cloves, peeled
1 bouquet garni★	1 bouquet garni★
3 whole cloves	3 whole cloves
pinch of freshly grated nutmeg	pinch of freshly grated nutmeg
pinch of ground mixed spice	pinch of ground allspice
salt	pinch of ground cinnamon
freshly ground black pepper	salt
1 bottle red wine	freshly ground black pepper
50 ml/2 fl oz armagnac or brandy	1 bottle red wine
	$\frac{1}{3}$ cup armagnac or brandy

Put the calf's (veal) foot in a pan, cover with water and bring to the boil. Boil for 15 minutes, then drain. Plunge the pork rinds into a pan of fresh boiling water to blanch them, then drain.

Melt the fat in a flameproof casserole. Add the beef, calf's foot, pork rinds, shallots (scallions), carrots, garlic and bouquet garni. Add the cloves, nutmeg, spice(s), and salt and pepper to taste. Pour in the wine and bring to the boil.

Cover with a tight-fitting lid, transfer to a preheated cool oven (140°C/275°F/Gas Mark 1) and cook for about 3 hours. Transfer the casserole to the top of the stove and stir in the *armagnac* or brandy. Simmer gently for 30 minutes.

To serve, place the beef in a warmed deep serving dish, taking great care to keep the pieces whole as they will be very tender. Keep hot.

Remove the bones from the calf's foot and dice the meat. Cut the pork rinds into very thin strips. Surround the beef with the calf's foot and pork rinds. Discard the garlic and bouquet garni from the cooking liquor, then taste and adjust seasoning. Pour over the beef.
SERVES 4 TO 6

VARIATION: In the Béarn region, *estouffat* is made with diced raw ham★ as well as beef, and slices of streaky (fatty) bacon are placed on top of the casserole before placing it in the oven.

Boeuf bourguignon; Carbonnades flamandes

[M]elt the fat in a large flameproof casserole, add the beef [an]d fry over brisk heat until browned on all sides. [R]emove with a slotted spoon and set aside.

Add the onions to the casserole and fry gently until [so]ft and lightly coloured. Stir in the sugar and fry until [th]e onions caramelize, then stir in the vinegar and scrape [u]p all the sediment from the bottom of the casserole.

Return the beef to the casserole and mix with the [o]nions. Add salt and pepper to taste, and the bouquet [ga]rni.

Spread one side of the bread with the mustard, then [p]lace on top of the beef and onions, mustard side down. [P]our in enough beer to come just level with the bread.

Cover the casserole with a lid, then seal around the [e]dge of the lid with a paste made from the flour and a few [d]rops of water.

Cook in a preheated moderate oven (160°C/ [32]5°F/Gas Mark 3) for 2 hours. Break the paste seal, [re]move the lid, then discard the bread and bouquet [ga]rni. Taste and adjust seasoning, then transfer to a [w]armed deep serving dish and sprinkle with chopped [p]arsley. Serve hot, with boiled potatoes and carrots or [p]etits pois.
[SE]RVES 4

BROUFADE DE NÎMES

Rump Steaks with Capers and Anchovies

Metric/Imperial	American
6 rump steaks (about 175 g/ 6 oz each and 1.5 cm/ ¾ inch thick)	6 top round steaks (about 6 oz each and ¾ inch thick)
1 bay leaf, crushed	1 bay leaf, crushed
3 whole cloves, lightly crushed	3 whole cloves, lightly crushed
8 garlic cloves, peeled and chopped	8 garlic cloves, peeled and chopped
150 ml/¼ pint oil	⅔ cup olive oil
5 onions, peeled and sliced into rings	5 onions, peeled and sliced into rings
salt	salt
freshly ground black pepper	freshly ground black pepper
150 ml/¼ pint red wine vinegar	⅔ cup red wine vinegar
100 g/4 oz capers, drained and finely chopped	¼ lb capers, drained and finely chopped
2 tablespoons plain flour	2 tablespoons all-purpose flour
300 ml/½ pint hot beef stock (page 42)	1¼ cups hot beef stock (page 42)
6 canned anchovy fillets, drained and desalted★	6 canned anchovy filets, drained and desalted★

Put the steaks in a deep bowl with the crushed bay leaf and cloves, 3 garlic cloves and the oil. Leave to marinate in a cool place for 8 hours or overnight, turning the steaks occasionally.

The next day, remove the steaks from the marinade, reserving the oil. Place a layer of onions in the bottom of a large flameproof casserole with a little of the remaining garlic. Place one or two steaks on top, then sprinkle with salt and pepper and a little of the vinegar. Continue with these layers until all the onions, garlic and steaks are used.

Cover the casserole with a concave lid or a deep ovenproof plate and fill this with water. Place the casserole over gentle heat and simmer very gently for 2 hours. Do not uncover the casserole during this time, but keep the lid or plate topped up with water as it evaporates during cooking.

Add the capers and sprinkle the flour over the steaks. Cook for 1 minute, stirring constantly, then gradually stir in the stock. Taste and adjust seasoning, then simmer for a further 15 minutes.

Place the steaks on a warmed serving platter and coat with the sauce. Place an anchovy on top of each steak, then sprinkle with the reserved oil from the marinade. Serve immediately.

SERVES 6

It is unusual to see a recipe for rump steaks which are cooked for 2 hours, but the secret of this dish lies in the special pot in which it is cooked. Called a *doufeu*, it is a casserole with an inverted lid. Water poured into the lid evaporates during cooking and the resultant condensation helps keep the meat succulent and tender. If you do not have a *doufeu*, use an upturned plate or dish for a lid, making sure it closely fits the rim of the cooking pot underneath.

Boeuf au cidre; Broufade
e Nîmes

FILET DE BOEUF AUX MORILLES

Fillet Steaks with Morel Mushrooms

Morel mushrooms are the wild, non-cultivated variety of mushrooms which have a unique and most delicate flavour. They are available in late spring in some specialist greengrocers and markets, and are well worth seeking out. They should be washed thoroughly under cold running water before use, to remove the sand that becomes trapped in their hollow shells. The stems should be trimmed at the bottom to remove any earth and sand that is clinging to them.

Metric/Imperial	American
225 g/8 oz morel mushrooms★	½ lb morel mushrooms★
250 ml/8 fl oz dry white wine	1 cup dry white wine
salt	salt
freshly ground black pepper	freshly ground black pepper
50 g/2 oz butter	¼ cup butter
6 fillet steaks (100–175 g/ 4–6 oz each)	6 filet steaks (4–6 oz each)

Put the mushrooms in a pan with the wine and salt and pepper to taste. Simmer gently for 20 minutes.

Meanwhile, melt the butter in a frying pan (skillet). Add the steaks and fry for 3 to 5 minutes on each side, according to taste.

Transfer the steaks to a warmed serving platter. Remove the mushrooms from their liquid with a slotted spoon and place around the steaks. Keep hot.

Stir the mushroom liquid into the steak frying pan and scrape up any sediment from the bottom. Increase the heat and cook rapidly until the liquid is glazed and reduced. Add salt and pepper to taste, then pour over the steak and mushrooms. Serve immediately.

SERVES 6

BOEUF AU CIDRE

Beef Cooked in Cider

Metric/Imperial	American
2 tablespoons goose fat★, dripping or butter	2 tablespoons goose fat★, drippings or butter
225 g/8 oz salt pork or streaky bacon, diced	½ lb salt pork or fatty bacon, diced
1.5 kg/3–3½ lb braising steak, cut into large chunks	3–3½ lb braising steak, cut into large chunks
3 onions, peeled and quartered	3 onions, peeled and quartered
450 g/1 lb carrots, peeled and sliced into rings	1 lb carrots, peeled and sliced into rings
1 bouquet garni★	1 bouquet garni★
1 tarragon sprig	1 tarragon sprig
salt	salt
freshly ground black pepper	freshly ground black pepper
1 litre/1¾ pints dry cider	4¼ cups hard cider

Melt the fat in a flameproof casserole, add the pork or bacon and fry over brisk heat until golden brown. Add the beef and fry until browned on all sides. Remove both pork and beef from the casserole with a slotted spoon; drain.

Add the onions to the casserole and fry gently until soft and lightly coloured. Add the carrots with the pork, beef, bouquet garni, tarragon, and salt and pepper to taste.

Stir in the cider, bring to the boil and cover with a tight-fitting lid. Cook in a preheated moderate oven (160°C/325°F/Gas Mark 3) for 2 to 2½ hours until the meat is tender. Discard the bouquet garni and tarragon. Taste and adjust seasoning, then serve straight from the casserole.

SERVES 6

VARIATION: Add about 225 g/½ lb sautéed mushrooms 15 minutes before the end of the cooking time.

BOEUF MIROTON

Gratin of Beef with Onions and Tomatoes

This is a good dish for using the beef left over from making beef stock (page 42). It can also be used for leftover roast beef, but the meat should be hot before coating with the sauce.

Metric/Imperial	American
75 g/3 oz butter	⅓ cup butter
350 g/12 oz onions, peeled and finely chopped	3 cups peeled and finely chopped onions
25 g/1 oz plain flour	¼ cup all-purpose flour
2 tablespoons wine vinegar	2 tablespoons wine vinegar
500 ml/18 fl oz beef stock (page 42)	2¼ cups beef stock (page 42)
3 tablespoons fresh tomato sauce (page 47)	3 tablespoons fresh tomato sauce (page 47)
salt	salt
freshly ground black pepper	freshly ground black pepper
750 g/1½ lb cooked beef, thinly sliced	1½ lb cooked beef, thinly sliced
3 tablespoons dried breadcrumbs	3 tablespoons dried bread crumbs

Melt 50 g/2 oz/¼ cup butter in a heavy pan, add the onions and fry gently until soft and lightly coloured. Sprinkle in the flour and cook for 1 minute, stirring constantly.

Stir in the vinegar and stock gradually, whisking vigorously after each addition, then stir in the tomato sauce, and salt and pepper to taste. Simmer gently for 20 minutes, stirring occasionally. Taste and adjust seasoning.

Spread half the sauce in the bottom of a flameproof baking dish. Arrange the slices of hot beef on top, then spread with the remaining sauce. Sprinkle with the breadcrumbs. Melt the remaining butter and pour over the top. Put under a preheated hot grill (broiler) for a few minutes until golden brown and bubbling. Serve immediately.

SERVES 4

NOTE: For additional flavour, add crushed garlic to the sauce according to taste. Mix a little chopped parsley with the breadcrumbs before sprinkling over the dish.

POT-AU-FEU

This famous dish is cooked throughout France, and each region has its own variation. It is really two dishes in one, because the cooking liquid or broth is served as a soup, then the meats and vegetables follow as the main course. The marrow from the beef bones is usually poured over baked bread which is served with the broth, although in this particular recipe the marrow bones are served along with the meats and vegetables. Accompaniments to the beef include mustard, horseradish, capers and gherkins (sweet dill pickles). A vinaigrette dressing (page 47) is sometimes poured over the vegetables just before serving.
A good pot-au-feu depends on very slow, even cooking. The cooking liquid should barely simmer.

Metric/Imperial	**American**
750 g/1½–1¾ lb flank of beef, in one piece	1½–1¾ lb flank of beef, in one piece
750 g/1½–1¾ lb silverside, in one piece	1½–1¾ lb silverside, in one piece
750 g/1½–1¾ lb shin of beef, in one piece	1½–1¾ lb shin of beef, in one piece
3 litres/5½ pints water	6½ pints water
2 onions, peeled and stuck with 4 whole cloves	2 onions, peeled and stuck with 4 cloves
1 bouquet garni★	1 bouquet garni★
4 garlic cloves	4 garlic cloves
1 tablespoon coarse sea salt	1 tablespoon coarse sea salt
12 black peppercorns	12 black peppercorns
1 bunch celery, trimmed, separated into sticks, then tied in a bundle	1 bunch celery, trimmed, separated into stalks, then tied in a bundle
4 leeks (white part only), tied in a bundle	4 leeks (white part only), tied in a bundle
12 young carrots, peeled	12 young carrots, peeled
8 small turnips, peeled	8 small turnips, peeled
8 potatoes, scrubbed	8 potatoes, scrubbed
4 pieces beef marrow bone★ (about 7.5 cm/3 inches long)	4 pieces beef marrow bone★ (about 3 inches long)
salt	salt

Tie the pieces of meat securely with string. Put the beef flank in a very large flameproof *pot-au-feu*, *marmite* or casserole. Pour in the water, then bring slowly to the boil. Skim off the scum, then lower the heat and simmer very gently for 1 hour, skimming occasionally.

Add the silverside, shin, onions, bouquet garni, unpeeled garlic cloves, sea salt and peppercorns. Bring to the boil and skim the surface again, then lower the heat and simmer gently, uncovered, for a further 1 hour.

Add the celery, leeks, carrots and turnips at 10 minute intervals, do not add them all at the same time as this will lower the temperature of the *pot-au-feu*. Continue simmering until the total cooking time is 4 hours, then remove from the heat and leave to stand for 15 minutes.

Meanwhile, cook the unpeeled potatoes in a separate pan of boiling water for 20 minutes until tender. Put the beef marrow bones in another pan, cover with cold salted water and bring to the boil. Simmer for 15 minutes.

Remove the meats and vegetables from the stock and discard all bones and string. Place the meats and vegetables in a warmed serving dish. Peel the potatoes while still warm, then add to the dish with the drained marrow bones. Sprinkle a little of the hot stock over the meats and vegetables; keep hot.

Degrease★ the stock, then pass through a sieve (strainer) lined with damp muslin (cheesecloth). Reheat the stock if necessary, then taste and adjust seasoning. Serve the stock hot as a soup, followed by the hot meat and vegetables for the main course.
SERVES 8

Pot-au-feu

FRAGINAT DE BOEUF À LA CATALANE

Beef Casserole with Aïoli

The usual accompaniment to this dish is boiled rice. Make the tomato purée by puréeing skinned and seeded tomatoes in a mouli-légumes (vegetable mill) or an electric blender.

Metric/Imperial
2 tablespoons saindoux★, dripping or butter
1 kg/2 lb chuck steak, cut into chunks
6 garlic cloves, peeled and crushed
1–2 tablespoons chopped parsley
1 tablespoon plain flour
250 ml/8 fl oz fresh tomato purée
freshly grated nutmeg
salt
freshly ground black pepper
450 g/1 lb small pickling onions, peeled
250 ml/8 fl oz aïoli (page 48)
3–4 tablespoons lukewarm water

American
2 tablespoons saindoux★, drippings or butter
2 lb chuck steak, cut into chunks
6 garlic cloves, peeled and crushed
1–2 tablespoons chopped parsley
1 tablespoon all-purpose flour
1 cup fresh tomato purée
freshly grated nutmeg
salt
freshly ground black pepper
1 lb baby onions, peeled
1 cup aïoli (page 48)
3–4 tablespoons lukewarm water

Melt half the fat in a flameproof casserole. Add the beef and fry over moderate heat until the juices run. Pour off the pan juices into a bowl and reserve.

Melt the remaining fat in the casserole. Mix the garlic and parsley together to make an *hachis*. Add to the casserole and fry over brisk heat for about 5 minutes, stirring constantly.

Sprinkle in the flour, cook for 1 minute, stirring constantly, then stir in the tomato purée and bring to the boil. Add nutmeg, salt and pepper to taste, lower the heat, cover and simmer gently for $1\frac{1}{2}$ hours.

Stir in the whole onions and simmer for a further 40 minutes or until the beef is tender. Meanwhile, mix the *aïoli* and warm water together and stir in the reserved pan juices from the beef.

Remove the beef from the cooking liquid with a slotted spoon and place in a warmed serving dish. Keep hot. Remove the casserole from the heat and stir the *aïoli* gradually into the cooking liquid. Taste and adjust seasoning. Serve the beef immediately, with the sauce handed separately.

SERVES 4 TO 6

Corsican cookery is noted for its strong, spicy flavours and this recipe for *alouettes sans têtes* is no exception. Allspice, cinnamon and nutmeg are combined with sausagemeat to make a stuffing which is not unlike the local spicy sausages which are so popular on the island.

ALOUETTES SANS TÊTES

Stuffed Beef Rolls

Literally translated, alouettes sans têtes, means 'larks without heads', and it is easy to see how the recipe came by its name. When the meat is rolled around the stuffing, it does indeed look like a small bird's body – without the head! For those who find the name offputting, the same beef rolls are also known as paupiettes. Veal escalopes are often used instead of beef.

Metric/Imperial	American
225 g/8 oz sausagemeat	*1 cup sausagemeat*
2 onions, peeled and very finely chopped	*2 onions, peeled and very finely chopped*
2 tablespoons dried breadcrumbs, soaked in 1 tablespoon milk	*2 tablespoons dried bread crumbs, soaked in 1 tablespoon milk*
1 bunch parsley, finely chopped	*1 bunch parsley, finely chopped*
pinch of ground mixed spice	*pinch of ground allspice*
pinch of freshly grated nutmeg	*pinch of ground cinnamon*
salt	*pinch of freshly grated nutmeg*
freshly ground black pepper	*salt*
6 rump steaks, about 100 g/ 4 oz each, beaten thin	*freshly ground black pepper*
2 tablespoons olive oil	*6 top round steaks, about $\frac{1}{4}$ lb each, beaten thin*
2 carrots, peeled and diced	*2 tablespoons olive oil*
6 tomatoes, skinned and roughly chopped	*2 carrots, peeled and diced*
1 garlic clove, peeled and crushed	*6 tomatoes, skinned and roughly chopped*
1 celery stick, finely chopped	*1 garlic clove, peeled and crushed*
1 thyme sprig	*1 celery stalk, finely chopped*
1 bay leaf	*1 thyme sprig*
150 ml/$\frac{1}{4}$ pint dry white wine	*1 bay leaf*
100 g/4 oz green olives, stoned	*$\frac{2}{3}$ cup dry white wine*
	$\frac{3}{4}$ cup pitted green olives

Put the sausagemeat in a bowl with half the onions, the soaked breadcrumbs, chopped parsley, spice(s), nutmeg, and salt and pepper to taste. Mix well with the hands until all the ingredients are thoroughly combined.

Spread out the steaks on a flat surface, then divide the sausagemeat mixture equally between them, placing it at one end of the meat, then rolling the meat around it to make a sausage shape. Tie them with string, tucking the meat in at the ends to prevent the stuffing from escaping during cooking.

Heat the oil in a frying pan (skillet), add the *alouettes* and fry over brisk heat until browned on all sides. Remove them from the pan with a slotted spoon and set aside.

Add the remaining onion and the carrots to the pan and fry gently until lightly coloured. Return the *alouettes* to the pan. Add the tomatoes, garlic, celery, thyme, bay leaf, and salt and pepper to taste. Simmer for 10 minutes, then pour in the wine. Cover and simmer very gently for 40 minutes. Add the olives and cook for a further 10 minutes or until the beef is tender.

Remove the *alouettes* from the sauce and untie and discard the string. Place the *alouettes* on a warmed serving platter. Discard the thyme sprig and bay leaf from the sauce, then taste and adjust seasoning. Pour the sauce over the *alouettes* and serve immediately.
SERVES 6

CÔTES DE VEAU À LA NANCÉENNE

Veal Chops with Mustard Sauce

Metric/Imperial	American
4 tablespoons dried breadcrumbs	*4 tablespoons dried bread crumbs*
1 shallot, peeled and very finely chopped	*1 scallion, peeled and very finely chopped*
1 tablespoon finely chopped parsley	*1 tablespoon finely chopped parsley*
4 veal chops	*4 veal chops*
salt	*salt*
freshly ground black pepper	*freshly ground black pepper*
1 egg, beaten	*1 egg, beaten*
75 g/3 oz butter	*$\frac{1}{3}$ cup butter*
3 tablespoons plain flour	*3 tablespoons all-purpose flour*
250 ml/8 fl oz chicken stock (page 42)	*1 cup chicken stock (page 42)*
1 teaspoon French mustard★	*1 teaspoon French mustard★*

Mix the breadcrumbs on a plate with the shallot (scallion) and parsley. Sprinkle the chops with salt and pepper to taste. Dip the chops into the beaten egg, then coat them in the breadcrumb mixture.

Melt two thirds of the butter in a large frying pan (skillet). Add the chops and fry over moderate heat until golden on both sides. Lower the heat and cook very gently for 10 minutes each side or until the veal is tender, taking care that the breadcrumbs do not become too brown.

Meanwhile, melt the remaining butter in a separate pan. Sprinkle in the flour and cook, stirring constantly, for 1 minute to obtain a smooth *roux* (paste). Pour in

the stock a little at a time, stirring vigorously after each addition. Bring slowly to the boil, stirring. Lower the heat and simmer for 5 to 6 minutes until the sauce thickens, stirring frequently.

When the chops are tender, transfer them to a warmed serving platter. Whisk the mustard into the sauce with salt and pepper to taste, then pour into a sauceboat. Serve immediately.

SERVES 4

NORMANDIE

CÔTES DE VEAU À LA NORMANDE

Veal Chops with Calvados and Apples

Serve with petits pois, braised chicory (Belgian endive), or lettuce hearts braised in cream.

Metric/Imperial	American
75 g/3 oz butter	$\frac{1}{3}$ cup butter
6 veal chops	6 veal chops
freshly grated nutmeg	freshly grated nutmeg
salt	salt
freshly ground black pepper	freshly ground black pepper
4 apples	4 apples
7 tablespoons calvados	7 tablespoons calvados
150 ml/$\frac{1}{4}$ pint dry cider	$\frac{2}{3}$ cup hard cider
3 tablespoons double cream	3 tablespoons heavy cream

Melt the butter in a large flameproof casserole, add the chops and fry over moderate heat for about 15 minutes or until tender and lightly coloured on both sides. Sprinkle with nutmeg, salt and pepper to taste, then transfer to a warmed serving platter. Cover with foil and stand over a pan of hot water to keep hot.

Peel and core the apples, slice thickly, then add to the casserole. Fry briskly until golden, turning the slices frequently. Arrange around the veal and keep hot.

Warm the *calvados*, pour into the casserole and ignite. Pour in the cider and boil rapidly for 2 to 3 minutes, scraping up the sediment from the bottom of the casserole with a wooden spoon.

Lower the heat and stir in the cream. Taste and adjust seasoning, then pour over the veal and apples. Serve immediately.

SERVES 6

VARIATION: In some parts of Normandy, mushrooms are used instead of apples. Slice 225 g/$\frac{1}{2}$ lb button mushrooms finely, then add to the casserole after sealing the chops in the butter. Cook for about 15 minutes with the chops.

ABOVE: **Côtes de veau à la nancéenne; Côtes de veau à la normande**
LEFT: **Alouettes sans têtes**

SAUTÉ DE VEAU MARENGO

Casseroled Veal with Onions and Mushrooms

Steamed or boiled new potatoes and a dish of mixed vegetables are the usual accompaniments to this dish.

Metric/Imperial	American
50 g/2 oz saindoux★, dripping or butter	¼ cup saindoux★, drippings or butter
1.5 kg/3–3½ lb pie veal, cut into chunks	3–3½ lb pie veal, cut into chunks
3 large onions, peeled and chopped	3 large onions, peeled and chopped
3 tablespoons plain flour	3 tablespoons all-purpose flour
1 tablespoon tomato purée	1 tablespoon tomato paste
2 cloves garlic, peeled and crushed	2 garlic cloves, peeled and crushed
1 bouquet garni★	1 bouquet garni★
200 ml/⅓ pint dry white wine	1 cup dry white wine
salt	salt
freshly ground black pepper	freshly ground black pepper
about 300 ml/½ pint chicken stock (page 42)	about 1¼ cups chicken stock (page 42)
GARNISH:	GARNISH:
24 small pickling onions, peeled	24 baby onions, peeled
60 g/2½ oz butter	5 tablespoons butter
1 tablespoon sugar	1 tablespoon sugar
225 g/8 oz button mushrooms	2 cups button mushrooms
1 tablespoon chopped tarragon or parsley	1 tablespoon chopped tarragon or parsley

Melt the fat in a large flameproof casserole, add the veal and fry over brisk heat until lightly coloured on all sides. Add the chopped onions and fry gently for a few minutes, stirring.

Stir in the flour and cook, stirring, for 3 minutes, then add the tomato purée (paste), garlic, bouquet garni, wine and salt and pepper to taste. Stir in enough stock to cover the meat, then bring to the boil. Cover and transfer to a preheated cool oven (150°C/300°F/Gas Mark 2). Cook for 2 to 2½ hours until the veal is tender.

About 20 minutes before the end of the cooking time, prepare the garnish: put the small onions in a heavy pan with half the butter and the sugar. Pour in enough water to just cover the bottom of the pan, then cook very gently for about 15 minutes until the onions have absorbed all the liquid. Shake the pan frequently so the onions become glazed on all sides.

Meanwhile, melt the remaining butter in a separate pan, add the mushrooms and fry over brisk heat until the juices run. Sprinkle with salt and pepper, then remove from the heat and keep hot.

When the veal is tender, discard the bouquet garni and taste and adjust seasoning. Transfer to a warmed serving dish, then top with the glazed onions and the mushrooms. Sprinkle over the tarragon or parsley and serve immediately.
SERVES 6

ESCALOPES À LA NORMANDE

Veal Escalopes (Scalloppini) with Mushrooms, Wine and Cream

This recipe is sometimes called Médaillons à la Normande, because of the medallion shape of the veal.

Metric/Imperial	American
225 g/8 oz mushrooms, sliced	2 cups sliced mushrooms
100 g/4 oz butter	½ cup butter
1 tablespoon lemon juice	1 tablespoon lemon juice
salt	salt
6 thick veal escalopes	6 thick veal scalloppini
freshly grated nutmeg	freshly grated nutmeg
freshly ground black pepper	freshly ground black pepper
150 ml/¼ pint dry white wine	⅔ cup dry white wine
2 teaspoons tarragon-flavoured mustard★	2 teaspoons tarragon-flavoured mustard★
3 tablespoons double cream	3 tablespoons heavy cream
1 egg yolk	1 egg yolk

Put the mushrooms in a heavy pan with 25 g/1 oz/2 tablespoons butter, the lemon juice and a little salt. Add just enough water to cover, then simmer gently for 5 minutes.

Meanwhile, melt the remaining butter in a large frying pan (skillet) until very hot. Add the veal and fry over brisk heat for 1 minute or until lightly coloured on each side. Sprinkle with nutmeg, salt and pepper to taste, then remove from the pan with a slotted spoon and keep hot.

Return the pan to the heat and pour in the wine. Boil rapidly for 2 to 3 minutes, scraping up the sediment from the bottom of the pan. Lower the heat slightly and stir in the mustard. Return the veal to the pan, cover and cook over a very low heat for a further 10 minutes.

Drain the mushrooms and add to the pan with the cream. Taste and adjust seasoning, then bring just to boiling point and immediately remove from the heat. Arrange the veal and mushrooms on a warmed serving platter and keep hot.

Put the egg yolk in a bowl, then stir in 2 tablespoons of the hot sauce. Stir this back into the sauce in the pan and heat through without boiling. Pour over the veal and mushrooms and serve immediately.
SERVES 6

Sauté de veau marengo is a much simplified version of the classic poulet sauté à la marengo, originally created for Napoleon after the battle of Marengo in June 1800.

Napoleon's chef Dunand could only muster an old hen, some crayfish, tomatoes and eggs for dinner that evening. Poulet sauté à la marengo was duly created using just these ingredients – with a little brandy and garlic thrown in for good measure. Napoleon was so pleased with the dish that he ordered Dunand to make it after every battle.

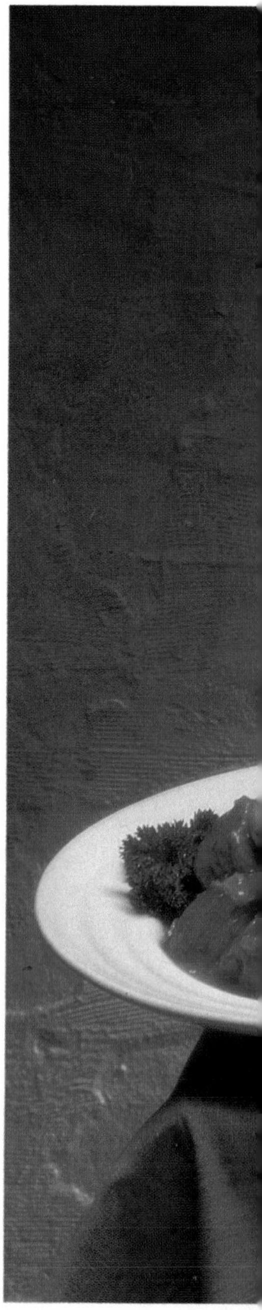

CÔTES DE VEAU À L'ÉTOUFFÉE

Braised Veal Chops with Ham and Parsley

Metric/Imperial	American
75 g/3 oz butter, softened	⅓ cup butter, softened
6 veal chops, boned	6 veal chops, boned
100 g/4 oz ham★, roughly chopped	½ cup roughly chopped ham★
1 onion, peeled and roughly chopped	1 onion, peeled and roughly chopped
2 garlic cloves, peeled and roughly chopped	2 garlic cloves, peeled and roughly chopped
1 tablespoon chopped parsley	1 tablespoon chopped parsley
salt	salt
freshly ground black pepper	freshly ground black pepper
7 tablespoons chicken stock (page 42)	7 tablespoons chicken stock (page 42)

Brush the inside of a large flameproof baking dish or roasting pan with the butter, then place the chops in a single layer in the dish.

Mix the ham, onion, garlic and parsley together and sprinkle over the chops with salt and pepper to taste.

Pour 4 tablespoons/¼ cup stock in the bottom of the dish. Cover and braise in a preheated moderate oven (180°C/350°F/Gas Mark 4) for 45 minutes to 1 hour until the chops are tender.

Transfer the chops to a warmed serving platter and keep hot. Transfer the baking dish to the top of the stove and stir in the remaining stock. Boil rapidly for 2 minutes, scraping up the sediment from the bottom of the dish with a wooden spoon. Taste and adjust seasoning, then pour over the chops. Serve immediately.

SERVES 6

**Sauté de veau marengo;
Escalopes à la normande**

POITRINE DE VEAU FARCIE

Stuffed Breast of Veal

*Get your butcher to make a 'pocket' in the veal so that the
stuffing can be placed inside. Alternatively, if the meat is a
neat rectangular shape, place it on a flat surface, spread the
stuffing over then roll the meat up with the stuffing inside.
The finished result is most attractive.*

*Serve with a platter of mixed fresh vegetables – celery
hearts, new potatoes, petits pois, salsify and chestnuts make
a good combination.*

Metric/Imperial	American
STUFFING:	STUFFING:
25 g/1 oz butter	2 tablespoons butter
shallots, peeled and very	2 scallions, peeled and very
finely chopped	finely chopped
100 g/4 oz streaky bacon,	½ cup ground fatty bacon
rind removed and minced	⅔ cup ground loin of pork
150 g/5 oz boned loin of	2 chicken livers, ground
pork, minced	salt
chicken livers, minced	freshly ground black pepper
salt	1 bottle dry white wine
freshly ground black pepper	
bottle dry white wine	2 lb boneless breast of veal
	⅓ cup butter
kg/2 lb boned breast of	2 onions, peeled and thinly
veal	sliced
75 g/3 oz butter	2 carrots, peeled and sliced
onions, peeled and thinly	into thin rings
sliced	1 celery stalk, thinly sliced
carrots, peeled and sliced	1 bouquet garni★
into thin rings	
celery stick, thinly sliced	
bouquet garni★	

Make the stuffing: melt the butter in a pan, add the
shallots (scallions), cover and cook gently for 10
minutes. Put the bacon, pork and chicken livers in a
bowl. Add the shallots with salt and pepper to taste and
tablespoons wine. Mix until all the ingredients are
thoroughly combined.

Push the stuffing inside the pocket in the veal, then
sew up the opening with trussing thread or fine string.
Melt the butter in a large flameproof casserole, add the
veal and fry over moderate heat until browned on all
sides. Remove from the casserole and set aside, then
add the onions, carrots and celery. Fry gently for
minutes, then return the veal to the casserole. Sprinkle
with salt and pepper and add the remaining wine and
the bouquet garni.

Bring to the boil, then cover and transfer to a
preheated moderate oven (180°C/350°F/Gas Mark 4).
Cook for 1½ hours or until the veal is tender.

Remove the meat from the casserole, slice neatly
and arrange on a warmed serving platter; keep hot.
Remove the bouquet garni from the cooking liquid,
then boil to reduce slightly. Taste and adjust seasoning,
then pour over the veal. Serve immediately.

SERVES 6

BLANQUETTE DE VEAU

Veal with Mushrooms in Cream Sauce

Metric/Imperial	American
1.5 kg/3 lb mixed veal (e.g.	3 lb mixed veal (e.g. leg,
leg, shoulder, breast), cut	shoulder, breast), cut into
into 5 cm/2 inch cubes	2 inch cubes
1 onion, peeled and stuck	1 onion, peeled and stuck
with 2 cloves	with 2 cloves
1 carrot, peeled	1 carrot, peeled
1 celery stick	1 celery stalk
1 leek (white part only)	1 leek (white part only)
1 bouquet garni★	1 bouquet garni★
200 ml/⅓ pint dry white wine	1 cup dry white wine
salt	salt
freshly ground black pepper	freshly ground black pepper
225 g/8 oz button	2–2½ cups button
mushrooms	mushrooms
juice of 1 lemon	juice of 1 lemon
60g/2½ oz butter	5 tablespoons butter
24 small pickling onions,	24 baby onions, peeled
peeled	7 tablespoons water
7 tablespoons water	LIAISON:
LIAISON:	3 egg yolks
3 egg yolks	⅔ cup heavy cream
150 ml/¼ pint double cream	freshly grated nutmeg
freshly grated nutmeg	

Put the veal in a flameproof casserole with the onion
and carrot. Tie the celery and leek around the bouquet
garni with thread or string, then add to the casserole
with the wine. Pour in enough water to just cover the
meat and add salt and pepper to taste. Bring slowly to
the boil, then skim the surface. Lower heat, cover and
simmer gently for 2 hours or until the veal is tender.

Forty-five minutes before the end of cooking, put
the mushrooms in a bowl and sprinkle with half the
lemon juice. Leave to stand for 20 minutes.

Melt half the butter in a heavy pan. Add the onions
and measured water and simmer gently for 25 minutes
until tender; do not allow the onions to brown.

Meanwhile, melt the remaining butter in a separate
pan. Add the mushrooms and lemon juice and simmer
for 15 minutes or until all the liquid has been absorbed
by the mushrooms. Add the onions, then cover the pan
and keep warm.

When the veal is tender, transfer to a warmed
serving dish with a slotted spoon. Sprinkle the onions
and mushrooms amongst the pieces of veal, cover the
dish and keep hot.

Make the liaison: put the egg yolks in a bowl with
1 tablespoon hot cooking liquid from the veal. Pass the
remaining cooking liquid through a fine sieve
(strainer) into a clean pan, then boil vigorously until
reduced to about 250 ml/8 fl oz/1 cup. Stir in the cream
and nutmeg to taste; simmer for 1 minute.

Whisk a ladleful of the hot sauce into the egg yolk
mixture, then whisk this back into the pan. Whisk
vigorously for 15 seconds over low heat; do not allow
the sauce to boil at this stage or it will curdle. Whisk in
the remaining lemon juice, then taste and adjust
seasoning. Pour the sauce over the veal and serve
immediately.

SERVES 6

Poitrine de veau farcie;
Blanquette de veau

**Veal is a very delicate
meat with a subtle
flavour which can be
easily masked by strong
or highly spiced
ingredients. Dry white
wine has a special affinity
with veal and it helps
keep the meat moist
(with little or no fat veal
has a tendency to dry out
during cooking). Choose
a light dry white wine
which is not too fruity.**

Meats/139

AGNEAU RÔTI DE PAUILLAC

Roast Leg of Lamb with Potatoes

Metric/Imperial	American
1 × 2 kg/4 lb leg of lamb	1 × 4 lb leg of lamb
8 garlic cloves, peeled	8 garlic cloves, peeled
50 g/2 oz butter, softened	$\frac{1}{4}$ cup softened butter
2 handfuls dried breadcrumbs	2 handfuls dried bread crumbs
4 tablespoons finely chopped parsley	$\frac{1}{4}$ cup finely chopped parsley
salt	salt
freshly ground black pepper	freshly ground black pepper
4 tablespoons oil	$\frac{1}{4}$ cup oil
1.5 kg/3–3$\frac{1}{2}$ lb new potatoes, peeled and sliced into thin rounds	3–3$\frac{1}{2}$ lb new potatoes, peeled and sliced into thin rounds
TO DEGLAZE:	TO DEGLAZE:
7 tablespoons wine vinegar	7 tablespoons wine vinegar
3 garlic cloves, peeled and crushed	3 garlic cloves, peeled and crushed
5 tablespoons boiling water	5 tablespoons boiling water

Place the lamb in a roasting pan. Cut two garlic cloves into quarters. Make 2 slits in the lamb alongside the bone with a sharp knife and insert a quarter of a garlic clove into each slit. Push the remaining quarters into the skin of the lamb. Spread the butter all over the lamb.

Crush the remaining 6 garlic cloves, then make a *hachis* by mixing them with the breadcrumbs, parsley, and salt and pepper to taste. Spread this *hachis* evenly over the lamb, then roast in a preheated moderately hot oven (200°C/400°F/Gas Mark 6) for 1$\frac{3}{4}$ to 2 hours, or according to your liking.

Meanwhile, heat the oil in a large frying pan (skillet). Add the potatoes and fry over brisk heat for a few minutes. Lower the heat, cover the pan and cook gently for 10 minutes or until the potatoes are golden brown on the underside. Turn the potatoes over with a spatula and cook the other side until tender.

Remove the lamb from the oven and carve into neat slices. Arrange the slices in a circle on a warmed serving platter. Remove the potatoes from the heat, sprinkle with salt and pepper, then pile onto the serving platter. Keep hot.

To deglaze★: boil the wine vinegar with the crushed garlic until reduced to one quarter of its original volume. Strain, add the boiling water and stir into the juices in the roasting pan, scraping up all the sediment and juices from the bottom. Pour into a sauceboat and serve hot, with the lamb.
SERVES 6

VARIATION: The potatoes can be sprinkled with the same *hachis* as the lamb, to give them extra flavour.

MOUTON GARDIANNE

Lamb Chops with Potatoes and Garlic

Metric/Imperial	American
2 tablespoons olive oil	2 tablespoons olive oil
4 large lamb chops, trimmed of fat	4 large lamb chops, trimmed of fat
4 potatoes, peeled and sliced into thick rounds	4 potatoes, peeled and sliced into thick rounds
3 garlic cloves, peeled and crushed	3 garlic cloves, peeled and crushed
2 thyme sprigs	2 thyme sprigs
1 bay leaf	1 bay leaf
1 rosemary sprig	1 rosemary sprig
salt	salt
freshly ground black pepper	freshly ground black pepper
about 300 ml/$\frac{1}{2}$ pint boiling hot beef stock (page 42)	about 1$\frac{1}{4}$ cups boiling hot beef stock (page 42)
1 tablespoon chopped parsley	1 tablespoon chopped parsley

Heat the oil in a large frying pan (skillet), add the chops and fry over brisk heat until browned on both sides. Remove from the pan and set aside.

Lower the heat and add the potatoes to the pan. Sprinkle with the garlic, then add the thyme, bay leaf and rosemary, and salt and pepper to taste. Place the chops on top and pour in enough stock to just cover.

Cook over brisk heat for about 40 minutes or until the lamb is tender. Press the chops into the potatoes occasionally to crush them to a purée.

Serve hot straight from the pan, sprinkled with the parsley.
SERVES 4

Gigot à la bretonne;
Agneau rôti de pauillac

GIGOT À LA BRETONNE

Leg of Lamb with White Haricot (Navy) Beans

Metric/Imperial
1 × 2 kg/4 lb leg of lamb
4 tablespoons olive oil
salt
freshly ground black pepper
450 g/1 lb dried white haricot beans, soaked overnight in cold water
3 onions, peeled
1 whole clove
1 bouquet garni★
1 garlic clove, peeled and chopped
3 tomatoes, skinned and roughly chopped
25 g/1 oz butter, softened

American
1 × 4 lb leg of lamb
¼ cup olive oil
salt
freshly ground black pepper
2¼ cups dried navy beans, soaked overnight in cold water
3 onions, peeled
1 whole clove
1 bouquet garni★
1 garlic clove, peeled and chopped
3 tomatoes, skinned and roughly chopped
2 tablespoons softened butter

Place the lamb in a roasting pan, then sprinkle with half the oil and salt and pepper to taste. Roast in a preheated moderately hot oven (200°C/400°F/Gas Mark 6) for 1¾ to 2 hours, or according to your liking.

Meanwhile, drain the haricots, rinse under cold running water, then place in a large pan and cover with fresh water. Add 1 onion stuck with the clove and the bouquet garni. Bring to the boil, then lower the heat, cover and simmer for 45 minutes to 1 hour until tender. Add salt to taste halfway through the cooking time.

Chop the remaining onions. Heat the remaining oil in a heavy pan, add the chopped onions and fry gently for 10 minutes. Add the garlic and tomatoes, and salt and pepper to taste, then cook gently until thick.

When the beans are tender, drain and discard the onion, clove and bouquet garni. Add the beans to the tomato mixture with the butter and stir well to mix. Heat through gently, then taste and adjust seasoning.

Place the lamb on a warmed serving platter and surround with the beans and tomatoes. Deglaze★ the juices in the roasting pan with a little boiling water, then pour into a sauceboat. Serve hot.
SERVES 6

Roast shoulder of lamb, although almost prohibitively expensive in France, still remains a popular favourite for Sunday lunch. Boned and rolled by the butcher it is simply roasted with garlic and rosemary, baked with onions and potatoes (*à la boulangère*) or stuffed with breadcrumbs, sausagemeat and herbs. The traditional Breton way to serve lamb is with haricot beans and onion sauce (*sauce soubise*), a popular method that helps make the meat go further!

PISTACHE DE MOUTON

Shoulder of Lamb with Haricot (Navy) Beans, Tomatoes and Garlic

Metric/Imperial	American
150 g/5 oz fresh pork rinds★ (optional)	5 oz fresh pork rinds★ (optional)
450 g/1 lb dried white haricot beans, soaked overnight in cold water	2¼ cups dried navy beans, soaked overnight in cold water
3 onions, peeled	3 onions, peeled
1 whole clove	1 whole clove
3 carrots, peeled and sliced into thick rounds	3 carrots, peeled and sliced into thick rounds
1 bouquet garni★	1 bouquet garni★
salt	salt
150 g/5 oz goose fat★, dripping or butter	⅔ cup goose fat★, drippings or butter
1.25 kg/2½–2¾ lb boned shoulder of lamb, cut into chunks	2½–2¾ lb boneless shoulder of lamb, cut into chunks
7 garlic cloves, peeled	7 garlic cloves, peeled
350 g/12 oz tomatoes, skinned, quartered and seeded	¾ lb tomatoes, skinned, quartered and seeded
250 ml/8 fl oz dry white wine	1 cup dry white wine
freshly ground black pepper	freshly ground black pepper
3 tablespoons breadcrumbs	3 tablespoons bread crumbs

If using the pork rinds, blanch by plunging them into boiling water for a few minutes, then drain. Roll the rinds together, then tie with thread or fine string.

Drain the haricots, rinse under cold running water, then place in a large pan. Cover with fresh water, then add the blanched pork rinds (if using), 1 onion stuck with the clove, the carrots and bouquet garni. Bring to the boil, lower the heat, cover and simmer for 40 minutes until the beans are almost tender. Add salt to taste halfway through the cooking time.

Meanwhile, melt 50 g/2 oz/¼ cup fat in a large flameproof casserole, add the lamb and fry over brisk heat until browned on all sides. Cut the remai 2 onions into quarters, add to the casserole and fry moderate heat until golden, stirring constantly.

Crush 6 garlic cloves, then add to the lamb onions with the tomatoes. Cook gently for a minutes.

Remove the pork rinds, onion, clove, carrots bouquet garni from the beans and discard. Drain beans and pour their cooking liquid into the casser Add the wine, stir well, then cover and simmer ge for 45 minutes. Add salt and pepper to taste after first 15 minutes' cooking time.

Rub an earthenware baking dish with the remai garlic clove, then brush with half the remaining Spread half the beans in the bottom of the dish, t spread the lamb on top. Cover the lamb with remaining beans, then moisten with 1 to 2 ladlefu the cooking liquid from the lamb.

Sprinkle the breadcrumbs over the top. Melt remaining fat, pour over the breadcrumbs, then b in a preheated cool oven (140°C/275°F/Gas Mark 1 1½ hours or until the lamb is tender and the beans moist and creamy. The breadcrumbs should for golden crust. Serve hot, straight from the baking d
SERVES 6

HOCHEPOT

Hot Pot of Meat and Vegetables

The choice of meats for this hot pot can vary according availability. If liked, the meats can be fried in saindoux dripping(s) beforehand, but care must be taken that the is not too fatty. The best way to ensure this is to cook hochepot the day before, then remove the surface fat when

Metric/Imperial	American
1 kg/2 lb oxtail, cut into chunks	2 lb oxtail, cut in chunk
350 g/12 oz shoulder of veal	¾ lb shoulder of veal
350 g/12 oz shoulder of lamb	¾ lb shoulder of lamb
1 pig's ear (optional)	1 pig's ear (optional)
1 pig's trotter, split	1 pig's foot, split
3 onions, peeled and stuck with 1 clove each	3 onions, peeled and stu with 1 clove each
10 whole juniper berries	10 whole juniper berries
1 bouquet garni★	1 bouquet garni★
3 celery sticks	3 celery stalks
few black peppercorns	few black peppercorns
6 carrots, peeled and cut into large chunks	6 carrots, peeled and cut large chunks
3 turnips, peeled and cut into large chunks	3 turnips, peeled and cut into large chunks
1 parsnip, peeled and cut into large chunks	1 parsnip, peeled and cu into large chunks
450 g/1 lb leeks (white part only), cut into large chunks	1 lb leeks (white part on cut into large chunks
1 green cabbage, quartered	1 green cabbage, quarter
225 g/8 oz salt belly pork	½ lb salt pork
1 × 450 g/1 lb French cooking sausage★	1 × 1 lb French cooking sausage★
salt	salt
freshly ground black pepper	freshly ground black pep
8 potatoes, peeled	8 potatoes, peeled
8 slices hot toast, to serve	8 slices hot toast, to serv

BAECKEOFFE

Three Meats Baked in Wine

Baeckeoffe, also sometimes called beckenoff, is from the German word baeckenofen meaning 'to bake in oven'.

Metric/Imperial	American
MARINADE:	MARINADE:
3 onions, peeled and sliced into rings	3 onions, peeled and sliced into rings
3 garlic cloves, peeled and crushed	3 garlic cloves, peeled and crushed
2 carrots, peeled and sliced into rings	2 carrots, peeled and sliced into rings
1 bouquet garni★	1 bouquet garni★
1 whole clove	1 whole clove
few black peppercorns	few black peppercorns
about 500 ml/18 fl oz dry white wine (preferably Alsace)	about $2\frac{1}{4}$ cups dry white wine (preferably Alsace)
salt	salt
600 g/1$\frac{1}{4}$ lb loin of pork, cut into serving pieces	1$\frac{1}{4}$ lb pork loin, cut into serving pieces
600 g/1$\frac{1}{4}$ lb boned shoulder of lamb, cut into serving pieces	1$\frac{1}{4}$ lb boneless shoulder of lamb, cut into serving pieces
600 g/1$\frac{1}{4}$ lb boned rib of beef, cut into serving pieces	1$\frac{1}{4}$ lb boneless rib of beef, cut into serving pieces
225 g/8 oz onions, peeled and thinly sliced	$\frac{1}{2}$ lb onions, peeled and thinly sliced
1.5 kg/3–3$\frac{1}{2}$ lb potatoes, peeled and cut into 5 mm/$\frac{1}{4}$ inch thick slices	3–3$\frac{1}{2}$ lb potatoes, peeled and cut into $\frac{1}{4}$ inch thick slices
2 garlic cloves, peeled and crushed	2 garlic cloves, peeled and crushed
2 parsley sprigs, chopped	2 parsley sprigs, chopped
1 bay leaf	1 bay leaf
freshly ground black pepper	freshly ground black pepper
2 tablespoons plain flour, for sealing	2 tablespoons all-purpose flour, for sealing

ABOVE: **Baeckeoffe**
LEFT: **Hochepot**

Put the oxtail, veal, lamb, pig's ear (if using) and trotter (foot) in a large flameproof casserole. Pour in enough water to come above the level of the meats, then add the whole onions, juniper berries, bouquet garni, celery and peppercorns. Bring slowly to the boil, then skim with a slotted spoon. Add the vegetables, except the cabbage and potatoes. Cover the pan and simmer gently for 2$\frac{1}{2}$ to 3 hours.

Plunge the cabbage into a separate pan of boiling water and simmer for 5 minutes. Drain and squeeze out as much moisture as possible. Put the belly pork in another pan, cover with cold water and bring to the boil. Lower the heat and simmer for 10 minutes; drain.

Add the pork and cabbage to the casserole, with salt and pepper to taste and simmer for 30 minutes. Prick the sausage skin with a fork, then add to the pan with the potatoes and cook for a further 30 minutes.

To serve, remove the meats from the liquid and cut into serving pieces – the pig's ear and trotter should be diced. Place in a warmed deep serving dish and surround with the vegetables. Strain the cooking liquid, taste and adjust seasoning, then pour over the toast in a warmed soup tureen. Serve hot as a soup, followed by the meat and vegetables as a main course.
SERVES 8

Put all the ingredients for the marinade in a large bowl, then add the meats and stir well. Add more wine if the meats are not completely covered. Cover and leave to marinate for 12 hours or overnight.

The next day, remove the meats from the marinade. Strain the marinade and reserve. Arrange the meats in layers in a large flameproof casserole with the sliced onions, potatoes, crushed garlic and chopped parsley. Add the bay leaf and salt and pepper to taste, then pour in the strained marinade. Add more wine if the ingredients in the casserole are not completely covered with liquid.

Cover the casserole with a lid, then seal around the edge of the lid with a paste made from the flour and a few drops of water. Bake in a preheated cool oven (150°C/300°F/Gas Mark 2) for 3 to 3$\frac{1}{2}$ hours until the meat and vegetables are tender.

Break the paste seal, discard the bay leaf, taste and adjust seasoning. Serve hot, straight from the casserole.
SERVES 8

Meats/143

ESCUEDELLA

Assorted Meat Casserole with Sausage

This very popular dish has numerous variations –
sometimes it is made with veal, sometimes with a lamb's
tail, and sometimes with a special local Roussillon sausage
known as botifarra. One version from Cerbère, known as
l'escuedella de nadal is made with beef and stuffed turkey,
and the pilota sausage is made from beef and eggs.

Metric/Imperial	American
1 × 450 g/1 lb salted knuckle of ham★	1 × 1 lb salted knuckle of ham★
450 g/1 lb shoulder of lamb	1 lb shoulder of lamb
150 g/5 oz fresh pork rinds★, blanched and thinly sliced (optional)	5 oz fresh pork rinds★, blanched and thinly sliced (optional)
225 g/8 oz belly pork thinly sliced	½ lb pork sides, thinly sliced
3 litres/5½ pints water	6½ pints water
1 small green cabbage, quartered	1 small green cabbage, quartered
2 leeks (white part only), quartered	2 leeks (white part only), quartered
6 carrots, peeled and halved lengthways	6 carrots, peeled and halved lengthways
2 turnips, peeled and halved	2 turnips, peeled and halved
1 onion, peeled and sliced	1 onion, peeled and sliced
3 tomatoes, skinned, quartered and seeded	3 tomatoes, skinned, quartered and seeded
1 celery stick, chopped	1 celery stalk, chopped
1 kg/2 lb potatoes, peeled and cut into small cubes	2 lb potatoes, peeled and cut into small cubes
2 chicken giblets	2 chicken giblets
50 g/2 oz streaky bacon, rinds removed and diced	¼ cup diced fatty bacon
1 tablespoon olive oil	1 tablespoon olive oil
2 pinches of powdered saffron	2 pinches of powdered saffron
salt	salt
freshly ground black pepper	freshly ground black pepper
PILOTA:	PILOTA:
1 tablespoon oil	1 tablespoon oil
1 onion, peeled and finely chopped	1 onion, peeled and finely chopped
450 g/1 lb sausagemeat	2 cups sausagemeat
2 garlic cloves, peeled and crushed	2 garlic cloves, peeled and crushed
1 tablespoon chopped parsley	1 tablespoon chopped parsley
1 egg, beaten	1 egg, beaten
3 tablespoons plain flour	3 tablespoons all-purpose flour

Put the ham, lamb, pork rinds (if using) and belly pork
(pork sides) in a very large pan and cover with the
measured water. Bring slowly to the boil, then lower
the heat, cover and simmer for 2 hours, skimming with
a slotted spoon from time to time.

Meanwhile, plunge the cabbage into a separate pan
of boiling water and simmer for 5 minutes. Drain,
squeeze out as much moisture as possible, then add to
the pan of meats with the other vegetables, except the
potatoes. Cover the pan and simmer gently for a
further 1 hour.

Meanwhile, prepare the *pilota*: heat the oil in a pan,
add the onion and fry gently until soft. Put the

sausagemeat in a bowl with the garlic and parsley and
mix well with the hands. Add the onion and cooking
juices, the egg and 2 tablespoons flour. Mix well, then
form into a sausage shape, squeezing it well with the
hands to ensure the mixture is firm. Roll the *pilota* in
the remaining flour.

Add the potatoes, giblets, bacon, oil and saffron to
the meat and vegetables, with salt and pepper to taste.
Add the *pilota*. Bring back to the boil, then cover and
simmer for a further 45 minutes.

To serve, remove the meats and *pilota* from the
liquid. Slice the meats neatly, cut the *pilota* into rings,
then place on a warmed serving platter; keep hot. Taste
and adjust the seasoning of the liquid, then pour into a
warmed soup tureen. Serve hot as a soup, with the
meats to follow as a main course.
SERVES 8

VARIATION: Ten minutes before the end of the
cooking time, add 4 tablespoons/¼ cup rice, vermicelli
or cooked chick peas.

CASSOULET TOULOUSAIN

There are numerous versions of this famous dish (see
above), but the cassoulet from Toulouse should always
contain breast of lamb and the characteristic Toulouse
sausage★. If you omit the pork rinds, grease the casserole
liberally with butter before adding the beans and meat.

slightly salted knuckle of ham	slightly salted knuckle of ham
750 g/1½ lb dried white haricot beans, soaked in cold water overnight	3½ cups dried navy beans, soaked in cold water overnight
600 g/1¼ lb boned breast of lamb	1¼ lb boneless breast of lamb
2 large leeks (white part only), sliced	2 large leeks (white part only), sliced
2 carrots, peeled and quartered lengthways	2 carrots, peeled and quartered lengthways
1 large onion, peeled and stuck with 2 whole cloves	1 large onion, peeled and stuck with 2 whole cloves
2 thyme sprigs	2 thyme sprigs
2 garlic cloves, peeled	2 garlic cloves, peeled
225 g/8 oz fresh pork rinds★, blanched (optional)	½ lb fresh pork rinds★, blanched (optional)
2 large firm tomatoes, skinned, quartered and seeded	2 large firm tomatoes, skinned, quartered and seeded
salt	salt
freshly ground black pepper	freshly ground black pepper
3 tablespoons goose fat★ or dripping	3 tablespoons goose fat★ or drippings
600 g/1¼ lb Toulouse sausage★	1¼ lb Toulouse sausage★
600 g/1¼ lb confit d'oie★ (optional)	1¼ lb confit d'oie★ (optional)
100 g/4 oz dried breadcrumbs	1 cup dried bread crumbs

Cassoulet is essentially a
country dish, perfect fo[r]
cold winter nights or
Sunday lunch for the
whole family. It is not a
dish to be made in smal[l]
quantities, for the
number of ingredients
requires would be wast[ed]
on anything less than
eight people.

Cassoulet improves [with]
keeping, however, so a[ny]
leftovers can be reheate[d]
next day. Before makin[g]
cassoulet, make sure yo[u]
have a casserole
(preferably earthenwar[e])
large enough to hold al[l]
the ingredients.

at the *jambonneau* in a large pan, cover with cold ater, then bring slowly to the boil. Boil for minutes, then drain.

Drain the haricots, rinse under cold running water, en place in a large pan. Add the *jambonneau*, lamb, ks, carrots, onion and thyme. Cover with fresh cold ater to come about 2.5 cm (1 inch) above the gredients, then bring to the boil. Lower the heat, ver and simmer gently for 1 hour. Skim with a tted spoon.

Rub the inside of a large earthenware casserole with e garlic. Line the bottom of the casserole with the ork rinds (if using), fat side downwards.

Remove the meats and beans from the cooking quid with a slotted spoon. Strain the liquid and serve. Cut the meats into serving pieces.

Put half the beans in the casserole, place the sliced eats and tomatoes on top, then cover with the maining beans. Add salt and pepper to taste (bearing in mind the saltiness of the ham and preserved goose). Dot the top with 2 tablespoons fat and sprinkle with 2 ladlefuls of the reserved cooking liquid.

Cover the casserole and bake in a preheated cool oven (140°C/275°F/Gas Mark 1) for 2 hours, skimming the surface with a slotted spoon every 30 minutes. If the beans become too dry, pour in a little of the reserved cooking liquid, which should be boiling hot.

Melt the remaining fat in a frying pan (skillet). Prick the sausage skin with a fork, add to the pan and fry over moderate heat until just golden on all sides. Remove from the pan and cut into 5 cm/2 inch thick slices. Cut the preserved goose into 8 pieces (if using).

Skim the surface of the casserole thoroughly then push the sausage and preserved goose into the beans and meats. Sprinkle the breadcrumbs over the top, then return to the oven and bake, uncovered, for a further 1 hour. Serve hot, straight from the casserole.
SERVES 8

BEUCHELLE TOURANGELLE

Kidneys, Sweetbreads and Cèpes or Mushrooms au Gratin

Cèpes★ are used in the original French recipe for this rich, creamy dish, but if cèpes are difficult to obtain, field or cultivated mushrooms can be used instead

Metric/Imperial	American
2 calf's sweetbreads	2 veal sweetbreads
2 tablespoons plain flour	2 tablespoons all-purpose flour
100 g/4 oz butter	½ cup butter
2 calf's kidneys, thinly sliced, with cores removed	2 veal kidneys, thinly sliced, with cores removed
salt	salt
freshly ground black pepper	freshly ground black pepper
2 tablespoons brandy, warmed	2 tablespoons brandy, warmed
2 boxed truffles★, sliced, with their juice (optional)	2 boxed truffles★, sliced, with their juice (optional)
250 ml/8 fl oz double cream	1 cup heavy cream
3 tablespoons oil	3 tablespoons oil
450 g/1 lb cèpes or mushrooms, sliced	1 lb sliced cèpes or mushrooms
75 g/3 oz Parmesan cheese, grated	¾ cup grated Parmesan cheese

Soak the sweetbreads in cold water for 3 hours, changing the water 2 or 3 times.

Drain the sweetbreads and rinse thoroughly under cold running water. Place them in a pan, cover with fresh water and bring slowly to the boil. Simmer for 5 minutes, then drain and rinse again under cold running water. Remove any fatty parts, place the sweetbreads between 2 plates and weight down. Leave for 1 hour.

Slice the sweetbreads the same thickness as the kidneys and coat in the flour. Melt half the butter in a frying pan (skillet), add the kidneys and fry over brisk heat for a few minutes on each side. Sprinkle with salt and pepper to taste, then lower the heat and fry for a further 2 minutes – the kidneys should still be pink in the centre. Pour over the brandy and ignite. Remove the kidneys and juices from the pan and keep hot. Melt the remaining butter in the pan, add the sweetbreads and fry until golden on each side.

Remove the sweetbreads from the pan with a slotted spoon. Stir the truffles and juice (if using), and 3 tablespoons cream into the pan. Simmer until reduced and thickened, then pour over the sweetbreads. Keep hot.

Meanwhile, heat the oil in another pan, add the mushrooms and fry over brisk heat for a few minutes. Lower the heat, cover and cook gently until tender. Remove from the pan and drain thoroughly.

Add the remaining cream to the rinsed-out pan and heat gently for 10 minutes, stirring constantly. Add salt and pepper to taste, then transfer to a heatproof serving dish and stir in the kidneys, sweetbreads and mushrooms. Sprinkle the Parmesan over the top.

Put the dish under a preheated hot grill (broiler) for a few minutes to brown the top. Serve immediately.
SERVES 6

**Rognons au genièvre;
Beuchelle tourangelle**

ROGNONS AU GENIÈVRE

Kidneys and Potatoes with Gin and White Wine

The white wine can be replaced by stock or beer, if liked

Metric/Imperial	American
750 g/1½ lb potatoes, peeled and cut into thin rounds	1½ lb potatoes, peeled and cut into thin rounds
3 tablespoons oil	3 tablespoons oil
salt	salt
freshly ground black pepper	freshly ground black pepper
50 g/2 oz butter	¼ cup butter
4 calf's kidneys, halved, with cores removed	4 veal kidneys, halved, with cores removed
7 tablespoons gin	7 tablespoons gin
120 ml/4 fl oz dry white wine	½ cup dry white wine

TRIPES À LA MODE DE CAEN

Tripe Baked in Calvados and Cider

Years ago, French housewives used to take this dish to the local baker, who would bake it in a special earthenware tripière (tripe pot) in his oven.

Metric/Imperial	American
100 g/4 oz butter	*½ cup butter*
450 g/1 lb onions, peeled	*1 lb onions, peeled*
450 g/1 lb carrots, peeled and sliced into rings	*1 lb carrots, peeled and sliced into rings*
225 g/8 oz leeks	*½ lb leeks*
2 kg/4 lb dressed tripe, cut into 5 cm/2 inch slices	*4 lb dressed tripe, cut into 2 inch slices*
1 calf's foot★, chopped, with bone removed and blanched (optional)	*1 veal foot★, chopped, with bone removed and blanched (optional)*
3 whole cloves	*3 whole cloves*
1 large bouquet garni★	*1 large bouquet garni★*
2 garlic cloves, peeled and crushed	*2 garlic cloves, peeled and crushed*
freshly grated nutmeg	*freshly grated nutmeg*
salt	*salt*
freshly ground black pepper	*freshly ground black pepper*
5 tablespoons calvados or brandy	*⅓ cup calvados or brandy*
about 2 litres/3½ pints dry cider	*about 4½ pints (9 cups) hard cider*
2 tablespoons plain flour, for sealing	*2 tablespoons all-purpose flour, for sealing*

Brush the inside of a large casserole with a little of the butter. Slice 2 onions into rings, then place a few rings in the bottom of the casserole with a few carrot slices. Slice the white part of the leeks, reserving the green tops. Sprinkle a few of the leek slices on top of the carrots and onions. Arrange a few pieces of tripe and calf's (veal) foot (if using) on top. Repeat these layers until half these ingredients are used.

Stick the cloves into the remaining whole onion. Tie the reserved green leeks around the bouquet garni. Place the onion, bouquet garni and garlic in the casserole. Cover with the remaining tripe, calf's foot and vegetables in layers, adding nutmeg, salt and pepper to taste.

Place the bone from the calf's foot on top, then sprinkle with the *calvados* or brandy and pour in enough cider to completely cover all the ingredients in the casserole. Dot the top with the remaining butter.

Cover the casserole with a lid, then seal around the edge of the lid with a paste made from the flour and a few drops of water. Bake in a preheated moderate oven (160°C/325°F/Gas Mark 3) for 6 hours.

Break the paste seal and remove the lid, then leave the casserole to cool. Remove the fat from the surface, then discard the bone, the whole onion and the bouquet garni. Reheat, taste and adjust seasoning. Serve hot.

SERVES 8

---

ake sure the potatoes are thoroughly dry by patting em with kitchen paper towels. Heat the oil in a ying pan (skillet), then place the potato slices in the n, layering them like a cake. Fry until golden on the nderside, then sprinkle with salt and pepper to taste.

Turn the potatoes over and fry until golden on the her side. Lower the heat, cover and continue cooking r about 20 minutes or until tender.

Meanwhile, melt the butter in a separate frying pan, d the kidneys and fry over brisk heat for a few inutes on each side. Lower the heat, sprinkle with salt d pepper to taste, then cover and cook gently for minutes.

Remove the kidneys from the pan with a slotted oon and slice them. Reserve the juices in the pan. urn the potatoes out onto a warmed serving platter, en place the kidneys on top. Keep hot.

Stir the gin into the kidney pan juices and boil pidly to deglaze★. Stir in the wine, return to the boil, ste and adjust seasoning. Pour over the kidneys and otatoes. Serve immediately.

RVES 4

The suet or fat from the outside of ox and veal kidneys is a popular cooking fat in France, particularly for deep-frying when it is known as *graisse de friture*. It is rendered down before use by being slowly melted in a heavy pan with a little water, then strained. Pork suet is also sometimes rendered and used in this way.

FOIE DE VEAU À LA LYONNAISE

Calf's (Veal) Liver with Onions

Metric/Imperial	American
450 g/1 lb calf's liver, sliced	1 lb veal liver, sliced
salt	salt
freshly ground black pepper	freshly ground black pepper
2 tablespoons plain flour	2 tablespoons all-purpose flour
50 g/2 oz butter	$\frac{1}{4}$ cup butter
4 onions, peeled and thinly sliced	4 onions, peeled and thinly sliced
2 tablespoons wine vinegar	2 tablespoons wine vinegar
chopped parsley, to garnish (optional)	chopped parsley, for garnish (optional)

Sprinkle the liver with salt and pepper to taste, then coat in the flour, shaking off the excess.

Melt half the butter in a frying pan (skillet), add the liver and fry over brisk heat for 2 minutes on each side. Transfer to a warmed serving platter and keep hot.

Melt the remaining butter in the pan. Add the onions and fry over very gentle heat until soft and lightly coloured, stirring frequently. Stir in the vinegar, and salt and pepper to taste.

Sprinkle the onions over the liver, then garnish with parsley, if liked. Serve immediately.

SERVES 4

LANGUE DE BOEUF SAUCE PIQUANTE

Calf's (Veal) Tongue with Piquant Sauce

Metric/Imperial	American
1 calf's tongue, dressed	1 veal tongue, dressed
2 carrots, peeled and sliced into rings	2 carrots, peeled and sliced into rings
2 leeks (white part only), sliced	2 leeks (white part only), sliced
2 onions, peeled and sliced into rings	2 onions, peeled and sliced into rings
2.5 litres/4$\frac{1}{2}$ pints water	5$\frac{1}{2}$ pints (11 cups) water
salt	salt
few black peppercorns	few black peppercorns
1 bouquet garni★	1 bouquet garni★
2 shallots, peeled and chopped	2 scallions, peeled and chopped
4 tablespoons wine vinegar	$\frac{1}{4}$ cup wine vinegar
1 tablespoon butter	1 tablespoon butter
1 tablespoon plain flour	1 tablespoon all-purpose flour
4 gherkins, diced	4 small dill pickles, diced
freshly ground black pepper	freshly ground black pepper

Put the tongue in a large pan, cover with cold water and bring to the boil. Boil for 20 minutes, skimming occasionally with a slotted spoon, then drain and rinse under cold running water.

Put the vegetables in a pan with the measured water, salt, peppercorns and bouquet garni. Bring to the boil, add the tongue and simmer for 3 hours or until tender.

Put the shallots (scallions) and wine vinegar in a separate small pan and boil rapidly until all the vinegar has evaporated.

Meanwhile, melt the butter in another pan. Sprinkle in the flour and cook, stirring, for 1 minute to obtain a smooth *roux* (paste). Gradually stir in about 300 ml/ $\frac{1}{2}$ pint/1$\frac{1}{4}$ cups of the boiling stock from the tongue. Bring slowly to the boil, stirring constantly, then add the shallots and gherkins (dill pickles), and salt and pepper to taste. Lower the heat and simmer for 5 to 6 minutes until thick, stirring frequently.

Drain the tongue and remove the outer skin. Slice the meat neatly, then place on a warmed serving platter. Pour over the sauce and serve immediately.

SERVES 8

RIS DE VEAU À LA NORMANDE

Calf's (Veal) Sweetbreads with Mushrooms and Cream

Metric/Imperial	American
4 calf's sweetbreads	4 veal sweetbreads, trimmed and sliced
150 g/5 oz butter	$\frac{2}{3}$ cup butter
225 g/8 oz mushrooms, trimmed and sliced	2 cups trimmed and sliced mushrooms
2 tablespoons plain flour	2 tablespoons all-purpose flour
salt	salt
freshly ground black pepper	freshly ground black pepper
7 tablespoons calvados or brandy	7 tablespoons calvados or brandy
200 ml/$\frac{1}{3}$ pint double cream	1 cup heavy cream

ANJOU
ANDOUILLETTES AU VOUVRAY
Sausages and Mushrooms with White Wine

Andouillettes are spicy sausages made from tripe or chitterlings. They are very popular in France, and can be found in almost every charcuterie there. Outside France they may occasionally be found in good French delicatessens or speciality shops, but if they are difficult to obtain, this dish can equally well be made with any other French sausage.

Only use the still Vouvray wine in cooking, not the sparkling variety. The usual accompaniment to a dish of andouillettes is creamed sorrel or spinach.

Metric/Imperial	American
2 tablespoons saindoux★, dripping or butter	2 tablespoons saindoux★, drippings or butter
6 andouillettes★, sliced	6 andouillettes★, sliced
3 shallots, peeled and chopped	3 scallions, peeled and chopped
225 g/8 oz mushrooms, sliced	$2-2\frac{1}{4}$ cups sliced mushrooms
300 ml/$\frac{1}{2}$ pint Vouvray (dry white) wine	$1\frac{1}{4}$ cups Vouvray (dry white) wine
salt	salt
freshly ground black pepper	freshly ground black pepper
2 tablespoons dried breadcrumbs	2 tablespoons dried bread crumbs

Melt half the fat in a frying pan (skillet), add the sausage and fry over moderate heat until golden brown and crisp. Pour a little of the cooking fat onto a heatproof serving platter, then arrange the sausage on the platter. Keep hot.

Add the shallots (scallions) to the pan and fry until lightly coloured. Add the mushrooms and fry until their juices run. Pour in the wine and add salt and pepper to taste. Cover and cook gently for 15 minutes.

Pour the mushroom mixture over the sausages, then sprinkle with the breadcrumbs and dot with the remaining fat. Put under a preheated hot grill (broiler) until the topping is golden brown. Serve immediately.
SERVES 6

Foie de veau à la lyonnaise; Andouillettes au Vouvray

Soak the sweetbreads in cold water for 3 hours, changing the water 2 or 3 times. Drain the sweetbreads and rinse thoroughly under cold running water. Place them in a pan, cover with fresh water, then bring slowly to the boil. Simmer for 5 minutes, then drain and rinse again under cold running water. Remove any fatty parts, then place the sweetbreads between 2 plates and weight them down. Leave for 1 hour.

Melt half the butter in a frying pan (skillet). Slice the sweetbreads and add to the pan. Fry over gentle heat until lightly coloured on both sides.

Coat the mushrooms in the flour, shaking off the excess. Add the mushrooms to the pan, sprinkle with salt and pepper to taste, then cover and simmer very gently for 15 minutes. Remove the sweetbreads and mushrooms from the pan with a slotted spoon and place on a warmed serving platter. Keep hot.

Stir the *calvados* or brandy into the pan and scrape up the sediment from the bottom. Stir in the cream and simmer until reduced by half. Remove from the heat, then add the remaining butter a little at a time, whisking vigorously. Taste and adjust seasoning, then pour over the sweetbreads. Serve immediately.
SERVES 4

VEGETABLES

To the French, vegetables are as important a part of the meal as the meat, fish, eggs or cheese, for rarely are they served simply as an accompaniment to a main course. Vegetables are a dish in their own right, and as much attention goes into their preparation and cooking as it does into any other part of the meal. Apart from their use in hors d'oeuvre dishes, the usual custom is to serve vegetables after the main dish of meat or fish, etc., so they can be appreciated on their own rather than being mixed with – and spoilt by – the sauces and gravies from other dishes.

French cooking methods for vegetables are different, but perhaps the main difference lies in the freshness and quality of the vegetables themselves. In France, vegetables are picked young and small. Courgettes (zucchini), for example, are never allowed to grow to the size of marrows (squash) in the way they are in other countries. They are picked while still tiny, sweet and full of flavour; the same rule applies to all the different types of beans and root vegetables – such as carrots, turnips and parsnips. But perhaps most important of all, they are eaten while still fresh, as soon as possible after picking, for the French housewife invariably buys her vegetables daily from the local vegetable market. Not for her the frozen vegetables available all year round, she prefers to use only fresh vegetables in season.

In order to make full use of each vegetable in season, the French have invented numerous ways of preparing and cooking each one, so that it is impossible to tire of them. Potato dishes are a fine example of French ingenuity, for there are literally hundreds of different ways to cook and serve them, each one deliciously different from the other.

Contrary to what you might expect, simplicity is always the keynote when cooking vegetables. First and foremost, it is essential to banish all thought of boiling vegetables in copious amounts of water. In France, if vegetables are to be boiled at all, they are simply thrown into a pan containing the minimum amount of boiling water, brought quickly back to the boil, then boiled briskly; the cooking time should be just sufficient to take away rawness, yet at the same time retain crispness. After draining, they are refreshed in a strainer held under cold running water, then left until the moment of serving when they can be quickly tossed in melted butter over moderate heat until heated through.

An equally popular method for cooking vegetables à la française is to braise or sweat them in a small amount of stock. This can be done on top of the stove or in the oven; the secret is to have a heavy-based pan (cast iron is best) with a tight-fitting lid so that the moisture from the vegetables is retained in the pan, then served with them. Glazing takes this method one step further, by adding sugar and sometimes butter to the stock. During cooking, the vegetable becomes coated in a sweet, shiny glaze – this is a favourite method for root vegetables, particularly carrots.

NICE

ARTICHAUTS À LA BARIGOULE
Artichokes Cooked in Wine with Garlic

In Provence, the small violet-coloured artichokes are always used for this dish, but any very young and tender artichoke will be suitable. The original recipe for artichauts à la barigoule is believed to be one of the oldest of Provençal dishes; in it the artichokes were cut in half lengthways, then brushed with oil and grilled (broiled). This is a more modern version.

Metric/Imperial	American
6 small globe artichokes	6 small globe artichokes
7 tablespoons oil	7 tablespoons oil
2 onions, peeled and chopped	2 onions, peeled and chopped
2 carrots, peeled and diced	2 carrots, peeled and diced
salt	salt
freshly ground black pepper	freshly ground black pepper
200 ml/⅓ pint dry white wine	1 cup dry white wine
2 garlic cloves, peeled and crushed	2 garlic cloves, peeled and crushed
7 tablespoons water	7 tablespoons water

emove the hard outer leaves from the artichokes. rim all the stalks to the same short length. Cut the tips ff the remaining leaves with scissors and scoop out the hokes with a sharp teaspoon. Plunge the artichokes nto a bowl of cold water and wash them thoroughly, rising the leaves apart so that the water penetrates eep into the base of the leaves. Drain the artichokes noroughly by standing them upside down in a olander.

Pour half the oil into a deep flameproof casserole, nen make a layer of the onions and carrots in the ottom. Place the artichokes on top, leaves uppermost, nen sprinkle with salt and pepper to taste and the emaining oil.

Cover the casserole and cook over moderate heat for 5 minutes, shaking the pan occasionally and making ure that the onions and carrots do not burn.

Pour in the wine, increase the heat and boil ncovered until the liquid has reduced by one third. dd the garlic and water, cover the casserole again, nen cook over moderate heat for 40 minutes or until ne artichokes are very tender and the liquid is almost ompletely absorbed. Transfer to a warmed serving ish. Serve hot.

ERVES 3

Artichauts à la languedocienne

ARTICHAUTS À LA LANGUEDOCIENNE
Artichokes with Pork, Ham and Wine

The perfect artichokes for this recipe are the very small violet-coloured variety which are most often sold in bunches. If only larger ones are obtainable, blanch them for a few minutes in boiling water to which a few drops of lemon juice have been added, then follow the recipe as for the small ones. In the Languedoc region, these artichokes are the traditional accompaniment to grilled (broiled) lamb cutlets.

Metric/Imperial	American
12 small globe artichokes	*12 small globe artichokes*
2 lemons	*2 lemons*
3 tablespoons olive oil	*3 tablespoons olive oil*
1 onion, peeled and chopped	*1 onion, peeled and chopped*
1 shallot, peeled and chopped	*1 scallion, peeled and chopped*
75 g/3 oz belly pork, diced	*$\frac{1}{3}$ cup diced pork sides*
100 g/4 oz raw ham★, diced	*$\frac{1}{2}$ cup diced raw ham★*
1 tablespoon plain flour	*1 tablespoon all-purpose flour*
750 ml/1$\frac{1}{4}$ pints dry white wine	*3 cups dry white wine*
little light stock or water, if necessary	*little light stock or water, if necessary*
freshly ground black pepper	*freshly ground black pepper*

Remove the hard outer leaves from the artichokes. Trim all the stalks to the same short length. Cut the tips off the remaining leaves with scissors. Cut the artichokes in quarters lengthways and scoop out the chokes with a sharp teaspoon.

Rub the cut surfaces of the artichokes with one of the lemons cut in half, then place in a bowl of cold water with the juice of the remaining lemon.

Heat the oil in a large heavy pan, add the onion and shallot (scallion) and fry gently until soft but not coloured. Add the pork and ham and fry for a further 5 minutes, stirring frequently.

Add the artichokes and fry gently for 10 minutes, stirring occasionally. Sprinkle in the flour and cook for 1 minute, stirring well to absorb all the fat in the pan.

Pour in the wine to just cover the artichokes, adding a little stock or water if there is not enough wine. Add pepper to taste, then cover and simmer for 30 minutes or until the artichokes are very tender. Transfer to a warmed serving dish. Serve hot.

SERVES 6

VARIATION: In Catalonia the artichokes are sprinkled with a *hachis* of breadcrumbs, garlic, parsley and belly pork, before cooking without liquid.

Morilles à la crème;
Endives à la flamande;
Cèpes à la bordelaise

CÈPES À LA BORDELAISE

Cèpes with Garlic and Parsley

The original French recipe for this famous dish calls for a special small variety of cèpes called têtes-de-nègre. If you are lucky enough to be able to buy any kind of cèpe in a specialist greengrocer or market, they will be just as good.

Metric/Imperial	American
450 g/1 lb cèpes★	1 lb cèpes★
salt	salt
freshly ground black pepper	freshly ground black pepper
5 tablespoons olive oil	5 tablespoons olive oil
1 garlic clove, peeled	1 garlic clove, peeled
1 tablespoon chopped parsley, to garnish	1 tablespoon chopped parsley, for garnish

Separate the caps from the stalks of the mushrooms, then wipe the caps clean, making a few incisions on the underside. Sprinkle the caps with salt and pepper to taste.

Heat half the oil in a heavy pan, add the mushroom caps and fry over brisk heat for 10 minutes, shaking the pan constantly and turning the mushrooms over from time to time.

Transfer the mushrooms to a frying pan (skillet) large enough to hold them easily without squashing together, then cook over very gentle heat for 10 minutes.

Meanwhile, peel the mushroom stalks and chop them with the garlic. Heat the remaining oil in a separate pan. Add the mushroom and garlic *hachis* and fry over brisk heat for a few minutes.

Sprinkle the *hachis* evenly over the mushroom caps, then transfer to a warmed serving dish and garnish with the parsley. Serve immediately.
SERVES 4

MORILLES À LA CRÈME

Morel Mushrooms with Cream

If fresh morels are difficult to obtain, use the dried variety instead, soaking them in lukewarm water for 3 hours beforehand.

Metric/Imperial	American
75 g/3 oz butter	⅓ cup butter
50 g/2 oz shallots, peeled and finely chopped	½ cup finely chopped scallions
450 g/1 lb morel mushrooms★, cleaned and quartered	1 lb morel mushrooms★, cleaned and quartered
juice of ½ lemon	juice of ½ lemon
salt	salt
cayenne pepper	cayenne pepper
freshly grated nutmeg	freshly grated nutmeg
200 ml/⅓ pint double cream	1 cup heavy cream

Cèpes, together with many other varieties of mushrooms and fungi, grow in abundance in the forests of the Bordeaux region in south-western France, but they can be difficult to find elsewhere. This simple recipe for *cèpes à la bordelaise* has become the classic way to cook *cèpes* in France.

Melt half the butter in a heavy pan, add the shallots (scallions) and fry gently until soft but not coloured.

Meanwhile, put the mushrooms in a separate pan with the remaining butter and the lemon juice. Add salt, cayenne and nutmeg to taste. Bring to the boil, stirring, then lower the heat and simmer for 10 minutes.

Remove the mushrooms from their juices with a slotted spoon, then add to the shallots. Boil the mushroom juices rapidly until reduced by half, then stir in the cream. Boil steadily until reduced by half, then add the mushrooms and shallots. Lower the heat and simmer for 2 minutes. Taste and adjust seasoning, then transfer to a warmed serving dish. Serve immediately.
SERVES 4

ENDIVES À LA FLAMANDE

Chicory (Belgian Endive) with Lemon Juice

This is a beautifully simple way of cooking chicory (Belgian endive), which does not detract from the bitter-sweet flavour of the vegetable.

Metric/Imperial	American
1 kg/2 lb chicory	2 lb Belgian endive
75 g/3 oz butter	⅓ cup butter
1 tablespoon sugar	1 tablespoon sugar
salt	salt
freshly ground black pepper	freshly ground black pepper
juice of 1 lemon	juice of 1 lemon

Cut off any damaged outer leaves from the chicory (endives), then make a slit along one side of each head with a sharp stainless steel knife. Wash thoroughly, drain upside down in a colander, then dry with kitchen paper towels.

Melt half the butter in a shallow flameproof casserole until frothy, then remove from the heat. Arrange the chicory heads in a single layer in the casserole. Sprinkle with the sugar, salt and pepper to taste, then with the lemon juice.

Cover the chicory with a sheet of buttered grease-proof (waxed) paper and bake in a preheated moderate oven (180°C/350°F/Gas Mark 4) for 30 minutes or until the chicory is tender.

Melt the remaining butter until quite hot and pour over the chicory just before serving. Serve immediately, straight from the casserole.
SERVES 4

VARIATION: Another popular way of serving chicory (Belgian endive) in Flandre is to cook it as above, then cover with a Béchamel sauce (page 44), grated cheese and breadcrumbs. The dish is then put under a preheated hot grill (broiler) until golden brown.

FARCUN ROUERGAT

Spinach and Ham in Béchamel Sauce

In the original recipe, the mixture is covered during baking, with a piece of pig's caul to add flavour. It is not essential, but if you use one, soak it in lukewarm water before use.

Metric/Imperial	American
1 kg/2 lb spinach, thinly sliced	2 lb spinach, thinly sliced
2 celery sticks, thinly sliced	2 celery stalks, thinly sliced
4 garlic cloves, peeled and finely chopped	4 garlic cloves, peeled and finely chopped
225 g/8 oz ham★, finely chopped	1 cup finely chopped ham★
2 parsley sprigs, finely chopped	2 parsley sprigs, finely chopped
2 thyme sprigs	2 thyme sprigs
freshly ground black pepper	freshly ground black pepper
25 g/1 oz butter	2 tablespoons butter
25 g/1 oz plain flour	¼ cup all-purpose flour
600 ml/1 pint milk	2½ cups milk
freshly grated nutmeg	freshly grated nutmeg
salt	salt
1 egg	1 egg
100 ml/4 fl oz double cream	½ cup heavy cream

Put the spinach in a bowl with the celery, garlic, ham and parsley. Rub the leaves from the thyme between your fingers over the bowl, add pepper to taste, then mix the ingredients well together.

Melt the butter in a heavy pan, sprinkle in the flour and cook, stirring constantly, for 1 minute to obtain a smooth *roux* (paste). Remove from the heat and add the milk gradually, stirring vigorously after each addition. Bring slowly to the boil, stirring constantly, then lower the heat and simmer, stirring, for 3 to 4 minutes. Add nutmeg, salt and pepper to taste, then remove from the heat.

Whisk the egg and cream together, then slowly stir into the sauce. Fold the vegetable mixture into the sauce until thoroughly incorporated.

Pour the mixture into a buttered gratin dish and level the surface. Cover with a lid and bake in a preheated moderate oven (160°C/325°F/Gas Mark 3) for 20 to 25 minutes. Serve hot, straight from the dish.

SERVES 4 TO 6

Farcun rouergat; Petits pois à la vendéene

CHOU AU LARD

White Cabbage with Bacon

Metric/Imperial	American
150 g/5 oz streaky bacon, rind removed and chopped	⅔ cup finely chopped fatty bacon
2 tablespoons red wine vinegar	2 tablespoons red wine vinegar
1 white cabbage, cored and shredded	1 white cabbage, cored and shredded
salt	salt
freshly ground black pepper	freshly ground black pepper

Put the bacon in a heavy pan and cook over moderate heat until the fat runs. Remove from the heat and add the wine vinegar.

Add the cabbage to the pan with salt and pepper to taste. Fry over high heat for 3 to 4 minutes, shaking the pan vigorously to mix the ingredients together. Serve immediately.

SERVES 4

PAPETON D'AUBERGINES

Aubergines (Eggplant) Baked with Parmesan and Eggs

This dish is usually served hot with a homemade tomato sauce (page 47), but it is equally good served cold, in which case it should be left to cool in the baking dish, then unmoulded before serving.

Metric/Imperial	American
7 tablespoons olive oil	7 tablespoons olive oil
1.5 kg/3–3½ lb aubergines, diced	3–3½ lb eggplant, diced
2 thyme sprigs	2 thyme sprigs
salt	salt
freshly ground black pepper	freshly ground black pepper
1 garlic clove, peeled and crushed	1 garlic clove, peeled and crushed
75 g/3 oz Parmesan cheese, grated	¾ cup grated Parmesan cheese
4 eggs, beaten	4 eggs, beaten

Heat the oil in a heavy pan, add the aubergines (eggplant) and fry over moderate heat for 20 minutes.

Work the aubergines and thyme leaves through the medium blade of a *mouli-légumes* (vegetable mill) or purée in an electric blender. Season with salt and pepper to taste. Add the garlic, Parmesan and eggs and beat well to mix.

Pour the mixture into an oiled baking dish, then bake in a preheated moderately hot oven (200°C/400°F/Gas Mark 6) for 20 to 30 minutes. The top of the *papeton* should be golden brown. Serve hot, straight from the baking dish.

SERVES 6

prigs of fresh thyme are sed frequently in French ecipes, not only as part f the traditional ouquet garni, but also as flavouring in their own ight. Thyme is an ssential herb in the Provençal mixture of ried herbs known as *erbes du midi* or *herbes du Provence*. It is a selection f Mediterranean herbs, mpossible to imitate lsewhere, but sachets nd pots are available at pecialist shops. The lavour of thyme goes vell with most green egetable dishes, and vith carrots. A sprig kept n a bottle of wine inegar gives the vinegar subtle flavour of thyme, erfect for vinaigrette.

PETITS POIS À LA VENDÉENNE

Petits Pois with Onions, Herbs and Lettuce

Metric/Imperial	American
50 g/2 oz butter	¼ cup butter
1 kg/2 lb petits pois, shelled	2 lb petits pois, shelled
12 small pickling onions, peeled	12 baby onions, peeled
finely chopped parsley, savory and thyme, to taste	finely chopped parsley, savory and thyme to taste
1 lettuce heart	1 lettuce heart
2 pinches of sugar	2 pinches of sugar
salt	salt
freshly ground black pepper	freshly ground black pepper

Melt the butter in a pan and add the peas, onions and herbs. Cook gently for 10 minutes, shaking the pan.

Tie the lettuce heart with fine string, then add to the pan. Add the sugar and salt and pepper to taste. Pour in enough boiling water to just cover the peas and simmer gently, uncovered, until the peas are tender.

Untie the lettuce heart and stir the leaves into the peas and onions. Serve immediately.

SERVES 6

Courgettes (zucchini), aubergines (eggplant), peppers, tomatoes, green beans and *petits pois* are the vegetables normally associated with French cooking, but cabbages are usually not. And yet in the inland mountainous regions of France, where poor soil and weather force the local people to rely on long-keeping vegetables, the cabbage is an immensely popular vegetable. Hundreds of ingenious ways of cooking cabbage are known to the French that would put our familiar 'boiled greens' to shame!

AUVERGNE

FARÇON DE CHOU

Cabbage and Bacon Pie

This dish is also sometimes called fouson de chou. In the Savoyarde region there is a similar recipe for gratin de chou in which the cabbage is boiled until tender, then the large outer leaves are stuffed with the inner leaves which have been chopped with bacon. The whole stuffed cabbage is then baked with a little stock in a moderate oven for 2 hours.

Metric/Imperial	American
1 tablespoon olive oil	1 tablespoon olive oil
2 onions, peeled and thinly sliced	2 onions, peeled and thinly sliced
150 g/5 oz smoked streaky bacon, rinds removed and cut into thin strips	$\frac{2}{3}$ cup smoked fatty bacon, cut into thin strips
1 white cabbage, finely shredded	1 white cabbage, finely shredded
2 garlic cloves, peeled and crushed	2 garlic cloves, peeled and crushed
salt	salt
freshly ground black pepper	freshly ground black pepper
2 eggs	2 eggs
150 ml/$\frac{1}{4}$ pint milk	$\frac{2}{3}$ cup milk
2 tablespoons dried breadcrumbs	2 tablespoons dried bread crumbs

Heat the oil in a heavy pan, add the onions and fry gently until golden, stirring occasionally. Add the bacon, cabbage and garlic, and salt and pepper to taste; stir well to mix. (Take care not to add too much salt because of the smoked bacon.) Fry gently for 20 minutes, stirring occasionally.

Whisk the eggs and milk together. Transfer the cabbage mixture to a buttered gratin dish, then pour the egg and milk mixture over the top. Sprinkle with the breadcrumbs and bake in a preheated moderate oven (160°C/325°F/Gas Mark 3) for 1 hour. Serve hot, straight from the gratin dish.
SERVES 6

PROVENCE

BOHÉMIENNE

Purée of Aubergines (Eggplant), Tomatoes and Parmesan

A speciality from the town of Avignon, la bohémienne is also sometimes known as gratin estrassaire. It can be eaten hot or cold.

Metric/Imperial	American
1 kg/2 lb aubergines, sliced into thin rounds	2 lb eggplant, sliced into thin rounds
salt	salt
3 tablespoons olive oil	3 tablespoons olive oil
1 onion, peeled and thinly sliced	1 onion, peeled and thinly sliced
4 tomatoes, skinned, chopped and seeded	4 tomatoes, skinned, chopped and seeded
2 garlic cloves, peeled and finely chopped	2 garlic cloves, peeled and finely chopped
chopped parsley	chopped parsley
75 g/3 oz Parmesan cheese, grated	$\frac{3}{4}$ cup grated Parmesan cheese
freshly ground black pepper	freshly ground black pepper

RATATOUILLE NIÇOISE

There are numerous versions of this famous vegetable dish from the Provence region of southern France. This recipe incorporates the usual summer vegetables, but it can equally well be made without some of them – use whatever is available at the time.

Metric/Imperial	American
120 ml/4 fl oz olive oil	½ cup olive oil
450 g/1 lb aubergines, thinly sliced or diced	1 lb eggplant, thinly sliced or diced
450 g/1 lb courgettes, sliced	1 lb zucchini, sliced
450 g/1 lb onions, peeled and thinly sliced	1 lb onions, peeled and thinly sliced
450 g/1 lb green peppers, cored, seeded and cut into thin strips	1 lb green peppers, cored, seeded and cut into thin strips
5 garlic cloves, peeled and crushed	5 garlic cloves, peeled and crushed
750 g/1½ lb tomatoes, skinned, halved and seeded	1½ lb tomatoes, skinned, halved and seeded
salt	salt
freshly ground black pepper	freshly ground black pepper
2 thyme sprigs	2 thyme sprigs
5 large basil leaves	5 large basil leaves
chopped parsley, to garnish	chopped parsley, for garnish

Heat half the oil in a large heavy pan, add the aubergines (eggplant) and fry over moderate heat until lightly coloured, stirring frequently. Add the courgettes (zucchini) and continue frying for 5 to 6 minutes until they are lightly coloured. Remove both aubergines and courgettes with a slotted spoon and set aside.

Add the remaining oil to the pan, then add the onions and fry gently until soft. Add the peppers and garlic, increase the heat and fry for a few minutes. Add the tomatoes and cook gently for 10 minutes, stirring frequently.

Return the aubergines and courgettes to the pan and stir well to mix with the other vegetables. Add salt and pepper to taste, then crumble in the thyme. Cook gently, uncovered, for 40 minutes or until the vegetables are soft, stirring occasionally.

Just before serving, crumble the basil leaves into the ratatouille, then taste and adjust seasoning. Transfer to a warmed serving dish and sprinkle with parsley. Serve hot or cold.

SERVES 6

ABOVE: **Ratatouille niçoise**
LEFT: **Farçon de chou**

...lace the aubergine (eggplant) slices in layers in a ...olander, sprinkling each layer with salt. Leave to ...égorge★.

Meanwhile, heat the oil in a large heavy pan, add the ...nion and fry gently until soft. Add the tomatoes and ...ook gently, stirring and pressing them firmly to ...educe them to a purée.

Drain the aubergines and rinse thoroughly under ...old running water. Dry with kitchen paper towels, ...hen add to the pan with the garlic, and parsley to taste. ...tir well, then cover and cook gently for 30 minutes. ...rush the mixture with a wooden spoon from time to ...me to mash the aubergines to a purée.

A few minutes before the end of cooking, stir in the ...armesan, then taste and adjust seasoning. Transfer to a ...armed serving dish and serve hot.

...ERVES 6

...ARIATION: Some versions of *la bohémienne* contain ...nchovies: Desalt★ canned anchovy fillets, then cook ...hem in a little olive oil, stirring with a wooden spoon ...ntil they are reduced to a purée. Mix with a little milk, ...hen with the Parmesan, and spread over the top of the ...ubergine purée in a gratin dish. Bake in a preheated ...ot oven (220°C/425°F/Gas Mark 7) for 10 minutes ...r until golden brown. Serve hot, straight from the ...ratin dish.

FABONADE

Broad (Lima) Beans with Ham and Garlic in Creamy Sauce

Metric/Imperial	American
50 g/2 oz saindoux★, dripping or butter	¼ cup saindoux★, drippings or butter
1 onion, peeled and finely chopped	1 onion, peeled and finely chopped
150 g/5 oz ham★, diced	⅔ cup diced ham★
4 garlic cloves, peeled and crushed	4 garlic cloves, peeled and crushed
1 kg/2 lb broad beans, shelled	2 lb lima beans, shelled
150 ml/¼ pint water	⅔ cup water
few savory sprigs	few savory sprigs
salt	salt
freshly ground black pepper	freshly ground black pepper
4 egg yolks	4 egg yolks
2 teaspoons wine vinegar or lemon juice	2 tablespoons wine vinegar or lemon juice
chopped parsley, to garnish	chopped parsley, for garnish

Melt the fat in a heavy pan, add the onion and ham and fry gently for a few minutes. Add the garlic and beans, then the water, savory, and salt and pepper to taste. Mix well.

Bring to the boil, then lower the heat, cover and simmer for 20 to 30 minutes until the beans are tender.

Discard the savory. Mix the egg yolks and vinegar or lemon juice together, then stir slowly into the beans. Heat through, but do not allow to boil. Taste and adjust seasoning, then transfer to a warmed serving dish and garnish with parsley. Serve immediately.

SERVES 6

CHOU ROUGE AUX POMMES

Braised Red Cabbage with Apples

Metric/Imperial	American
25 g/1 oz goose fat★, dripping or butter	2 tablespoons goose fat★, drippings or butter
1 large onion, peeled and sliced	1 large onion, peeled and sliced
1 red cabbage, coarsely shredded	1 red cabbage, coarsely shredded
salt	salt
freshly ground black pepper	freshly ground black pepper
200 ml/8 fl oz chicken stock (page 42)	1 cup chicken stock (page 42)
pinch of sugar	pinch of sugar
1 bay leaf	1 bay leaf
1 whole clove	1 whole clove
3 cooking apples, peeled, cored and thinly sliced	3 tart apples, peeled, cored and thinly sliced

Melt the fat in a large flameproof casserole, add the onion and fry gently until soft but not coloured. Add the cabbage with salt and pepper to taste, then moisten with half of the stock. Stir in the sugar, bay leaf and clove, then cover and cook very gently for 45 minutes.

Add the apples to the casserole, folding them in gently to mix with the cabbage. Cover again and cook for a further 45 minutes or until the cabbage and apples are tender. Add the remaining stock a little at a time during cooking as the cabbage becomes dry.

Discard the bay leaf and clove, then taste and adjust seasoning. Serve hot, straight from the casserole.

SERVES 4 TO 5

Fabonade; Tian de légumes

The word *tian* is
Provençal dialect, for
which there is no direct
translation. It is used to
describe a kind of gratin
dish, both the vessel in
which the food is cooked
and the food itself. A *tian*
is usually a mixture of
vegetables and eggs
topped with grated
cheese and breadcrumbs;
spinach is probably the
best-known *tian* but it is
equally delicious made
with courgettes
(zucchini) or a mixture
of different vegetables.

TIAN DE LÉGUMES

Spinach au Gratin

Metric/Imperial	American
4 tablespoons olive oil	$\frac{1}{4}$ cup olive oil
1.5 kg/3–3$\frac{1}{2}$ lb spinach, thinly sliced	3–3$\frac{1}{2}$ lb spinach, thinly sliced
2 garlic cloves, peeled and bruised	2 garlic cloves, peeled and bruised
salt	salt
freshly ground black pepper	freshly ground black pepper
1 egg, beaten	1 egg, beaten
50 g/2 oz fresh breadcrumbs	1 cup fresh bread crumbs
50 g/2 oz Gruyère cheese★, grated	$\frac{1}{2}$ cup grated Gruyère cheese★

Heat half the oil in a large heavy pan. Add the spinach with just the water clinging to the leaves after washing, the garlic and a little salt and pepper. Cook, uncovered, over brisk heat for 10 minutes until all the water from the spinach has evaporated.

Discard the garlic, then leave the spinach to cool slightly. Stir in the beaten egg, reheat gently, then taste and adjust seasoning.

Transfer the spinach to an oiled gratin dish and level the surface. Mix together the breadcrumbs and cheese, sprinkle over the top, then sprinkle with the remaining oil. Put under a preheated hot grill (broiler) for 5 minutes or until the topping is golden brown. Serve hot.
SERVES 6

Tian aux oeufs: Make as above, adding a layer of 6 sliced hard-boiled eggs in the middle of the spinach.
Tian de courgettes (zucchini): Make as above, but use 1 kg/2 lb courgettes (zucchini) instead of the spinach. Cut the courgettes diagonally into 5 mm/$\frac{1}{4}$ inch thick slices and cook for 10 minutes as for spinach.

COUSINAT

Mixed Vegetable Casserole

Any young, tender vegetables can be used for this vegetable dish, the important factor is that they should be as small and fresh as possible. If the small violet-coloured artichokes are not available, lettuce hearts can be used instead.

Metric/Imperial	American
6 small globe artichokes	6 small globe artichokes
1 kg/2 lb fresh vegetables (e.g. carrots, broad and French beans)	2 lb fresh vegetables (e.g. carrots, lima and snap beans)
2 tablespoons pork dripping or butter	2 tablespoons pork drippings or butter
2 thick slices raw ham★, diced	2 thick slices raw ham★, diced
6 small pickling onions, peeled	6 baby onions, peeled
2 tomatoes, skinned, quartered and seeded	2 tomatoes, skinned, quartered and seeded
2 green or red peppers, cored, seeded and thinly sliced	2 green or red peppers, cored, seeded and thinly sliced
about 200 ml/⅓ pint chicken stock (page 42)	about 1 cup chicken stock (page 42)
salt	salt
freshly ground black pepper	freshly ground black pepper
120 ml/4 fl oz dry white wine	½ cup dry white wine

Remove the hard outer leaves from the artichokes. Trim all the stalks to the same short length. Cut the tips off the remaining leaves with scissors and scoop out the chokes with a sharp teaspoon. Plunge the artichokes into a bowl of cold water and wash them thoroughly, prising the leaves apart so that the water penetrates deep into the base of the leaves. Drain the artichokes thoroughly by standing them upside down in a colander.

Prepare the vegetables: peel the carrots, shell the broad (lima) beans and top and tail the French (snap) beans.

Melt the fat in a heavy pan, add the ham and onions, and fry gently until lightly coloured. Add all the prepared vegetables, then enough stock to just cover them. Add salt and pepper to taste. Bring to the boil, then lower the heat, cover and simmer for 30 minutes.

Pour in the wine, then cover again and cook gently for a further 10 to 15 minutes until all the vegetables are just tender. Taste and adjust seasoning, then transfer to a warmed serving dish. Serve immediately.
SERVES 6

Cousinat; Farcis provençaux

PIPÉRADE

Pipérade is best served straight from the pan, but if it is necessary to wait a while before eating it, then it can be ke warm by standing the pan in a hot bain marie★.

Metric/Imperial	American
4 large green or red peppers	4 large green or red pepper
about 7 tablespoons olive oil	about 7 tablespoons olive
4 large onions, peeled and thinly sliced	4 large onions, peeled and thinly sliced
1 hot pimento, thinly sliced	1 hot pimento, thinly slice
2 garlic cloves, peeled and crushed	2 garlic cloves, peeled and crushed
pinch of sugar	pinch of sugar
1 kg/2 lb tomatoes, skinned, chopped and seeded	4 cups skinned, chopped a seeded tomatoes
1 bouquet garni★	1 bouquet garni★
salt	salt
6 thick slices Bayonne ham★ (optional)	6 thick slices Bayonne han (optional)
6 eggs, lightly beaten	6 eggs, lightly beaten
freshly ground black pepper	freshly ground black peppe

FARÇIS PROVENÇAUX

Provençal Stuffed Vegetables

The large Spanish or Bermuda onions with a mild flavour are the best variety for stuffing.

Metric/Imperial	American
3 aubergines	3 eggplant
6 large onions, peeled	6 large onions, peeled
6 large tomatoes	6 large tomatoes
salt	salt
freshly ground black pepper	freshly ground black pepper
7 tablespoons olive oil	7 tablespoons olive oil
STUFFING:	STUFFING:
225 g/8 oz boned loin of veal	½ lb boneless loin of veal
75 g/3 oz boned belly pork, rind removed	1 slice of pork sides, bone and rind removed
1 onion, peeled	1 onion, peeled
2 garlic cloves, peeled	2 garlic cloves, peeled
few parsley sprigs	few parsley sprigs
2 tablespoons grated Parmesan cheese	2 tablespoons grated Parmesan cheese
2 tablespoons boiled long-grain rice	2 tablespoons boiled long-grain rice
2 thyme sprigs	2 thyme sprigs
2 eggs, beaten	2 eggs, beaten

Cut the aubergines (eggplant) in half lengthways, scoop out the flesh and reserve.

Plunge the onions into a pan of boiling water for a few minutes, then drain. Cut a hole in the top of each onion, then hollow out the centres with a sharp teaspoon, reserving the flesh that is removed. Cut a hole in the top of each tomato, scoop out the flesh and reserve. Sprinkle salt, pepper and a little oil inside the hollowed-out vegetables.

Prepare the stuffing: mince (grind) together the veal, pork, onion, garlic, parsley and the reserved flesh from the hollowed-out vegetables.

Heat 1 tablespoon oil in a pan, add the minced (ground) mixture and fry gently for a few minutes, stirring constantly. Remove from the heat, then stir in the cheese, rice and the crumbled thyme leaves. Stir in the eggs and salt and pepper to taste.

Stand the hollowed-out vegetables in a single layer in a buttered gratin dish. Divide the stuffing equally between them, then sprinkle with a little oil. Bake, uncovered, in a preheated moderate oven (180°C/350°F/Gas Mark 4) for 45 minutes. Sprinkle with more oil from time to time to prevent the stuffing from becoming dry.

Transfer the vegetables carefully to a warmed serving platter and serve immediately.
SERVES 6

VARIATION: If liked, pour 1 to 2 tablespoons home-made fresh tomato sauce (page 47) over each stuffed vegetable before baking. Tomato sauce can also be poured into the bottom of the baking dish halfway through the cooking time or, if preferred, it can be served separately in a sauceboat.

lace the peppers under a preheated hot grill (broiler) ntil the skins become charred, turning them requently. Remove from the heat, then remove the kins by rubbing the peppers with kitchen paper owels.

Cut the peppers in half, then remove the cores and eeds. Slice the flesh thinly. Heat the oil in a frying pan skillet), add the peppers and fry over moderate heat or a few minutes, stirring frequently.

Add the onions, pimento and garlic and fry for a urther 10 minutes, stirring all the time. Add the sugar, omatoes and bouquet garni, and salt to taste. Cook ently for a further 10 minutes stirring frequently.

If using the ham, heat it through gently in a separate an with a little oil.

Meanwhile, pour the eggs into a lightly oiled' or reased frying pan (skillet) and cook for 2 to 3 minutes ithout stirring. Discard the bouquet garni from the egetable mixture, then add to the eggs, stirring to mix he two together so that the eggs become scrambled nd cooked to your liking. Taste and adjust seasoning.

Serve the pipérade straight from the pan or, if using he ham, transfer the pipérade to a warmed serving latter and surround with the slices of ham. Serve mmediately.
ERVES 6

Pipérade, which originated in the Basque country of south-western Béarn, is often referred to as *Pipérade Basquaise*, yet it is one of those regional dishes which has travelled all over France to become almost a national dish. It takes its name from the word *piper* (meaning hot red pepper), which is one of its essential ingredients.

Haricots en garniture
tourangelle; Oignons
sous la cendre; Palets de
marrons

HARICOTS EN GARNITURE TOURANGELLE

Haricot (Navy) Beans with French Beans

Metric/Imperial	American
450 g/1 lb dried white haricot beans, soaked in cold water overnight	*2¼ cups dried white navy beans, soaked in cold water overnight*
1 garlic clove, peeled	*1 garlic clove, peeled*
1 bouquet garni★	*1 bouquet garni★*
salt	*salt*
450 g/1 lb French green beans, topped and tailed	*1 lb green beans, topped and tailed*
75 g/3 oz butter	*⅓ cup butter*
75 g/3 oz plain flour	*¾ cup all-purpose flour*
750 ml/1¼ pints vegetable stock (page 43)	*3 cups vegetable stock (page 43)*
freshly ground black pepper	*freshly ground black pepper*

Drain the haricots, rinse under cold running water, then place in a large pan. Cover with fresh water and add the garlic and bouquet garni. Bring to the boil, lower the heat, cover and simmer for 45 minutes to 1 hour or until just tender. Add salt to taste halfway through the cooking time.

Meanwhile, cook the green beans in boiling salted water for 10 minutes or until just tender. Drain both kinds of beans, discarding the garlic and bouquet garni, then mix together.

Melt the butter in a clean heavy pan, sprinkle in the flour and cook, stirring constantly, for 1 minute to obtain a smooth *roux* (paste). Pour in the stock a little at a time, stirring vigorously after each addition. Bring slowly to the boil, stirring constantly, then lower the heat and simmer for 5 to 6 minutes until the sauce thickens, stirring frequently. Add salt and pepper to taste, bearing in mind the seasoning of the stock.

Stir the beans into the sauce and heat through gently without boiling. Transfer to a warmed serving dish and serve immediately.
SERVES 6

VARIATION: In Bas-Maine, this dish is served with butter and flavoured with chopped fresh herbs.

Soaking dried haricot beans helps tenderize them and thus shortens cooking time. If you do not have time to soak the beans in cold water overnight, put the beans in a large pan, cover with cold water and bring to the boil. Drain and repeat this process, then remove from the heat, cover the pan and leave the beans to stand in the hot water for 2 hours. Drain and rinse thoroughly, then proceed with the recipe.

OIGNONS SOUS LA CENDRE
Onions Baked in Cinders

A recipe to reserve for the summertime, when using the barbecue or charcoal fire for cooking meat.

Metric/Imperial	American
12 medium onions	12 medium onions
6 tablespoons olive oil	6 tablespoons olive oil
2 tablespoons wine vinegar	2 tablespoons wine vinegar
3 garlic cloves, peeled and crushed	3 garlic cloves, peeled and crushed
chopped parsley	chopped parsley
salt	salt
freshly ground black pepper	freshly ground black pepper

Wrap the unpeeled onions individually in kitchen foil, then push into the coals of the fire. Leave for 30 to 40 minutes.

Meanwhile, make the dressing: whisk together the oil and vinegar until thick, then whisk in the garlic with parsley, salt and pepper to taste.

Unwrap the onions carefully, remove the skins and serve hot, with a little of the dressing poured over each one.
SERVES 6

PALETS DE MARRONS
Chestnut Patties

Called palets or quoits because of their shape, these patties of chestnut purée are the traditional accompaniment to game dishes.

Metric/Imperial	American
1 kg/2 lb chestnuts	2 lb chestnuts
1 celery stick, sliced	1 celery stalk, sliced
salt	salt
freshly ground black pepper	freshly ground black pepper
100 g/4 oz butter	$\frac{1}{2}$ cup butter
3 egg yolks	3 egg yolks

Plunge the chestnuts, a few at a time into a pan of boiling water and boil for 10 minutes. Remove from the pan with a slotted spoon, then peel off both outer and inner skins.

Put the skinned chestnuts in a clean pan, just cover with water, then add the celery, salt and pepper to taste and 25 g/1 oz/2 tablespoons butter. Bring to the boil, then lower the heat, cover and simmer for 15 minutes or until tender.

Drain the chestnuts thoroughly, then work to a purée in an electric blender or *mouli-légumes* (vegetable mill). Stir in the egg yolks, then leave until completely cold.

Form the purée into flat quoit shapes. Melt the remaining butter in a frying pan (skillet), add the *palets* and fry until golden brown on both sides. Transfer to a warmed serving dish and serve hot.
SERVES 6

Fèves en ragoût;
Porrosalda

SALADE TIÈDE DE LENTILLES

Lentils with Bacon

Although lentils are usually sold pre-washed, it is advisable
to rinse them thoroughly before cooking, and to pick them
over to remove any particles of stone or grit.

Metric/Imperial	American
450 g/1 lb brown or green lentils	*2 cups brown or green lentils*
2 onions, peeled	*2 onions, peeled*
1 whole clove	*1 whole clove*
2 carrots, peeled and thinly sliced	*2 carrots, peeled and thinly sliced*
1 bouquet garni★	*1 bouquet garni★*
1 × 100 g/4 oz piece smoked bacon	*1 × ¼ lb piece smoked bacon*
2 garlic cloves, peeled	*2 garlic cloves, peeled*
salt	*salt*
1 teaspoon prepared hot mustard	*1 teaspoon prepared hot mustard*
4 tablespoons vinegar	*¼ cup vinegar*
120 ml/4 fl oz oil	*½ cup oil*
1 bunch chives, snipped	*1 bunch chives, snipped*
freshly ground black pepper	*freshly ground black pepper*
chopped parsley, to garnish	*chopped parsley, for garnish*

Put the lentils in a pan, cover with cold water and bring to the boil. Stud 1 onion with the clove, then add to the pan with the carrots, bouquet garni, bacon, 1 whole garlic clove and a little salt. Lower the heat, cover the pan and simmer for 40 minutes or until the lentils are tender.

Meanwhile, chop the remaining onion and garlic finely. Put the mustard in a large serving bowl. Stir in the vinegar, then the oil, chopped onion and garlic, and the chives.

Drain the lentils and discard the whole onion, garlic and bouquet garni. Cut the bacon into bite-sized pieces, discarding any rind, then add to the serving bowl with the lentils.

Toss gently to mix, adding salt and pepper to taste. Serve immediately, while still warm, sprinkled liberally with parsley.
SERVES 6

Melt the fat in a heavy pan, add the bacon, beans and garlic. Cook gently for a few minutes, stirring constantly, then add the remaining ingredients with salt and pepper to taste. Mix well.

Bring to the boil, lower the heat, cover and simmer for 20 to 30 minutes until the beans are tender. Discard the bouquet garni and savory, then taste and adjust seasoning. Transfer to a warmed serving dish and serve immediately.

SERVES 6

VARIATION: Often broad (lima) beans are served as a purée: cook as above, but until very soft, then work through a fine sieve (strainer). Reheat, then add sautéed diced ham to taste. Bind the purée by adding 2 eggs beaten with a little double (heavy) cream.

AQUITAINE

PORROSALDA

Leek and Potato Ragoût

Metric/Imperial	American
2 tablespoons pork dripping or goose fat★	2 tablespoons pork drippings or goose fat★
150 g/5 oz streaky bacon in the piece, rind removed and diced	$\frac{2}{3}$ cup thickly diced fatty bacon
6 medium potatoes, peeled and sliced into rounds	6 medium potatoes, peeled and sliced into rounds
1 kg/2 lb leeks (white part only), sliced into rings	2 lb leeks (white part only), sliced into rings
3 tablespoons plain flour	3 tablespoons all-purpose flour
200 ml/$\frac{1}{3}$ pint vegetable stock or water (page 43)	1 cup vegetable stock or water (page 43)
2 garlic cloves, peeled and crushed	2 garlic cloves, peeled and crushed
1 bouquet garni★	1 bouquet garni★
salt	salt
freshly ground black pepper	freshly ground black pepper

Melt the fat in a large heavy pan, add the bacon and fry over brisk heat until golden brown. Reduce the heat to moderate, add the potatoes and leeks and fry until lightly coloured.

Sprinkle in the flour and cook for 1 minute, stirring constantly. Stir in the stock or water gradually, then add the garlic, bouquet garni, and salt and pepper to taste. Cover and simmer gently for 20 to 30 minutes or until the potatoes are tender.

Discard the bouquet garni, then taste and adjust seasoning. Transfer to a warmed serving dish and serve immediately.

SERVES 6

Whenever broad beans are served in France, it is traditional to flavour them with *sarriette* or savory. This rather bitter-tasting herb seems to marry well with the delicate flavour of broad beans, but it should be used with caution because it has a strong flavour. There are two varieties of savory, summer and winter, the latter being the stronger of the two.

PÉRIGORD

FÈVES EN RAGOÛT

Broad (Lima) Bean Ragoût

Metric/Imperial	American
50 g/2 oz goose fat★, dripping or butter	$\frac{1}{4}$ cup goose fat★, drippings or butter
100 g/4 oz bacon, rinds removed and diced	$\frac{1}{2}$ cup diced bacon
1 kg/2 lb broad beans, shelled	2 lb lima beans, shelled
2 garlic cloves, peeled and crushed	2 garlic cloves, peeled and crushed
150 ml/$\frac{1}{4}$ pint water	$\frac{2}{3}$ cup water
3 carrots, peeled and cut into thin rounds	3 carrots, peeled and cut into thin rounds
6 small pickling onions, peeled	6 baby onions, peeled
1 bouquet garni★	1 bouquet garni★
1 savory sprig	1 savory sprig
pinch of sugar	pinch of sugar
salt	salt
freshly ground black pepper	freshly ground black pepper

GRATIN DAUPHINOIS

Layered Potatoes with Cream and Garlic

Metric/Imperial	American
1 garlic clove, peeled	1 garlic clove, peeled
75 g/3 oz butter	⅓ cup butter
1 kg/2 lb waxy potatoes, peeled and sliced into thin rounds	2 lb waxy potatoes, peeled and sliced into thin rounds
freshly grated nutmeg	freshly grated nutmeg
salt	salt
freshly ground black pepper	freshly ground black pepper
about 250 ml/8 fl oz hot milk	about 1 cup hot milk
about 250 ml/8 fl oz single cream	about 1 cup light cream

Rub the inside of an earthenware or enamel baking dish with the garlic, then brush thickly with butter.

Place the potato slices in the dish in layers, sprinkling each layer with nutmeg, salt and pepper to taste.

Mix the milk and cream together, then pour over the potatoes, making sure the potatoes are completely covered with the liquid. Dot the top with the remaining butter.

Bake uncovered, in a preheated moderate oven (180°C/350°F/Gas Mark 4) for 1 to 1¼ hours until the potatoes are tender when pierced with a skewer. Increase the heat to moderately hot (200°C/400°F/Gas Mark 6) for the last 10 minutes' cooking time to brown the top layer of potatoes. Serve hot, straight from the baking dish.

SERVES 4 TO 6

LENTILLES DU PUY

Lentils Auvergne-Style

Lentils from Le Puy in the Auvergne are the small dark green variety, not to be confused with other brown, red or yellow lentils. Lentilles du Puy can be bought in good French delicatessens. They are sold ready to cook, with grit removed, but before cooking, wash them in a bowl of warm water and discard any that float to the surface.

Metric/Imperial	American
450 g/1 lb green lentils	2 cups green lentils
2 litres/3½ pints water	4½ pints (9 cups) water
salt	salt
freshly ground black pepper	freshly ground black pepper
100 g/4 oz belly pork	¼ lb pork sides
2 onions, peeled	2 onions, peeled
2 whole cloves	2 whole cloves
2 carrots, peeled and halved lengthways	2 carrots, peeled and halved lengthways
1 celery stick	1 celery stick
1 bouquet garni★	1 bouquet garni★
1 tablespoon saindoux★, dripping or butter	1 tablespoon saindoux★, drippings or butter
2 garlic cloves, peeled and thinly sliced	2 garlic cloves, peeled and thinly sliced
2 tablespoons plain flour	2 tablespoons flour
300 ml/½ pint vegetable stock (page 43)	1¼ cups vegetable stock (page 43)

Soak the lentils in cold water for 1 hour. Drain and place in a large pan. Add boiling water to cover and simmer just below boiling point for 5 minutes. Drain.

Bring the measured water to the boil in the rinsed-out pan. Add salt and pepper to taste, the pork, 1 onion stuck with the cloves, the carrots, celery and bouquet garni. Bring back to the boil, then add the lentils. Simmer, covered, for 1¼ hours or until the lentils and pork are tender.

Meanwhile, melt the fat in a flameproof casserole, slice the remaining onion, then add to the fat with the garlic. Fry gently until golden, then sprinkle in the flour. Cook, stirring, for 1 minute to obtain a smooth *roux* (paste). Stir in the stock gradually, then bring slowly to the boil, stirring. Lower the heat and simmer for 5 to 6 minutes, stirring frequently.

Drain the lentils and discard the whole onion, cloves, carrots, celery and bouquet garni. Dice the pork. Stir the lentils and pork into the sauce and heat through gently. Taste and adjust seasoning, then transfer to a warmed serving dish. Serve hot.

SERVES 6

TRUFFIAT

Potato Cake

Metric/Imperial	American
1 kg/2 lb floury old potatoes, peeled	2 lb floury old potatoes, peeled
3 eggs, beaten	3 eggs, beaten
150 g/5 oz butter, softened	⅔ cup softened butter
freshly grated nutmeg	freshly grated nutmeg
salt	salt
freshly ground black pepper	freshly ground black pepper
250 g/9 oz plain flour	2¼ cups all-purpose flour

Steam the potatoes, in a pressure-cooker if possible, or cook in a small amount of water until just tender, to avoid them becoming too moist. Mash or purée them in an electric blender or *mouli-légumes* (vegetable mill). Beat in the eggs (reserving a little for the glaze), then 50 g/2 oz/¼ cup butter and nutmeg, salt and pepper to taste.

Mix the flour and the remaining butter together with a little water to form a soft dough. Mix the potato purée with the dough, then knead until smooth.

Form the potato dough into a rectangular shape about 2 cm/¾ inch thick in a buttered baking dish. Make criss-cross incisions in the top, then brush with the reserved beaten egg.

Bake in a preheated moderate oven (180°C/350°F, Gas Mark 4) for about 45 minutes or until the top is golden brown. The inside of the cake should still be quite moist. Serve hot, straight from the baking dish.

SERVES 6

VARIATION: A little grated cheese can be added to the dough while mixing.

Rather than mixing the two doughs together, the flour dough can be formed into a rectangular shape and placed in the baking dish, then the potato purée spread on top.

French potato dishes are often flavoured with nutmeg. Never use the ready-ground nutmeg sold in drums or jars; follow the French tradition – buy whole nutmegs and grate them on the fine side of a conical or box cheese grater. Better still, buy a special nutmeg grater or grinder to encourage you to grate nutmeg freshly as and when required. The difference in flavour between ground and freshly grated nutmeg is incomparable.

GALETTE LYONNAISE
Potato and Onion Bake

Metric/Imperial	American
1 kg/2 lb floury old potatoes, peeled	2 lb floury old potatoes, peeled
150 g/5 oz butter	⅔ cup butter
about 250 ml/8 fl oz hot milk	about 1 cup hot milk
freshly grated nutmeg	freshly grated nutmeg
salt	salt
freshly ground black pepper	freshly ground black pepper
3 large onions, peeled and sliced into thin rings	3 large onions, peeled and sliced into thin rings

Steam the potatoes, in a pressure cooker if possible, or cook in a small amount of water until tender, to avoid them becoming too moist. Mash or purée them in an electric blender or *mouli-légumes* (vegetable mill). Beat in 25 g/1 oz/2 tablespoons butter, then add the milk a little at a time until a firm purée is obtained. Add nutmeg, salt and pepper to taste.

Melt 25 g/1 oz/2 tablespoons butter in a large heavy pan. Add the onions and fry gently until soft, stirring frequently. Add the potato purée and stir well to mix with the onions. Heat through gently for a few minutes, turning the mixture over constantly.

Taste and adjust seasoning, then turn the mixture into a buttered gratin dish and level the surface. Dot with the remaining butter, then put under a preheated hot grill (broiler) for a few minutes until the top is golden brown. Serve hot, straight from the gratin dish.

SERVES 4 TO 6

POMMES SARLADAISES
Fried Potato Slices with Garlic and Parsley

The quantity of garlic and parsley is a matter of personal taste – use as much or as little as you like!

Metric/Imperial	American
50 g/2 oz goose fat★, dripping or butter	¼ cup goose fat★, drippings or butter
750 g/1½ lb waxy potatoes, peeled and sliced into thin rounds	1½ lb waxy potatoes, peeled and sliced into thin rounds
garlic cloves, peeled	garlic cloves, peeled
parsley sprigs	parsley sprigs
salt	salt
freshly ground black pepper	freshly ground black pepper

Melt the fat in a frying pan (skillet), add the potato slices and cook over moderate heat for about 20 minutes until tender, turning the potatoes over frequently so that they are golden on all sides.

Meanwhile, chop the garlic and parsley together to make a *hachis*. When the potatoes are cooked, sprinkle the *hachis* over them, with salt and pepper to taste. Cover the pan tightly, remove from the heat and leave to stand for 5 minutes before serving. Serve hot, straight from the pan.

SERVES 4

GNOCCHI NIÇOISE

These gnocchi are delicious served with grated cheese, or a homemade fresh tomato sauce (page 47); they make an unusual alternative to potatoes, rice or noodles.

Metric/Imperial	American
1 kg/2 lb waxy potatoes	2 lb waxy potatoes
250 g/9 oz plain flour, sifted	2¼ cups all-purpose flour, sifted
2 tablespoons oil	2 tablespoons oil
1 egg, beaten	1 egg, beaten
salt	salt
50 g/2 oz butter	¼ cup butter
chopped parsley, to garnish	chopped parsley, for garnish

Although *potato gnocchi* are associated with Italian food, they are enjoyed on both sides of the Franco-Italian border. Pasta is also popular along the south coast of France.

Cook the potatoes in their skins in boiling water for about 20 minutes until tender. Drain them and remove their skins, then work to a fine purée in an electric blender or *mouli-légumes* (vegetable mill). Leave to cool.

Put the potato purée in a bowl, then gradually work in the flour, using the palms of your hands. Add the oil

d egg with salt to taste, then knead the dough with
e hands until smooth.

Place a quarter of the dough on a floured work
rface. Roll the dough with floured hands into a long
usage shape, 1 cm/½ inch thick. Repeat with the
maining dough.

Cut the rolls into small circles about 2 cm/¾ inch
ick, then spread them out on a floured surface. Using
fork, twist each gnocchi from left to right to make a
ated shell shape – this will make the dough more
pple and thus easier to cook.

Plunge half the gnocchi carefully into a pan of
iling salted water. Simmer for about 5 minutes, until
e gnocchi rise to the surface of the water. Remove
om the pan with a slotted spoon. Keep hot on a
armed serving platter while cooking the remainder.
ot with butter and garnish with chopped parsley.
rve immediately.

RVES 6

**Pommes sarladaises;
Criques ardéchoises;
Gnocchi niçoise**

GRATIN SAVOYARD
Potato and Cheese Casserole

Metric/Imperial	American
75 g/3 oz butter	⅓ cup butter
1 kg/2 lb waxy potatoes, peeled and sliced into thin rounds	2 lb waxy potatoes, peeled and sliced into thin rounds
150 g/5 oz Gruyère cheese★, grated	1¼ cups grated Gruyère cheese★
freshly grated nutmeg	freshly grated nutmeg
salt	salt
freshly ground black pepper	freshly ground black pepper
600 ml/1 pint hot chicken stock (page 42)	2½ cups hot chicken stock (page 42)

Brush the inside of an earthenware or enamel baking
dish thickly with butter.

Place the potato slices in the dish in layers, sprinkling
each layer with cheese, and nutmeg, salt and pepper to
taste. Cover the top layer of potatoes with cheese, then
pour the stock carefully into the dish. Dot the top with
the remaining butter.

Bake, uncovered, in a preheated moderate oven
(180°C/350°F/Gas Mark 4) for 1 to 1¼ hours or until the
potatoes are tender when pierced with a skewer.
Increase the heat to moderately hot (200°C/400°F/Gas
Mark 6) for the last 10 minutes' cooking time to brown
the top.

Serve hot, straight from the baking dish.

SERVES 4 TO 6

CRIQUES ARDÉCHOISES
Potato, Bacon and Garlic Croquettes

Metric/Imperial	American
5 large waxy potatoes, peeled and grated	5 large waxy potatoes, peeled and grated
50g/2 oz streaky bacon, derinded and finely chopped	¼ cup finely chopped fatty bacon
1 garlic clove, peeled and crushed	1 garlic clove, peeled and crushed
1 egg, beaten	1 egg, beaten
chopped parsley	chopped parsley
salt	salt
freshly ground black pepper	freshly ground black pepper
olive oil, for shallow frying	olive oil, for shallow frying

Drain the potatoes in a sieve (strainer), then dry them
in a clean tea towel.

Put the potatoes in a bowl with the bacon, garlic and
egg and stir well to mix. Add parsley, salt and pepper
to taste.

Form the mixture into small balls with the hands,
then flatten them. Heat a little oil in a frying pan
(skillet), add the *criques* and fry until golden brown on
both sides. Drain on kitchen paper towels, then pile
into a warmed serving dish. Serve immediately.

SERVES 4

DESSERTS

The French prefer cheese and fresh fruit to desserts, the cheese being served after the main course to finish up the last of the wine, and the fruit after the cheese to cleanse the palate. Sometimes, especially in summer, the fruit comes in the form of a chilled compote, a simple dish of fresh fruit poached with sugar and water or wine, occasionally with a dash of brandy or liqueur added. In winter, dried fruits are sometimes poached and served warm. Poached fruit bears little or no resemblance to its stewed counterpart so frequently served in Britain – the fruit is cooked very gently so that it retains its shape and texture.

If you are serving a meal in the French style, with an hors d'oeuvre or soup followed by a main dish of meat, poultry or fish, a separate vegetable dish, then a French cheese or two, you will quickly find that a rich, creamy dessert is almost impossible to eat! For everyday meals, the French housewife occasionally makes a light creamy dessert, a milk-based pudding or a crème caramel (page 172), especially if there are children, but in most cases there will only be a fruit yoghurt or a soft creamy cheese such as a petit-suisse sprinkled with sugar or topped with some poached fruit. The dessert course only really comes into its own at dinner parties and on special occasions, when fruit-filled crêpes, a crème brûlée or a sweet soufflé might be served. Fresh fruit tarts with crème patissière are also popular, but in many cases when a French housewife is entertaining, she will send out to the local pâtisserie for her pastries, tarts and gâteaux.

Every French town, however small, sports its own pâtisserie, and the visitor to France cannot help but notice the sumptuous array of tarts, pastries, gâteaux and sweetmeats that are displayed in the window. In France it is just as acceptable to offer your guests a tart bought from the pâtissier, as it is to serve a home-made one, for the quality is at least comparable. Unfortunately fine pâtisserie is not so easy to find in this country and elaborate desserts are best prepared at home.

ILE DE FRANCE

CRÊPES SUZETTE

Orange-flavoured liqueur and the zest and juice of oranges is the traditional flavouring for this classic dish, but some people may prefer the more unusual flavour of mandarins – the choice is up to you!

Metric/Imperial	American
BATTER:	BATTER:
125 g/4½ oz plain flour	1 cup plus 2 tablespoons all-purpose flour
¼ teaspoon salt	¼ teaspoon salt
3 eggs	3 eggs
2 tablespoons oil	2 tablespoons oil
50 g/2 oz butter, melted	¼ cup melted butter
1 tablespoon caster sugar	1 tablespoon sugar
2 teaspoons vanilla sugar★	2 teaspoons vanilla sugar★
350 ml/12 fl oz milk	1½ cups milk
1 tablespoon rum	1 tablespoon rum
25 g/1 oz butter, for frying	2 tablespoons butter, for frying
SYRUP:	SYRUP:
100 g/4 oz butter, softened and diced	½ cup softened butter, diced
100 g/4 oz caster sugar	½ cup sugar
6 tablespoons Cointreau or Grand Marnier	6 tablespoons Cointreau or Grand Marnier
3 tablespoons brandy	3 tablespoons brandy
1 orange or 2 mandarins	1 orange or 2 mandarins

For the batter, sift the flour and salt into a bowl and make a well in the centre. Add the remaining batter ingredients, then beat well to mix until smooth, using an electric mixer if available. Pass the batter through a fine sieve (strainer) to remove any lumps.

Melt the butter for frying in a 20 cm/8 inch crêpe
~~pan~~ or frying pan (skillet). Pour off the butter into
~~a~~ warmed jug.

Pour a small ladleful of batter into the pan, then tilt
~~th~~e pan from side to side so that the batter runs and
~~co~~vers the base of the pan evenly. Fry over brisk heat
~~fo~~r 10 to 15 seconds until golden brown on the
~~un~~derside, then turn or toss the crêpe over and fry the
~~ot~~her side for 10 to 15 seconds until golden brown.

Slide the crêpe onto a warmed platter and keep hot
~~w~~hile frying the remainder. Pour a little melted butter
~~in~~to the pan in between making the crêpes as the pan
~~be~~comes dry.

Ten minutes before serving, make the syrup. Put the
~~bu~~tter in the pan in which the crêpes were cooked. Add
~~th~~e sugar, 2 tablespoons liqueur and 1 tablespoon
~~br~~andy. Grate the zest★ of the orange or mandarins
~~fin~~ely into the pan, then squeeze in the juice from the
~~fr~~uit.

Place the pan over brisk heat and boil rapidly for
~~1~~ minute until a thick syrup is obtained. Lower the heat
~~an~~d leave to simmer.

Add the crêpes to the pan one at a time to coat them
~~in~~ the syrup, fold each one in half, then in half again to
~~m~~ake a triangular shape. Place on a warmed serving
~~pl~~atter and keep hot by standing the platter over a pan
~~of~~ gently simmering water. Repeat with the remaining
~~cr~~êpes, pouring any remaining syrup over the finished
~~cr~~êpes.

Warm the remaining liqueur and brandy in a
~~se~~parate small pan. Set light to the liqueur in the pan,
~~th~~en pour over the crêpes at the table. Serve as soon as
~~th~~e flames have died down.

SERVES 6 to 8

Crêpes suzette

CRÊPES BRETONNES
Apple Crêpes

*In Brittany these crêpes are often served as a dessert with
jam, honey, chocolate sauce or fruit in syrup.*

Metric/Imperial	American
250 g/9 oz wholewheat flour	2¼ cups wholewheat flour
4 eggs	4 eggs
2 tablespoons oil	2 tablespoons oil
5 tablespoons caster sugar	5 tablespoons sugar
150 g/5 oz butter	⅔ cup butter
250 ml/8 fl oz warm milk	1 cup warm milk
1 teaspoon orange flower water★	1 teaspoon orange flower water★
450 g/1 lb eating apples, peeled, cored and thinly sliced	1 lb dessert apples, peeled, cored and thinly sliced

Put the flour in a bowl and make a well in the centre.
Add the eggs, oil and sugar, then beat until smooth,
using an electric mixer if available.

Melt 50 g/2 oz/¼ cup butter in the warm milk, then
whisk into the batter with a fork until thoroughly
incorporated. Pass the batter through a fine sieve
(strainer) to remove any lumps, then whisk in the
orange flower water. If the batter seems too thick, add
a little cold water until a thin, pouring consistency is
obtained.

Melt 50 g/2 oz/¼ cup butter in a heavy pan, add the
apple slices and fry gently until golden. Keep hot in the
pan.

Melt the remaining butter in a 20 cm/8 inch crêpe
pan or frying pan (skillet). Pour off the butter into
a warmed jug.

Pour a small ladleful of batter into the pan, then tilt
the pan from the side to side so that the batter runs and
covers the base of the pan evenly. Sprinkle a few apple
slices over the crêpe, then fry over brisk heat for 10 to 15
seconds until golden brown on the underside. Turn or
toss the crêpe over and fry the other side for 10 to 15
seconds until golden brown. Keep hot while frying the
remaining batter and apples, pouring a little melted
butter into the pan in between making the crêpes, as
the pan becomes dry. Serve hot.

SERVES 8

CRÈME CARAMEL

A classic French dessert with many variations.

Metric/Imperial	American
CUSTARD:	CUSTARD:
1 litre/1¾ pints milk	4¼ cups milk
1 vanilla pod★, split in half lengthways	1 vanilla bean★, split in half lengthways
8 eggs	8 eggs
100 g/4 oz sugar	½ cup sugar
CARAMEL:	CARAMEL:
100 g/4 oz sugar	½ cup sugar
2 tablespoons water	2 tablespoons water
1 teaspoon lemon juice	1 teaspoon lemon juice

Put the milk in a heavy pan with the vanilla and bring slowly to the boil. Remove from the heat and leave to infuse.

Meanwhile, make the caramel: put the sugar, water and lemon juice in a small heavy pan. Cook over moderate heat until a rich golden caramel colour is obtained. Remove from the heat and pour immediately into a warmed 2 litre/3½ pint/9 cup charlotte or ring mould, soufflé dish or *moule à manqué*. Rotate the mould or dish quickly so that the caramel coats the base and sides evenly. Set aside.

Make the custard: whisk the eggs and sugar together in a bowl until thoroughly combined. Discard the vanilla from the infused milk, then whisk the milk into the egg and sugar mixture. Pass the mixture through a fine sieve (strainer) into the caramelized mould.

Stand the mould in a hot *bain marie* and place in a preheated moderate oven (180°C/350°F/Gas Mark 4). Immediately lower the temperature to cool (150°C/300°F/Gas Mark 2). Cook for about 1 hour or until set; to test if the custard is set, insert a knife into the centre – it should be clean when withdrawn.

Remove the *crème caramel* from the *bain marie* and leave until cold. Leave in a cool place or chill in the refrigerator for 4 hours before unmoulding onto a deep serving dish. To unmould easily, dip the base of the mould into a bowl of hot water for 30 seconds.

Serve *crème caramel* at room temperature or chilled, according to taste.
SERVES 8

VARIATIONS:
1. *Crème caramel* can be baked in 8 individual ramekins or soufflé dishes if preferred, in which case the cooking time should only be 45 minutes.
2. If a more solid custard is preferred, use 4 whole eggs and 8 egg yolks instead of the 8 whole eggs suggested above.
3. The milk can be infused with orange or lemon zest★ as well as, or instead of, the vanilla.
4. The custard can be baked on its own without the caramel, in which case it is called *oeufs au lait*. Brush the mould lightly with butter before pouring in the custard – without the caramel it is likely to stick. If liked, a caramel sauce can be made separately and poured over the custard before serving. Make the caramel sauce by cooking 150 g/5 oz/⅔ cup sugar with 7 tablespoons water until a golden caramel liquid is obtained.
5. If baking the custard on its own without the caramel sauce, the custard itself can be flavoured with chocolate or coffee. Whisk 50 g/2 oz/½ cup cocoa powder or 2 tablespoons instant coffee powder into the eggs and sugar. Increase the quantity of sugar in the custard to 50 g/2 oz/¼ cup.

CLAFOUTIS
Cherry Custard Pudding

It is traditional to remove the stalks from the cherries, but not to stone (pit) them. The size of the baking dish is important when making clafoutis – it should be shallow, but large enough to contain all the cherries in a single layer so that the custard sets evenly around the fruit. Do not use a deep dish in which the cherries have to be piled on top of each other.

Metric/Imperial	American
50 g/2 oz butter, softened	¼ cup softened butter
750 g/1½ lb ripe black cherries	1½ lb ripe black cherries
2 eggs	2 eggs
1 egg yolk	1 egg yolk
100 g/4 oz caster sugar	½ cup sugar
pinch of salt	pinch of salt
50 g/2 oz plain flour	½ cup all-purpose flour
250 ml/8 fl oz milk	1 cup milk
2 teaspoons vanilla sugar★	2 teaspoons vanilla sugar★

Brush the inside of a large shallow baking dish or mould with a little of the softened butter. Arrange the cherries in the bottom of the dish side by side, keeping them in a single layer.

Put the whole eggs and egg yolk in a bowl, add the sugar and salt, then whisk together until light and fluffy.

Melt the remaining butter and whisk into the egg mixture. Whisk in the flour, then add the milk and continue whisking until the batter is smooth.

Pour the batter over the cherries, then bake uncovered in a preheated moderately hot oven (190°C/375°F/Gas Mark 5) for 40 minutes, or until the *clafoutis* is puffed and golden brown. Remove from the oven and leave to cool slightly, until warm.

Sprinkle with the vanilla sugar just before serving. Serve warm, straight from the baking dish.
SERVES 6

Crème caramel; Crème champenoise

CRÈME CHAMPENOISE
White Wine and Lemon Cream

If possible, use a still white wine from the Champagne region (not champagne) for this light, creamy dessert.

Metric/Imperial	American
6 eggs, separated	6 eggs, separated
2 tablespoons cornflour	2 tablespoons cornstarch
grated rind and juice of 1 lemon	grated rind and juice of 1 lemon
100 g/4 oz caster sugar	$\frac{1}{2}$ cup sugar
350 ml/12 fl oz dry white wine	$1\frac{1}{2}$ cups dry white wine

Place 2 egg yolks and the cornflour in a bowl and beat until smooth. Add the remaining egg yolks, lemon rind and juice, and 2 tablespoons of the sugar; beat thoroughly. Heat the wine in a pan to just below boiling, then gradually stir in the egg yolk mixture.

Stand the bowl over a pan of hot water and continue whisking until the mixture is thick and creamy. Remove the bowl from the heat and continue whisking until cool.

Whisk the egg whites in a separate bowl until stiff, then whisk in the sugar a little at a time. Fold 2 tablespoons of the egg white mixture into the custard, then carefully fold in the remaining mixture. Turn into a serving bowl. Chill in the refrigerator for up to 1 hour. Serve with thin crisp biscuits (cookies).
SERVES 8

CRÉMETS D'ANGERS
Whipped Cream Dessert

Sometimes the simplest dishes are the most delicious and crémets is no exception, served with fresh strawberries or raspberries, or simply with sugar and cream.
In France, crémets are made in special porcelain or metal moulds (page 24), which have holes in the base to allow for drainage. Although the moulds can be bought outside France, you can improvise and make your own by punching holes in a small plastic container. Remember to stand the mould over a dish to catch the drips from the cream.

Metric/Imperial	American
120 ml/4 fl oz double cream, chilled	$\frac{1}{2}$ cup heavy cream, chilled
1 egg white	1 egg white
sugar and cream, to serve	sugar and cream, to serve

Whip the cream until stiff. Beat the egg white in a separate bowl until stiff, then fold into the cream until thoroughly incorporated.

Turn the mixture into a muslin (cheesecloth) lined mould, then cover and place in the refrigerator. Leave to drain for 3 to 6 hours.

Turn the *crémets* onto a serving dish and serve immediately, with sugar and cream.
SERVES 2

SOUFFLÉ GLACÉ AUX MIRABELLES

Iced Plum Soufflé

Alsace-Lorraine is famous for its small garden plums known as mirabelles, which are perfect for this recipe. If they are not available, other varieties can be used. Mirabelles are used extensively in the cooking of this region; they are also made into a liqueur known as eau-de-vie de mirabelles. In this recipe the liqueur gives the finished soufflé a heady plum flavour, but if it is difficult to obtain, use kirsch instead.

Metric/Imperial
500 g/1 lb fresh plums, halved and stoned
300 ml/½ pint double cream, chilled
2 tablespoons eau-de-vie de mirabelles or kirsch
4 egg whites
175 g/6 oz caster sugar
TO DECORATE:
about 25 g/1 oz finely chopped nuts or crushed ratafias
about 120 ml/4 fl oz double or whipping cream, whipped

American
1 lb fresh plums, halved and pitted
1¼ cups heavy cream, chilled
2 tablespoons eau-de-vie de mirabelles or kirsch
4 egg whites
¾ cup sugar
TO DECORATE:
about ¼ cup finely chopped nuts or crushed ratafias
about ½ cup heavy or whipping cream, whipped

Prepare a 1.2 litre/2 pint/5 cup freezerproof soufflé dish: cut a strip of doubled greaseproof (waxed) paper long enough to go around the outside of the dish and stand 5 cm/2 inches higher. Tie this securely around the outside of the dish and brush the inside above the rim with melted butter.

Work the fruit in an electric blender or *mouli-légumes* (vegetable mill), then sieve (strain) to remove the skins. Whip the cream until it just holds its shape, then fold into the fruit purée until thoroughly incorporated. Whisk in the liqueur. Set aside.

Beat the egg whites in a separate bowl until stiff and standing in peaks, then add the sugar a little at a time, beating constantly after each addition until thoroughly incorporated.

Fold the egg whites into the fruit purée mixture a little at a time. Do not whisk the mixture as this will knock the air out of the egg whites and cause the soufflé to lose body and lightness.

Spoon the mixture into the prepared soufflé dish, then freeze for at least 4 hours until firm. Thirty minutes before serving, carefully peel off the greaseproof paper and place the soufflé in the refrigerator to soften.

Press nuts or ratafias around the edge and decorate the top with piped whipped cream before serving.
SERVES 6 to 8

ABRICOTS À L'ALSACIENNE

Apricots Baked with Sugar and Kirsch

Metric/Imperial	American
750 g/1½ lb ripe fresh apricots, halved and stoned	1½ lb ripe fresh apricots, halved and pitted
4 tablespoons water	¼ cup water
150 g/5 oz sugar	⅔ cup sugar
2 tablespoons kirsch	2 tablespoons kirsch

Put the apricots, cut side down, in a baking dish. Mix the water and half the sugar together, then pour over the apricots.

Bake in a preheated moderately hot oven (200°C/400°F/Gas Mark 6) for about 30 minutes until the apricots are tender.

Pour the kirsch into the bottom of the dish, then sprinkle the apricots with the remaining sugar. Put under a preheated hot grill (broiler) as close to the flame as possible, then grill (broil) for a few minutes until browned. Serve hot or cold, straight from the baking dish.

SERVES 6

Charlotte aux framboises; Soufflé glacé aux mirabelles

CHARLOTTE AUX FRAMBOISES

Raspberry Cream Charlotte

If liked, serve this spectacular-looking dessert with crème anglaise (page 50)

Metric/Imperial	American
4 egg yolks	4 egg yolks
100 g/4 oz caster sugar	½ cup sugar
250 ml/8 fl oz boiling hot milk	1 cup boiling hot milk
15 g/½ oz gelatine	2 envelopes gelatin
120 ml/4 fl oz cold water	½ cup cold water
150 ml/¼ pint double cream, chilled	⅔ cup heavy cream, chilled
about 2 teaspoons vanilla sugar★	about 2 teaspoons vanilla sugar★
350 g/12 oz fresh raspberries, hulled	2½ cups hulled fresh raspberries
4 tablespoons kirsch	¼ cup kirsch
about 28 (2 packets) sponge fingers	about 28 ladyfingers
TO DECORATE:	TO DECORATE:
about 150 ml/¼ pint double cream, whipped	about ⅔ cup heavy cream, whipped
100 g/4 oz fresh raspberries	1 cup fresh raspberries

Whisk the egg yolks and sugar together in a heatproof bowl until thick and pale. Pour in the milk a little at a time, stirring constantly with a wooden spoon. Stand the bowl over a pan of gently simmering water and cook gently, stirring, until the custard coats the back of the spoon; this may take up to 20 minutes.

Meanwhile, sprinkle the gelatine over 4 table-spoons/¼ cup of the water in a small heatproof bowl and leave to soak for a few minutes. Stand the bowl in a pan of hot water until the gelatine has dissolved, stirring if necessary. Remove the thickened custard from the heat and stir in the dissolved gelatine. Leave until cold.

Whip the cream until it just holds its shape, then whip in the vanilla sugar. Fold into the cold custard with the raspberries and half of the kirsch.

Pour the remaining kirsch and water into a shallow dish. Dip the sponge fingers (ladyfingers) one at a time into the liquid, then use to line the base and sides of a lightly oiled 15 to 18 cm/6 to 7 inch charlotte mould or soufflé dish, reserving a few for the top. Stand the biscuits upright, sugared side outwards, as close together as possible and trimming them to fit if necessary.

Fill the centre of the mould with the raspberry cream mixture, level the top, then cover with the reserved sponge fingers. Chill in the refrigerator for at least 3 hours until the filling is set.

To serve, unmould the charlotte onto a chilled serving platter. Decorate with the whipped cream and raspberries. Serve chilled.

SERVES 6 to 8

ABOVE: **Sorbet au champagne**
RIGHT: **Poires 'belle-angevine'; Soupe aux cerises**

MOUSSE DE CHOCOLAT AU COGNAC

Chocolate and Brandy Mousse

Metric/Imperial	American
200 g/7 oz plain chocolate, broken into small pieces	7 squares semi-sweet chocolate, broken into small pieces
250 ml/8 fl oz milk	1 cup milk
5 eggs, separated	5 eggs, separated
50 g/2 oz caster sugar	¼ cup sugar
500 ml/18 fl oz double cream, chilled	2¼ cups heavy cream, chill
7 tablespoons brandy	7 tablespoons brandy
pinch of salt	pinch of salt

Put the chocolate and milk in a heatproof bowl, th
stand the bowl in a pan of hot water until the chocol
melts, stirring occasionally.

Put the egg yolks and sugar in a bowl and whi
together until light and fluffy. Whisk in the war
chocolate and milk mixture, then leave to cool. Wh
the cream until thick, then fold into the chocola
mixture, with the brandy.

Beat the egg whites with the salt until stiff a
standing in peaks, then fold into the chocolate; do n
whisk the mixture at this stage or it will lose volume

Pour the mousse into a large serving bowl or in
6 individual ramekins or serving dishes. Chill in t
refrigerator for at least 4 hours until set. Serve chilled
SERVES 6

POIRES 'BELLE-ANGEVINE'

Pears Poached in Wine with Cinnamon and Lemon

*This recipe takes its name from a variety of French pear
known as 'belle angevine', although any firm cooking pear
such as Conference may be used instead. If liked, serve the
pears with crème anglaise (page 50) flavoured with lemon
zest★.*

Metric/Imperial	American
1 litre/1¾ pints red wine (preferably Chinon)	4¼ cups red wine (preferably Chinon)
225 g/8 oz sugar	1 cup sugar
1 cinnamon stick	1 cinnamon stick
1 lemon, blanched and thinly sliced	1 lemon, blanched and thinly sliced
6 firm cooking pears	6 firm cooking pears

Put the wine in a saucepan with the sugar, cinnamon
stick and lemon slices. Heat gently until the sugar has
dissolved, then boil rapidly for a few minutes until
syrupy. Discard the cinnamon and lemon.

Peel the pears and scoop out the cores carefully from
the base, leaving the stems. Place the pears in a saucepan
into which they fit snugly, standing upright. Pour the
red wine over the pears, cover and simmer gently for
25 to 45 minutes or until the pears are tender when
tested with a knife. Cooking time depends on the
variety and ripeness of the pears.

Remove the pears from the wine with a slotted
spoon and place in a warmed serving dish. Keep hot.
The cooking liquid should be thick and syrupy – boil
to reduce if it seems too thin. Pour over the pears to
coat them thickly. Serve hot, warm or cold, according
to taste.
SERVES 6

SORBET AU CHAMPAGNE

*Many French cooks have a sorbetière or sorbet-making
machine in their kitchens. The sorbet mixture is simply
placed in the machine, which does all the work for you an
produces a less granular result than hand beating. If you
make sorbets and ice creams regularly it is worth investin
in a sorbetière; if not, then follow these instructions for
making the sorbet by hand. The more often you beat the
sorbet, the smoother it will be at the finish!*

Metric/Imperial	American
250 g/9 oz caster sugar	1 cup plus 2 tablespoons sugar
300 ml/½ pint water	1¼ cups water
juice of 2 lemons	juice of 2 lemons
500 ml/18 fl oz champagne	2¼ cups champagne
a little chilled champagne, to serve	a little chilled champagne, to serve

If using a refrigerator, turn it to its coldest setting. P
the sugar and water in a heavy pan and heat gently un
the sugar has dissolved. Boil rapidly for a few minut
until syrupy. Leave until cold.

Whisk the lemon juice and champagne into the co
sugar syrup, then pour the mixture into a freez
container. Chill in the refrigerator for at le
30 minutes, then transfer to the freezing compartme
or freezer. Freeze for 1 to 2 hours or until half-frozen

Turn the sorbet mixture into a large bowl, then beat again to break up the ice crystals. Return to the freezer container, cover and freeze again for at least 4 hours or until firm.

Transfer the sorbet to the main body of the refrigerator to soften for a few minutes before scooping into individual serving dishes. Sprinkle each serving with a little champagne and serve immediately.
SERVES 6

FRANCHE-COMTÉ

SOUPE AUX CERISES

Cherries in Red Wine with Kirsch

Metric/Imperial	American
750 g/1½ lb black cherries	1½ lb black cherries
500 ml/18 fl oz red wine (e.g. Montigny)	2¼ cups red wine (e.g. Montigny)
4 tablespoons kirsch	¼ cup kirsch
1 strip lemon rind	1 strip lemon rind
175–225 g/6–8 oz caster sugar	¾–1 cup sugar
1 small cinnamon stick	1 small cinnamon stick
700 ml/1¼ pints water	3 cups water
croûtons★ to serve (optional)	croûtons★ to serve (optional)

Stone (pit) half of the cherries and crack half of the stones (pits), using a mortar and pestle. Discard the other stones.

Bring the wine to the boil in a pan, add the cracked stones and the kirsch, and boil for 5 minutes. Remove from the heat, cover and leave to infuse for 20 minutes.

Meanwhile, put the stoned (pitted) cherries in a large pan with the lemon rind, sugar, cinnamon stick and water. Boil rapidly for 10 minutes.

Discard the lemon rind and cinnamon, then work the cherries and liquid through a fine sieve (strainer). Return to the rinsed-out pan and bring to the boil. Add the reserved whole cherries and simmer gently for 6 minutes.

Divide between individual serving bowls. Serve hot, with croûtons fried in butter if liked, or cold.
SERVES 6

Soupe aux cerises **is an unusual dessert, traditionally poured over croûtons and served hot. It is equally delicious served chilled as a summer dessert.**

In Franche-Comté tart cherries are used. If only slightly sweet ones are available, reduce the sugar accordingly.

SOUFFLÉ AU KIRSCH

Metric/Imperial	American
300 ml/½ pint milk	1¼ cups milk
50 g/2 oz sugar	¼ cup sugar
1 vanilla pod★, split in two lengthways	1 vanilla bean★, split in half lengthways
75 g/3 oz butter	⅓ cup butter
50 g/2 oz plain flour	½ cup all-purpose flour
6 egg yolks	6 egg yolks
6 tablespoons kirsch	6 tablespoons kirsch
7 egg whites	7 egg whites
pinch of salt	pinch of salt

Brush the inside of a 1.5 litre/2½ pint/6¼ cup soufflé dish with butter, then sprinkle with sugar, shaking off the excess.

Put the milk, sugar and vanilla in a pan. Bring to the boil, then remove from the heat and leave to infuse.

Melt the butter in a heavy pan, sprinkle in the flour and cook, stirring constantly, for 1 minute to obtain a smooth *roux* (paste). Remove from the heat. Strain the infused milk and add to the *roux* a little at a time, stirring vigorously after each addition. Bring slowly to the boil, stirring constantly, then remove from the heat and beat into the egg yolks. Stir in the kirsch.

Put the egg whites and salt in a bowl and beat until stiff and standing in peaks. Fold into the white sauce gently until thoroughly incorporated. Do not whisk or beat the mixture.

Turn the mixture into the prepared soufflé dish and level the surface. Bake in a preheated moderately hot oven (200°C/400°F/Gas Mark 6) for 25 minutes or until well risen and golden. Serve immediately.

SERVES 6

PESCAJOUN AUX FRUITS

Fresh Fruit Fritter Cake

Metric/Imperial	American
225 g/8 oz dessert pears	½ lb dessert pears
225 g/8 oz peaches	½ lb peaches
225 g/8 oz plums	½ lb plums
60 g/2½ oz sugar	⅓ cup sugar
2 tablespoons eau-de-vie de prunes or kirsch	2 tablespoons eau-de-vie de prunes or kirsch
100 g/4 oz plain flour	1 cup all-purpose flour
3 eggs, separated	3 eggs, separated
2 tablespoons milk	2 tablespoons milk
25 g/1 oz butter	2 tablespoons butter

Peel the fruits, then cut the flesh into 1 cm/½ inch cubes, discarding the cores and stones. Place in a bowl with 2 tablespoons sugar and half the liqueur. Fold gently to mix.

Sift the flour into a separate bowl, then add 2 tablespoons sugar and the egg yolks. Stir well with a wooden spoon, adding the milk a little at a time.

Press the fruit through a fine sieve (strainer) to extract the juices. Stir these into the batter. Beat the egg whites in a separate bowl until stiff and standing in peaks, then fold gently into the batter.

Melt the butter in a large frying pan (skillet) and pour in the fruit batter. Cover the pan and cook gently for 10 minutes or until just set. Place under a preheated moderate grill (broiler) for 1 to 2 minutes until golden brown.

Slide the *pescajoun* onto a warmed serving platter and sprinkle with the remaining sugar. Heat the remaining liqueur in a small pan, pour over the *pescajoun* and set alight. Serve immediately.

SERVES 6

Eaux-de-vie are colourless liqueurs made from distilled fruit, popular in France as *digestifs* and in cooking, because of their concentrated flavour. Kirsch, the best known *eau-de-vie*, is distilled from cherries, *quetsch* from the purple-skinned quetsch plums, and *mirabelle* from the yellow plums of the same name. *Framboise*, made from raspberries, has one of the best flavours.

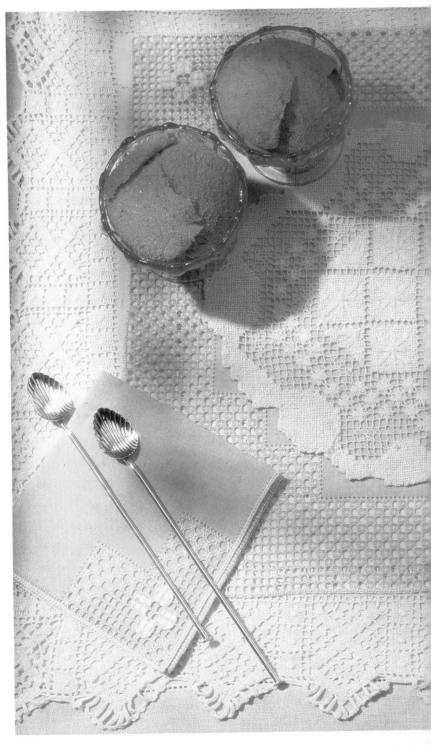

SORBET DE PLOUGASTEL

Strawberry Sorbet

Plougastel is a region famous for its strawberries. As with Sorbet au Champagne (page 176), this sorbet is best made in a sorbetière.

Metric/Imperial	American
1.5 kg/3–3½ lb fresh strawberries	3–3½ lb fresh strawberries
1 litre/1¾ pints milk	4¼ cups milk
200 g/7 oz caster sugar	1 cup sugar
juice of 1 lemon	juice of 1 lemon

Sorbet de Plougastel;
Tarte au fromage blanc

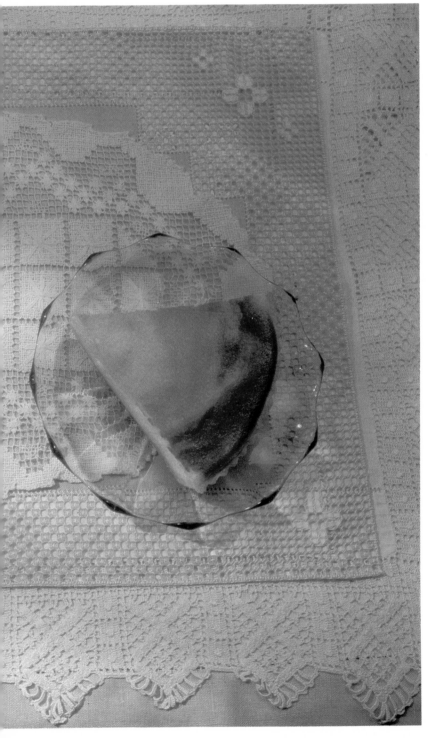

If using a refrigerator, turn to its coldest setting. Work the strawberries through the fine blade of a *mouli-légumes* (vegetable mill), or purée in an electric blender.

Put the strawberry purée in an electric mixer with the remaining ingredients and work until the mixture is smooth.

Turn the mixture into a freezer container and chill in the refrigerator for at least 30 minutes. Transfer to the freezing compartment or freezer and freeze for 1 to 2 hours or until half-frozen.

Turn the sorbet mixture into a large bowl, then beat again to break up the ice crystals. Return to the freezer container, cover and freeze again for at least 4 hours or until firm.

Transfer the sorbet to the main body of the refrigerator to soften for a few minutes before scooping into individual serving dishes. Serve immediately.
SERVES 6 to 8

TARTE AU FROMAGE BLANC

Baked Lemon Cheesecake

Metric/Imperial	American
PÂTE SABLÉE:	PÂTE SABLÉE:
225 g/8 oz plain flour	2 cups all-purpose flour
pinch of salt	pinch of salt
100 g/4 oz butter, cut into small pieces	½ cup butter, cut into small pieces
1 egg yolk	1 egg yolk
50 g/2 oz caster sugar	¼ cup sugar
a little iced water, to mix	a little iced water, to mix
FILLING:	FILLING:
375 g/12 oz fromage blanc★ or other cream cheese	2 cups fromage blanc★ or other cream cheese
3 eggs, separated	3 eggs, separated
75 g/3 oz caster sugar	⅓ cup sugar
150 ml/¼ pint double cream	⅔ cup heavy cream
zest of 1 lemon	zest of 1 lemon

To make the *pâte sablée*, sift the flour and salt into a bowl and make a well in the centre. Add the butter, egg yolk and sugar, then work the ingredients together with the fingertips, adding the water gradually until a smooth, soft dough is obtained. Leave in the refrigerator for at least 1 hour.

Meanwhile, make the filling: Beat the cheese and egg yolks together in a bowl. Add the sugar, cream and lemon zest and beat again until thoroughly incorporated.

Roll out the dough on a floured surface and use to line the base and sides of a buttered 25 cm/10 inch flan dish or tart pan. Prick the base and line with greaseproof (waxed) paper or foil and baking beans. Bake blind in a preheated moderately hot oven (200°C/400°F/Gas Mark 6) for 15 minutes. Remove the beans and cook for a further 5 minutes.

Beat the egg whites until stiff and standing in peaks. Fold gently into the filling, then pour into the flan dish. Bake immediately in a preheated moderately hot oven (190°C/375°F/Gas Mark 5) for 40 to 45 minutes. Serve at room temperature.
SERVES 8

VACHERIN

Strawberry Meringue Gâteau

In France, the meringue base and shells for vacherin can be bought ready made at most pâtisseries.

Metric/Imperial	American
MERINGUE:	MERINGUE:
3 egg whites	3 egg whites
75 g/3 oz icing sugar, sifted	¾ cup sifted confectioner's sugar
75 g/3 oz caster sugar	⅓ cup sugar
TO FINISH:	TO FINISH:
250 ml/8 fl oz crème chantilly (page 50)	1 cup crème chantilly (page 50)
100 g/4 oz sugar	½ cup sugar
7 tablespoons water	7 tablespoons water
450 g/1 lb fresh strawberries	3 cups fresh strawberries
about 500 ml/18 fl oz vanilla ice cream	about 2¼ cups vanilla ice cream
about 500 ml/18 fl oz strawberry ice cream	about 2¼ cups strawberry ice cream

Make the meringue: beat the egg whites until stiff and standing in peaks, then fold in the sugars gradually until thoroughly incorporated.

Place a sheet of non-stick parchment paper on a baking sheet. Draw an 18 cm/7 inch circle on the paper, then spread with half of the meringue mixture.

Put the remaining meringue into a piping bag fitted with a 2.5 cm/1 inch fluted nozzle. On a separate sheet of parchment paper, pipe the remaining meringue into shell shapes, about 5 cm/2 inches long. Bake the circle and the shells in a preheated cool oven (140°C/275°F/Gas Mark 1) for 1 hour or until the meringue is firm and dry but still white. Leave until cold before peeling off the paper.

Place the meringue circle on a serving platter. Sandwich the shells together in pairs with a little of the *crème chantilly*, then stick around the edge of the circle with more *crème chantilly*.

Put the sugar and water in a heavy pan and heat gently until the sugar has dissolved. Bring to the boil and boil rapidly until thick and syrupy. Remove from the heat and leave to cool.

Reserve 12 whole strawberries for the decoration, then work the remaining strawberries through the fine blade of a *mouli-légumes* (vegetable mill) or purée in an electric blender. Stir in the sugar syrup to make a strawberry sauce or *coulis*.

Scoop the ice cream into the centre of the *vacherin* and dot with some of the reserved whole strawberries. Pour over about one third of the strawberry sauce, then decorate with the remaining whole strawberries and the remaining *crème chantilly*. Serve immediately, with the remaining strawberry sauce handed separately in a sauceboat.

SERVES 6

TARTE AUX POMMES

Creamy Apple Flan

In Alsace-Lorraine this flan is often given the name 'chaude'. Sometimes the custard topping is flavoured with a local eau-de-vie, cinnamon or vanilla, then the flan takes the name of 'migaine'.

Metric/Imperial	American
PÂTE SABLÉE:	PÂTE SABLÉE:
250 g/9 oz plain flour	2¼ cups all-purpose flour
pinch of salt	pinch of salt
125 g/4½ oz butter, cut into small pieces	½ cup plus 1 tablespoon butter, cut into small pieces
1 egg yolk	1 egg yolk
50 g/2 oz caster sugar	¼ cup sugar
3–4 tablespoons iced water	3–4 tablespoons iced water
FILLING:	FILLING:
juice of 1 lemon	juice of 1 lemon
750 g/1½ lb crisp eating apples	1½ lb crisp dessert apples
75 ml/3 fl oz milk	⅓ cup milk
75 ml/3 fl oz double cream	⅓ cup heavy cream
2 eggs, beaten	2 eggs, beaten
50 g/2 oz caster sugar	¼ cup sugar

To make the *pâte sablée*, sift the flour and salt into a bowl and make a well in the centre. Add the butter, egg yolk and sugar, then work the ingredients together with the fingertips, adding the water gradually until a smooth, soft dough is obtained. Leave in the refrigerator for at least 1 hour.

Roll out the dough on a floured surface and use to line the base and sides of a buttered 25 cm/10 inch flan dish or tart pan (preferably with a removable base). Set aside.

For the filling, pour the lemon juice into a large bowl. Peel, quarter and core the apples one at a time, then slice thinly into the bowl of lemon juice, stirring to prevent discoloration.

Arrange the apple slices in the flan dish in a circular pattern, working from the edge of the dish inwards, and overlapping the slices slightly. Stand the dish on a baking sheet and bake in a preheated hot oven (230°C/450°F/Gas Mark 8) for 10 minutes.

Meanwhile, put the remaining filling ingredients in a bowl and whisk together. Pour over the apples in the flan dish and bake in a moderately hot oven (200°C/400°F/Gas Mark 6) for a further 30 minutes. Leave to cool slightly, then serve straight from the dish or transfer to a serving platter. Serve warm.

SERVES 8

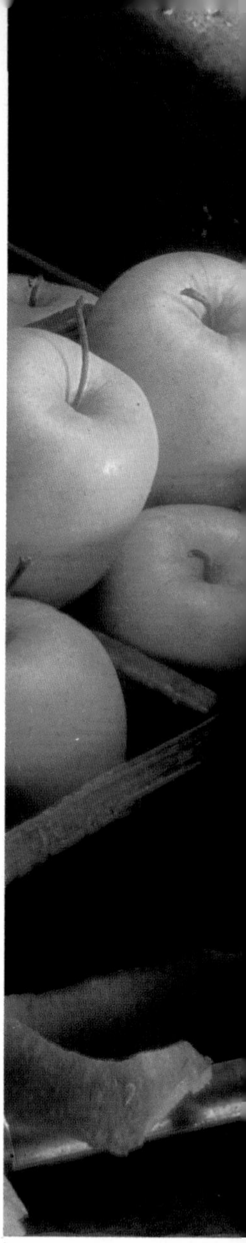

Alsace-Lorraine is the real home of *tartes* and *quiches*, both sweet and savoury. The basic filling for both of these is egg custard, the difference is simply that fruit and sugar are added for a sweet flan, whereas cheese, onion and bacon are more usual for a savoury filling. Fruit orchards are as prolific in the region as *quiches*, and all kinds of fruit are used to make creamy *tartes*, including cherries, apricots and bilberries, as well as apples.

NORMANDIE

DOUILLONS

Baked Apple Parcels

*Douillons are often made with whole pears instead of
apples as in this recipe, and sometimes the shortcrust pastry
(pie dough) is replaced by pâte feuilletée (puff pastry).*

Metric/Imperial	American
PÂTE SABLÉE:	PÂTE SABLÉE:
250 g/9 oz plain flour	2¼ cups all-purpose flour
pinch of salt	pinch of salt
125 g/4½ oz butter, cut into small pieces	½ cup plus 1 tablespoon butter, cut into small pieces
1 egg yolk	1 egg yolk
25 g/1 oz caster sugar	2 tablespoons sugar
a little iced water, to mix	a little iced water, to mix
APPLE FILLING:	APPLE FILLING:
50 g/2 oz caster sugar	¼ cup sugar
50 g/2 oz butter, softened	¼ cup softened butter
1 teaspoon ground cinnamon	1 teaspoon ground cinnamon
4 large eating apples	4 large dessert apples
juice of 1 lemon	juice of 1 lemon
GLAZE:	GLAZE:
1 egg	1 egg
1 tablespoon water	1 tablespoon water

To make the *pâte sablée*, sift the flour and salt into a
bowl and make a well in the centre. Add the butter, egg
yolk and sugar, then work the ingredients together with
the fingertips, adding the water gradually until a
smooth, soft dough is obtained. Leave in the refrigerator for at least 1 hour.

Meanwhile, make the apple filling. Mix together the
sugar, butter and cinnamon. Peel and core the apples,
making enough room in the centre of each one for the
butter and sugar mixture. Sprinkle the apples immediately with the lemon juice to prevent
discoloration.

Roll out the dough on a floured surface until very
thin, then cut into 4 equal squares. Place 1 apple in the
centre of each square, then divide the butter and sugar
mixture equally between them, pushing it well down
into the central cavity. If there is any mixture left over,
spread it over the top of the apples.

Wrap the dough around the apples to enclose them
completely, then moisten the edges with water and
press together to seal. Stand the parcels on a dampened
baking sheet and decorate with leaves cut from the
pastry trimmings. Beat together the egg and water
for the glaze and brush all over the dough.

Bake in a preheated moderately hot oven
(200°C/400°F/Gas Mark 6) for 30 minutes. Serve hot or
cold.
SERVES 4

Tarte aux pommes;
Douillons

Desserts/181

TARTE TATIN

Upside-Down Apple Tart

This tart is named after the young ladies Tatin, who owned
a restaurant in Sologne at the beginning of this century
called 'Le Motte-Beuvron'.

Metric/Imperial	American
100 g/4 oz butter, softened	*½ cup softened butter*
100 g/4 oz caster sugar	*½ cup sugar*
1.5 kg/2½ lb small crisp dessert apples	*2½ lb small crisp dessert apples*
225 g/8 oz pâte brisée (page 52)	*½ lb pâte brisée (page 52)*

Brush the base of a 23 to 25 cm/9 to 10 inch round flameproof baking dish with two thirds of the butter. Sprinkle with two thirds of the sugar.

Peel, halve and core the apples. Arrange the apple halves in the dish, cut sides facing upwards and pressing them firmly together. (It does not matter if they come above the edge of the dish – they will shrink down during cooking.) Sprinkle with the remaining sugar, then dot with the remaining butter.

Cook the apples over moderate heat for about 20 minutes until they begin to caramelize underneath. Transfer to a preheated moderately hot oven (200°C/400°F/Gas Mark 6) and bake for about 5 minutes until the apples become caramelized on top. Remove from the oven and set aside.

Roll out the pastry (dough) thinly on a floured surface to a circle large enough to cover the baking dish. Place the pastry over the dish, then trim around the edge with a knife so that the pastry falls inside the dish to enclose the apples.

Return the dish to the hot oven and bake for a further 20 minutes or until the pastry is crisp and golden. Remove from the oven and immediately invert the dish onto a serving platter. Leave to cool slightly. Serve warm.

SERVES 6

POIRAT DU BERRY

Pear Tart with Brandy and Cream

Metric/Imperial	American
1 kg/2 lb firm cooking pears	*2 lb firm cooking pears*
4 tablespoons brandy	*¼ cup brandy*
100 g/4 oz caster sugar	*½ cup sugar*
pinch of pepper	*pinch of pepper*
350 g/12 oz pâte brisée (page 52)	*¾ lb pâte brisée (page 52)*
2 tablespoons double cream	*2 tablespoons heavy cream*
GLAZE:	GLAZE:
1 egg yolk	*1 egg yolk*
1 tablespoon milk	*1 tablespoon milk*

Peel and quarter the pears, removing the cores, and place in a bowl. Mix together the brandy, sugar and pepper and pour over the pears. Cover and leave to macerate for 3 hours.

Roll out the dough on a floured surface to a rectangle about 1 cm/½ inch thick. Place on a baking (cookie) sheet. Drain the pears, reserving the juices,

Beignets de fromage
blanc; Pithiviers

then pile them up in the centre of the dough. Gather the dough up around the pears to enclose them completely like a parcel. Moisten the edges with water and pinch them together to seal at the top, leaving a 1 cm (½ inch) hole in the centre.

Beat together the egg yolk and milk for the glaze and brush all over the dough. Bake in a preheated moderately hot oven (200°C/400°F/Gas Mark 6) for 30 minutes.

Remove the *poirat* from the oven and place on a warmed serving platter. Mix together the cream and the reserved juices from the pears, then pour slowly into the *poirat* through the hole in the centre. Serve warm.

SERVES 6

PITHIVIERS

Almond and Puff Pastry Gâteau

This cake takes its name from the town of Pithiviers,
80 kilometres south of Paris, where it was originally created.

Metric/Imperial	American
PÂTE FEUILLETÉE:	PÂTE FEUILLETÉE:
450 g/1 lb plain flour	4 cups all-purpose flour
½ teaspoon salt	½ teaspoon salt
450 g/1 lb unsalted butter	2 cups sweet butter
2 teaspoons lemon juice	2 teaspoons lemon juice
about 250 ml/8 fl oz iced water	about 1 cup iced water
ALMOND FILLING:	ALMOND FILLING:
150 g/5 oz butter	⅔ cup butter
150 g/5 oz icing sugar, sifted	1 cup sifted confectioner's sugar, firmly packed
2 small eggs, beaten	2 small eggs, beaten
2 tablespoons rum	2 tablespoons rum
150 g/5 oz ground almonds	1¼ cups ground almonds
GLAZE:	GLAZE:
1 egg	1 egg
1 tablespoon water	1 tablespoon water
2 tablespoons icing sugar	2 tablespoons confectioner's sugar

Make the *pâte feuilletée* according to the method on page 53. Chill for 1 hour.

For the almond filling, cream the butter in a bowl until soft. Add the icing (confectioner's) sugar and beat until soft, then beat in the eggs and rum. Stir in the ground almonds.

Cut the dough in two, one piece slightly larger than the other. Roll out the larger piece of dough on a floured surface to a circle about 30 cm/12 inches in diameter. Place on a dampened baking (cookie) sheet, then spread the almond filling over the top to within 1 cm/½ inch of the edge. Brush the edge with water.

Roll out the remaining piece of dough to a circle the same size and place on top of the almond filling. Trim the edges of the dough, press together firmly to seal, then flute with a knife at 1 cm/½ inch intervals.

Beat together the egg and water for the glaze and brush over the dough. With the point of a knife, score the top of the dough in curves from the centre outwards, like the spokes of a wheel, taking care not to cut right through to the filling.

Bake in a preheated hot oven (220°C/425°F/Gas Mark 7) for 30 minutes until well risen and golden. Remove from the oven, sprinkle the sugar over the cake, then bake for a further 10 minutes. Transfer carefully to a warmed serving platter. Serve warm.

SERVES 8

BEIGNETS DE FROMAGE BLANC

Deep-Fried Cheese Puffs

Metric/Imperial	American
450 g/1 lb fromage blanc★, well drained	2 cups fromage blanc★, well drained
25 g/1 oz caster sugar	2 tablespoons sugar
100 g/4 oz plain flour	1 cup all-purpose flour
2 eggs	2 eggs
oil for deep-frying	oil for deep-frying
caster sugar, for sprinkling	sugar, for sprinkling

Put the cheese in a bowl and beat in the sugar with a wooden spoon until soft and smooth. Stir in the flour a little at a time, beating constantly after each addition. Beat in the eggs one at a time until thoroughly incorporated, then leave the mixture to stand for 1 hour.

Heat the oil in a deep-fat fryer to 190°C/375°F, or until a stale bread cube dropped into the oil turns golden in 10 to 15 seconds. Put teaspoonfuls of the cheese mixture into the hot oil a few at a time and deep-fry for a few minutes until puffed and golden. Remove from the oil with a slotted spoon and drain on kitchen paper towels. Keep warm while frying the remainder.

Pile the cheese puffs in a warmed serving dish and sprinkle with sugar to taste. Serve immediately.

SERVES 6

PARIS-BREST

Choux Ring with Praline Meringue Filling

Metric/Imperial	American
PÂTE À CHOUX:	PÂTE À CHOUX:
150 ml/¼ pint water	⅔ cup water
50 g/2 oz butter	¼ cup butter
¼ teaspoon salt	¼ teaspoon salt
125 g/4½ oz plain flour	1 cup + 2 tablespoons all-purpose flour
2 large eggs	2 large eggs
GLAZE:	GLAZE:
1 egg white	1 egg white
25 g/1 oz blanched slivered almonds	¼ cup blanched slivered almonds
PRALINE MERINGUE FILLING:	PRALINE MERINGUE FILLING:
100 g/4 oz sugar	½ cup sugar
7 tablespoons water	7 tablespoons water
2 egg whites	2 egg whites
200 g/7 oz praline (page 52)	7 oz praline (page 52)
200 g/7 oz butter, softened	1 cup softened butter
icing sugar, for sprinkling	confectioner's sugar, for sprinkling

Make the *pâte à choux* according to the method on page 53 and put into a piping bag fitted with a 1 cm/½ inch plain nozzle. Pipe a 20 cm/8 inch ring onto a lightly oiled baking sheet. Pipe another ring inside the first, then pipe a third ring on top to cover the join.

Whisk the egg white just until frothy, then brush over the dough. Sprinkle the almonds over the top. Bake in a preheated hot oven (220°C/425°F/Gas Mark 7) for 10 minutes, then reduce the temperature to moderately hot (190°C/375°F/Gas Mark 5) and continue baking for a further 20 to 25 minutes until well risen and golden brown.

Meanwhile, make the filling: put the sugar and water in a heavy pan over low heat until the sugar has dissolved. Increase the heat and cook until the syrup reaches the ball stage; i.e. when a little of the syrup, dropped into cold water, forms a ball. Whisk the egg whites until stiff, then whisk in the syrup. Continue whisking until the meringue is completely cold. Stir the praline into the softened butter, then whisk into the meringue. Chill until firm.

Slice the choux ring in half horizontally, making the bottom twice as thick as the top. Put the praline meringue filling into a piping bag fitted with a 2 cm/¾ inch fluted nozzle and pipe onto the bottom half of the choux ring. Place the top in position and sprinkle with icing (confectioner's) sugar to serve.

SERVES 6

RIGHT: **Macarons**
BELOW: **Saint-Honoré**

SAINT-HONORÉ

Choux Pastry Gâteau with Cream

This classic confection is named after Saint-Honoré, the patron saint of bakers and patissiers (pastry chefs).

Metric/Imperial	American
PÂTE SABLÉE:	PÂTE SABLÉE:
100 g/4 oz plain flour	1 cup all-purpose flour
pinch of salt	pinch of salt
50 g/2 oz butter, cut into small pieces	¼ cup butter, cut into small pieces
1 egg yolk	1 egg yolk
2 teaspoons caster sugar	2 teaspoons sugar
a little iced water, to mix	a little iced water, to mix
PÂTE À CHOUX:	PÂTE À CHOUX:
300 ml/½ pint water	1¼ cups water
pinch of salt	pinch of salt
1 teaspoon caster sugar	1 teaspoon sugar
100 g/4 oz butter, cut into small pieces	½ cup butter, cut into small pieces
150 g/5 oz plain flour	1¼ cups all-purpose flour
4 eggs	4 eggs
beaten egg, for brushing	beaten egg, for brushing
CARAMEL:	CARAMEL:
225 g/8 oz sugar	1 cup sugar
7 tablespoons water	7 tablespoons water
TO FINISH:	TO FINISH:
250 ml/8 fl oz double cream, chilled	1 cup heavy cream, chilled
3 tablespoons milk	3 tablespoons milk
75 g/3 oz caster sugar	⅓ cup sugar

Make the *pâte sablée* according to the method on page 52. Chill in the refrigerator for 1 hour. Make the *pâte à choux* according to the method on page 53.

Roll out the *pâte sablée* for the base on a floured surface to a circle about 20 cm/8 inches in diameter. Place the circle on a buttered baking sheet and prick with a fork.

Put the choux pastry in a piping bag fitted with a 1.5 cm/½ inch plain nozzle and pipe small mounds in a crown shape around the edge of the pastry base. Pipe the remaining choux dough in small mounds straight onto the baking sheet.

Brush the pastry base and choux mounds with beaten egg. Bake in a preheated hot oven (220°C/425°F/Gas Mark 7) for 15 minutes, then lower the heat to moderately hot (200°C/400°F/Gas Mark 6) and continue baking for a further 10 minutes for the small choux mounds and a further 15 to 20 minutes for the base and choux crown. Leave the small choux mounds to cool on a wire rack.

Make the caramel: put the sugar and water in a heavy pan and cook until thick and caramel in colour. Place the gâteau base on a serving platter. Spoon a little caramel over the mounds on the base. Dip the small choux mounds quickly into the caramel, then stick them side by side on top of the choux crown. Stick the remaining small choux in the centre of the pastry base, making a pyramid shape. Leave to harden.

To finish: whip the cream and milk together until thick, adding the sugar a little at a time. Put into a piping bag fitted with a fluted nozzle and pipe over the choux. Serve as soon as possible.

SERVES 8

MACARONS

Macaroons

Macaroons used to be made by pounding whole blanched almonds with lump sugar – this way the almond oil was freshly released into the sugar and the finished macaroons had a better flavour and texture. Nowadays, ground almonds are more frequently used for convenience, but only the freshest are suitable. Macaroons are best eaten soon after baking, but they will keep fresh for a few days if stored in an airtight metal container.

Metric/Imperial	American
112 g/4 oz ground almonds	1 cup ground almonds
225 g/8 oz caster sugar	1 cup sugar, firmly packed
2 small egg whites	2 small egg whites
icing sugar, for sprinkling	confectioner's sugar, for sprinkling

Pound the almonds, preferably in a wooden mortar and pestle, to release their oil. Add the sugar a little at a time, pounding constantly until well mixed. Transfer to a bowl and beat in the egg whites with a wooden spoon.

Line a baking sheet with lightly oiled non-stick parchment (waxed) paper. Using 2 teaspoons, place 15 mounds of the macaroon mixture on the paper, spacing them well apart. Brush the top of each mound with a little water, then sprinkle lightly with icing (confectioner's) sugar.

Bake in a preheated moderate oven (180°C/350°F/Gas Mark 4) for about 15 minutes or until the macaroons are light golden. Leave to cool before peeling off the paper.

MAKES 15

The macaroon is a French confection with a long tradition closely connected with abbeys and convents – strange though it may seem! Originally, they were made by the monks at the abbey of Cormery in Touraine, and though imitations of these famous macaroons were produced, only those from Cormery bore the special trademark of a monk's navel!

Nowadays, macaroons from Nancy, the capital of Lorraine, are considered amongst the best in France. Originally created by nuns in a Nancy convent, they are still made today in the same bakery where the nuns set up business during the French revolution.

KUGELHOPF

Yeast Cake with Almonds and Raisins

This cake is baked in a special mould, usually earthenware or copper, which is known as a kugelhopf. It has a fluted bottom and sides, and a tube or funnel in the centre which gives the cake a hole in the middle when it is turned out. Remember to start making this cake 24 to 36 hours before required, because it needs time to mature before serving.

Metric/Imperial	American
15 g/½ oz fresh yeast	½ cake compressed yeast
7 tablespoons lukewarm milk	7 tablespoons lukewarm milk
250 g/9 oz plain flour	2¼ cups all-purpose flour
½ teaspoon salt	½ teaspoon salt
65 g/2½ oz sugar	5 tablespoons sugar
2 eggs, beaten	2 eggs, beaten
100 g/4 oz butter, softened	½ cup softened butter
2 tablespoons slivered blanched almonds	2 tablespoons slivered blanched almonds
75 g/3 oz raisins, soaked overnight in 2 tablespoons kirsch	½ cup seedless white raisins, soaked overnight in 2 tablespoons kirsch
icing sugar, for sprinkling	confectioner's sugar, for sprinkling

Dissolve the yeast in half the lukewarm milk. Sift the flour into a large bowl, make a well in the centre and add the salt, sugar, eggs and remaining milk. Work the ingredients together with the hands, then knead vigorously for 5 minutes. Add the yeast mixture and knead again for a further 5 minutes. Cover the bowl with a clean cloth and leave to rise in a warm place for 1 hour or until doubled in bulk.

Brush the inside of a 23 cm/9 inch *kugelhopf* mould with butter, then sprinkle with flour, shaking off the excess. Press the almonds into the grooves in the mould.

Work the butter and raisins into the dough by kneading lightly, then place in the prepared mould. Cover with a clean cloth and leave to rise in a warm place for 1 hour or until the dough has risen to about 2 cm/¾ inch from the top of the mould.

Bake in a preheated moderately hot oven (190°C/375°F/Gas Mark 5) for 40 minutes. Turn out onto a wire rack and leave to cool. Leave to mature for 24 hours.

Sprinkle with icing (confectioner's) sugar before serving.
SERVES 6

Kugelhopf is sometimes spelt *kougloff*, *kouglof* or even *kougelhopf*, depending on regional spelling differences. An Alsatian pastry made with risen dough, it is now made all over France. Originally of Austrian origin, its arrival and subsequent popularity in Paris seems clouded with confusion. Some say it was made popular by Marie Antoinette who had a passion for it, others say it was the international chef Carême who popularized it.

Gâteau de Savoie;
Fougasse

GÂTEAU DE SAVOIE
Savoie Whisked Sponge

*This light, airy sponge can be served simply sprinkled
with icing (confectioner's) sugar; or split, filled and topped
with whipped cream, jam, fresh fruit or a light fruit mousse.
It can therefore be used for making sumptuous gâteaux.*

Metric/Imperial	American
6 eggs, separated	6 eggs, separated
200 g/7 oz sugar	scant 1 cup sugar
125 g/4½ oz plain flour, sifted	1 cup plus 2 tablespoons all-purpose flour, sifted
pinch of salt	pinch of salt

Put the egg yolks and sugar in a bowl and whisk
together until light, fluffy and doubled in volume. Fold
in the flour until thoroughly incorporated.

Put the egg whites in a separate bowl with the salt.
Beat until stiff and standing in peaks, then fold gently
into the egg yolk mixture.

Turn the mixture into a buttered and floured
23 cm/9 inch *moule à manque*★ or loose-bottomed flan
tin (pan). Bake in a preheated moderate oven
(160°C/325°F/Gas Mark 3) for 50 minutes to 1 hour or
until a skewer inserted in the centre comes out clean.

Turn off the oven, open the door and leave for
10 minutes to prevent the cake from sinking due to
sudden change in temperature. Remove from the tin
carefully (the cake is very fragile), then leave to cool on
a wire rack.
SERVES 6

VARIATIONS: The mixture can be flavoured with
lemon zest★ or vanilla according to taste.

MADELEINES DE COMMERCY
Madeleines

*French madeleines need to be baked in special fluted
madeleine tins, which are available from specialist kitchen
shops. They are not to be confused with the coconut-covered
English madeleine cakes which are baked in castle (dariole)
moulds. French madeleines are crisp and light on the
outside, slightly soft in the centre; they will keep fresh for
several days if stored in an airtight metal container.*

Metric/Imperial	American
3 eggs	3 eggs
pinch of salt	pinch of salt
100 g/4 oz caster sugar	½ cup sugar
100 g/4 oz plain flour	1 cup all-purpose flour
2 pinches of bicarbonate of soda	2 pinches of sodium bicarbonate
75 g/3 oz butter, melted	⅓ cup butter, melted
zest of 1 lemon	zest of 1 lemon

Put the eggs, salt and sugar in a bowl and whisk
together until light and fluffy. Sift the flour and
bicarbonate of soda (sodium bicarbonate) together,
then carefully fold into the whisked mixture. When
almost completely incorporated, fold in the butter and
lemon zest.

Divide the mixture equally between 36 well-
buttered madeleine moulds. Do not overfill the
moulds or the mixture will spill out during baking.
Bake in a preheated moderate oven (180°C/350°F/Gas
Mark 4) for 12 to 15 minutes until golden.

Remove the madeleines carefully from their moulds
and leave to cool on a wire rack.
MAKES 36

VARIATION: Add a few drops of orange flower water★
to the mixture with, or instead of, the lemon zest.

FOUGASSE
Yeast Cake with Glacé (Candied) Fruits

*Fougasse is a kind of brioche, a speciality of the Var in
Provence. Some recipes for fougasse include eggs in their
ingredients, thus making a rich brioche dough – this one is
lighter. Saffron is not absolutely essential, but it gives
fougasse its characteristic golden colour.*

Metric/Imperial	American
20 g/¾ oz fresh yeast	¾ cake compressed yeast
3 tablespoons lukewarm water	3 tablespoons lukewarm water
450 g/1 lb plain flour	4 cups all-purpose flour
pinch of salt	pinch of salt
1½ tablespoons caster sugar	1½ tablespoons sugar
pinch of powdered saffron (optional)	pinch of powdered saffron (optional)
2 tablespoons olive oil	2 tablespoons olive oil
2 tablespoons orange-flower water★	2 tablespoons orange-flower water★
120 ml/4 fl oz lukewarm water	½ cup lukewarm water
75 g/3 oz glacé fruits (cherries, pears, lemons, oranges, etc. cut into small pieces)	3 oz candied fruits (cherries, pears, lemons, oranges, etc.), cut into small pieces
TO GLAZE:	TO GLAZE:
100 g/4 oz sugar	½ cup sugar
2 tablespoons water	2 tablespoons water

Work the yeast and lukewarm water together in a
small bowl. Sift 100 g/4 oz/1 cup flour into a separate
bowl, then work in the yeast mixture. Cover with a
cloth, then leave to rise in a warm place for 1 to 2 hours
or until doubled in bulk.

Sift the remaining flour into a large bowl, then stir in
the salt, sugar and saffron (if using). Stir in the oil a little
at a time, then the orange flower water and yeast
batter. Mix to a soft, pliable dough, adding the
lukewarm water. Form the dough into a ball, place in a
clean bowl, then cover with a cloth and leave to rise in a
warm place for 45 minutes.

Place the dough on a dampened baking sheet, then
form into a figure of eight shape with floured hands.
Leave to rise in a warm place for 40 minutes.

Press the pieces of fruit lightly into the dough, then
bake in a preheated moderately hot oven (200°C/
400°F/Gas Mark 6) for 30 minutes. Meanwhile, make
the glaze: dissolve the sugar in the water over low
heat, then boil for 2 to 3 minutes until syrupy.

Transfer the *fougasse* to a wire rack and brush with
the glaze. Leave to cool. Serve warm or cold.
SERVES 6 to 8

INDEX

ACKNOWLEDGMENTS

Special photography by Robert Golden
Photographic stylist: Antonia Gaunt
Food prepared by Mary Cadogan, Caroline Ellwood
and Carole Handslip

The publishers would like to thank the following individuals for their permission to reproduce the location photographs in this book: Robert Golden 11 above, 12 below, 20, 21, 23, 43, 46, 51, 52–3: Paul Williams 12 above, 14 above, 15 above, 16–17, 49; Tessa Traeger 13, 31, 45; Bill Mason 8, 9 left, 11 below; Adam Woolfitt (Susan Griggs Agency) 14 below, 15 below, 18–19; John Bulmer (Susan Griggs Agency) 9 right, 10; Bridgeman Art Library 7.

The publishers would also like to express their gratitude to the following companies for the loan of accessories for photography: Coppershop, 48 Neal St, London WC2; Covent Garden Kitchen Supplies, 3 North Row, The Market, Covent Garden, London WC2; Elizabeth David Ltd, 46 Bourne St, London SW1; Divertimenti, 68 Marylebone Lane, London W1.

PDO 82-0015